Meta-Analytics

Meta-Analytics

Consensus Approaches and System Patterns for Data Analysis

Steven Simske

MORGAN KAUFMANN PUBLISHERS

AN IMPRINT OF ELSEVIER

Morgan Kaufmann is an imprint of Elsevier
50 Hampshire Street, 5th Floor, Cambridge, MA 02139, United States

Notices

Knowledge and best practice in this field are constantly changing. As new research and experience broaden our understanding, changes in research methods, professional practices, or medical treatment may become necessary.

Practitioners and researchers must always rely on their own experience and knowledge in evaluating and using any information, methods, compounds, or experiments described herein. In using such information or methods they should be mindful of their own safety and the safety of others, including parties for whom they have a professional responsibility.

To the fullest extent of the law, neither the Publisher nor the authors, contributors, or editors, assume any liability for any injury and/or damage to persons or property as a matter of products liability, negligence or otherwise, or from any use or operation of any methods, products, instructions, or ideas contained in the material herein.

Library of Congress Cataloging-in-Publication Data
A catalog record for this book is available from the Library of Congress

British Library Cataloguing-in-Publication Data
A catalogue record for this book is available from the British Library

ISBN: 978-0-12-814623-1

For information on all Morgan Kaufmann publications
visit our website at https://www.elsevier.com/books-and-journals

Working together
to grow libraries in
developing countries

www.elsevier.com • www.bookaid.org

Publisher: Jonathan Simpson
Acquisition Editor: Glyn Jones
Editorial Project Manager: Aleksandra Packowska
Production Project Manager: Punithavathy Govindaradjane
Cover Designer: Matthew Limbert

Typeset by SPi Global, India

This book is dedicated to Tess, my partner for 30 years and my best friend in life.

Contents

Acknowledgments

No man is an island, and a book is definitely a human archipelago. I owe so much to so many for this book being completed and hopefully of high relevance to the reader. I am especially happy with the advancements in clustering and classification that show in here, along with a wide variety of analytic approaches based on great work in disparate fields of science. If I have seen anything well here, to paraphrase the late, great Newton, it is because I am *understanding* on the shoulders of giants.

Thanks to the team at Elsevier for their prodding, probing, professionalism, and promptness. In particular, I'd like to thank Brian Guerin, Glyn Jones, Sabrina Webber, Peter Llewellyn, and Aleksandra Packowska for their important roles in seeing this book through its more than 2-year incubation and birth.

Thanks to many, many encouraging colleagues and friends—from universities, from HP Inc., and from so many groups and activities here in Fort Collins. Hundreds of people who've made my life better during the writing of this book may not all be named here, but rest assured that you are appreciated! Without having had the chance to participate in so many different activities and professions over the years, I would never have been able to see the connections between them.

Thanks to all the great folks at Colorado State University, which I made my professional home at the beginning of the writing phase of this book. In particular, thanks to the systems engineering staff and faculty (featuring Jim Adams, Ann Batchelor, Mike Borky, Ingrid Bridge, Jim Cale, Mary Gomez, Greg "Bo" Marzolf, Erika Miller, Ron Sega, and Tom Bradley) for providing me with a home and classroom suitable for elaboration of key parts of the book, not to mention their support and friendship, which seem the rule at CSU.

Special thanks indeed to my Irish trio of great friends: Paul Ellingstad, Mick Keyes, and Gary Moloney. Their wisdom, friendship, kindhearted cynicism, energy, and inability to lose their optimism in the face of the grittiness of reality have always been a wind in my sails. Special thanks also to my non-Irish support team of friends and intellectual guides: Reed Ayers, Dave Barry, Gary Dispoto, Matt Gaubatz, Ellis Gayles, Stephen Pollard, Tom Schmeister, Steve Siatczynski, Dave Wright, and Bob Ulichney. Thank you, brothers!

Some of our best friends come from professional organizations. From ACM Doc Eng, I have lifelong friends in Steve Bagley, the Balinskys, Dave and Julie Brailsford, Alexandra Bonnici, Tamir Hassan, Rafael Lins, Cerstin Mahlow, Ethan Munson, Michael Piotrowski, and so many more. Thank you all! From IS&T, Suzanne Grinnan and staff (Jenny O'Brien, Diana Gonzalez, Roberta Morehouse, Donna Smith, and Marion Zoretich chief among them), Alan Hodgson, Robin Jenkin, Susan Farnand, and many others have helped guide my research and professional career with friendship and advice.

A friend and IS&T colleague who I've worked with for 10 years played a huge role in this book. Thanks, and then, more thanks goes to Marie Vans for proofreading this entire book from start to finish. If errors remain, they are of course my evil

Acknowledgments

spawn, but thanks to Marie; an unholy horde of heuristic horrors has already been eliminated. Marie, thank you so much! Having someone as talented as you are in the research area of this book go through it with a fine-tooth comb was wonderful.

Finally, this book is dedicated to Tess, my life partner for 30 years. I cannot thank you enough for your patience, encouragement, and occasional hard reset. Along with Tess, I can trust my two amazing sons (Kieran and Dallen) and my great friend, Doug Heins, to keep me on track—in life and in learning, which is really the same. Your talents, feedback, investment, and love of learning are not just inspiring—they are the breath inspired. Thank you!

Steve Simske
Fort Collins, CO
18 November 2019

Introduction, overview, and applications

1

It is a capital mistake to theorize before one has data
Arthur Conan Doyle (1887)
Numquam ponenda est pluralitas sine necessitate
William of Ockham, Duns Scotus, et al. (c. 1300)
E pluribus unum
US Motto

1.1 Introduction

We live in a world in which more data have been collected in the past 2–3 years than were collected in the entire history of the world before then. Based on the trends of the past few years, we'll be saying this for a while. Why is this the case? The confluence of nearly limitless storage and processing power has, quite simply, made it far easier to generate and preserve data. The most relevant question is, perhaps, not whether this will continue, but rather how much of the data will be used for anything more than filling up storage space.

The machine intelligence community is, of course, interested in turning these data into information and has had tremendous success to date albeit in somewhat specific and/or constrained situations. Recent advancements in hardware—from raw processing power and nearly limitless storage capacity, to the architectural revolution that graphics processing units (GPUs) bring, to parallel and distributed computation—have allowed software developers and algorithm developers to encode processes that were unthinkable with the hardware of even a decade ago. Deep learning and in particular convolutional neural networks, together with data-flow programming, allow for an ease of rolling out sophisticated machine learning algorithms and processes that is unprecedented, with the entire field having by all means a bright future.

Taking the power of hybrid architectures as a starting point, analytic approaches can be upgraded to benefit from all components when employing a plurality of analytics. This book is about how simple building blocks of analytics can be used in aggregate to provide systems that are readily optimized for accuracy, robustness, cost, scalability, modularity, reusability, and other design concerns. This book covers the basics of analytics; builds on them to create a set of meta-analytic approaches; and provides straightforward analytics algorithms, processes, and designs that will bring a neophyte up to speed while augmenting the arsenal of an analytics authority.

Meta-Analytics. https://doi.org/10.1016/B978-0-12-814623-1.00001-0

The goal of the book is to make analytics enjoyable, efficient, and comprehensible to the entire gamut of data scientists—in what is surely an age of data science.

1.2 Why is this book important?

First and foremost, this book is meant to be accessible to anyone interested in data science. Data already permeate every science, technology, engineering, and mathematics (STEM) endeavor, and the expectations to generate relevant and copious data in any process, service, or product will only continue to grow in the years to come. A book helping a STEM professional pick up the art of data analysis from the ground up, providing both fundamentals and a roadmap for the future, is needed.

The book is aimed at supplying an extensive set of patterns for data scientists to use to "hit the ground running" on any machine-learning-based data analysis task and virtually ensures that at least one approach will lead to better overall system behavior (accuracy, cost, robustness, performance, etc.) than by using traditional analytic approaches only. Because the book is "meta-" analytics, it also must cover general analytics well enough for the reader to engage with and comprehend the hybrid approaches, or "meta-" approaches. As such, the book aims to allow a relative novice to analytics to move to an elevated level of competency and "fluency" relatively quickly. It is also intended to challenge the data scientist to think more broadly and more thoroughly than they might be otherwise motivated.

The target audience, therefore, consists of data scientists in all sectors—academia, industry, government, and NGO. Because of the importance of statistical methods, data normalization, data visualization, and machine intelligence to the types of data science included in this book, the book has relevance to machine translation, robotics, biological and social sciences, medical and health-care informatics, economics, business, and finance. The analytic approaches covered herein can be applied to predictive algorithms for everyone from police departments (crime prediction) to sport analysts. The book is readily amenable to a graduate class on systems engineering, analytics, or data science, in addition to a course on machine intelligence. A subset of the book could be used for an advanced undergraduate class in intelligent systems.

Predictive analytics have long held a fascination for people. Seeing the future has been associated with divinity, with magic, with the occult, or simply—and more in keeping with Occam's razor—with enhanced intelligence. But is Occam's razor, or the law of parsimony, applicable in the age of data science? It is no longer necessarily the best advice to say "Numquam ponenda est pluralitas sine necessitate," or "plurality is never to be posited without necessity," unless, of course, one uses "goodness of fit to a model," "output of sensitivity analysis," or "least-squares estimation," among other quantitative artifacts, as proxies for "necessity." The concept of predictive analytics, used at the galactic level and extending many thousands of years into the future, is the basis of the Foundation trilogy by Isaac Asimov, written in the middle of the 20th century. Futurist—or should we say mathematician?—Hari Seldon particularized the science of psychohistory, which presumably incorporated an extremely multivariate analysis intended to remove as much uncertainty from the future as possible for those privy to his output. Perhaps, the only prediction he was unable to make was the randomness of the personality of the "Mule," an überintelligent, übermanipulative leader of the future. However, his ability to estimate the future in probabilistic terms led to the (correct) prediction of the collapse of the Galactic Empire and so included a manual to abbreviate the millennia of chaos expected to follow. In other words, he may have foreseen not the "specific randomness" of the Mule, but constructed his psychohistory to be optimally robust to the unforeseen. That is, Hari Seldon performed "preflight sensitivity analysis" of his predictive model. Kudos to Asimov for anticipating the value of analytics in the future. But even more so, kudos for anticipating that the law of parsimony would be insufficient to address the needs of a predictive analytic system to be insensitive to such "unpredictable" random artifacts (people, places, and things). The need to provide for the simplest model reasonable—that is, the law of model parsimony—remains. However, it is evident that hybrid systems, affording simplicity where possible but able to handle much more complexity where appropriate, are more robust than either extreme and ultimately will remain relevant longer in real-world applications.

This book is, consequently, important precisely because of the value provided by both the Williams of Ockham and the Hari Seldon. The real world is dynamic and ever-changing, and predictive models must be preadapted to change in the assumptions that underpin them, including but not limited to the drift in data from that used to train the model; changes in the "measurement system" including sampling, filtering, transduction, and compression; and changes in the interactions between the system being modeled and measured and the larger environment around it. I hope that the approaches revisited, introduced, and/or elaborated in this book will aid data scientists in their tasks while also bringing non-data scientists to sufficient data "fluency" to be able to interact intelligently with the world of data. One thing is certain—unlike Hari Seldon's Galactic Empire, the world of data is not about to crumble. It is getting stronger—for good and for bad—every day.

1.3 Organization of the book

This, the first, is the critical chapter for the entire book and takes on a disproportionate length compared with the other chapters intentionally, as this book is meant to stand on its own, allowing the student, data enthusiast, and even data professional to use it as a single source to proceed from unstructured data to fully tagged, clustered, and classified data. This chapter also provides background on the statistics, machine learning, and artificial intelligence needed for analytics and meta-analytics.

Additional chapters, then, elaborate further on what analytics provide. In Chapter 2, the value of training data is thoroughly investigated, and the assumptions around the long-standing training, validation, and testing process are revisited. In Chapter 3, experimental design—from bias and normalization to the treatment of data experiments as systems of data—is considered. In Chapter 4, meta-analytic approaches are introduced, with primary focus being on cumulative gain, or lift, curves. Chapters 5–10 focus on other key aspects of systems around analytics, including the broad but very approachable field of sensitivity analysis (Chapter 5); the powerful family or "platform" of patterns for analytics loosely described as predictive selection (Chapter 6); a consideration of models, model fitting, and how to design models to be more robust to their environment (Chapter 7); addition analytic design patterns (Chapter 8); the recursive use of analytics to explore the efficacy of employed analytics (Chapter 9); and optimization of analytic system design (Chapter 10), which is a natural follow-on to Chapter 9. Chapter 11 is used to show how optimized system designs not only provide a better "buffer" to unanticipated random artifacts (these are called "aleatory techniques" here) but also do a better job of ingesting domain expertise from decidedly nonrandom artifacts, that is, from domain experts and requirements. In Chapters 12–13, the analytic approaches introduced in the preceding chapters are applied to specific technical fields (Chapter 12) and to some broader fields (Chapter 13). In Chapter 14, the contributions of this book are discussed in a larger context, and the future of data in the age of data is described.

A note on what is meant by meta-analytics is worth providing. Essentially, "meta-analysis" has two broad fields of study/application:

1. Meta- in the sense of meta-algorithmics, where we are combining two or more analytic techniques (algorithms, processes, services, systems, etc.) to obtain improved analytic output.
2. Meta- in the sense of being outside, additional, and augmentative to pure analytics, which includes fields such as testing, ground truthing, training, and sensitivity analysis and optimization of system design.

With this perspective, analytics is more than just simply machine learning: it is also learning in the correct order. It is not only knowledge extraction but also extraction of knowledge in the correct order. It is not only creating information but also creating information in the correct order. This means that analytics is more than simple descriptive or quantitative information. It is meant to extract and tell a story about the data that someone skilled in the field would be able to provide, including modifying the analysis in light of changing data and context for the data.

1.4 Informatics

Occasionally, data science will be used interchangeably with the term "informatics." Informatics, however, is a branch of information engineering/science/systems concerned with the impact of data on humans (and presumably the impact of humans on data!). Informatics is concerned with the interaction between humans and relevant information, particularly in how humans process information digitally. Thus, an important aspect of informatics is the study of the social implications of information technologies. From this broad perspective, then, analytics gathered to determine how digital technologies affect humans [Carr11] are an important part of informatics.

In this book, informatics will only be addressed peripherally, that is, as an integrated part of the example, which is instead focused on the algorithmic, process, or system approach to generating information from a data set. This does not mean we are allowed to operate in a vacuum as data scientists; rather, it simply means that this book will not have as a general concern the specific manner in which data are presented nor with which software the data are processed, etc.

1.5 **Statistics for analytics**

In this section, a quick summary (and, for many readers, a high-level recapitulation) of statistics relevant to data science is given. The main topics covered will be value (mean and estimate), variability, degrees of freedom, analysis of variance, and the relationship of these statistics to information and inferences that can be drawn from the data.

1.5.1 **Value and variance**

The value is an individual datum, typically binary, numerical, alphanumeric, or a word, depending on the data-type definition. The first-order descriptor of a plurality of values is the mean, μ, which is distinctly different from the "average":

$$\mu = \bar{x} = \sum_{n=1}^{n_{samples}} \frac{x_i}{n_{samples}} \tag{1.1}$$

For example, the "average" income, house price, or cost of goods is generally given as the median, not the mean. The "average" day that the trash collector comes is usually the mode, not the mean. But in most analytics—that is, in parametric analytics—the mean is our "average of choice." In nonparametric statistics, the median is often of concern, since the ranked order of values is important. Still on other occasions, the mean does not need to be computed but is instead a specification that a system is required to meet, for example, miles per gallon, cycles before failure, or bends before fatigue. In these cases, a single type of event is monitored and its mean calculated, and this mean is compared with this "specification as mean."

Of course, two populations can share the same mean and still be quite different. This is because most populations (and all nontheoretical populations) have variability around the mean. The second moment of the distribution is the variance, usually denoted by σ^2, whose square root the standard deviation σ, defined in Eq. (1.2), is an important characterizing datum of a distribution:

$$\sigma = \sqrt{\frac{\sum_{n=1}^{n_{samples}} (x_n - \mu_0)^2}{n_{samples} - 1}} \tag{1.2}$$

For a Gaussian, or normal, distribution, roughly 68% of the samples fall within the range $\{\mu-\sigma, \mu+\sigma\}$. Note in Eq. (1.2) that the degrees of freedom, or *df* for short, are equal to *(number of samples)-1*. This is intuitive since you can only choose the first *(number of samples)-1* samples and then the last one is already determined. Degrees of freedom are always important in statistical analyses, since confidence in the result is directly related to the number of times a result has been repeated. While "confidence" is not a quantitative statistical measure (though confidence intervals are!), generally, confidence increases with degrees of freedom and inversely with variability. The highest possible confidence, then, comes when you repeat the exact same result many, many times.

It is usually quite important to distinguish between comparing means and comparing variances. For example, this distinguishes between weather and climate: if, in a locale, the mean temperature is the same but the variance increases significantly over time, then the mean "weather" does not change, but the climate does. Similarly, higher variability in a genome more likely leads to new speciation than lower variability.

Another example may be for an engine used for transportation or for hauling materials. For example, the modal and median engine revolutions per minute (RPM), when measured over a day or even over a driving/on-cycle session, may be well within the safety range. But this does not account for the variability. In some short driving sessions, the standard deviation may be as high as the mean, and so, a more important measure might be percent of time spent above a given value, which may be, for example, 1.2 standard deviation above the mean. Here, the nature of the distribution (the "shape" of the variance) is far more important than the mean. As a general rule, for nonnegative data sets, whenever $\mu \leq \sigma$, what you are measuring requires further elaboration to be useful from an analytic viewpoint.

1.5.2 Sample and population tests

This type of confidence directly factors in when we consider the first quantitative measurement for determining whether a sample belongs to a given population. This measure, the z-score, is given in Eq. (1.3), where we see that the numerator is the difference between the sample value, x, and the mean of the population, μ. The denominator is the standard deviation, σ, divided by the square root of the number of samples being compared with the population (which is effectively the degrees of freedom for comparing the sample x to the population having n samples):

$$z = \frac{x-\mu}{\sigma/\sqrt{n}} \tag{1.3}$$

Note that the value of z can be positive or negative depending on whether x is greater than the mean of the population. The z-score is used to *decide with a given level of confidence that a sample does not come from a population.* As such, the absolute value of the z-score in Eq. (1.3) is typically our concern. Table 1.3 provides a few of the most important probabilities and their corresponding z-scores. Two-tailed probability means that we do not know beforehand (*a priori*) whether a sample is being tested to be above or below the mean of the population; one-tailed probability means that we *a priori* are testing in a single direction from the mean. For example, a two-tailed test might be "it's not a normal temperature for this day of the year," while a one-tailed test might be "it's warmer than usual for this day of the year." In general, from a "conservative" statistical standpoint, it is better to use a two-tailed test than a one-tailed test unless you already have a hypothesis, model, or regulation guiding your comparison. You are less likely to have "false positives" for declaring a sample statistically significantly different from a population this way. Note that the probability of a one-tailed test is halfway to 100% from that of a two-tailed test. Thus, for $z = 1.96$, we are 95% certain that a sample did not come from a specific population, and we are 97.5% certain that it comes from a second population with a higher mean value if $z = 1.96$ (and not -1.96). This makes sense, because we are effectively getting another 50% probability "correct" if the sign of the calculation z-value is correct. In this case, had z been -1.96, we would not be able to support our hypothesis since the direction from the mean of the population of size n to which we compare the sample contradicts our hypothesis. (See Table 1.1.)

Eq. (1.3) relies on some assumptions that are worth discussing, as there are several factors that affect the z-score in addition to the degrees of freedom. The first is the possibility of non-Gaussian (nonnormal) behavior of the population with which the sample is compared (and the population from which the sample actually comes, although we may have no way of knowing/estimating this population yet). When we consider third- and fourth-order moments such as skew and kurtosis, we may uncover non-Gaussian behavior such as left skew (long tail left), right skew (long tail right), bimodality (two clusters of data, implying that the population represents two subpopulations with different attributes), and other non-Gaussian behaviors (e.g., exponential, uniform, logistic, Poisson, and symmetrical distributions). These *distribution deviations* from assumed Gaussian behavior impact the interpretation of the z-score (generally undermining the *p*-value, or probability). Secondly, a *temporal drift* in the samples belonging to the population will undermine the z-score, since the sample may be compared with data that are no longer relevant. For this reason, the population and sample to compare should be time (and other experimental factor) matched whenever possible. Thirdly, an *imbalanced training set* or population sample bias

Table 1.1 Z-scores (absolute values) and some important probabilities

Absolute value of z-score	Probability, two-tailed	Probability, one-tailed
1.645	0.90	0.95
1.96	0.95	0.975
2.326	0.98	0.99
2.576	0.99	0.995

The probability is not used to establish whether a sample belongs to a population; rather, it provides the probability that a single sample was not drawn from the population having mean μ and standard deviation σ per Eq. (1.3)

will impact the z-score. If the population is meant to cover a specific range of input and does not, it can introduce distribution deviation and/or temporal drift or hide the same.

In practice, z-scores are very important for process control and for identifying outliers. A brief example is given here. Suppose we represent a surface-based forensic, such as you might get using a high-resolution imager [Sims10] and image analysis that subtracts the actual postprinting or postmanufacturing micron-scale surface texture to that of a model [Poll10]. The so-called forensic signature (derived from the variations in electromagnetic spectrum, ultrasound, or other salient physical property) of the surface is represented as a bitstream, with 1024 bits in the string. When a new image is captured, its binary surface detail string is compared with that of the candidate (matched) sample and with the population of (unmatched) samples. The expected Hamming distance to the population of unmatched samples has an expected value of 512 bits (i.e., with random guessing, precisely 50% of the bits should match, and the other 50% should be in error). In our test of binary string descriptors for a large set of surfaces, we obtained a mean Hamming distance to unmatched samples of 509.7 (very close to the expected value of 512, with a standard deviation of 31.6). The number of test samples in the population is 100. Next, we measure a value, 319.4, for the Hamming difference between a surface that we wish to prove is authentic with a forensically relevant probability (typically $p = 10^{-9}$, meaning there is one chance in a billion of a false-positive match). Plugging into Eq. (1.3), we get Eq. (1.4):

$$z = \frac{319.4 - 509.7}{31.6 \Big/ \sqrt{1}} \tag{1.4}$$

So, $z = -6.02$. Note that we use $n = 1$ (not $n = 100$, which is the number of samples to determine the population mean and standard deviation) here, since it is the number of samples that we are comparing with the population. Since $z = -5.997932$ corresponds to $p = 10^{-9}$, we have (just barely!) forensic authentication ($p < 10^{-9}$).

Even though there is a term for n, the number of samples, in the z-score, when the number of samples in a second population increases, we generally employ another statistical test for comparing two populations. This test, the t-test, is given by Eq. (1.5):

$$t = \frac{\mu_1 - \mu_2}{\sqrt{\dfrac{(n_1 - 1)\sigma_1^2 + (n_2 - 1)\sigma_2^2}{n_1 + n_2 - 2}} \sqrt{\dfrac{1}{n_1} + \dfrac{1}{n_2}}} \tag{1.5}$$

In the t-test statistic, the means of the two populations are denoted by the symbol μ, the standard deviations by the symbol σ, and the number in each sample by the symbol n (each with the appropriate numerical subscript). The overall degree of freedom (df) for comparison is $n_1 + n_2 - 2$ (this is needed when looking up the corresponding probability, or p, value from a t-table). The -2 indicates the -1 degree of freedom lost for selecting from each of the two populations. Statistical significance for one-tailed and two-tailed comparisons is determined as for z-values. Generally, t-tables, whether online or in a text, require the three data: *df*, *t*-score, and tailedness (1 or 2). For example, for $df=11$, a two-tailed $p=0.01$ requires $|t|>3.106$.

Next, we consider what happens when there are several populations to compare simultaneously. In this case, we generally employ analysis of variance (or "ANOVA"), which is a collection of statistical models and their associated procedures (such as "variation" among and between groups) that are used to analyze the differences among group means. As with many other statistical approaches, ANOVA was originally developed for quantitative biological applications. A convenient means of calculating the necessary elements of an ANOVA is the tabular arrangement shown in Table 1.2. Here, a particular variable's variance (sum squared variability about its mean) is partitioned into components attributed to the different sources of the variation (usually from within the groups or from between the groups). Groups can be clusters, classes, or other labeled sets. ANOVA provides a statistical test for whether the means of several groups are equal, providing a logical extension of the *z*-score (one dimension) to the *t*-test (two dimensions) to the comparing (testing) of three or more means for statistical significance.

As shown in Table 1.2, the sums of squares (around the means) between groups and within groups are calculated. Dividing these by the degrees of freedom gives us the mean squared variance (akin to mean squared error), and the ratio of mean squared error between and within groups gives us an *F*-score (named for Fisher, who was the first to systematize the ANOVA) to test if there are groups statistically significantly different from each other. High ratios of between-group to within-group variance are the basis of clustering, segmentation, and optimized partitioning. Thus, the *F*-score used for statistical analysis with the ANOVA is confluent with the aggregation approaches used for clustering.

Additional calculations may be required for follow-on tests that determine the statistically significant differences between the groups, such as the Tukey; Student-Newman-Keuls (SNK); Fisher's least significant difference (LSD); and Dunnett, Holm, Bonferroni, or Duncan's multiple range test (MRT) [Ott08]. A variety of follow-on tests allow the statistician to trade off between false positives and false negatives. For example, Duncan's MRT rank orders the clusters and compares each cluster pair with a critical value determined from a studentized range distribution. This has greater

Table 1.2 Necessary (though not always sufficient) calculations for performing an ANOVA

Source of variance	Sum of squares	Degrees of freedom (*df*)	Estimate of variance (mean square)	F-score (or F-ratio)
Between groups	SS_B	N_G-1	$MS_B=SS_B/(N_G-1)$	MS_B/MS_W
Within groups	SS_W	N_S-N_G	$MS_W=SS_W/(N_S-N_G)$	
Total	$SS_T=SS_B+SS_W$	N_S-1		

See text for details.

statistical power than the SNK but results in, statistically, more false positives. Tukey's test is based on the z-test and is functionally akin to pairwise z-tests. The SNK test modifies Tukey's test to have a more relaxed difference for more closely ranked samples, providing a bias toward false positives for closely ranked samples and the same bias toward false negatives for less closely ranked samples.

1.5.3 Regression and estimation

Regression techniques [Hast09] are used to provide predictive output for input across a broad range of values. There are many flavors of regression, including the familiar *linear*, *polynomial*, and *logistic* regressions that match curve descriptors for the relationship between independent (covariate) and dependent variables. *Ridge regression*, which is also known as weight decay, adds a regularization term that effectively acts like a Lagrange multiplier to incorporate one or more constraints to a regression equation. The least absolute shrinkage and selection operator (*lasso*) regression and *stepwise selection* perform both feature selection (dimensionality reduction, in which only a subset of the provided covariates are used in the final model, rather than the complete set of them) and regularization (which allows the regression to avoid overfitting by introducing, for example, interpolated information). Advanced forms of lasso alter the coefficients of the regression rather than setting some to zero as in stepwise selection. Finally, the *elastic net* adds penalty terms to extend lasso and provides a combination of lasso and ridge functionality.

In this section, important aspects of regression for prediction—in particular sensitivity of the estimation—will be discussed using linear and logistic regression as the exemplars. Figs. 1.1 and 1.2 provide a simple linear and logistic, respectively,

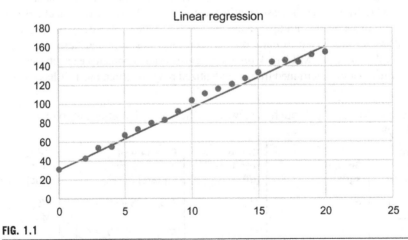

FIG. 1.1

Example linear regression where the line of best fit for the filled circular points is indicated. The line is determined using least squared error as the cost function.

curve, along with the sample points from which the curve was defined. For linear regression, the line of best fit is described by Eq. (1.6):

$$\hat{y} = \beta_0 + \beta_1 x \tag{1.6}$$

For the logistic regression curve of Fig. 1.2, the relationship between the dependent and independent variables is given by Eq. (1.7):

$$\hat{y} = \frac{1}{1 + e^{-(\beta_0 + \beta_1 x)}} \tag{1.7}$$

Once the regression curve (center curves in Figs. 1.3 and 1.4) is determined, the curve is subtracted from the observations, and the mean and standard deviation of the errors, $|x_i - \mu|$, is computed. The error bars shown in Figs. 1.3–1.6 are the 99% error bars, that is, 2.576 standard deviations above and below the regression curves.

The 99% confidence interval in Fig. 1.3 should contain 99% of all samples as the number of samples gets very large. The 20 data points collected are insufficient for truly defining or testing these intervals for confidence—generally, it will take 10–20 times the inverse of the error to have statistical confidence in an error rate or in this case 1000–2000 samples. But the lines are useful for determining sensitivity even with the small number of samples. In Fig. 1.4, another curve, this time a logistic curve, is provided along with its 99% confidence interval.

Elaborating on the confidence intervals of Figs. 1.3 and 1.4, the confidence interval around an estimate of y is treated as "uncertainty" in Figs. 1.5 and 1.6. It is important to remember that the regression curve is based on observing many values of x and y and then building a model of $y = f(x)$. However, when deployed, the regression models are used for prediction, or estimation, of what x is given an observation y.

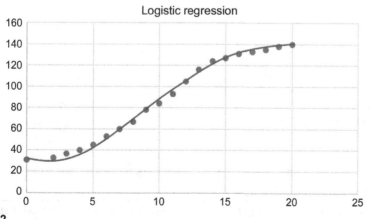

FIG. 1.2

Example logistic regression where the logistic curve of best fit for the filled circular points is indicated. The curve is determined using least squared error as the cost function.

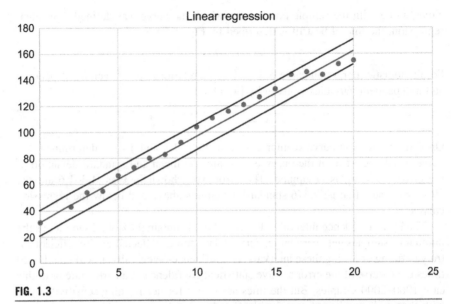

FIG. 1.3

Example linear regression of Fig. 1.1 with 99% confidence interval lines indicated. These are 2.576 standard deviations to either side of the regression line.

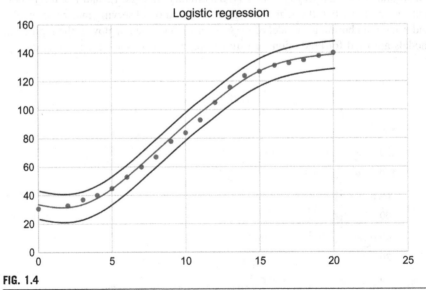

FIG. 1.4

Example logistic regression of Fig. 1.2 with 99% confidence interval lines indicated. These are 2.576 standard deviations to either side of the regression curve.

$$\hat{y} = \beta_0 + \beta_1 X$$

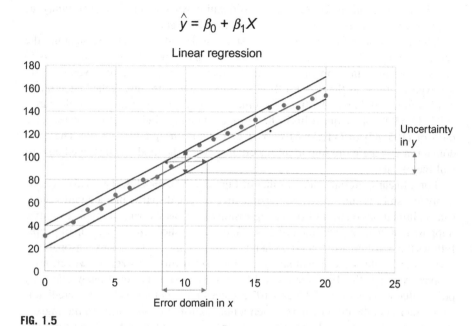

FIG. 1.5

Example linear regression of Fig. 1.1 with sensitivity lines indicated. See text for details.

$$\hat{y} = \frac{1}{1 + e^{-(\beta_0 + \beta_1 x)}}$$

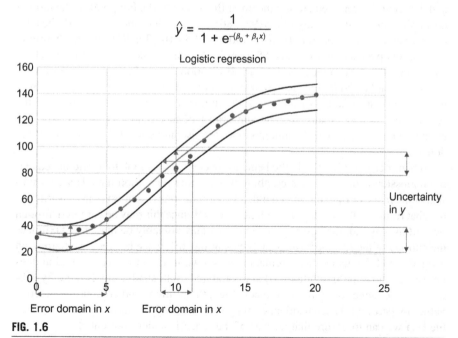

FIG. 1.6

Example logistic regression of Fig. 1.2 with sensitivity lines indicated. See text for details.

That is, $x=g(y)$. This is an important consideration when it comes to uncertainty, as the relative sensitivity of $y=f(x)$ is the inverse of $x=g(y)$.

This is shown in Fig. 1.5 where the slope of the line $y=\beta_0+\beta_1 x$, meaning the value β_1, is roughly 6.75. The uncertainty in y, therefore, should be roughly 6.75 times uncertainty in x. In the "forward" direction, we can see that when $x=10$, we expect y to be in the domain 85–105 99% of the time (this is the "uncertainty in y" in Fig. 1.5). For $y=95$ (the middomain value), we expect to see x in the range 8.5%–11.5 99% of the time (this is the "error domain in x" in Fig. 1.5). As we see, the ratio of (105–85) to (11.5–8.5) is 6.67 or roughly the predicted 6.75. The error domain in x is the more important uncertainty when the model is deployed against real (new) data.

For a linear regression such as that of Figs. 1.1, 1.3, and 1.5, the relative uncertainty in x and y is uniform across the domain of y. The disparity in uncertainty alone can put limitations on the utility of a regression model, as shown in a simple example. Suppose that in our regression model, we find that the shoe size for a group of people follows the equation size$=6+0.08$(height in inches)±1.2. This seems reasonable—given your height, we can estimate your shoe size within 1.2 sizes. However, now, suppose we know that Bob wears size 13 shoes. Reversing the equation, we can only predict that he is between 72.5 and 102.5 inches tall—not a very precise predictor!

Further complicating matters, when a nonlinear regression, such as the logistic regression of Figs. 1.2, 1.4, and 1.6, is performed, we no longer have a uniform relative uncertainty across the domain. This is illustrated in Fig. 1.6, which shows two distinct measures of uncertainty: One is centered around the point A$(x,y)=(10,89)$, and the second is centered around the point B$(x,y)=(2.5,31)$. For point A, the ratio of uncertainty in y to uncertainty in x is $(98-80)/(11-9)=9.0$, and for point B, the ratio of uncertainty in y to uncertainty in x is $(40-22)/(5-0)=3.6$. We can see, therefore, that our relative uncertainty in x is 2.5 times higher for a value of $y=31$ than it is for a value of $y=89$. We can see that given an observation, y, for a logistic curve, its uncertainty is complicated by the change in slope, or the derivative, across the domain of the independent variable, particularly with saturation or "asymptotic behavior" at the start and end of the domain. Such nonuniformity in uncertainty is even further exacerbated in functions with nonmonotonic or discontinuous behavior across the domain.

When such complexities in the behavior occur, we may look to hybrid or sequential regression approaches that combine two or more regression models across subsets of the range or domain. In general, an "optimal" regression is not necessarily the one that results in the smallest confidence interval since this may be garnered through overfitting. Instead, the best regression model may arguably be that that maximizes the entropy of the *residuals* (measurements of the difference between the regression estimates and the actual measurements), as shown in Eq. (1.8). This equation does not specify how the individual $p(i)$ are computed, but usually, this is done by subdividing the range (or domain) into equal length partitions and computing the error values by partition. When residual entropy is maximized, we have presumably done the best we can to ensure that no part of the range is underrepresented:

$$\text{Residual\_entropy} = \sum_{i=1}^{i=N} P_{residual(i)} \ln\left(p_{residual(i)}\right) \tag{1.8}$$

We can extend the utility of entropy further by modeling the residual with a noise model. Here, the entropy is calculated on the residuals when the model is subtracted from the data. Of course, a linear or logistic regression can be considered a form of model, in which case Eq. (1.9) devolves into Eq. (1.8). But Eq. (1.9) allows for a model of any complexity to be applied to data, with the model residual entropy describing the goodness of fit of the model across the range or domain:

$$\text{Model\_residual\_entropy} = \sum_{i=1}^{i=N} P_{model\_residual(i)} \ln\left(p_{model\_residual(i)}\right) \tag{1.9}$$

Finally, a data model and noise model can be combined in an overall objective function and optimized using, for example, a least-squared-error (LSE) approach as in Eq. (1.10), wherein the lasso regression model is coupled with a noise model based on noise η.

$$J = \min_{\beta_0, \beta, \eta} \left\{ \frac{1}{N_s} \sum_{i=1}^{N_s} \left(y_i - \beta_0 - x_i^T \beta - \left(x_i^T\right)^2 \eta \right)^2 \right\} \text{subject to } \|\beta\|_1 < threshold \tag{1.10}$$

Linear and logistic regressions describe many trends. Linear regression is often used to assess direct correlation, while logistic regression is used for assessment of growth rates and saturation. Both are important for prediction, or "estimation." As with the F-score for the analysis of variance (ANOVA) above, the ability to estimate accuracy is a function of "local variance" compared with "overall variance." In Fig. 1.6, we see that the ability to estimate the x-value from a given measured value of y is higher in the middle portion of the logistic curve and much poorer at the beginning and end, due to differences in slope. The overall predictability therefore depends on the sub-range, and if our goal is to have equal predictability across the range of inputs, we will need a hybrid regression model.

The usefulness of a regression model over time can be addressed by assessing the drift in the data that the process/analytic system is meant to handle. This requires training data to be organized based on its time of creation, and a *predictive model* of when the data will drift far enough for the current system to no longer satisfactorily handle the data should be gleaned. This is "introspective prediction" on the system itself. That is, we predict the ability of a predictive system to predict well over time. This is temporal prediction of the model's domain predictive capabilities.

The usefulness of a predictive model when scaling is best addressed by "under-training" the data. Ideally, this means using as small of a percentage of the ground truth as training data as possible, so that a much larger percentage of the ground truth can be used for validation and/or testing. This generally leads to greater robustness for system scaling and allows the model to be tested for temporal drift (though it is acceptable to "repurpose" the training data for testing of temporal drift anyway).

The usefulness of a regression model for distributed applications can be viewed from the perspective of modularity. The more modular an approach is, the more it can be distributed. For nearly any algorithmic task, there is domain specificity; for example, text algorithms are generally quite different from those used for extracting information from images or sensor information. Domain specificity is not, therefore, a sign of nonmodularity. However, high sensitivity to context shifts (such as moving to a different but related language or moving from one camera to another) are indicators that an analytic approach is overfitted to its task. This may be acceptable for a high-value, high-security, etc. process, but it should be understood in those overtrained circumstances that the approach adopted is likely not generalizable.

Finally, the usefulness of a regression model for reliability can be tested by specific apportionment of training data. Training and validation sets that are not highly correlated can be used to test the reliability of the analytic approach. This type of robustness is almost certainly not garnered when a k-fold cross validation is used to train and test the analytic approach, since in that case, too large of a portion of the labeled (ground truth) data are used for the training and no ability to validate the system for robustness is possible.

1.6 Algorithms for analytics

1.6.1 *k*-Means and *k*-nearest neighbor clustering

One of the most important tasks in analytics is the clustering of data. As described above (Table 1.2), the task of clustering is analogous to the task of determining which groups are statistically significantly different from each other in the finishing stage of an analysis of variance (ANOVA).

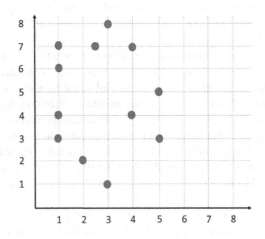

FIG. 1.7

Example array of 12 points having two dimensions that will be assigned to clusters based on their distances from other samples.

For k-means clustering, an iterative algorithm called expectation-maximization is generally employed. This iterative algorithm comprises two steps per iteration: (1) assign every sample to the closest cluster centroid and (2) redefine the cluster centroid based on the set of samples that are now assigned to it. There are several issues with this process, however:

(a) How are the original set of centroids assigned?
(b) How many centroids should there be?
(c) How are the iterations terminated?

For (a), there are many reasonable means of initiating the centroids. Among the methods that I have implemented with some success are to pick a sample at random as the first centroid and then select k-1 more centroids as the samples the farthest overall distance from the existing set of centroids. This approach works well when a bit of "noise" is added to the centroids so chosen—for example, randomly add an offset in each dimension equal to a small percentage (typically 10%–20% of the mean intercentroid distance) after the entire initial set of centroids is defined.

Fig. 1.8 uses a different method of initiating the centroids. Here, a random number generator (RNG) is used to create an n-tuple in the n dimensions of the data, and the locations are identified by the n-tuple. In Fig. 1.8, the range in $x=[0.0, 6.0]$, and the domain in $y=[0.0, 9.0]$. This is typical—a "buffer" around the extrema of a range is added inversely proportional to the number of samples and/or proportional to the mean distances between samples. Regardless, for the initial centroid that eventually became the "A" cluster in Fig. 1.8, the RNG delivered a value of [0.535, 0.590], resulting in an initial value of [3.21, 5.31] as shown where $x=0.0+0.535*(6.0-0.0)$

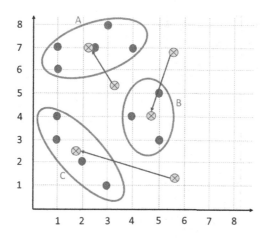

FIG. 1.8

k-Means clustering of the 12 data points from Fig. 1.7 where $k=3$. The solid circles are the data samples, and the X-filled circles are the initial cluster centroids and the final cluster centroids (arrow shows net progression of the centroid). Please see text for details.

and $y=0.0+0.590*(9.0-0.0)$. Similarly, the RNG delivered [0.916, 0.763] for eventual B cluster centroid and [0.924, 0.144] for eventual C cluster centroid.

The same approach was taken for $k=4$ in Fig. 1.9. Comparing Figs. 1.8 and 1.9 allows us to start addressing question (b), regarding how many clusters there should be. The simplest answer is, given a reasonable range of k values tested, select the one that provides the highest ratio of between-centroid variability to within-cluster variability. Adding one or more regularization methods to provide an optimal k will be discussed in Chapter 10. Finally, we need to answer question (c) and determine when to terminate the iterating. Generally, this is accomplished by checking to see whether the current set of clusters is a repeat of a previous set, in which case the iteration having the highest ratio of between-centroid variability to within-cluster variability between repeats is chosen. With very large data sets, a minimum change criterion can be used, terminating the process when the iteration changes by less than this. In all cases, an absolute maximum number of iterations should be set.

Once the clusters are formed, new points can be added to the existing clusters. The simplest form of clustering new points, however, does not even rely on the "between group" variance; instead, it simply tabulates the group membership of the k-nearest neighbors to it in the overall population. Note the same letter, k, is used here, but this is a different k entirely from the k-means k. There are two variables in this clustering approach: (1) the number of nearest neighbors, k, and (2) the definition of nearness. Each of these can be varied during the clustering process and afford some type of goodness of fit measurement. The assignment of a new sample can consider any of the following metrics for cluster belonging: (1) minimum L1-norm (absolute value of differences), per Eq. (1.11); (2) minimum L2-norm

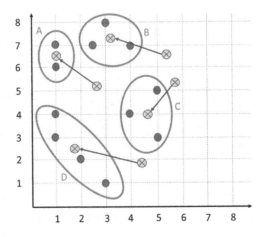

FIG. 1.9

k-Means clustering of the 12 data points from Fig. 1.7 where $k=4$. The solid circles are the data samples, and the X-filled circles are the initial cluster centroids and the final cluster centroids (arrow shows net progression of the centroid). Please see text for details.

(sum of squared differences), per Eq. (1.12); and (3) cluster with maximum number of k-nearest neighbors to the sample:

$$\min \sum_{i=1}^{n_{clusters}} \left| x_{cluster(i)} - x_{sample} \right| + \left| y_{cluster(i)} - y_{sample} \right| + \ldots \tag{1.11}$$

$$\min \sum_{i=1}^{n_{clusters}} \left(x_{cluster(i)} - x_{sample} \right)^2 + \left(y_{cluster(i)} - y_{sample} \right)^2 + \ldots \tag{1.12}$$

Clustering will be revisited in a later chapter (Chapter 10) in the context of system optimization. There, we will be optimizing system clustering by using multiple forms of regularization.

1.6.2 Unclustering

One last item related to clustering will be covered in this section. This is the concept of "unclustering," in which 100% accuracy in clustering is obtained by adding child clusters until every sample belongs to the correct family of clusters. This concept is illustrated in Fig. 1.10, where two clusters that originally had a third-order curve as the boundary (and incorrectly clustered 3 of the 35 samples) are replaced by two families of clusters having no clustering errors.

A convex hull subcluster model is chosen, and so, the parent clusters have four or five subclusters, as shown. New samples are assigned to the subcluster to which they

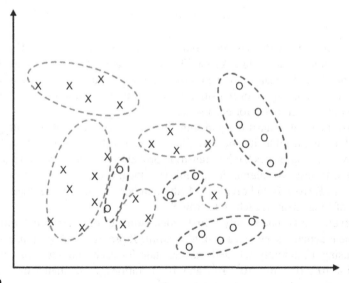

FIG. 1.10

Example of a two-class distribution that is "unclustered," in this case using a convex hull approach. Please see text for details.

are closest. While this "unclustering" approach is more complex of a model for the data than a single boundary that distinguishes all the samples, it has the additional advantage of allowing the individual subclusters to be "data mined" to see if they actually should be splinter clusters. That is, the actual data may be more fairly represented as three or more classes, which themselves may comprise multiple clusters. Various knowledge generation techniques suitable to determining the correct number of classes (e.g., by comparing the similarity of the subclusters) will be discussed in later chapters. It is clear that the unclustering approach also has the advantage of being preadapted to scaling, since as more samples are added, the statistical power of being able to ascertain the similarity among a family of subclusters will only increase.

1.6.3 Markov models

Markov models are convenient diagrams for illustrating systems with a finite number of states, and from the transition probabilities, they are convenient for determining how long a system resides in each state (or "node"). The state-state transitions are given by conditional probabilities, with an entire sequence of length S having the probability given in Eq. (1.13). Such Markov sequences are used extensively in linguistics (part of speech detection, semantics, etc.) and are used to determine other complicated sequences, like managing multiple queues simultaneously or controlling traffic flow for a large number of intersections:

$$p(o_1, o_2, ..., o_S) = p(o_1) \prod_{k=2}^{S} p(o_k \mid o_{k-1}) \qquad (1.13)$$

For our example, we will consider a four-state Markov model given in Fig. 1.11. In this model, let us consider state A first. The arrows leading from state A are the marginal probabilities for state A to remain in state A (0.33), transition to state B (0.25), transition to state C (0.22), or transition to state D (0.20). These marginal probabilities, of course, sum to 1.0 for each state.

The 16 state-state transitions and some interesting column statistics are given in Table 1.3. From the table, it is observed that the system has a positive "bias" toward state A, with all four states having transition probabilities above the expected value of 0.25. The lowest two columns in the table sum the transition probabilities for states A, B, C, and D (row 7) and divide by 4 (the number of states) to get the first-order estimate of time spent in each state (row 8).

However, this is indeed only a first-order estimate. In order to determine how much time is actually spent in each state, a simple R program was written, and a simulation, using a randomly selected starting state for each individual run, was performed for 10^2, 10^3, 10^4, 10^5, 10^6, and 10^7 iterations, as tabulated in Table 1.4. The values were very near asymptotic by 10^5 iterations.

In Table 1.5, the predicted, observed, and corresponding difference between predicted and observed times spent in each state after 10^7 iterations is tabulated.

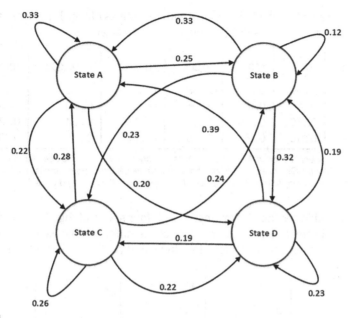

FIG. 1.11

Markov model with four states. State-state transition probabilities are adjacent to the direction of transition.

Table 1.3 Table for the Markov model with four states of Fig. 1.11, with all state-state transition probabilities

		State n			
		A	**B**	**C**	**D**
State n − 1	A	0.33	0.25	0.22	0.20
	B	0.33	0.12	0.23	0.32
	C	0.28	0.24	0.26	0.22
	D	0.39	0.19	0.19	0.23
Simplest estimate		1.33	0.80	0.90	0.97
Percent		0.3325	0.20	0.225	0.2425

The lowest two rows indicate the first-order estimate of how much time the system will spend in each state. Please see text for further details.

The values are generally close to the first-order prediction, although state B was observed 3.4% more than predicted and state D was observed 2.5% less than predicted. Not surprisingly, perhaps, these are the two states with the highest and second highest variance, respectively, in their state transition probabilities (Table 1.3).

Table 1.4 Table for the Markov model with four states of Fig. 1.11, with random starting states and between 100 and 10 million iterations

State/iterations	100	1000	10,000	100,000	1,000,000	10,000,000
A (pct)	0.340	0.327	0.338	0.332	0.333	0.3330
B (pct)	0.190	0.190	0.205	0.205	0.206	0.2068
C (pct)	0.260	0.215	0.222	0.223	0.224	0.2238
D (pct)	0.210	0.268	0.235	0.240	0.236	0.2364

Percent of time spent in each state is given. Results will vary depending on the seed for the random number generator (RNG), but any simulation should asymptotically behave the same as the last column here (this column is given to four decimal places to compare with the predicted values).

Table 1.5 Table for the Markov model with four states of Fig. 1.11, with the predicted, observed, and absolute value of the difference between predicted and observed time spent in each state indicated (10^7 iterations of the simulation)

Pct/state	A	B	C	D
Predicted	0.3325	0.20	0.225	0.2425
Observed	0.3330	0.2068	0.2238	0.2364
|Difference|	0.0005	0.0068	0.0012	0.0061

   Markov models are useful for predicting how long a system will stay in different states. If, for example, the four states in Table 1.3 correspond to four different gear ratios in an engine, then we may need to focus our postmanufacturing inspection on the gears engaged in state A, since all other factors being identical, these will wear out 41% faster than those of any other gears (those corresponding to state D).

1.7 Machine learning

In this and the next section, many of the most familiar approaches in machine learning and artificial intelligence will be covered at a largely overview level. The key here will not be to cover the topics exhaustively—as there are hundreds of new books each year on these topics—but to provide the interested reader with enough familiarity to talk intelligently on the topics, interact with experts on the topics, and know which topics to pursue further in their own work going forward. I make a somewhat arbitrary distinction between machine intelligence and artificial intelligence, not for taxonomic reasons, as likely most machine learning experts would disagree with my naming choice. For organizing these broad topics into two sections, I define machine intelligence as the algorithms and processes for turning data into information with known processes. Also, I define artificial intelligence as the processes for turning data into information with "unknown," nature-inspired processes. Thus, in this section, I cover entropy, probability, dimensionality reduction, information gain, optimization, search, data mining, recognition, and ensemble learning. Each of these is compatible with ingesting expert knowledge. In the next section, I address the broad, nature-inspired areas of genetic algorithms, artificial neural networks, and immunologically inspired algorithms.

1.7.1 Entropy

Entropy is a measurement that we have spent some time discussing above, particularly as a means of measuring the goodness of fit of a model. Entropy as a tool for use in information science and knowledge generation originated with Claude Shannon and his groundbreaking work on information theory in communications [Shan48]. Entropy is related to the maximum amount of information that can be conveyed by a certain number of bits. As such, a completely random distribution has maximum entropy, because it cannot be compressed without the loss of some aspect of its information. Entropy has, in some sense, made its fame in compression, where we can talk about a compression ratio—for example, a compression ratio of 8:1, or 800%, indicates that on the mean, we can represent a byte in a data set with a single bit. For a given discrete distribution, D, with N elements, we compute the probabilities of each event in the distribution as $p(i)$. For a simple distribution where each event is mutually exclusive, the entropy **e** is defined as in Eq. (1.14):

$$e = -\sum_{i=1}^{N} p(D_i) \ln(p(D_i)) \tag{1.14}$$

For binary systems (e.g., in communications), the log base 2 is often used in place of the natural log, and so here, the entropy is defined by Eq. (1.15):

$$e = -\sum_{i=1}^{N} p(D_i) \log_2(p(D_i)) \tag{1.15}$$

The maximum value of the entropy is therefore $\log_2(N)$, which explains why the log of 2 rather than the natural log is a convenient means of defining entropy.

As a simple example, suppose that you have a histogram with 10 bins and in those bins are distributed 100 events. The entropy associated with two different events has a maximum value of 2.303 (for natural log) or 3.322 (for log base 2). Table 1.6 illustrates a poorly randomized distribution, in which the clear majority of events accumulate in histogram bins 3, 4, and 5. The entropy of this distribution is 1.776, or 0.527 less than fully random (2.303). Table 1.7 illustrates a much more randomly distributed event set. For this distribution, the entropy is 2.285, or 0.018 less than fully random. From an entropy measurement, this is more than 29 times better than for the Table 1.6 (since $0.527/0.018 > 29$).

Entropy can be extended to multiple distributions (joint entropy) and to conditional events (conditional entropy) readily. Since almost any analytic task is amenable to some form of entropy measurement, it should always be considered as a tool for assessment.

Table 1.6 Poorly randomized distribution with overall entropy=1.776, or 22.9% less than the theoretical maximum of 2.303

Histogram bin #	$p(i)$	$\ln(p(i))$	$-p(i)\ln(p(i))$
1	0.04	−3.219	0.129
2	0.02	−3.912	0.078
3	0.24	−1.427	0.343
4	0.33	−1.109	0.366
5	0.21	−1.561	0.328
6	0.05	−3.000	0.150
7	0.04	−3.219	0.129
8	0.02	−3.921	0.078
9	0.04	−3.219	0.129
10	0.01	−4.605	0.046
Sums	1.00	NA	1.776

Table 1.7 Effectively randomized distribution with overall entropy=2.285, or 0.8% less than the theoretical maximum of 2.303

Histogram bin #	$p(i)$	$\ln(p(i))$	$-p(i)\ln(p(i))$
1	0.12	−2.120	0.254
2	0.10	−2.303	0.230
3	0.08	−2.526	0.202
4	0.11	−2.207	0.243
5	0.13	−2.040	0.265
6	0.11	−2.207	0.243
7	0.08	−2.526	0.202
8	0.07	−2.659	0.186
9	0.11	−2.207	0.243
10	0.09	−2.408	0.217
Sums	1.00	NA	2.285

1.7.2 SVM and kernels

Support vector machines (SVMs) are two-class, or binary, classifiers, although with decision tree, voting, or other ensemble approaches, they can be used to perform any level of classification. However, the manner in which multiple SVMs are aggregated may have undesirable averaging, which might mean a different ensemble approach (e.g., boosting or bagging) will perform better. Regardless, SVMs are designed to provide an adaptable approach to decision boundaries between two classes. Support vectors create boundaries for which the margin between the two classes is maximized, creating what is termed "optimal separation." While this approach can provide excellent results in training data, it can also be highly sensitive to noise for small- and medium-sized data sets. This is because the only relevant subset of input data—the support vectors—are used to define the boundary and its margin (spacing to either side of the decision boundary). In my experience, adjustment of the boundary, for example, by weighting the proximity of the boundary based on the number of samples nearby the boundary on either side (using a "repelling" force assigned to each sample) produces a more robust boundary.

Overall, the solution of the optimization problem created by the search for an optimum margin is highly complex—as a meta-analyst, you may prefer genetic, near-exhaustive, and/or artificial neural network (ANN) approaches to the mathematically precise approach of the SVM. The complexity can be moderated, however, by reducing the SVM optimization equation to what is known as the canonical representation of the decision hyperplane. This means the optimization is now recrafted as a familiar quadratic programming problem—a second-order function is optimized subject to a set of first-order inequality constraints.

As noted, the support vector machine originated from the need to determine an optimal separation between two apposed classes. The margin is the largest region with which we can separate two classes, and so, the data points closest to the margin are the support vector. The "kernel trick" is used to effectively add "extra dimensions" to the margin by introducing a kernel (Gram) matrix such as those provided in Eqs. (1.16), (1.17), and (1.18):

$$K(x, y) = (1 + x \cdot y)^S \tag{1.16}$$

$$K(x, y) = \tan h(\kappa x \cdot y - \delta) \tag{1.17}$$

$$K(x, y) = \exp\left(-(x - y)^2 / 2\sigma^2\right) \tag{1.18}$$

In these kernels, s is the degree of the polynomial in the x_k input elements. In Eq. (1.17), $K(x, y)$ is a sigmoid function in the x_k input elements with parameters κ and δ. Finally, in Eq. (1.18), $K(x, y)$ is a radial basis function (RBF) in the x_k input elements with parameter σ. The kernel trick allows us to apply an order (d) rather than order (d^2) matrix to the margin.

1.7.3 Probability

Bayesian statistics are probably the most popular approach to statistical inference in the predeep learning days. The basic Bayesian probability equation is a simple rearrangement of the law of independence, Eq. (1.19):

$$P(x \mid y)P(y) = P(y \mid x)P(x) \tag{1.19}$$

Rearranged, the equation becomes

$$P(x, y) = \frac{P(y \mid x)P(x)}{P(y)} \tag{1.20}$$

As a simple example, consider computing the probability of having a face card in a standard deck of cards given the card is a king. Obviously, this should be true every time. Here are the steps:

(1) Probability of king given a face card $=1/3=P(K|FC)$
(2) Probability of a face card $=3/13=P(FC)$
(3) Probability of a king $=1/13=P(K)$
(4) Probability of a face card given a king $=P(FC|K)$

$$P(FC|K)=\frac{P(K|FC)P(FC)}{P(K)}=\frac{\left(\frac{1}{3}\right)\left(\frac{3}{13}\right)}{\left(\frac{1}{13}\right)}=\frac{\left(\frac{1}{13}\right)}{\left(\frac{1}{13}\right)}=1 \qquad (1.21)$$

As expected, the probability $P(FC|K)$ is exactly 1. We next consider a simple example that may be less intuitive. Here, we wish to compute the probability that it was a young driver, given a car accident occurred:

(1) Probability of a car accident given a young driver $=1/3000=P(CA|YD)$
(2) Probability of a young driver $=1/12=P(YD)$
(3) Probability of a car accident $=1/4500=P(CA)$
(4) Probability of a young driver given a car accident $=P(YD|CA)$

$$P(YD|CA)=\frac{P(CA|YD)P(YD)}{P(CA)}=\frac{\left(\frac{1}{3000}\right)\left(\frac{1}{12}\right)}{\left(\frac{1}{4500}\right)}=\frac{\left(\frac{1}{36000}\right)}{\left(\frac{1}{4500}\right)}=\left(\frac{1}{8}\right) \qquad (1.22)$$

We see from the example of Eq. (1.22) that even though young drivers may be more likely to be in an accident, they are by no means in most of the accidents.

It is worth noting here that we can use two Bayesian equations together to find a relative probability of two events. Two Bayesian probabilities, those of events A and C occurring when event B occurs, are given in Eqs. (1.23) and (1.24):

$$p(A|B)=\frac{p(B|A)p(A)}{p(B)} \qquad (1.23)$$

$$p(C|B)=\frac{p(B|C)p(C)}{p(B)} \qquad (1.24)$$

Equating the $p(B)$ terms in Eqs. (1.23) and (1.24), we obtain Eq. (1.25), which is a ratio that can be used to assess the relative value of features for a Bayesian classifier:

$$\frac{p(A|B)}{p(C|B)}=\frac{p(B|A)p(A)}{p(B|C)p(C)} \qquad (1.25)$$

This rearrangement can be used readily to solve event probabilities, as well. In "person in the crow" tracking, we are looking for "continuity items" that allow us to track people through space and time, even when we can't see them for some of the time—for example, moving through a tunnel and obfuscated by another object or person. So in a large set of images, we note that a face shows up in 25% of images and a shirt shows up in 30% of images. A woman is in 80% of the facial images and in 45% of the shirt images. Given this, what are the odds of a woman's face but not a woman's shirt being present in an image? This gives us the relative likely utility of using face recognition versus clothing recognition as a tracking artifact. For this example, A=face, C=shirt, and B=woman and $p(A)$=0.25, $p(C)$=0.30, and $p(B)$=unknown. We also see that $p(B|A)$=0.80 and $p(B|C)$=0.45. Eq. (1.26) performs the calculation for us:

$$\frac{p(A|B)}{p(C|B)} = \frac{p(B|A)p(A)}{p(B|C)p(C)} = \frac{(0.80)(0.25)}{(0.45)(0.30)} = 1.48 \tag{1.26}$$

Thus, if each of the events measured is independent (which may well be the case for a large image set), the woman's face occurs in 0.48 without a shirt and 1.00 with a shirt, so 32.4% of the time a woman's face is identified, but no shirt is identified.

1.7.4 Dimensionality reduction and information gain

A fundamental, though perhaps glib, rule of thumb for analytics is that "just because you measure something doesn't mean you should use it." In this section, we consider dimensionality reduction, which is the means to remove measurements or at least dimensions that do not contribute significantly to the analysis. Dimensionality reduction reduces the number of dependent variables under consideration by obtaining a set of principal variables (either selected or composed somehow of the dependent variables). For feature selection, we rank order the features and attach a value to each feature indicative of its overall contribution to the decision. This enables a straightforward feature extraction process, wherein the remaining set of features defines the order of the dimensionality. For feature selection and extraction, at least three strategies are relevant and often deployed:

(1) Filtering, in which information gain, driven by measurements of entropy, is used as the decision criterion (see Eq. 1.27 below).
(2) Wrapping, for example, based on accuracy ranking, is used to rank order and then extract features (e.g., any feature with more than N times the error rate may be pruned).
(3) Embedding, in which features are added/removed during model construction based on the prediction errors, can be a dynamic selection process, updated based on the overall statistics over time.

If the information can be described using a histogram, with each element, i, in the histogram having probability $p(i)$, then the information gain can be viewed as the absolute value of the change of the entropy, per Eq. (1.27). Typically, information gain is due to an increase in entropy, but in the case of correctly assigning samples to their classes, a perfect classification has no entropy, and so, in that case, information gain is due to a *decrease* in entropy:

$$\text{Information gain} = \left| \sum_{final} p_i \ln(p_i) - \sum_{initial} p_i \ln(p_i) \right| \qquad (1.27)$$

A simple example of information gain is illustrated in Table 1.8. Information gain is here determined based on how well three different classifiers (row results) do on assigning samples to three different clusters A, B, and C, corresponding to Classes a, b, and c. The original cluster has 10 samples each from Classes a, b, and c, and so, the entropy of three such clusters $=3.300$. The maximum information gain is thus 3.300 if a classifier perfectly assigns each sample, generating cluster $A=\{10,0,0\}$, cluster $B=\{0,10,0\}$, and cluster $C=\{0,0,10\}$. Actual (realized) information gain is 3.300 (entropy sum), or 0.507 for distribution 1, 1.081 for distribution 2, and 1.535 for distribution 3. Distribution 3 thus has the maximum information gain and therefore performs the best classification. Note that these values correlated with the observed accuracies of 60%, 70%, and 77%, respectively, for distributions 1, 2, and 3, respectively.

1.7.5 Optimization and search

Much research has been performed in optimization, and it will be revisited in Section 1.8 with regard to genetic algorithms. Suffice it to say that this is a huge area of research, and its scope is often underestimated. Elements of optimization that are often underappreciated include considerations of (a) sensitivity analysis of the optimal algorithm or system design; (b) the robustness and relevance of the ground truth, or training data; (c) determining the breadth of the search space and performing an exhaustive "presearch" (usually as part of the training or validation); and (d) estimating the lifetime of the system and periodically ensuring that prediction meets

Table 1.8 Information gain for a classification problem

Original cluster = {10,10,10} distribution among the three classes	Cluster A	Cluster B	Cluster C	Sum of A,B,C
{a,b,c} Distribution 1	{6,2,1}	{2,6,3}	{2,2,6}	{10,10,10}
Entropy of distribution 1	0.848	0.995	0.950	2.793
{a,b,c} Distribution 2	{7,0,3}	{2,8,1}	{1,2,6}	{10,10,10}
Entropy of distribution 2	0.611	0.760	0.848	2.219
{a,b,c} Distribution 3	{8,1,1}	{0,9,3}	{2,0,6}	{10,10,10}
Entropy of distribution 3	0.639	0.563	0.563	1.765

The original cluster comprises an equal amount (10 each) of samples from each of three classes. Three different classifiers result in three different distributions of assignment, where a perfect assignment would be {10,0,0}, {0,10,0}, and {0,0,10}, with a resulting entropy of 0.000 for the distribution. Distribution 3 clearly moves the distribution entropy closest to 0.000 and so is judged the best classifier.

expectation. For (a), it is always recommended that the validation stage, if possible, be used to determine which factor(s) the optimization is most sensitive to, which can help in (b). For (b), a general rule is that the more highly optimized the system, the more sensitive it is to data drift, and there is usually a trade-off between robustness and the amount of detail provided in the description of the optimized system. For (c), the validation data are checked for how well they explore the overall anticipated range of input. Finally, for (d), the training and validation should be segmented wherever possible to account for differences in time and other input variation.

Among the considerations for optimization is how to ensure that the means of measuring/ensuring optimization does not bias the way in which optimization occurs. This means that the objective function should be made, where possible, as independent from the mechanisms for optimization as possible. This is the Stockholm syndrome of analytics, wherein an optimization approach can fall in love with the means of assessing optimization. This could, at a more mundane level, be seen analogous to teachers with "teach to the exam" rather than providing a broader set of skills. Another term for this is the *objective function paradox*. As discussed next, this is an important justification for the use of functional means of assessing optimization.

As an example of functional means of assessing a given optimization instance, let us consider functional search here. In this approach, after all the search queries have been defined, they are performed on the one or search engines of interest. For example, if the query set includes "Michigan" and "Michigan State," we perform separate searches for each of these two terms (one simple and one compound). All the queries in the set are provided as input for the search engine, and the search engine returns the web sites, documents, etc. that it determines to be best matches. These matches are typically presented in order of relevance, utility, hit frequency, or other reasonable metric and are presented to the user ranked from 1 to M, where M is the number of "hits" or "matching pages" found. Note that the "hits" or "matching pages" can be additional and otherwise ranked, for example, by their overall relevance in the data set, akin to the page rank approach. Additionally, the following modifications of the functional ranking can be employed:

(1) The engines themselves may be weighted by the relative confidence in the engines—this can be discretized by subtopic, etc., as the amount of data and confidence in the accuracy of the engines grow.
(2) The order of the results may be weighted by various manners, according to their rank in the output set provided by the search engine.

Search behavior can then be compared with the behavior of the larger document corpus, and we can determine the optimal search structure based on analyzing the differences in behavior of one or more search responses with the linking behavior of the document corpus. For example, the document corpus may be linked by metadata (author name, author provided tag, etc.).

An example of how search behavior can be used as a functional measurement for document corpus tagging is given in Table 1.9. Here, the documents have been

Table 1.9 Two different methods of comparing search behavior with the top 10 ranked documents in a corpus

Best rank "Michigan"	Rank Search1	Rank Search2	Delta rank Search1	Delta rank Search2	Weighted delta Search1	Weighted delta Search2
1 (0.345)	1 (0.233)	2 (0.147)	0	1	0.112	0.198
2 (0.217)	4 (0.145)	1 (0.404)	2	1	0.072	0.187
3 (0.145)	2 (0.217)	3 (0.145)	1	0	0.072	0.000
4 (0.078)	3 (0.194)	4 (0.112)	1	0	0.116	0.034
5 (0.045)	6 (0.052)	5 (0.088)	1	0	0.007	0.043
6 (0.033)	5 (0.065)	6 (0.033)	1	0	0.032	0.000
7 (0.031)	7 (0.025)	7 (0.025)	0	0	0.006	0.006
8 (0.017)	9 (0.011)	9 (0.007)	1	1	0.006	0.010
9 (0.009)	10 (0.007)	8 (0.010)	1	1	0.002	0.001
10 (0.008)	8 (0.019)	10 (0.003)	2	0	0.011	0.005
Top 10 (0.928)	– (0.968)	– (0.974)	10	4	0.436	0.484

Based on raw ranking differences (fourth and fifth columns from the left), Search2 is the better search engine, as its ranking difference is only 4, compared with a ranking difference of 10 for Search1. However, when the actual weighting for each document is accounted for, the difference for Search2 is now 0.484, more than the 0.436 for Search1.

ranked for their relevance to the top document for a given search term ("Michigan") based on their metadata, which has been painstakingly entered by a human operator as part of the process to establish the links between documents. Next, two distinct search engines are used, and the top 10 documents are returned in order with ranking (1–10) and relevance (summing to 1.000 for all documents in the database). As shown in Table 1.9, the differences in ranking (sum of the absolute ranking differences in comparing the search results with the metadata results) indicate that the second search engine is better; however, the differences in relevance indicate that the first search engine is better. If the relevance values are reliable, using them is generally a more appropriate functional means of assessing optimization than simply ranking results.

1.7.6 Data mining and knowledge discovery

The distinction between data mining and knowledge discovery is largely one of timing. Data mining is the process by which substantial amounts of data are organized, normalized, tabulated, and categorized; in short, it is analyzing large databases in order to generate additional information. Knowledge discovery, however, can be associated with specific context (e.g., can be guided by the vernacular of a particular specialty, organization, or practice), making it both quantitative and qualitative.

Knowledge can—and should—be viewed as having a personality. For knowledge, people are the primary resource: They provide the domain expertise that can be converted into rules, and these rules are used to guide the manner in which the knowledge is employed after its generation. Therefore, for knowledge generation, human expertise guides the input and the manner in which the input is converted into useful, *actionable* output. Knowledge generated is often the composite of several data streams, for example, publications, patents, salubrious hiring decisions, and connecting smart people in networks.

An often underappreciated part of knowledge generation is that it must be archived carefully, such that it can be reused or repurposed, with different context in the future. This requires the association of attributes and features with the data. Attributes are tags or metadata that are generally reusable in processes such as search and categorization. Features, on the other hand, can be derived (including long after the data are collected) in light of new context. Generally, when data elements are used as features, they are normalized, and missing data are filled in (a process called imputation). Features also are usually considered together with other features. This may involve principal component approaches that "dissolve" features into a mixed solution, but it can also involve decision trees in which feature-based decisions are used to reach conclusions about the data. The tree branches are often based on the optimal reduction of entropy in the remaining data set. Feature-based decision trees are particularly useful for deriving classification and association rules:

(a) Classification: if j and k, then it belongs to Class C.
(b) Association: if p and q, then it has attribute A.

For both of these, properly constructed tables allow the mapping of variables with attributes, features, categories, clusters, partitions, and classes, as appropriate. For our purposes, partitions are means of segmenting data based on *a priori* rules, while clusters are data segmentation rules learned *a posteriori*. Partitions and clusters are integral to recognition, the topic of the next section.

1.7.7 Recognition

Recognition is the assignment of data—usually compound data such as an image, a video, an audio clip, and a document—to a partition of the overall domain to which the data could possibly be assigned. Structured data will typically involve predefined and thus generally well-understood partitions in the data space, while unstructured data will typically require the generation of clusters. Classification is an advanced partition in which the partition is labeled and represented by categorization descriptives that allow it to be distinguished from other classes. Classes therefore provide both absolute and relative partitioning. Classes can be related to clusters, but they don't have to be. Clusters need not be tagged and can be differentiated solely based on absolute and relative location within a domain.

Thus, we can cluster solely based on a set of ranged values (multithresholding). We can follow clustering with the definition of classes, if we perform what I herein designate *attribute-based a posteriori construction* of classes (or, more simply, labeling).

The example of image recognition is illustrative of a broader set of recognition approaches, and as such merits some discussion here. The first step in image recognition is often the binarization, or thresholding, step. The threshold distinguishes background (below threshold) from foreground (above threshold) and can be used more generally with any type of signal, image, or volume processing. In 1-D signal processing, for example, the DC level can be subtracted from the overall signal as a threshold. The next step is segmentation, which can use the foreground (positive segmentation) or the background (negative segmentation). Segmentation results in connected components, which are often aligned with the particular elements of classification (e.g., objects). However, these components can be parts of objects or aggregates of objects depending on how well foreground and background are distinguishable and on the quality of the original images. For example, blurring can merge objects, and oversaturation can break up objects.

Key-point detection is often an important next step in the image recognition problem. A common approach to image recognition currently is to use point clouds, which are, for example, produced by 3-D scanners when they are mapping the surfaces of scanned objects. In some ways, this is analogous to a Monte Carlo simulation, in which many events are accumulated and their statistics compared with a model. The point cloud is readily compared with a model of the object to be recognized. However, the key points to be detected need not be "randomly" distributed. They can instead be part of the model for the object [Walk98], and as such recognition can be turned into an optimization (e.g., least-squared-error comparison) exercise. The object "recognized" is thereby the object whose model has the least squared error for the salient points.

The approach just mentioned is confluent with the process of classification. For image classification, there are, not surprisingly, multiple factors to be considered. Among these are whether there are multiple images available including multiple perspectives or views on the object; whether the object has a specific, generic, or no representation in the training data; and whether a single process or multiple analytic processes should be used. Whatever the choice on these options, classification is a process that benefits from continually updated training data. The number of features that can be used for image classification is quite large, running the gamut from well gamut to saturation, chroma, intensity, texture, edges, and many other image features. An algorithm such as scale-invariant feature transform (SIFT) can be used to determine the most salient features.

The training data can be used to "reset" the image recognition process in several ways. First off, the new training data can be compared with the existing training data, and nonrelevant training data can be pruned (more on this topic in Section 3.3). Secondly, the new training data can be used to "reset" the settings of the classification algorithm(s). Thirdly, the new data can be used in synchrony with the prior training data to determine if a *new architecture* for image recognition should be adopted.

For example, if the amount of training data increases significantly, the analytics architect may decide to adopt a deep learning approach instead of, for example, an SVM or boosting approach. Fourthly, more training data allow additional recognition steps—for example, skew and orientation detection and correction—to be applied, which may significantly improve recognition accuracy.

New training data will also affect the existing analytic model, irrespective of any decision to update the image recognition approach. The additional training data can improve any recognition steps that are dependent on pattern matching, since presumably better estimates of the salient points for object identification will result. Also, non-pattern-based matching is almost certainly improved. Texture matching, albedo determination, and optimization of the binarization settings are examples of matching that does not involve an object recognition step.

Recognition is not, of course, limited to 2D images (photos, maps, and video). Recognition in 1D includes voice and speech recognition (voice being a biometric and speech being a linguistic recognition process), electrocardiograms (ECGs), electroencephalograms (EEGs), telecommunications, and a wide variety of other environmental sensors (thermistors, humistors, chemosensors, etc.). The concepts applied to 2D image recognition are meaningful for 1D signal recognition. As mentioned above, subtracting out the "DC" or baseline value is a form of thresholding. Filtering, separating signal-related information from noise (random, periodic, coherent, drifting, etc.), is a form of segmentation. With the EEG, this is even more directly analogous: the alpha, beta, delta, gamma, and theta bands correspond to segmentations in both frequency and in partitioning. Identifying specific temporal landmarks (e.g., the P, Q, R, S, and T waves in an ECG) is a form of key-point detection. The concepts of classification, pattern matching, and augmenting training data are directly analogous for 1D, 2D, and 3D recognition.

Recognition in higher dimensions (3D and above, where 4D is, e.g., a 3D-over-time model) has similar approaches as for 2D. Three-dimensional object and motion recognition, for example, benefit from the same types of binarization as 2D object recognition, although they can have the binarization change by each (tomographic) slice or onion layer through the 3D object. This can incorporate a transparency model, an albedo model, or even in the case of fluorescence an absorption/emission model. Segmentation can be done in the 3D volume or can stitch together tomographic segments.

1.7.8 Ensemble learning

Ensemble learning is a form of hybrid learning system in which multiple analytics are combined intelligently with the purpose of obtaining better (more accurate, more robust, etc.) results than a single analytics can provide. Three types of ensemble learning are overviewed here: bagging, boosting, and stacking. In some ways, meta-algorithmic approaches [Sims13] can be considered specialized forms of ensemble learning; however, in this book, both meta-algorithmics and meta-analytics will be considered in their much broader system optimization context.

In a *bagging* process, random sets of samples are drawn N times *with replacement*, and nonpruned classification (decision) trees are created from these subsets. Replacement is important as it ensures that each possible decision tree branching has equal probability of being represented in the ensemble. This is meant to provide optimal coverage of the domain space. This process is repeated N times, after which the classification for each sample in the overall data set is decided by majority voting of its classification from the decision trees. Incidentally, the many decision trees so formed can be ranked for their overall accuracies and a subpopulation of them kept as a model for the classifier (if needed). Overfitting during bagging is avoided by the central limit theorem, which accompanies the averaging of the many decision trees. If the domain space is large, it may happen that samples are not incorporated into sufficient decision tree(s) for a classification to be assigned. Should this occur for any samples, they can be assigned by nearest neighbor or other decisioning approaches. Randomization (adding a small random bias to decision tree node splits) can add further robustness and path coverage to this simple but often effective design. Overall, bagging does not necessarily provide a significant improvement in accuracy, but it usually provides excellent rank bias, moving the correct classification higher up in ranking.

Boosting is an alternative form of ensemble learning in which the weighting of the samples changes over time to allow the system to optimize its decision by considering the results from the samples in proportion to their (positive) impact on overall system accuracy. In boosting, initially, the samples are equally weighted. After each iteration of the algorithm, the samples that are correctly assigned are weighted lower than the incorrectly assigned samples. This is analogous to the formation of a support vector, except that in the case of a support vector, the samples are zero-weighted unless they are abutting the boundary zone between two classes. With boosting, the approach is innately scalable to any number of classes. Weighting factors often employed for the correctly classified samples are $e/(1-e)$ and $1+\log[e]$, where e is the error rate of the current iteration classifier. These factors quickly scale over the error range of 0.1–0.9, as shown in Table 1.10. The first, $e/(1-e)$, has a range of $[0.0, +\infty)$, whereas the second, $1+\log_{10}[e]$, has a range of $[0.0, 1.0]$.

Table 1.10 Error rate, e, and two different weightings for a boosting approach

Error rate e	Weight $=e/(1-e)$	Weight $=1+\log_{10}[e]$
0.1	0.111	0.000
0.3	0.429	0.477
0.5	1.000	0.699
0.7	2.333	0.845
0.9	9.000	0.954

Both weights are much higher for a higher error weight, except that e/(1−e) scales from 0.0 to +infinity, whereas 1+log10[e] scales from 0.0 to 1.0. Regardless, the overall sum of weights for all samples is scaled to 1.0 after the weights in this table are computed and assigned.

After computing the weights as in Table 1.10, the final weights for each sample are normalized, for example, so that the sum of weights is 1.0. The boosting approach is amenable to the multiplicity of decision trees as for bagging and like bagging tends to provide good rank bias for intelligent systems.

The third ensemble approach discussed in this section is stacking, which is also known as stacked generalization. This approach is difficult to analyze theoretically, as it is applied to multiple models that are built by two or more learning algorithms—for example, a Bayesian and a decision tree approach. Stacking leads toward the architectural approaches associated with meta-algorithms, except that stacking does not provide specific design patterns to employ. Traditional stacking approaches end with the application of output probabilities for every class and weighted voting based on summing these probabilities for each sample and each algorithm. As with bagging and boosting, stacking tends to provide good rank bias for intelligent systems.

In addition to these well-known ensemble approaches, there are some other topics to consider for ensemble or at least hybrid approaches to analytics. The first is to employ sensitivity analysis wherever possible, to see where the analytic model is most sensitive to changes in the input. This can be readily performed by adding slight changes to the training data (e.g., by feature) and then analyzing the first derivative of the model across the domain. The model with the smallest mean first derivative (best when applied to data that has been normalized to have a mean of 0.0 and a standard deviation of 1.0, of course) is generally the model least sensitive to changes in the input. This then identifies the model that is "most robust" and complements the ensemble methods of bagging, boosting, and stacking, which generally focus on accuracy.

Another ensemble method is a spatial-continuity hybrid. Multiple models for a data set are hypothesized, and among the domain of the input, the models are weighted differently (still normalized to sum to 1.0 for all models) with any settings (e.g., coefficients) adjusted to make the hybrid model behavior be contiguous across the boundaries of the subdomain. In general, the "adjusting" needed for continuity should be relatively minor: adjustments of more than a few percent of the standard deviation of the variable or feature are generally indicative of a poor subdomain boundary having been chosen. This ensemble method is generally used for classification, but it can be applied to clustering, as well. With clustering, the settings that are checked for continuity across the spatial subdomain boundaries are not the weightings of the individual analytics, however. For clustering, a k-nearest neighbors (kNN) approach may be used for cluster assignment, and an F-score computing the ratio of within-cluster to between-cluster variance is used to determine the value of k. For spatial ensemble methods, we may choose to provide a moving average of F-score and/or k across subdomain boundaries. However, clustering also can be guided by temporal continuity hybridization, wherein a moving average of F-score and k over time is used to guide the reformation of clusters (unclustering and merging clusters).

1.8 Artificial intelligence

As mentioned above, for purposes of organization of this chapter, I define artificial intelligence (AI) as the processes for turning data into information employing nature-inspired processes. A relative disadvantage of artificial intelligence compared with the machine learning approaches of Section 1.7 is that we often do not have a good understanding of how the AI is making its decision. This makes the pruning of training data, the selection of new features, and performing sensitivity analysis more difficult with AI than with machine learning. In this admittedly abbreviated/superficial section, I consider genetic algorithms, artificial neural networks, and immunologically inspired analytics.

1.8.1 Genetic algorithms

Genetic algorithms incorporate concepts from the world of mitosis and meiosis. Chromosomes, of which there are 23 pairs in most human cells (except germ and anucleate cells), carry long strings of quaternary (two bits) base pairs, totaling 3×10^9 in the human genome. This corresponds to 6×10^9 bits, or 750 M bytes. Effectively, then, DNA (and RNA, with simply one nucleotide, thymine, replaced by uracil) is a long binary string. Individual locations in the string are called loci (singular locus), and different substrings occupying the same location within a chromosome are called alleles. The binary strings are readily altered from generation to generation by the following mechanisms:

(1) Mutation, in which one of the loci is randomly altered to another of the allowed elements. In DNA, this might mean a thymine is replaced by a guanine, cytosine, or adenine. In a binary string, it can only mean that a "0" is replaced by a "1" or a "1" is replaced by a "0." However, in some advanced genetic algorithms, we can change the length of the bit string, too. Thus, we can allow insertions and deletions as well as substitutions for mutations in the broadest sense. As an example, suppose that we have a string encoded by "0001101011." A mutation (substitution) at the fifth locus changes the string to "0001001011." An insertion of a "1" before the seventh locus changes the string to "00011011011." A deletion of the third locus changes the string to "001101011."

(2) Crossover, in which strings exchange substrings. Usually, the amount of material exchanged is aligned and of the same length for the two chromosomes. For the string "000110110111101010111" and the string "11001110111101001000," if we crossover loci 6–9, then the first string becomes "000111101111101010111," and the second string becomes "11001011011101001000." Crossover can result in several mutations simultaneously—the expected value of the number of mutations is half the length of the crossover for binary strings.

(3) Inversion, in which substrings are reversed in order. For the string "110010110111101001000" in the previous example, suppose that we invert loci 7–12. We thereby obtain "110010111101101001000" that only changes two of the six bits in the run. In general, the expected number of loci changed during an inversion is half of the length of the inversion range for binary strings.

(4) Alleles, which are highly related chromosomes differing only in short substrings and which can also be designated "traits" or "genes." "11001011101101001000" and "11001011101101111010" are two alleles of "11001011101101," one with the allele (at the end) of "001000" and the other with allele at the end of "111010." Alleles are highly useful when a part of the overall optimization space is "known good"—in this example, the "11001011101101"—but the rest of the space is less optimized. The "known good" substring can preferentially survive into the next iteration, which will make sense after we see how a genetic algorithm (GA) works.

(5) The concepts of incomplete dominance and codominance also afford us with differential survivability methods across iterations. Incomplete dominance means that certain substrings—whether alleles (locked in a particular place) or "peptides" (having the same sequence but not in a fixed location in the overall string)—survive better into the next iteration. Codominance means that two alleles or paired peptides survive with the same rate into the next iteration.

We will learn more about how genetic algorithms (hereafter "GAs") by example. The example given is extremely simplified, so the reader can focus on the main points, rather than getting lost in the data.

Step 1 is creating a population of chromosomes. For our example, we will have only five chromosomes per generation, each 15 bits in length. More typical applications may have hundreds of chromosomes, although the length of each chromosome is somewhat domain-dependent. Our starting population of "randomly" defined chromosomes is given here:

1. 100011000111101
2. 001001110110110
3. 110111010111011
4. 001011101000111
5. 101010100010100

These 15 loci represent a 15-element string. Although we do not know the "optimal solution" before evaluating, let us suppose that the optimal solution is actually "101110011000110" and that the "value" of having each of the loci correct is 5 each for the first 5 loci, 10 each for the second 5 loci, and 20 each for the third 5 loci, that is, getting the initial "10111" exactly right has a benefit of 25, getting the next "00110" exactly right has a benefit of 50, and getting the final "00110" correct has a benefit of 100. The maximum score obtainable is thus $25+50+100=175$, although we cannot tell that *a priori*. This value, 175, is therefore the maximum fitness of a chromosome, and the individual fitness can be determined by adding up the

Table 1.11 Iteration 1, original bit strings, their Hamming distance from the ideal string of "101110011000110" (which we have no way of computing until the ideal string is found, if indeed it is, at the end of the iterations), and their measure of fitness, which presumably can be measured at the end of each iteration

String	Hamming distance	Fitness
100011000111101	10	45
001001110110110	8	100
110111010111011	9	55
001011101000111	6	115
101010100010100	6	100

5s, 10s, and 20s of the fitness whenever the value is correct. Table 1.11 tabulates the Hamming distance (number of bits with different values—i.e., "1" instead of "0" or "0" instead of "1") of each of the five original bit strings and the fitness. While the Hamming distance is unknown during the iterations, since we do not know the "optimal" 15-bit sequence, the fitness can be measured after each iteration, and so, we have a means of assessing the relative fitness for survival into the next iteration of each of the strings. As we can see, Hamming distance does not always inversely correlate with fitness, even though the optimal string has a Hamming distance of 0 and the worst possible string has a Hamming distance of 15.

Step 2 is determining which chromosomes survive to be the beginning pool of the next iteration. Note that in this example problem, there are 15 bits in the string. For a binary string, there are 2^N unique chromosomes, where N=length or the number of bits. Since N=15, there are 32,768 different chromosomes—for example, corresponding to 15 distinctive design choices by the system architect. We really do not want to simulate (let alone build) all 32,768 systems, so we are hoping that the optimization converges quickly. As such, we define and calculate a measure of goodness of fit for each of the chromosomes produced. As mentioned above, getting one of the optimal values in the first five loci adds 5 to the fitness; in the next 5 loci, 10 to the fitness; and in the last 5 loci, 20 to the fitness. All nonmatches contribute 0 to the fitness. Table 1.11, column 3, tabulates these, and we see that they range from 45 to 115, with a mean of 83.0. This fitness is slightly less than the expected value of fitness for pure guessing, which is 175/2 = 87.5. We also note in Table 1.11 that the mean Hamming distance, 7.8, is just above the expected value of 7.5 obtained for pure guessing. We have no way of knowing this until after the optimal string is discovered, but it is a valuable means of assessing how the GA works during the iterative process. We assign a survival weight to each of the five chromosomes based on their relative fitness. In this simple example, we simply compute the relative fitness of each chromosome, based on its percentage of the total summed fitness of all chromosomes (Table 1.12).

Table 1.12 Iteration 1, fitness, relative fitness, and number surviving for each of the five chromosomes

String	Fitness	Relative fitness	Number surviving
100011000111101	45	0.108	0
001001110110110	100	0.241	1
110111010111011	55	0.133	0
001011101000111	115	0.277	2
101010100010100	100	0.241	2

In this iteration, one copy of chromosome 2 and two copies of chromosomes 4 and 5 survived for modification and reiteration.

Next, we use the relative fitness of each chromosome and a random number generator (RNG) to determine how many of each chromosome, if any, survive into the next iteration. Our RNG produces a value between 0.0 and 1.0, and we therefore assign the following ranges:

1. RNG output=[0.0, 0.108]; chromosome 1 survives.
2. RNG output=[0.108, 0.349]; chromosome 2 survives.
3. RNG output=[0.349, 0.482]; chromosome 3 survives.
4. RNG output=[0.482, 0.759]; chromosome 4 survives.
5. RNG output=[0.759, 1.0]; chromosome 5 survives.

Running the RNG, we observed these five values: 0.511, 0.893, 0.277, 0.663, and 0.905, which means a copy of chromosomes 4, 5, 2, 4, and 5, respectively, survive.

Step 3 involves passing along something good to the children. Survival of the fittest does not usually imply parthenogenesis. That is, the genes are not passed along unchanged to the offspring (why should they be? We already know what the fitness will be!). Instead, they are modified somewhere in the range between minor and substantially, and these modified offspring are then the evaluated pool for the next generation. The alterations start with mutations (Table 1.13), where for purposes of

Table 1.13 Iteration 1 initial survivors, number of mutations, new string, and the Hamming distance and fitness of the new string when compared with the ideal string of "101110011000110"

String	No. of mutations	New string	Hamming distance	Fitness
001001110110110	1	001001110110111	9	80
001011101000111	3	101011111000110	3	150
001011101000111	1	001010101000111	5	125
101010100010100	2	101000110010100	6	105
101010100010100	2	101010100000110	4	140

The realized mutation rate was 12%. Mutated loci are indicated by boldface in column 3.

illustration, we are using a high mutation rate of 10%. Random mutations with a probability of 0.10 in Table 1.13 led to a realized mutation rate of 0.12 (i.e., 12%). Even before the mutations, the mean fitness of the surviving strings (two sets of which were identical chromosomes) rose to 106 from 83. After the mutations shown in Table 1.13, the mean fitness rose further to 120. The mean Hamming distance—which again we cannot assess in real time since we still don't know the actual optimal string— dropped considerably to 5.4.

Mutation, of course, is only the first step in adding some genetic variability for the next generation. In addition to mutation, we can consider crossover. Two crossover events occur in Table 1.14, both of which swap four-bit substrings between two strings. The first, designated crossover event A, is between the first and third chromosomes, loci 7–10. The second crossover occurs between strings 4 and 5 (before mutation, the same chromosomes), loci 6–9. Since crossovers exchange, but do not change, the overall collective set of matching loci, the mean Hamming distance (5.4) and mean fitness (120) do not change in Table 1.14 relative to Table 1.13. However, after crossover, two new strings have fitness of 150 or more. The overall crossover rate here is also quite high for purposes of illustration—16 out of 75 or 21.3% of loci are involved in crossover.

The last operation to perform in this iteration is inversion, should one be indicated by the output of the RNG. In this example, one inversion is indicated by the RNG, and it affects loci 4–7 of string 2. As shown in Table 1.15, this further improves the fitness of string 2 to 165.0.

At this point, iteration 1 is complete, and we can calculate how much an iteration has brought us. The mean Hamming distance has improved from 7.8 to 5.0, and the mean fitness has increased from 83.0 to 123.0. New goodness of fit for the output strings of Table 1.15, based on their relative fitness, is 0.146, 0.268, 0.187, 0.154, and 0.244, respectively. These are more uniform than for the original set of strings, and the difference between the most fit string and the optimal string has dropped

Table 1.14 Iteration 1 survivors, after mutations, with two crossover events (bold and italic) occurring between strings 1 and 3 (crossover A) and between two mutated versions of the same surviving chromosome, strings 4 and 5 (crossover B)

String	Crossover?	New string	Hamming distance	Fitness
001001110110111	Yes (A)	001001*101*010111	8	90
101011111000110	No	101011111000110	3	150
001010101000111	Yes (A)	001010*110*100111	6	115
101000110010100	Yes (B)	10100*0100*010100	7	95
101010100000110	Yes(B)	10101*0110*000110	3	150

Since crossover exchanges substrings, it does not alter the mean Hamming distance (still 5.4) or the mean fitness (still 120), though the individual string values for Hamming distance and fitness may change.

Table 1.15 Iteration 1 survivors, after mutations and crossover occurring in Tables 1.13 and 1.14, with a single inversion event affecting string 2, loci 4–7

String	Inversion?	New string	Hamming distance	Fitness
001001101010111	No	001001101010111	8	90
101011111000110	Yes	101**1110**11000110	1	165
001010110100111	No	001010110100111	6	115
101000100010100	No	101000100010100	7	95
101010110000110	No	101010110000110	3	150

Since this event improved string 2's fitness, the mean Hamming distance is now 5.0, and the mean fitness is now 123.0. Moreover, the fitness of string 2 is now within 10 of the absolute optimum value of 175.

from 60 to 10. Continuing along this path, the optimal string might be obtained in 4–5 iterations, required only 20–25 candidates to be simulated and/or built and tested, rather than the 32,768 required for exhaustive search.

This relatively simple example outlines some of the basics of a genetic approach, particularly for optimization. However, as implemented, the GA is not going to be particularly useful for a wide variety of optimization situations, since it requires them to be reduced to a single binary string. However, we rarely need to use just a single GA in a robust, hybrid system. There, we typically use the GA for one or more of the following:

1. Separate out the decision tasks and use the genetic algorithms to optimize the decisions against a reasonable cost function. Traditional clustering, classification, and segmentation approaches can be used to identify the separable decision tasks for the GA to tackle.
2. Ensure that the GA task space is as small as possible—whenever possible, break up the overall optimization into multiple GA processes (genetic algorithms along the lines of those illustrated herein do not generally scale well).
3. Use neural networks, boosting, SVM, and/or meta-algorithmic patterns for classification, regression approaches for estimation, etc., and only deploy the GA where absolutely needed. Genetic algorithms are not "one size fits all" and are a useful tool, but not hardware store, for the analytic expert.

In this section, I have scratched the surface of genetic and evolutionary algorithms, introducing the relatively straightforward processes of mutation, crossover, and inversion. Clearly, the role of these processes is to provide "just enough" variability in the offspring of a generation of chromosomes to allow these "child chromosomes" to effectively explore both the local optima that might be near the higher-fitness parent generation chromosomes while still searching for the global optima if it is distinct from any of the local optima. There are many additional approaches in genetic and evolutionary programming, including specific replication of high-fitness strings (rather than just using a "lottery" or RNG-based system for survival), which is a form of codominance in which both direct and RNG-based inheritance is allowed. Substitution, deletion, and insertion processes can be extended to nonbinary strings, if, for example, evolutionary approaches are used on linguistic applications. Additional means of hybridizing survival populations include regrouping, colonization-extinction, and migration [Akba11]. In regrouping, there are several "groups" of strings evaluated simultaneously (e.g., multiple sets of five strings using our example), and all groups are mixed together, and then, new groups are formed. For migration, the same type of grouping is used, and at the end of each iteration, an individual is encouraged to leave its own group and move to one of its neighbor groups. Finally, for the extinction-colonization process, a group is selected as extinct (due to low fitness) and replaced by offspring of a colonist group.

Evolutionary algorithms, of which genetic algorithms are a straightforward example, are useful in optimization processes, especially when—as in the example—the options at each step can be assigned to a small dictionary: binary as used in the example being the simplest, but ASCII, alphanumeric, numeric, and other dictionaries are acceptable, as well. These dictionaries should be as small as possible for performance reasons, but the ability to support dictionaries of varied sizes is a benefit of genetic and evolutionary approaches. Evolutionary approaches are also useful in search, which can be viewed in some ways as an inverse process to optimization. In search, the proximity of content can be used to weight the operators (mutation, crossover, inversion, etc.).

1.8.2 Neural networks

Neural networks, or artificial neural networks (ANNs), are roughly based on the connectivity within biological nervous systems. To understand some of the principles of neural networks, we provide here an overview of the human visual system, as its architecture and processes are used to model many ANNs, including convolutional neural networks.

The retina, a sensory extension of the brain, comprises several special types of cells, including the photoreceptor cells. These are the sensory cells of the visual system, comprising the rods and cones. There is one type of rod, which is sensitive to incident light of 400–700 nm (510 nm peak), and three types of cones: beta (blue, 420 nm), gamma (green, 531 nm), and rho (red, 558 nm). The cones are not equally distributed, with there being twice as many rho receptors as gamma receptors and many less beta receptors. This is why people can read red text better than blue text. The rods and cones are not evenly distributed, with their absolute and relative (to rods) concentration decreasing with distance from the fovea.

After photoreception, the array of light on the photoreceptors forms a pattern, matching the light pattern in the visual field. Each photoreceptor is effectively a pixel in the 2-D array on the retina, which is a photosensor with a pixel resolution of 400 pixels/mm (1.6×10^5 cones/mm^2) or 10,000 pixels/inch in the fovea (the part of the retina normal "focused" best). This photoreceptor-level information is then parallel processed with both a direct pathway and with "receptive fields" that surround each photoreceptor (acting as a convolution window around the photoreceptor). Anatomically, the direct path of visual information to the lateral geniculate nucleus (LGN) of the thalamus follows the bipolar and ganglion cells, while horizontal and amacrine cells lead to edge enhancement through lateral inhibition and to ON/OFF "receptive fields" via excitatory/inhibitory interconnections. Interplexiform cells feedback information from the ganglion cell level to the horizontal cell level. Thus, the architecture of the retina, while only three cells thick, provides a powerful gain and feedback design.

Embryologically, an extension of the brain's tissue, the retina, is architected "inside out," with the rod and cone pigment epithelium being the farthest from the iris, where light enters the eye. The photoreceptor cells are just above the epithelium, in the outer nuclear layer. The next layer is the outer plexiform layer, which includes the horizontal cells, enabling convolution-like effects, which are called the lateral pathway. The inner nuclear layer, comprising the bipolar cells, is the first vertical pathway cells. Because they receive input from multiple cones, they may blur or compress the information, particularly when farther from the fovea. Compression in the fovea is generally 1:1, but in the periphery of the retina (where you are tested for "peripheral vision"), the compression may be as high as 1000:1. The convolution-like effects are modulated by the inner plexiform layer, comprising amacrine cells, which are also part of the lateral pathway. The third direct-in-line cells are the ganglion cells, whose axons are bundled together into the optic nerve, which exits the retina in the so-called blind spot.

From a signal processing standpoint, then, the photoreceptors are the sensors, the bipolar and ganglion cells are compression algorithms, and the horizontal and amacrine cells are convolution algorithms. ANNs are at least roughly based on the connectivity within biological nervous systems. The bipolar cells are effectively a "hidden layer" between the photoreceptors as input layers and the ganglion cells as output layers. Horizontal and amacrine cells are analogous to the weighted connections of ANNs. Interplexiform cells are analogous to the back-propagation (of error, used for training) functions in ANNs. In the human brain, of course, most of the visual processing occurs in the occipital lobe, which is much more complex than the retina (six-layered instead of three-layered). The visual cortex I and its hypercolumns for massive series-parallel processing are where movement and color are determined.

The concept of the receptive field is important for the retina and for the ANN. A receptive field is defined as an area that affects a sensory cell. For the retina, this is the set of photoreceptors that can affect the output of a subsequent bipolar, ganglion, or other cell. Bipolar and ganglion cells near the fovea have much smaller receptive fields than peripheral ones, and in general, ganglion cells have larger receptive fields than bipolar cells. Convergence (or compression) is proportional to the receptive field size and is >1000 in the periphery but 1 in the foveola. Divergence also occurs simultaneously, due to overlap of the receptive fields of neighboring cells. However, simple compression is not sufficient—there must be intelligent compression taking into account surrounding cells to incorporate motion across a receptive field as part of the compressed data. The retina has ON-center and OFF-center ganglion cells, which respond differently to provide the analogue of sharpening (ON center) and blurring (OFF center). In the retina, these center/surround structures provide lateral inhibition, edge and motion detection, and general light-intensity information at the ganglion level.

For the purposes of our brief tutorial on ANNs, we need to consider the following definitions:

(1) Inputs: An input vector is one input to the system usually written as vector $\mathbf{x}$ where $x_i =$ one element, $i = \{1,\dots,m\}$.
(2) Weights: w_{ij} is the weighted connection between nodes i and j. Modeled after synapses in a nervous system. Arranged as matrix $\mathbf{W}$.
(3) Outputs: An output vector $\mathbf{y}$ is the output vector $y_i =$ one element, $j = \{1,\dots,n\}$, formally $\mathbf{y}(\mathbf{x},\mathbf{W})$ since the vector is a function of $\mathbf{x}$ and $\mathbf{W}$.
(4) Targets: A target vector $\mathbf{t}$ contains extra data needed for supervised learning—contains the "correct" or training data. Note that $t_j =$ one element, $j = \{1,\dots,n\}$.
(5) Activation function: A mathematical function, usually given as $g()$ for gain or conductance, describing the firing of the neuron in response to the weighted inputs. Often a simple binary decision or threshold. If the sum of $w_{ij}x_i$ coming to node y_j exceed a threshold, provide output $= 1$; else, output $= 0$. Formally, $A = f(\mathbf{x},\mathbf{W})$.
(6) Error: Usually a function, E, which computes the inaccuracies of the network as a function of targets $\mathbf{t}$ and outputs $\mathbf{y}$; that is, $E = f(\mathbf{t},\mathbf{y})$.

The interplay of these elements of an ANN is shown in Fig. 1.12.

We start with a small section of a relatively complicated neural network (the multilayer perceptron) and describe how it works next. The base network showing the nodes (filled circles) and the connections (line segments with arrows pointing to the output) are shown in Fig. 1.13.

The ANN of Fig. 1.13 has the input, connection weight, and output notation added in Fig. 1.14. The input to $\mathbf{y}$ is $\mathbf{x}$, and to $\mathbf{z}$, it is $\mathbf{y}$. The output to $\mathbf{x}$ is $\mathbf{y}$, and to $\mathbf{y}$, it is $\mathbf{z}$. Overall, $\mathbf{x}$ is the input, $\mathbf{y}$ the hidden layer, and $\mathbf{z}$ the output of the ANN.

Next, for the labeled ANN of Fig. 1.14, we compute the path gains. For one specific input vector $\mathbf{x}$:

$$y_1 = w_{11}x_1 + w_{21}x_2 + w_{31}x_3 + w_{41}x_4$$

$$y_2 = w_{12}x_1 + w_{22}x_2 + w_{32}x_3 + w_{42}x_4$$

$$y_3 = w_{13}x_1 + w_{23}x_2 + w_{33}x_3 + w_{43}x_4$$

And for the hidden layer vector $\mathbf{y}$:

$$z_1 = \hat{w}_{11}y_1 + \hat{w}_{21}y_2 + \hat{w}_{31}y_3$$

$$z_2 = \hat{w}_{12}y_1 + \hat{w}_{22}y_2 + \hat{w}_{32}y_3$$

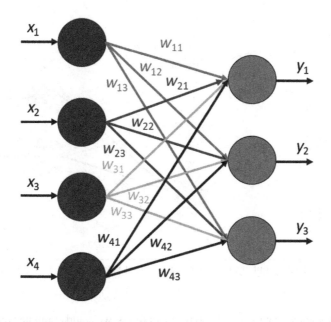

FIG. 1.12

Simple artificial neural network (ANN) illustrating two layers. The input vector is **x**, the output vector **y**, and the weights **w** on the connections from the input nodes (circles on left) and output nodes (circles on right).

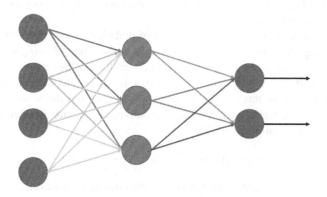

FIG. 1.13

Section of a larger multilayered perceptron ANN illustrating input *(left)*, hidden *(center)*, and output *(right)* nodes (filled circles) and the connections between them, shown as line segments with arrows pointing from the input to the output of a stage in the ANN. The hidden layer is the output to the input layer, and the output layer is the output to the hidden layer.

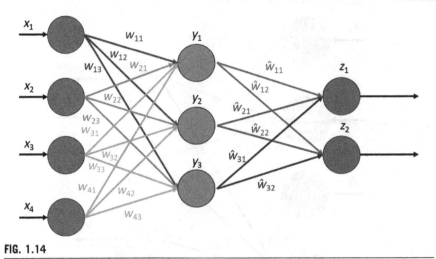

FIG. 1.14

ANN of Fig. 1.13 with input layer, hidden layer, output layer, and weighting indicated.

If we really wanted to write out the long calculations, we could compute z_1 as follows (and z_2 in like fashion):

$$z_1 = \hat{w}_{11}(w_{11}x_1 + w_{21}x_2 + w_{31}x_3 + w_{41}x_4) + \hat{w}_{21}y(w_{12}x_1 + w_{22}x_2 + w_{32}x_3 + w_{42}x_4)$$
$$+ \hat{w}_{31}y(w_{13}x_1 + w_{23}x_2 + w_{33}x_3 + w_{43}x_4)$$

Generally, however, the hidden layer makes some decisions of its own, which means a closed-form expression for the relationship between **x** and **z** is not advantageous and perhaps not possible.

Next, we need an algorithm for setting and updating the weights. First, we initialize the weights of the connections randomly in the range of $-1/\sqrt{m}$ to $+1/\sqrt{m}$. The value of m is often chosen to be 1. We then randomize the order of inputs from one iteration to the next. Next, an input vector, **x**, is put into the input nodes, and the inputs are fed forward through the network—the inputs and the **w** weights decide whether the hidden nodes **y** fire or not. The activation function is often a sigmoid function such as given in Eq. (1.28).

$$a(j) = g\left(h(j) = \sum_{i=1}^{m} w_i x_i \middle| j\right) = \frac{1}{1 + e^{-\beta hj}} \tag{1.28}$$

The outputs of these neurons, either $g(h)$ or usually the all-or-none (thresholded) version of $g(h)$, multiplied by the $\hat{w}$ weights, are then used to decide if the output **z** nodes fire or not. The error is computed as the sum-of-squares difference between the training targets **t** and the output **z** nodes, and the error is back propagated (fed backward) through the network so as to update the $\hat{w}$ weights using Eq. (1.29):

$$\delta_{ok} = (t_k - y_k)y_k(1 - y_k) \tag{1.29}$$

The error in the **y** layer is computed using Eq. (1.30):

$$\delta_{hj} = a_j(1-a_j)\sum_k \hat{w}jk\delta_{ok} \qquad (1.30)$$

The $\hat{\mathbf{w}}$ weights are updated using Eq. (1.31):

$$\hat{w}jk = \hat{w}jk + \eta\delta_{ok}a_j \qquad (1.31)$$

Finally, update the **w** weights using Eq. (1.32):

$$wjk = wjk + \eta\delta_{hj}x_i \qquad (1.32)$$

Note that eta, η, is typically a small fraction, for example, 0.1, 0.2, or 0.3. An example of how this comes together will be instructive. For this example, we consider the ANN shown in Fig. 1.15. The input is the representation of the first third of a letter, and so, for H, the input $\mathbf{x}=[1\ 1\ 1\ 1]$, and for T, the input $\mathbf{x}=[1\ 0\ 0\ 0]$.

The artificial neural network in Fig. 1.15 is then trained to recognize different input sets, including those for T and H. The weights learned are shown in Fig. 1.16.

In Fig. 1.16, we see that the sums for y_1 are 3.4 for H and 1.0 for T. This is because $y_1=(1.0)1+(0.8)1+(0.8)1+(0.8)1=3.4$ for H and $y_1=(1.0)1+(0.8)0+(0.8)0+(0.8)0=1.0$ for T. Similarly, the sums $y_2=(0.5)1+(0.5)1+(0.5)1+(0.5)1=2.0$ for H, and $y_2=(0.5)1+(0.5)0+(0.5)0+(0.5)0=0.5$ for T; the sums $y_3=(0.3)1+(0.2)1+(0.1)1+(0.0)1=0.6$ for H, and $y_3=(0.3)1+(0.2)0+(0.1)0+(0.0)0=0.3$ for T.

We then threshold the values for **y** to binarize each of $\{y_1, y_2, y_3\}$ to be 0 or 1. If the threshold is in the range [2.0, 3.4], then $y_1=1$ and $y_2=y_3=0$ for H, and $y_1=y_2=y_3=0$ for T. In this case, $z_1=1.0$ for H and 0.0 for T, and $z_2=0.6$ for H and 0.0 for T. If instead the threshold on **y** is in the range [1.0, 2.0], then $y_1=y_2=1$ and $y_3=0$ for H, and $y_1=y_2=y_3=0$ for T. In this case, $z_1=2.0$ for H

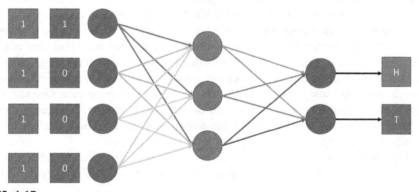

FIG. 1.15

ANN, for example, where the input is the first third of a character. For the H, it is all 1s since the first third of an H looks like "I." For the T, it is all 0s except for the top fourth since only the left side of the crossbar of the T is nonbackground. Regardless, the input $\mathbf{x}=[1\ 1\ 1\ 1]$ for H, and $\mathbf{x}=[1\ 0\ 0\ 0]$ for T.

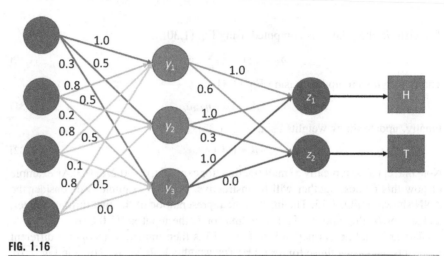

FIG. 1.16

ANN of Fig. 1.15 after weights have been learned for distinguishing *H*, *T*, and some other possible inputs for **x**. See text for details, please.

and 0.0 for *T*, and $z_2 = 0.9$ for *H* and 0.0 for *T*. So, across a wide range of thresholds, we readily distinguish *H* and *T* at **z**. Note that we can only distinguish a maximum of four inputs (or input classes) at **z** since **z** is just two bits. We therefore must compress a four-bit input to a three-bit hidden layer to a two-bit output.

We have several design options here—the number of nodes at input and output, degree of connectivity between layers, number of hidden layers, gain and back-propagation algorithm, etc. We can add more hidden layers for scalability and robustness. We can also use it to prune some of the connections between layers, sometimes speeding training. The back-propagation algorithm generally contains terms that are meant to provide a good balance between fast convergence and convergence to a nonglobal optimum. The error term can also include a regularization term to prevent overtraining. Also, it is worth noting that the activation term often uses tanh() in place of the sigmoid function described above. Another design option worth noting is that we can use convolution at a hidden layer and at the input layer to provide different "sharpness" or conversely "blur" to the training data. One reason convolutional neural networks work well on very large data sets is because they "expand" the amount of a convolved layer used to train on each sample, thereby preventing overtraining through isolation of input within the net.

I finish this section with a quick overview of the connectivity of the ANN. Suppose we have a single input layer, a single hidden layer, and a single output layer:

(1) Input layer: N_{Input} nodes
(2) Hidden layer: N_{Hidden} nodes
(3) Output layer: N_{Output} nodes

Here, the total number of connections between input and hidden layers is $N_{Input}*N_{Hidden}$, and the total number of connections between hidden and output layers is $N_{Hidden}*N_{Output}$. This means that there are $N_{Input}*(N_{Hidden})^2*N_{Output}$ total pathways through the neural network. If this value, $N_{Input}*(N_{Hidden})^2*N_{Output}$, is greater than the number of inputs, we have more degrees of freedom for the network than we have for the problem space. If not, we have more degrees of freedom for the problem space than for the network. Thus, two or more input samples will be recognized as "the same." In our example, we had 16 possible inputs but only four possible outputs. Therefore, a mean value of four inputs would map to each output, and we cannot distinguish every possible input. Regardless, in an ANN, by adding more layers, we have a geometric increase in the number of pathways through the network and can adjust the relative degrees of freedom based on the needs of the problem. In some cases, we will want more outputs than inputs and vice versa. Clearly, ANNs provide us with a tremendous amount of flexibility in analytic system design.

1.8.3 Immunological algorithms

Immunologic algorithms are based on the *distributed, recognition-based, layered* system of memory that is your immune system. This system includes innate memory (the family of complement proteins), collaborative memory (ligand-receptor binding), and learned memory (including unlearned memory). The immune system, in fact, is capable of *deep unlearning*, which in physiological terms is called clonal deletion and is how the immune system learns not to attack the self.

In this section, biological immune system concepts will be introduced, and AI immune system architectures and processes inspired by these concepts will be described. The goal is to stimulate further research in this area, because one thing is certain—hundreds of millions of years of evolution have certainly made the natural immune systems robust.

The first of these is antigens (also haptens and epitopes), which are fragments of information that can be recognized by the antigen-binding site on the antibody. Antigens are often "residues" of the digestion of nonself particles (viruses, proteins, etc.), or they can be surface-presented molecules of living nonself cells. In the context of AI, an antigen is a specific element or combination of elements that trigger a set of activities by the AI immune system. This may mean the occurrence of a rare event triggers a different response—for example, a different analytics algorithm or design pattern—to be applied. One example is a "trigger" word that indicates switching between monolingual and bilingual analysis of text or speech.

The second concept of interest is that of antibodies. These are molecules with the ability to recognize (antigen) and the ability to moderate behavior, location, and scalability of the response to the antigen. That is, antibodies are molecules with different sections, or sites, which enable them to participate in different chemical reactions, or "binding." The primary binding sites are the antigen-binding sets, which are at the ends of the two prongs of the "Y" shape of an IgG antibody; the complement-binding site in the middle part of the molecule, just below the fork of the "Y"; and the receptor-binding site at the bottom of the "Y," which allows the antigen binding of multiple antibodies to trigger other reactions, such as macrophage cell endocytosis of the antigen-antibody complex and the resultant destruction of the antigen-presenting cells. Applied to AI, these are potentially powerful concepts, which can be used to guide the generation of hybrid algorithms that may be simultaneously useful in search, recognition, clustering, and other knowledge generation. The AI equivalent of antigen binding, for example, may be the detection of a specific pattern of data in a sample. This antigen binding triggers a complement cascade of relevant analytics, which are used to further validate that the antigen-antibody complex is a correct match. The receptor-binding site then attaches the antibody as sample to its category, cluster, and/or class set and adds its analytics to those of the set.

Antigen-based sites are the sites of recognition for the antibody and the epitope (attachment-specific portion) of the antigen or the hapten bound to a facilitating protein (on an antigen-presenting cell such as a macrophage or dendritic cell), simplified in the previous discussion as being "antigens." As the recognition sites, they are important for clustering, classifying, and categorizing. In AI, the part of a search, recognition, or knowledge-generating algorithm or process that extracts the specific element and/or distinguishes its content relevance is a form of antigen-binding site. One example used in text analytics is $tf*idf$, or term frequency times inverse document frequency. This approach identifies terms that are rare in the overall corpus but commonplace in a specific cluster, class, or category. As with the natural immune system, there is the possibility of ectopic or false binding, but subsequent validation steps can further assess the sample and ensure the correctness of the assignment.

Contextual reaction is an important concept in the immune system, and it is the expression for the fact that different elements of the immune system have different specificity of reaction. The process of inflammation is a good case study for this specificity. Complement proteins attract neutrophils and macrophages and attach to antigens, marking them for phagocytosis by macrophages in a process called opsonization. Neutrophils, basophils, and mast cells release chemical agents that cause increased blood flow, swelling, and extravasation of other immune cells. Macrophages target the opsonized cells and perform cleanup of foreign bodies. Finally, T and B memory cells recognize viruses and bacteria, and both prevent their spread and lead to their destruction. This contextual reaction is readily borrowed by analytic and AI approaches. Generic approaches, like $tf*idf$ mentioned above and k-means clustering, can be used to broadly tag data content. Based on the tags applied (analogous to opsonization), different analytics, algorithms, and processes can be brought to bear on the data. The concept of tagging content with multiple descriptors allows multiple hypotheses (models, classification, categorizations, etc.) about the data to be tested simultaneously. Once the hypotheses have been tested, much more specific analytics (akin to T and B cells) can be performed.

Complement, already mentioned herein, is a family of more than 30 proteins that are involved in many innate immune processes, particularly in the activation of other innate immune responses (inflammation) and labeling foreign elements for phagocytosis (opsonization). For analytics and AI, this concept is directly borrowed for the meta-analytic approach, wherein a modular set of general tools or patterns for approaching system problems is employed in order to efficiently roll out a hybrid system comprising two or more processes. Obviously, meta-analytics are the primary subject of this book.

Another concept from the immune system is that of a learned response. For the immune system, the T and B cells are the primary mediators of the learned response. They learn, through their T-cell receptors and antibodies, respectively, about specific elements (antigens) of a somatic threat and remembering these for future. They also mediate unlearning where appropriate—the T and B cells that are exposed to their specific antigen during their development undergo apoptosis, or programmed cell death, so that they will not later mediate an autoimmune response. Learned specificity for an analytic or AI problem will be tied to a general recognition of the context first so the right refining response is taken.

Clusters of differentiation (CDs) are cell surface, usually transmembranous, proteins that indicate a stage of maturation, differentiation, and/or functionality of a cell. CDs differ by cell type, and so, the CDs on the surface are also shorthand of sort for cell typing. In analytics, processes such as search, recognition, or knowledge generation algorithms can come online at appropriate stages in a project or learning process. CDs can represent how far along they are in the analytic process and what degree of categorization confidence they have. The concept of CDs can also be borrowed as a means of showing multicategory membership.

Surface proteins are the superclass for clusters of differentiation, and in biology, these are the proteins along the surface of a cell that are used to bind to specific ligands (other binding molecules) in the surrounding milieu. The binding of ligand and receptor generally leads to additional reactivity, often mediated by intracellular second messenger pathways. There is clearly a strong analogy here for multistep, hybrid, meta-analytic approaches in analysis and AI. Secondary algorithms or analytics specific to germane environment events, processes, signals, etc. can be triggered based on the positive or negative assignment of data to a cluster, class, or category; in addition, these further downstream steps can be indicated or contraindicated based on the overall statistics. For example, if the goodness of fit of a data set to a particular category is above a particular threshold, then we are comfortable with its membership and proceed with the indexing, content extraction, and other operations consistent with membership to be performed. If, however, the goodness of fit is below the threshold, we "mine deeper" into the data set to further discriminate membership among the highest ranked candidates.

The last concept borrowed from the immune system here is the concept of mediated responses. In immunology, responses that are mediated are physiological events that occur after the binding of surface receptors to ligands. These secondary events are often metabolic, growth-related, or secretory (packaging of synthesized products) in nature. In analytics, downstream workflows, events, additional analytics, etc., can be triggered by the positive recognition of events, processes, signals, and other context. Analytic system designers can incorporate hard-won domain expertise into downstream rules that are applied only when a certain set of (statistical) confidence has been achieved for the data's classification, cluster membership, categorization, or other tagging.

1.9 A platform for building a classifier from the ground up (binary case)

In this section, I pull together a number of concepts to create a classifier from the ground up. While this may not be a particularly elegant classifier from the aesthetics of the design, it will provide very comparable results with top-level classification approaches such as LDA, Adaboost, SVM and ANNs because of its innate flexibility and its ability to ingest domain expertise into the composition of the feature set and the feature weighting. We are most interested in a classifier that simultaneously addresses five major desired attributes for a generalized classifier:

(1) Three or more classes can be distinguished. This is necessary to provide functionality beyond that provided by a nonprobabilistic binary linear classifier such as a support vector machine. The preferred classifier will be able to distinguish as many classes as necessary, with linear scale-up if possible.

(2) Graded weighting of the samples based on their distance from the expected values of each class. Samples should have nuanced classification probabilities, such that the farther the samples are from a given class, the lower the probability of belonging to the class. This means that sample assignment is graded, or analogue, and not binary, or digital.

(3) Feature selection should have an unambiguous, easy-to-employ process. Preferably, a single metric can be used to decide which feature(s) to include in the overall classification set.

(4) Ability to create noncorrelated features from a smaller set of features. As opposed to the determination of principal components that are weighted combinations of multiple features and/or required to be orthogonal features, we would like to have an uncomplicated way to generate a large set of potential features from the measured data and then refine the set based on the degrees of freedom in the measurement.

(5) Ability to ingest expert system rules from domain experts. If an observer, analyst, or other domain expert, for example, notices that certain measurements are correlated with specific classes or that there are requirements for specific measurements to place the so-measured samples into specific classes, then these rules should be readily incorporated into the overall classifier. This means that the features used for classification can be tagged, or labeled, with a real name.

In order to address these attributes, we begin with a simple binary classification model the rudimentary elements of which were first introduced in 2005. Before we proceed to more than two classes, we show how a critical point (hereafter "CPt") between the populations that represent two classes is derived. The simple set we will use for illustration is given in Table 1.16. This is a very simple classification design in which there are only two classes (a binary classification problem) and there are only two measurements made for each sample (the only simpler design would be for one feature). For this example, we may be measuring both

Table 1.16 Statistics for two classes and two measured features

Sample	Feature1, Class A	Feature1, Class B	Feature2, Class A	Feature2, Class B	Feature ratio, Class A	Feature ratio, Class B	Feature product, Class A	Feature product, Class B
1	141	165	31	22	4.55	7.5	4.37	3.63
2	155	178	23	19	6.74	9.37	3.57	3.38
3	164	185	25	15	6.56	12.33	4.10	2.78
4	165	201	41	26	4.02	7.73	6.77	5.23
5	178	221	37	31	4.81	7.13	6.59	6.85
6	189	227	29	28	6.52	8.11	5.48	6.36
7	203	235	37	29	5.49	8.10	7.51	6.82
8	211	244	46	33	4.59	7.39	9.71	8.05
9	217	253	39	36	5.56	7.03	8.46	9.11
10	229	266	51	31	4.49	8.58	11.68	8.25

Data in the last two columns on the right are divided by 1000 simply for convenience in the table. The data are ordered for Feature1, as is evident from columns 2 and 3. Columns 4 and 5 are the corresponding measurements for Feature2, ordered identically as columns 2 and 3, respectively, so that columns 6–9, the ratios and products of these features, can be readily calculated.

temperature (Feature1) and volume (Feature2) in a chamber (e.g., an ideal gas equation). We will consider only 10 samples from each class, so that the total number of samples is 20. In preparation for the classification task, we have ordered the 10 samples from Class A and, separately, from Class B so that they are in sorted (ascending) order in columns 2 and 3 of Table 1.16. These are the columns corresponding to Feature1.

We note that the two classes have different behavior for the two measured features. The second measured feature is provided in columns 4 and 5 of Table 1.16. We then provide two derived features from Feature1 and Feature2. The first, the ratio of Feature1/Feature2, is presented in columns 6 and 7. This particular feature has a physical meaning, since temperature/volume is proportional to pressure in the chamber. The second derived feature, the product of Feature1 and Feature2, does not in this case have a physical meaning in the example (where we are considering temperature, pressure, and volume), but as it is not a linear combination of the two features and the first derived feature, it may have some unique contribution to classification accuracy from that of the other three features. In general, we can derive features from measured features using a variety of mathematical transformations, including exponential and logarithmic products and quotients; periodic functions; trigonometric functions; and other products, quotient, and exponential series, so long as no derived feature is a linear combination of existing measured or derived features. More will be said on this later in this section.

For each measured and derived feature, we then determine a unique critical point, CPt, for separating any two classes. For purposes of consistency, we define the means

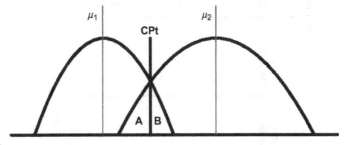

FIG. 1.17

Illustration demonstrating the critical point CPt (vertical line segment between A and B), along with the "error areas" A and B. Thus, CPt is defined as the point between the two means that is equidistant from the two means in multiples of their standard deviations (the two populations need not have equal variance). As such, CPt is selected so that the distance from the mean of each population to CPt is the same in terms of standard deviations of the means. The number of standard deviations from each mean, $n\sigma_{CPt}$, and then the actual value of the critical point, CPt, is determined by Eqs. (1.33), (1.34), and (1.35). Please see text for details.

of the sample populations of any two classes as μ_1 and μ_2, where the class with the lower mean is assigned the index "1"; that is,

$$\mu_1 < \mu_2 \tag{1.33}$$

This allows us to readily compute the number of standard deviations that the critical point between the two classes is from the mean of each class, as in Eq. (1.34):

$$n\sigma_{CPt} = (\mu_2 - \mu_1)/(\sigma_1 + \sigma_2) \tag{1.34}$$

Here, σ_1 is the standard deviation of the class with mean μ_1, and σ_2 is the standard deviation of the class with mean μ_2. This critical point (CPt) is the value that is the same multiple of standard deviations away from the means of both classes in the standard deviation *specific to that class*. We can determine the value of CPt from either of the two classes as follows:

$$CPt = \mu_1 + n\sigma_{CPt}\sigma_1 = \mu_2 - n\sigma_{CPt}\sigma_2 \tag{1.35}$$

The relative "separation" of the two classes is defined by the single derived value, $n\sigma_{CPt}$. Two classes are, in general, more readily distinguished by a (measured or derived) feature when $n\sigma_{CPt}$ is larger and less readily distinguished by a (measured or derived) feature when $n\sigma_{CPt}$ is smaller.

The next step in this classification approach is to compute the means and standard deviations ("stds") of each measured and derived feature for each class and, from Eqs. (1.33), (1.34), and (1.35), compute the values CPt and $n\sigma_{CPt}$ for each feature. Table 1.17 provides these values for the data of Table 1.16. Note in Table 1.17 that the two values for the critical point (CPt), as must be, are identical—for all four metrics, $\mu_1 + n\sigma_{CPt}\sigma_1 = \mu_2 - n\sigma_{CPt}\sigma_2$. This is in accord with Eq. (1.35).

In Table 1.17, the derived value, n_{CPt}, can be used to compare the measured and derived features for their likely utility in overall classification. Among the four features Feature1, Feature2, feature ratio, and feature product, the n_{CPt} values are 0.524, 0.563, 1.181, and 0.160, respectively. The largest value, 1.181, corresponds to Feature1/Feature2, which using our ideal gas example is directly proportional to pressure. The n_{CPt} values for Feature1 and Feature2 are similar, implying each of these (both measured) features will have similar value for classification accuracy. Finally, the derived feature, the product of temperature and volume, appears to have limited value for classification accuracy, since its value for n_{CPt} is 0.160.

In Table 1.18, we use the individual critical points to estimate the accuracy of each feature, used by itself, for classification. Samples from the class with mean μ_1 are correctly assigned if they are below the critical point, and samples from the class with mean μ_2 are correctly assigned if they are above the critical point. Samples directly on the critical point are ignored. It is worth noting when looking at Table 1.18 that the class with mean μ_1 is not always Class A (e.g., for Feature2 and the feature product in Table 1.18, Class A have the higher mean values, and so, Class A provides mean μ_2 in the simple classification model).

Table 1.17 Statistics for two classes and two measured features

Statistic	Feature1, Class A	Feature1, Class B	Feature2, Class A	Feature2, Class B	Feature ratio, Class A	Feature ratio, Class B	Feature product, Class A	Feature product, Class B
Mean	185	218	36	27	5.33	8.33	6.82	6.05
Std	29	34	9	7	0.97	1.57	2.60	2.21
$n\sigma_{CPt}$	0.524		0.563		1.181		0.160	
$\mu_1 + n\sigma_{CPt}\sigma_1$	200		31		6.48		6.40	
$\mu_2 - n\sigma_{CPt}\sigma_2$	200		31		6.48		6.40	
Physical analogue	Temperature		Volume		Pressure		No direct analogue	

In our example, Feature1 is temperature, and Feature2 is volume, meaning the feature ratio is proportional to pressure and feature product does not have a simple physical analogue. The relative values for $n\sigma_{CPt}$ in the fourth row imply that pressure provides the best binary classification accuracy for the two classes among the four features, with temperature and volume of intermediate binary classification accuracy, and the "feature product" having the lowest binary classification accuracy. Rows 4 and 5 are identical since they are two means of computing the critical point, CPt.

Table 1.18 Predicted accuracy of each of the features on the training data

Sample	Feature1, Class A	Feature1, Class B	Feature2, Class A	Feature2, Class B	Feature ratio, Class A	Feature ratio, Class B	Feature product, Class A	Feature product, Class B
1	141	**165**	31	22	4.55	7.5	**4.37**	3.63
2	155	**178**	**23**	19	**6.74**	9.37	**3.57**	3.38
3	164	**185**	**25**	15	**6.56**	12.33	**4.10**	2.78
4	165	201	41	26	4.02	7.73	6.77	5.23
5	178	221	37	31	4.81	7.13	6.59	**6.85**
6	189	227	**29**	28	**6.52**	8.11	**5.48**	6.36
7	**203**	235	37	29	5.49	8.10	7.51	**6.82**
8	**211**	244	46	**33**	4.59	7.39	9.71	**8.05**
9	**217**	253	39	**36**	5.56	7.03	8.46	**9.11**
10	**229**	266	51	31	4.49	8.58	11.68	**8.25**
CPt	200		31		6.48		6.40	
n_{CPt}	0.524		0.563		1.181		0.160	
Accuracy	13/20=0.65		12/17=0.71		17/20=0.85		11/20=0.55	
Improved Accuracy	0.30		0.42		0.70		0.10	

Accuracy is the percent of correct assignments over the total number of assignments. Improved accuracy is the percentage above guessing (0.50) toward perfect accuracy (1.00) as given in Eq. (1.36). In the case of Feature2, three samples are precisely on the critical point, and so are not assigned. Boldface data are assigned to the incorrect class based solely on the critical point. Note that Class A has the lower mean for Feature1 and feature ratio and the higher mean for Feature2 and feature product.

Not surprisingly, the predicted accuracy of the features is correlated with the value of n_{CPt} in Table 1.18. In sorted order, the values for n_{CPt} are ranked in the same order as the accuracy. When we consider that accuracy is 50% for simple random guessing for a binary classifier, we can further compute the improved accuracy as given by Eq. (1.36):

$$\text{Improved accuracy} = (\text{Accuracy} - 0.50)/(1.0 - 0.50) \tag{1.36}$$

These calculations are given in the last row of Table 1.18 and plotted against n_{CPt} in Fig. 1.18. The monotonic relationship (and linear regression R^2 value of 0.97) between accuracy and n_{CPt} is encouraging for the use of n_{CPt} as a metric for identifying good features for classification, as will be described in more detail.

Once the accuracies are computed, we can compute and assign weights (coefficients) to each of the features so that they can be used together to make an overall decision, with each feature contributing its appropriate relative share to the overall decision. Customarily, the weights are normalized to sum to 1.0 for all the features, as presented in Table 1.19. Two different sets of weights are computed, which we will compare. The first makes the relative weighting proportional to the accuracy of the feature, as given in Eq. (1.37):

$$Weighting_{accuracy(i)} = \frac{accuracy(i)}{\sum_{k} accuracy(k)} \tag{1.37}$$

The second set of weights is computed so that the weights are inversely proportional to the error rate of the features, as given in Eq. (1.38).

$$Weighting_{error(i)} = \frac{1/error(i)}{\sum_{k} 1/error(k)} \tag{1.38}$$

The weights so computed are given in Table 1.19.

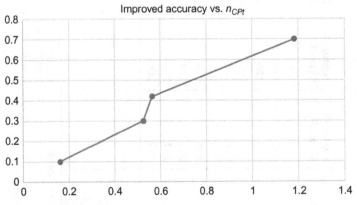

FIG. 1.18

Percent improvement in accuracy (y-axis) versus n_{CPt} (x-axis) for the data in Table 1.18. The equation of the regression line is $y = 0.583x + 0.0261$, with $R^2 = 0.9687$.

The weights in Table 1.19, as expected, are ordered identically to n_{CPt}-based ordering for the features, being highest for the feature ratio and lowest for the feature product. While this is a nice result, for a simple binary classification problem like this (two classes and two measured features), where the weighting of the features is based on a very simple binary boundary for each of the four metrics, even with relative weighting approaches employed, we do not obtain a particularly sophisticated model for the classification. In fact, we can boil the classification down to one simple rule for both weighting approaches: if the "feature ratio" and one other feature vote one way, the overall classifier does. This is true since $0.308 + (0.236$ or 0.257 or $0.199) > 0.500$ for accuracy weighting and $0.439 + (0.188$ or 0.227 or $0.146) > 0.500$ for (inverse) error weighting. Only if the other three features (Feature1, Feature2, and feature product) agree will the opposing classification of the feature ratio be "overruled."

Next, we compare what we have observed for n_{CPt} and the weighting to the simple statistical analysis afforded by the t-test. The t-test is a good measurement choice to validate the selection of features normally based on the number of standard deviations to the critical point, CPt, or n_{CPt}. Note that remapping the data to a normal distribution before performing the t-test (e.g., when distributions are skewed and bimodal and show kurtosis) is good practice before computing the t-statistics so that the features will be ordered in a meaningful manner. Regardless, the t-statistics and corresponding two-tailed p-values are provided in Table 1.20. The t-statistic is, of course, computed according to Eq. (1.39):

$$t = \frac{\mu_1 - \mu_2}{\sqrt{\dfrac{(n_1 - 1)\sigma_1^2 + (n_2 - 1)\sigma_2^2}{n_1 + n_2 - 2}} \sqrt{\dfrac{1}{n_1} + \dfrac{1}{n_2}}} \tag{1.39}$$

Unsurprisingly, the p-values of the t-tests track nicely with the features most useful for the classification. The feature ratio is most significant, with a p-value of 0.000121. Next is the Feature2 feature, with a still statistically significant $p = 0.0293$, followed by Feature1, which also has a statistically significant result ($p = 0.0399$). Feature product is not statistically significant ($p > 0.05$).

In this example, we see that the final choice of classification largely depends on the binary decision for the "feature ratio"-derived feature, having the same performance (85% accuracy) on the training data as any combination of features. In a real classification problem, we would then test on a separate (validation or testing) set, which we will formalize in the next section. Here, we did not weight the samples additionally based on how far they are from the decision boundary (the CPt). As noted in Fig. 1.19., the actual sample, S, would be weighted more heavily for population 1 the further left it is on the line graph, and by symmetry, it would be weighted more heavily for population 2 the further right it is on the line graph. For the example shown in Fig. 1.19, the "S" above would be weighted more heavily for population 1 than if it was directly next to the CPt. This consideration will be very important in the general case.

We did not prune the features, even though we only measured two features (Feature1 and Feature2) and derived the other two (feature ratio and feature product) from these

Table 1.19 Table showing the weighting of the features in Table 1.18, as determined by Eq. (1.37) (third row) and Eq. (1.38) (fifth row)

Sample	Feature1, Class A	Feature1, Class B	Feature2, Class A	Feature2, Class B	Feature ratio, Class A	Feature ratio, Class B	Feature product, Class A	Feature product, Class B
Accuracy	13/20=0.65		12/17=0.71		17/20=0.85		11/20=0.55	
Weighting	0.236		0.257		0.308		0.199	
Error rate	1−0.65=0.35		1−0.71=0.29		1−0.85=0.15		1−0.55=0.45	
Weighting	0.188		0.227		0.439		0.146	

In both cases, the ranking of the weights is feature ratio followed by Feature2, Feature1, and feature product in that order.

Table 1.20 Mean, standard deviation (std), degrees of freedom (*df*), *t*-statistic, and two-tailed *p*-value for the data from Table 1.18

Sample	Feature1, Class A	Feature1, Class B	Feature2, Class A	Feature2, Class B	Feature ratio, Class A	Feature ratio, Class B	Feature product, Class A	Feature product, Class B
Mean	185	218	36	27	5.33	8.33	6.82	6.05
Std	29	34	9	7	0.97	1.57	2.60	2.21
$df=n_1+n_2-2$	18		18		18		18	
t-Statistic	2.215		2.368		4.877		0.677	
Two-tailed *p*-value	0.0399		0.0293		0.000121		0.507	

The order of the t-tests is the same as for nCPt and the weightings in Table 1.19.

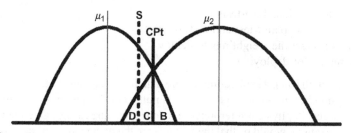

FIG. 1.19

This represents Fig. 1.17 with an actual sample introduced. The sample S is to the left of the critical point CPt, meaning that it will be assigned to the class with the smaller mean μ_1. However, in this section, we have no process for showing additional confidence that the sample S belongs to one class versus the other as it moves further from the CPt—though we certainly should.

two. In reality, we would likely drop two of the features … keeping Feature2 and feature ratio. The number of retained features would equal the number of actual measurements performed or less. Since we would still employ relative weighting, we would not lose any of the benefit of the two measurements, and statistically, only two features are merited anyway. In the next section, we will learn how to handle more than two features and how to weight the sample, S, for distance from the decision boundary.

1.10 A platform for building a classifier from the ground up (general case)

As we move into an even more in-depth description of how to build a classifier from the ground up, you may be wondering why so much time is being spent on this topic. At the most expansive level, I would argue that what Shakespeare is to drama, what the symphony is to music, what Jane Austen is to characterization, what the novel is to writing, and what La Pieta is to sculpture—classifiers are to analytics. They are where art, design, and understanding of data come together. In this section, we build on the principles introduced in the previous section to describe how to build an "infinitely scalable" classifier from the ground up, with separate training and validation in addition to the testing and deployment.

1.10.1 Training and validation

For the training and validation stage, there are eight steps we will describe here that, as an output, provide a fully characterized classification model that can then be deployed on new data:

1. Collect feature data for all classes
2. Compute all μ and σ values
3. Order all populations by means
4. Determine critical points

5. Compute all *p*-values for *t*-tests
6. Compute and compare *t*-test and *nSTD-CPt*
7. Validation: select the weightings to deploy
8. Define model for deploying

We begin with (Step 1) collecting feature data for all classes. In this example, we expand the number of classes to three and simultaneously the number of measured features to three. A physical interpretation of these features is not given here, but a very simple example would be that the features are the mean values of the red, green, and blue channels of an image. The data for Classes A, B, and C are given in Tables 1.21, 1.22, and 1.23.

Table 1.21 Measured feature values for the 10 training samples for Class A

Class A measured feature values			
Item	**Feature1**	**Feature2**	**Feature3**
1	25.00	6.00	30.00
2	23.00	14.00	12.00
3	17.00	13.00	18.00
4	27.00	9.00	27.00
5	33.00	8.00	25.00
6	30.00	11.00	23.00
7	24.00	15.00	17.00
8	29.00	7.00	22.00
9	19.00	5.00	15.00
10	35.00	13.00	26.00

There are no missing or out-of-bound data, so no data imputation is required.

Table 1.22 Measured feature values for the 10 training samples for Class B

Class B measured feature values			
Item	**Feature1**	**Feature2**	**Feature3**
1	20.00	9.00	15.00
2	39.00	20.00	28.00
3	25.00	18.00	16.00
4	29.00	11.00	22.00
5	34.00	10.00	21.00
6	22.00	15.00	36.00
7	36.00	16.00	17.00
8	25.00	13.00	24.00
9	31.00	19.00	33.00
10	38.00	15.00	30.00

There are no missing or out-of-bound data, so no data imputation is required.

Table 1.23 Measured feature values for the 10 training samples for Class C

	Class C measured feature values		
Item	Feature1	Feature2	Feature3
1	44.00	3.00	11.00
2	33.00	8.00	18.00
3	39.00	4.00	22.00
4	26.00	5.00	17.00
5	41.00	3.00	20.00
6	35.00	6.00	16.00
7	36.00	8.00	15.00
8	29.00	5.00	14.00
9	40.00	7.00	13.00
10	27.00	8.00	17.00

There are no missing or out-of-bound data, so no data imputation is required.

As noted in Tables 1.21, 1.22, and 1.23, we have a complete data set for the admittedly modest set of training samples. No imputation is required, and we have 10 sets of three measurements for each of the three classes. If, for example, the classes were images, then Class A might be a set of images from location A, Class B a set of images from location B, and Class C a set of images from location C.

Next, we take the simplest equations containing two or more of the Features 1, 2, and 3. These are the multiplication of two features, designated 1*2, 1*3, and 2*3, and the ratio of three pairs of classes, designated 1/2, 1/3, and 2/3. There are other, more complex, equations possible—for example, 1*2*3, 1*2/3, 1*3/2, and 2*3/1—but these are generally only used if domain expertise input supports them, and the nine already defined should suffice to hone in on three final features. A set of derived features for Classes A, B, and C are shown in Tables 1.24, 1.25, and 1.26, respectively.

Table 1.24 Derived features 1*2, 1*3, 2*3, 1/2, 1/3, and 2/3 for the original Features 1, 2, and 3 for Class A presented in Table 1.21

	Class A derived feature values (computed from measured feature values)					
Item	Product 1*2	Product 1*3	Product 2*3	Ratio 1/2	Ratio 1/3	Ratio 2/3
1	150.00	750.00	180.00	4.17	0.83	0.20
2	322.00	276.00	168.00	1.64	1.92	1.17
3	221.00	306.00	234.00	1.31	0.94	0.72
4	243.00	729.00	243.00	3.00	1.00	0.33
5	264.00	825.00	200.00	4.13	1.32	0.32
6	330.00	690.00	253.00	2.73	1.30	0.48
7	360.00	408.00	255.00	1.60	1.41	0.88
8	203.00	638.00	154.00	4.14	1.32	0.32
9	95.00	285.00	75.00	3.80	1.27	0.33
10	455.00	910.00	338.00	2.69	1.35	0.50

Table 1.25 Derived Features 1*2, 1*3, 2*3, 1/2, 1/3, and 2/3 for the original Features 1, 2, and 3 for Class B presented in Table 1.22

	Class B derived feature values (computed from measured feature values)					
Item	Product 1*2	Product 1*3	Product 2*3	Ratio 1/2	Ratio 1/3	Ratio 2/3
1	180.00	300.00	135.00	2.22	1.33	0.60
2	780.00	1092.00	560.00	1.95	1.39	0.71
3	450.00	400.00	288.00	1.39	1.56	1.13
4	319.00	638.00	242.00	2.64	1.32	0.50
5	340.00	714.00	210.00	3.40	1.62	0.48
6	330.00	792.00	540.00	1.47	0.61	0.42
7	576.00	612.00	272.00	2.25	2.12	0.94
8	325.00	600.00	312.00	1.92	1.04	0.54
9	589.00	1023.00	627.00	1.63	0.94	0.58
10	570.00	1140.00	450.00	2.53	1.27	0.50

Table 1.26 Derived Features 1*2, 1*3, 2*3, 1/2, 1/3, and 2/3 for the original Features 1, 2, and 3 for Class C presented in Table 1.23

	Class C derived feature values (computed from measured feature values)					
Item	Product 1*2	Product 1*3	Product 2*3	Ratio 1/2	Ratio 1/3	Ratio 2/3
1	132.00	484.00	33.00	14.67	4.00	0.27
2	264.00	594.00	144.00	4.13	1.83	0.44
3	156.00	858.00	88.00	9.75	1.77	0.18
4	130.00	442.00	85.00	5.20	1.53	0.29
5	123.00	820.00	60.00	13.67	2.05	0.15
6	210.00	560.00	96.00	5.83	2.19	0.38
7	288.00	540.00	120.00	4.50	2.40	0.53
8	145.00	406.00	70.00	5.80	2.07	0.36
9	280.00	520.00	91.00	5.71	3.08	0.54
10	216.00	459.00	136.00	3.38	1.59	0.47

In Step 2 of the training and validation phase, we compute all of the μ and σ values for the features. These values are provided in Table 1.27.

For Step 3, we order the populations by their means. These are indicated in the parentheses in Table 1.28. In general, Class C has the highest values, followed by Classes A and B.

From the ranked order of the means, we define pairs of classes to compute CPt values. One example "data model," for Feature2, is shown in Fig. 1.20. This figure

Table 1.27 The μ and σ values for the three measured and six derived features of Classes A, B, and C

Item	Feature1	Feature2	Feature3	Product 1*2	Product 1*3	Product 2*3	Ratio 1/2	Ratio 1/3	Ratio 2/3
Class A									
μ	26.2	10.1	21.5	264	582	210	2.92	1.28	0.53
σ	5.8	3.6	5.8	106	240	72	1.12	0.30	0.31
Class B									
μ	29.9	14.6	24.2	446	731	364	2.14	1.32	0.64
σ	6.8	3.8	7.3	180	283	168	0.61	0.41	0.23
Class C									
μ	35	5.7	16.3	194	568	92	7.26	2.25	0.36
σ	6.2	2.0	3.3	66	154	34	4.02	0.76	0.14

Table 1.28 Classes ranked by mean, with the rank of their means in parentheses

Item	Feature1	Feature2	Feature3	Product 1*2	Product 1*3	Product 2*3	Ratio 1/2	Ratio 1/3	Ratio 2/3
Class A									
μ	26.2 (1)	10.1 (2)	21.5 (2)	264 (2)	582 (2)	210 (2)	2.92 (2)	1.28 (1)	0.53 (2)
σ	5.8	3.6	5.8	106	240	72	1.12	0.30	0.31
Class B									
μ	29.9 (2)	14.6 (3)	24.2 (3)	446 (3)	731 (3)	364 (3)	2.14 (1)	1.32 (2)	0.64 (3)
σ	6.8	3.8	7.3	180	283	168	0.61	0.41	0.23
Class C									
μ	35 (3)	5.7 (1)	16.3 (1)	194 (1)	568 (1)	92 (1)	7.26 (3)	2.25 (3)	0.36 (1)
σ	6.2	2.0	3.3	66	154	34	4.02	0.76	0.14

Class C has the highest values, followed by Classes A and B, for both Features 2 and 3. For Feature1, Class A is the highest and Class C the lowest. This means that critical points between Classes A and C will not be computed for Feature1. Critical points between Classes B and C will not be computed for Features 2 and 3.

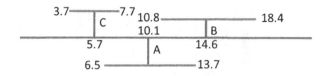

FIG. 1.20

Data model for Feature2, showing the standard deviations (± 2.0 for Class C, ± 3.6 for Class A, and ± 3.8 for Class B) in the shorter horizontal bars above or below the longer axis and showing the means along the axis: 5.7 for Class C, 10.1 for Class A, and 14.6 for Class B. From this, we can see that two *CPt* values will be computed, one between Classes C and A and the other between Classes A and B.

shows the standard deviations (which are ± 2.0 for Class C, ± 3.6 for Class A, and ± 3.8 for Class B) in the shorter horizontal bars above or below the longer horizontal bar representing the feature axis. Fig. 1.20 also shows the means along the axis: 5.7 for Class C, 10.1 for Class A, and 14.6 for Class B. From this, we can see that two *CPt* values will be computed, one between Classes C and A and the other between Classes A and B.

As such, for Step 4, we compute the critical points. The critical points are an equal multiple of standard deviations away from the means of their two defining classes, in the specific standard deviation of each class. There are, in this model, $N-1$ critical points, where $N=$number of classes. The 18 *CPt* values, two for each feature, are given in columns 3 and 6 of Table 1.29.

In Table 1.29, we can see that there is a third critical point that is between the means of the classes in columns 2 and 8, which could be computed if desired. However, this critical point is not generally used for assessing which features to employ in the classification model. The critical point generally has the least valuable input, the exception being where the mean of one of the classes is relatively much farther from the means of the other two classes than those two are from each other. Nevertheless, it does constitute a "variation" on the classification model provided here and can be considered when the classes are not evenly spaced in their means.

A key metric of interest is the sum of *nSTD-CPt*s in columns 4 and 7 of Table 1.29. Summing these two columns, the set of values in order from top to bottom is {0.686, 1.394, 0.777, 1.043, 0.321, 1.755, 1.295, 0.865, 0.582}, with Features 2*3, 2, and 1/2 being the three largest values in order. This is {7, 2, 6, 4, 9, 1, 3, 5, 8} in rank order (e.g., the sixth position, Feature2*3, with a sum of 1.752, has rank order 1 since it is the highest sum) and will be compared with the *p*-values of the tests, which are described next.

In Step 5, we compute all *p*-values for *t*-tests. These are compiled in Table 1.30. Note the *p*-values for the *T*-scores given in columns 3 and 6. If we choose $p<0.05$ as an indicator of statistically significant differences, we see that 11 of the 20 comparisons are statistically significant. If we compared columns 2 and 8, we'd have another 9 of 10 comparisons that are statistically significant (this is another piece of evidence for why we don't need to compute a critical point between the highest and lowest

Table 1.29 Critical points (CPts) for the three measured features and the six derived features of the example

Feature	$\mu \pm \sigma$ (Class)	CPt_1	$nSTD\text{-}CPt_1$	$\mu \pm \sigma$ (Class)	CPt_2	$nSTD\text{-}CPt_2$	$\mu \pm \sigma$ (Class)
1	26.2±5.8 (A)	27.9	0.294	29.9±6.8 (B)	32.6	0.392	35.0±6.2 (C)
2	5.7±2.0 (C)	7.3	0.786	10.1±3.6 (A)	12.3	0.608	14.6±3.8 (B)
3	16.3±3.3 (C)	18.2	0.571	21.5±5.8 (A)	22.7	0.206	24.2±7.3 (B)
1*2	194±66 (C)	221	0.407	264±106 (A)	331	0.636	446±180 (B)
1*3	568±154 (C)	573	0.036	582±240 (A)	650	0.285	731±283 (B)
2*3	92±34 (C)	130	1.113	210±72 (A)	256	0.642	364±168 (B)
1/2	2.14±0.61 (B)	2.42	0.451	2.92±1.12 (A)	3.87	0.844	7.26±4.02 (C)
1/3	1.27±0.30 (A)	1.29	0.070	1.32±0.41 (B)	1.65	0.795	2.25±0.76 (C)
2/3	0.36±0.14 (C)	0.41	0.378	0.53±0.31 (A)	0.59	0.204	0.64±0.23 (B)

There are two critical points for each feature. The third critical point, between the means of the classes in columns 2 and 8, is not generally used for assessing which features to employ in the classification model.

Table 1.30 Statistical p-values for the t-tests comparing populations on either side of the 18 critical points reported in Table 1.29

Feature	$\mu \pm \sigma$ (Class)	$p(t)$	$nSTD\text{-}CPt_1$	$\mu \pm \sigma$ (Class)	$p(t)$	$nSTD\text{-}CPt_2$	$\mu \pm \sigma$ (Class)
1	26.2±5.8 (A)	0.103	0.294	29.9±6.8 (B)	0.048	0.392	35.0±6.2 (C)
2	5.7±2.0 (C)	0.002	0.786	10.1±3.6 (A)	0.007	0.608	14.6±3.8 (B)
3	16.3±3.3 (C)	0.012	0.571	21.5±5.8 (A)	0.187	0.206	24.2±7.3 (B)
1*2	194±66 (C)	0.046	0.407	264±106 (A)	0.007	0.636	446±180 (B)
1*3	568±154 (C)	0.442	0.036	582±240 (A)	0.110	0.285	731±283 (B)
2*3	92±34 (C)	0.000	1.113	210±72 (A)	0.008	0.642	364±168 (B)
1/2	2.14±0.61 (B)	0.035	0.451	2.92±1.12 (A)	0.002	0.844	7.26±4.02 (C)
1/3	1.27±0.30 (A)	0.380	0.070	1.32±0.41 (B)	0.002	0.795	2.25±0.76 (C)
2/3	0.36±0.14 (C)	0.070	0.378	0.53±0.31 (A)	0.190	0.204	0.64±0.23 (B)

Column 3 represents p-values for t-test comparing columns 2 and 5, while column 6 represents p-values for t-test comparing columns 5 and 8. t-Tests comparing columns 2 and 8 are not needed for the classifier model, but are statistically significant ($p < 0.05$) for all but Feature1*3.

Table 1.31 In this table, the sum of *nSTD-CPt* values {0.686, *1.394*, 0.777, 1.043, 0.321, *1.755*, *1.295*, 0.865, 0.582} shows that Features 2*3, 2, and 1/2 have the maximum values, indicating these are the three best features for classification

Feature	$nSTD\text{-}CPt_1 + nSTD\text{-}CPt_2$	$p(t\text{-}score_1) + p(t\text{-}score_2)$
1	0.686	0.151
2	1.394	0.009
3	0.777	0.199
1*2	1.043	0.053
1*3	0.321	0.552
2*3	1.755	0.008
1/2	1.295	0.037
1/3	0.865	0.382
2/3	0.582	0.260

*The sum of p(t-score) values {0.151, 0.009, 0.199, 0.053, 0.552, 0.008, 0.037, 0.382, 0.260} also shows that Features 2*3, 2, and 1/2 have the minimum values, indicating these are the three best features for classification.*

mean populations). The sum of the two *t*-tests is, from top to bottom, {0.151, 0.009, 0.199, 0.053, 0.552, 0.008, 0.037, 0.382, 0.260}, which gives a rank order of {5, 2, 6, 4, 9, 1, 3, 8, 7}, similar to those for sum of *nSTD-CPt*s (and exactly the same for ranks 1, 2, 3, and 4).

In Step 6, we compute and compare the *t*-tests and the *nSTD-CPt*. Discussed above, these are tabulated in Table 1.31.

In Step 7, the weightings to deploy are selected. We only measured three features (1–3), and deriving the other six. As such, we will keep only three of the measured and derived features. Both *nSTD-CPt* and *p*-value of *t*-test indicated keeping Features 2, 2*3, and 1/2. Nicely, these three incorporate Features 1, 2, and 3, so that none are left out. Feature2 is represented in all of them.

There are several ways of selecting the relative weights for the surviving features, involving *nSTD-CPt*, the *p*-value of *t*-tests, or even other methods (e.g., *F*-score for classes as clusters). We choose the relatively simple sum of squares of the *nSTD-CPt* values, shown in Table 1.32. The last column normalizes the weights to sum to 1.0.

Table 1.32 Features selected and their relative weights as determined by the sum of squares of the *nSTD-CPt* values, normalized to sum to 1.0

Feature	$nSTD\text{-}CPt_1$	$nSTD\text{-}CPt_2$	$(nSTD\text{-}CPt_1)^2 + (nSTD\text{-}CPt_2)^2$	$\frac{(nSTD-CPt_1)^2 + (nSTD-CPt_2)^2}{\sum((nSTD-CPt_1)^2 + (nSTD-CPt_2)^2)}$
2	0.786	0.608	0.987	0.987/3.554=0.278
2*3	1.113	0.642	1.651	1.651/3.554=0.464
1/2	0.451	0.844	0.916	0.916/3.554=0.258

Table 1.33 Model for deployment (features and weights, in columns 1 and 2)

Feature	Weight	Coefficient of variance {Classes A, B, C}
2	0.278	{0.351, 0.356, 0.260}
2*3	0.464	{0.370, 0.343, 0.462}
1/2	0.258	{0.285, 0.384, 0.554}

The third column gives the coefficient of variance (ratio of standard deviation to mean) for each selected feature by class.

In Step 8, the model is defined for deploying. Based on the training data, the model for deployment is capture succinctly in Table 1.33. The measured feature is used with weight 0.278, and the two derived Features 2*3 and 1/2 are used with weights 0.464 and 0.258, respectively. Note that for the purposes of this particular classification process, we used the results from the training set for the validation step, also. We could have chosen to keep aside a portion of the original data set to determine the weights of Features 2, 2*3, and 1/2, after using the (different) training data to determine which features to keep. However, given the problem at hand, we would just as likely have merely combined the training and validation data, anyway, to obtain a better estimate of weight on as much of the labeled (ground truth, training, and validation) data as possible. This is one of the advantages of this classification approach—training and validation data can be combined since the two processes are related to each other. Regardless, we now have our features and their weights and can now use this for testing and deployment in the field.

1.10.2 Testing and deployment

For testing and deployment, we also have an eight-step process. These eight steps are given here and described in detail in this section:

1. Compute all μ and σ values.
2. Ensure test data have not drifted.
3. Compute z-value for each sample's features.
4. Compute $f(z)$ for each sample's features.
5. Weight the $f(z)$ by feature weights.
6. Sum the weighted feature $f(z)$ values for each class.
7. Assign the class based on max sum.
8. Testing and proofing: feedback test results.

For Step 1, we compute all of the μ and σ values here for the model testing data. These data are 10 new samples for each of the three classes, which we did not use for training. Note that in the binary classifier example (Section 1.9), we performed the so-called testing on the same samples used for training, which is both overfitting and statistically irrelevant. However, "testing on training" data do give a nice upper limit of accuracy for which to aim. The data sets for the test data are shown in Tables 1.34, 1.35, and 1.36 for Classes A, B, and C, respectively.

Table 1.34 Measured feature values for the 10 test samples for Class A

Class A measured feature values			
Item	Feature1	Feature2	Feature3
1	19.00	8.00	13.00
2	25.00	5.00	27.00
3	22.00	14.00	28.00
4	16.00	11.00	21.00
5	34.00	10.00	25.00
6	18.00	9.00	17.00
7	31.00	13.00	18.00
8	24.00	12.00	19.00
9	29.00	6.00	13.00
10	30.00	15.00	22.00

There are no missing or out-of-bound data, so no data imputation is required.

Table 1.35 Measured feature values for the 10 test samples for Class B

Class B measured feature values			
Item	Feature1	Feature2	Feature3
1	24.00	21.00	14.00
2	34.00	8.00	19.00
3	39.00	20.00	28.00
4	21.00	15.00	22.00
5	41.00	16.00	18.00
6	36.00	14.00	33.00
7	34.00	12.00	29.00
8	35.00	18.00	24.00
9	24.00	10.00	17.00
10	29.00	19.00	29.00

There are no missing or out-of-bound data, so no data imputation is required.

Next, the derived features are computed for all of the test samples. These are computed as above for the training data and are tabulated in Tables 1.37, 1.38, and 1.39.

Computing the mean and standard deviation of each feature for the data for each class is next. These values are compiled in Table 1.40.

Step 2 of the deployment and testing phase is to ensure that the test data have not drifted. Here, we use t-tests for comparing the combined training+validation data with the test data. The t-test values computed for comparing these sets are given in Table 1.41.

Table 1.36 Measured feature values for the 10 test samples for Class C

Item	Feature1	Feature2	Feature3
	Class C measured feature values		
1	29.00	5.00	15.00
2	46.00	6.00	16.00
3	34.00	7.00	12.00
4	33.00	6.00	16.00
5	39.00	4.00	17.00
6	31.00	5.00	10.00
7	28.00	6.00	23.00
8	26.00	8.00	17.00
9	41.00	9.00	20.00
10	43.00	4.00	19.00

There are no missing or out-of-bound data, so no data imputation is required.

Table 1.37 Derived Features 1*2, 1*3, 2*3, 1/2, 1/3, and 2/3 for the original Features 1, 2, and 3 for Class A presented in Table 1.34

Item	Product 1*2	Product 1*3	Product 2*3	Ratio 1/2	Ratio 1/3	Ratio 2/3
	Class A derived feature values (computed from measured feature values)					
1	152.00	247.00	104.00	2.38	1.46	0.62
2	125.00	675.00	135.00	5.00	0.93	0.19
3	308.00	616.00	392.00	1.57	0.79	0.50
4	176.00	336.00	231.00	1.45	0.76	0.52
5	340.00	850.00	250.00	3.40	1.36	0.40
6	162.00	306.00	153.00	2.00	1.06	0.53
7	403.00	558.00	234.00	2.38	1.72	0.72
8	288.00	456.00	228.00	2.00	1.26	0.63
9	174.00	377.00	78.00	4.83	2.23	0.46
10	450.00	660.00	330.00	2.00	1.36	0.68

Interestingly, in Table 1.41, every statistical p-value is $\gg 0.200$. For two-tailed t-tests, setting alpha $= 0.20$ and $df = 18$, we need a t-value of 1.330 to declare a statistically significant difference even with this paltry 80% confidence that it is real. We are fairly confident, therefore, that the training and testing samples are drawn from the same, larger, population and they are not biased one way or the other comparatively. In Table 1.42, the calculations for the $nSTDs$ apart, given by $n\sigma_{CPt} = |\mu_2 - \mu_1|/(\sigma_1 + \sigma_2)$, are shown for comparison with the p-values of Table 1.41.

Table 1.38 Derived Features 1*2, 1*3, 2*3, 1/2, 1/3, and 2/3 for the original Features 1, 2, and 3 for Class B presented in Table 1.35

	Class B derived feature values (computed from measured feature values)					
Item	Product 1*2	Product 1*3	Product 2*3	Ratio 1/2	Ratio 1/3	Ratio 2/3
1	504.00	336.00	294.00	1.14	1.71	1.50
2	272.00	646.00	152.00	4.25	1.79	0.42
3	780.00	1092.00	560.00	1.95	1.39	0.71
4	315.00	462.00	330.00	1.40	0.95	0.68
5	656.00	738.00	288.00	2.56	2.28	0.89
6	504.00	1188.00	462.00	2.57	1.09	0.42
7	408.00	986.00	348.00	2.83	1.17	0.41
8	630.00	840.00	432.00	1.94	1.46	0.75
9	240.00	408.00	170.00	2.40	1.41	0.59
10	551.00	841.00	551.00	1.53	1.00	0.66

Table 1.39 Derived Features 1*2, 1*3, 2*3, 1/2, 1/3, and 2/3 for the original Features 1, 2, and 3 for Class C presented in Table 1.36

	Class C derived feature values (computed from measured feature values)					
Item	Product 1*2	Product 1*3	Product 2*3	Ratio 1/2	Ratio 1/3	Ratio 2/3
1	145.00	435.00	75.00	5.80	1.93	0.33
2	276.00	736.00	96.00	7.67	2.88	0.38
3	238.00	408.00	84.00	4.86	2.83	0.58
4	198.00	528.00	96.00	5.50	2.06	0.38
5	156.00	663.00	68.00	9.75	2.29	0.24
6	155.00	310.00	50.00	6.20	3.10	0.50
7	168.00	644.00	138.00	4.67	1.22	0.26
8	208.00	442.00	136.00	3.25	1.53	0.47
9	369.00	820.00	180.00	4.56	2.05	0.45
10	172.00	817.00	76.00	10.75	2.26	0.21

In Table 1.42, the largest value of *nSTD-CPt* is only 0.170. For a normal distribution, this means that 57% of the distribution is to one side of the critical point and 43% of the distribution is to the other side of the critical point. Thus, in no case is there even a 4:3 ratio of guessing correctly whether a sample came from the training or testing class based solely on a single feature. As for Table 1.41, then, Table 1.42 provides strong support for the training and test sets having been drawn from the same larger population.

Table 1.40 The mean (μ) and standard deviation (σ) values for the three measured and six derived features of Classes A, B, and C, test data sets

Item	Feature1	Feature2	Feature3	Product 1*2	Product 1*3	Product 2*3	Ratio 1/2	Ratio 1/3	Ratio 2/3
Class A									
μ	24.8	10.3	20.3	258	508	214	2.70	1.29	0.53
σ	6.1	3.3	5.3	115	195	99	1.28	0.45	0.16
Class B									
μ	31.7	15.3	23.3	486	754	359	2.26	1.43	0.70
σ	6.8	4.3	6.3	177	291	142	0.90	0.41	0.32
Class C									
μ	35	6	16.5	208	580	100	6.30	2.22	0.38
σ	6.9	1.6	3.7	70	181	40	2.39	0.60	0.12

Table 1.41 Statistical *t*-tests comparing the training and test data as compiled in Tables 1.27 and 1.40

Feature	1	2	3	1*2	1*3	2*3	1/2	1/3	2/3
Class A	0.53	0.13	0.48	0.12	0.76	0.10	0.41	0.06	0.00
Class B	0.59	0.39	0.30	0.50	0.18	0.07	0.35	0.60	0.48
Class C	0.00	0.37	0.13	0.46	0.16	0.48	0.65	0.10	0.34

In spite of 27 t-tests being performed, none are even "borderline" statistically significant (p>0.20 for all comparisons). Note that every t-value here is ≪1.330, which the minimum t-value for confidence p=0.200 (two-tailed). Thus, there is no statistically significant difference between two populations. We are fairly confident, then, that the training and testing samples are drawn from the same, larger, population.

Table 1.42 Number of standard deviations apart from the critical point, *nSTD-CPt*, for the training and test data as compiled in Tables 1.27 and 1.40

Feature	1	2	3	1*2	1*3	2*3	1/2	1/3	2/3
Class A	0.118	0.029	0.108	0.027	0.170	0.023	0.092	0.013	0.000
Class B	0.132	0.086	0.066	0.112	0.040	0.016	0.080	0.134	0.109
Class C	0.000	0.083	0.029	0.103	0.036	0.108	0.150	0.022	0.077

In spite of 27 t-tests being performed, the largest number of standard deviations apart for any comparison is 0.170, a value at which a critical point only separates 43% of the distribution from 57% of the distribution.

In Step 3, the task is to compute the z-value for each sample's features. This is the first real break from the procedures used on the training set, and so, it requires some additional attention. In order for the classification approach to be scalable, universally applicable, and easy to use, we perform the classification by computing a comparative measurement for the following:

1. Each sample
2. Each feature employed for each sample
3. Each possible class

By this, we mean that every test sample is treated as if we don't know which class it came from (an absolute necessity for deployment, since we really don't know what class each sample belongs to in the deployment of the system). For each of the remaining features (recall that we reduced the set of measured and derived features back to the same number as the measured features in the model defining the end of the training and validation process), we compute a z-distance to (the mean of) each of the possible classes to which we can assign the data. In our example, this means that we compute a z_A, z_B, and z_C, defined by Eqs. (1.40), (1.41), and (1.42):

$$z_A = \frac{|S - \mu_A|}{\sigma_A / \sqrt{n_A}} = \frac{|S - \mu_A| \sqrt{n_A}}{\sigma_A} \qquad (1.40)$$

$$z_B = \frac{|S - \mu_B|}{\sigma_B / \sqrt{n_B}} = \frac{|S - \mu_B| \sqrt{n_B}}{\sigma_B} \tag{1.41}$$

$$z_C = \frac{|S - \mu_C|}{\sigma_C / \sqrt{n_C}} = \frac{|S - \mu_C| \sqrt{n_C}}{\sigma_C} \tag{1.42}$$

where z_A is the z-value of the distance from the sample value, S, and the mean of the feature for Class A training data. Similarly, z_B is the z-value of the distance from the sample value, S, and the mean of the feature for Class B training, and z_C is the z-value of the distance from the sample value, S, and the mean of the feature for Class C training data. This set of z-values for the new test samples is given in Table 1.43 (for test samples that are actually from Class A), Table 1.44 (for test samples that are actually from Class B), and Table 1.45 (for test samples that are actually from Class C).

The z-scores computed are used as input for the next step, but that does not mean that the z-score is the only reasonable metric to use as input. There are other "independent" and "dependent" scores that can be used in place of the z-score. By independence, we mean measurements that are computed independently for each class. The z-score measurements are independent of each other, since z_A does not consider anything in common with z_B or z_C in its calculation (except of course the single sample S). Other independent scores include the simple distance ($L1$) or squared distance ($L2$) between S and the means of (training) Classes A, B, and C. These distances appear less satisfactory than z-scores, since they do not account for the standard deviation; however, if the classes are expected/assumed to have the same variance, then the $L2$ distance should work rather well. Other independent measurements can take into account any non-Gaussian behavior in the distribution of the classes, and so replace the variance with the area under the (empirical or modeled) distribution curve. Dependent scores, on the other hand, depend on the other measurements for their calculations. This is different than simple normalization; for example, dividing the z-scores by the sum of all the z-scores so that they sum to 1.0 does not make them dependent. A dependent score will often be a conditional score and thus involve a conditional (e.g., if/else if/else) expression. One example is setting one of the z-score values to a maximum value if it exceeds it or to a minimum value if it is below it. This is useful if and only if multiple features are being used, and the features have widely different weights. In our example, the weights are 0.294, 0.433, and 0.273, so this may have limited benefit. However, if the weights were widely different—say, 0.6, 0.3, and 0.1—then we may wish to "limit the bias" that a single feature can do by restricting the z-score to a given range such as [0.1, 3.0]. Another example of a dependent score is adjusting the z-score for one class based on the z-score of another class. This can be done when two features are highly correlated, and we wish to penalize large distances between their z-scores.

In Step 4, we create a function of the z-score (or a suitable replacement for the z-score, as just described), designated here as $f(z)$. This is computed by feature, and so,

Table 1.43 Distances from the means of Classes A, B, and C in terms of z-score for samples that actually came from the Class A test set

Feature	Feature2 z-values			Feature2*3 z-values			Feature1/2 z-values		
Sample	z_A	z_B	z_C	z_A	z_B	z_C	z_A	z_B	z_C
1	1.845	5.492	3.637	4.656	4.894	1.116	1.525	1.244	3.839
2	4.480	7.989	1.107	3.294	4.310	3.999	5.873	14.826	1.778
3	3.426	0.499	13.123	7.994	0.527	27.902	3.812	2.955	4.476
4	0.791	2.996	8.380	0.922	2.503	12.928	4.150	3.577	4.570
5	0.088	3.828	6.799	1.757	2.146	14.695	1.355	6.532	3.036
6	0.966	4.660	5.218	2.503	3.972	5.673	2.598	0.726	4.138
7	2.547	1.331	11.542	1.054	2.447	13.207	1.525	1.244	3.839
8	1.669	2.164	9.961	0.791	2.560	12.649	2.598	0.726	4.138
9	3.601	7.157	0.474	5.798	5.383	1.302	5.393	13.945	1.912
10	4.304	0.333	14.705	5.270	0.640	22.136	2.598	0.726	4.138

The z_A, z_B and z_C values are defined by Eqs. (1.40), (1.41), and (1.42), and here, μ_A, μ_B, and μ_C are the means of the training data (see Table 1.27). If the classification is proceeding accurately, then the values for z_A should be lower than the values for z_B and z_C.

Table 1.44 Distances from the means of Classes A, B, and C in terms of z-score for samples that actually came from the Class B test set

Feature	Feature2 z-values			Feature2*3 z-values			Feature1/2 z-values		
Sample	z_A	z_B	z_C	z_A	z_B	z_C	z_A	z_B	z_C
1	9.575	5.326	24.191	3.689	1.318	18.788	5.026	5.184	4.814
2	1.845	5.492	3.637	2.547	3.990	5.580	3.755	10.938	2.368
3	8.696	4.494	22.610	15.372	3.689	43.528	2.739	0.985	4.177
4	4.304	0.333	14.705	5.270	0.640	22.136	4.292	3.836	4.610
5	5.183	1.165	16.286	3.426	1.431	18.230	1.016	2.177	3.697
6	3.426	0.499	13.123	11.068	1.845	34.413	0.988	2.229	3.689
7	1.669	2.164	9.961	6.061	0.301	23.810	0.254	3.577	3.485
8	6.939	2.829	19.448	9.750	1.280	31.623	2.767	1.037	4.185
9	0.088	3.828	6.799	1.757	3.652	7.255	1.468	1.348	3.823
10	7.818	3.662	21.029	14.977	3.520	42.691	3.935	3.162	4.507

The z_A, z_B and z_C values are defined by Eqs. (1.40), (1.41), and (1.42), and here, μ_A, μ_B, and μ_C are the means of the training data (see Table 1.27). If the classification is proceeding accurately, then the values for z_B should be lower than the values for z_A and z_C.

Table 1.45 Distances from the means of Classes A, B, and C in terms of z-score for samples that actually came from the Class C test set

Feature	Feature2 z-values			Feature2*3 z-values			Feature1/2 z-values		
Sample	z_A	z_B	z_C	z_A	z_B	z_C	z_A	z_B	z_C
1	4.480	7.989	1.107	5.929	5.440	1.581	8.132	18.974	1.148
2	3.601	7.157	0.474	5.007	5.045	0.372	13.411	28.668	0.323
3	2.723	6.325	2.055	5.534	5.270	0.744	5.478	14.101	1.888
4	3.601	7.157	0.474	5.007	5.045	0.372	7.285	17.418	1.384
5	5.358	8.821	2.688	6.237	5.572	2.232	19.284	39.451	1.959
6	4.480	7.989	1.107	7.027	5.910	3.906	9.261	21.047	0.834
7	3.601	7.157	0.474	3.162	4.254	4.278	4.941	13.116	2.037
8	1.845	5.492	3.637	3.250	4.292	4.092	0.932	5.754	3.154
9	0.966	4.660	5.218	1.318	3.463	8.185	4.630	12.545	2.124
10	5.358	8.821	2.688	5.885	5.421	1.488	22.108	44.635	2.745

The z_A, z_B and z_C values are defined by Eqs. (1.40), (1.41), and (1.42), and here, μ_A, μ_B and μ_C are the means of the training data (see Table 1.27). If the classification is proceeding accurately, then the values for z_C should be lower than the values for z_A and z_B.

we first explain how $f(z)$ was selected. First, since we chose z-score as the computed metric to factor into this function, it is important to realize that z-score is linear in the distance from the means of each class. This means that a function in z will be in the order of the distance from the means to each class. Since Gaussian curves have density that is infinitely differentiable, with "supersmoothness" of order 2, we are encouraged to model $f(z)$ with order 2. Because the z-score grows the farther the sample gets from the mean, we need an inverse function. So, the simplest order 2 inverse function is $f(z)=1/z^2$, which we choose to employ here. The values of $f(z)$ for the test data of Classes A, B, and C are given in Tables 1.46, 1.47, and 1.48, respectively.

Next, we normalize the values of $f(z)$ to sum to 1.0 for every sample and for each of the features for every sample. This means $f(z_A)+f(z_B)+f(z_C)=1.0$ for every feature. These values are tabulated in Tables 1.49, 1.50, and 1.51 for test samples originating from Classes A, B, and C, respectively.

In Step 5, we weight the $f(z)$ values by the feature weights as derived in Table 1.32. The feature weights are {0.278, 0.464, 0.258} for Features 2, 2*3, and 1/2, respectively. After this weighting, then, $f(z_A)+f(z_B)+f(z_C)=0.278$ for Feature2, $f(z_A)+f(z_B)+f(z_C)=0.464$ for Feature2*3, and $f(z_A)+f(z_B)+f(z_C)=0.258$ for Feature1/2. These values are shown in Tables 1.52, 1.53, and 1.54, for Classes A, B, and C, respectively.

In Step 6, we sum the weighted feature $f(z)$ values for each class. From Tables 1.52, 1.53, and 1.54, we compare the following sums:

$$\text{Sum weight}(A) = f(z_A)_{Feature2} + f(z_A)_{Feature2*3} + f(z_A)_{Feature1/2}$$

$$\text{Sum weight}(B) = f(z_B)_{Feature2} + f(z_B)_{Feature2*3} + f(z_B)_{Feature1/2}$$

$$\text{Sum weight}(C) = f(z_C)_{Feature2} + f(z_C)_{Feature2*3} + f(z_C)_{Feature1/2}$$

For Step 7, the maximum value of (1.), (2.), and (3.) is used to select the class assignment for the test data. The sums and the classification results for test samples from Classes A, B, and C are tabulated in Tables 1.55, 1.56, and 1.57.

The final step in the testing process is in tabulating the results and feeding back the test results. The confusion matrix for the test results is provided in Table 1.58.

From the data in Table 1.58, the sum of the diagonals (21) divided by the total number of samples (30) yields the overall accuracy, which is 70%. The recall is computed from the rows and is 50% for Class A, 80% for Class B, and 80% for Class C. Precision is computed from the columns and is 56% for Class A, 80% for Class B, and 73% for Class C. Thus, these data indicate that Class A overlaps the other two classes rather pronouncedly and that Classes B and C have very little overlap. The lack of confusion between Classes B and C is emphasized in Table 1.59, where the confusion matrix is the normalized sum of weighted feature f(z) values from summing Tables 1.55, 1.56, and 1.57 and dividing by 10. In Table 1.59, the off-diagonal confusion values for Classes B and C are only 0.065 and 0.069. These are less than a

Table 1.46 Values of $f(z)=1/z^2$, calculated for the z-scores of Table 1.43 (Class A)

Feature	Feature2 f(z) values			Feature2*3 f(z) values			Feature1/2 f(z) values		
Sample	$f(z_A)$	$f(z_B)$	$f(z_C)$	$f(z_A)$	$f(z_B)$	$f(z_C)$	$f(z_A)$	$f(z_B)$	$f(z_C)$
1	0.294	0.033	0.076	0.046	0.042	0.803	0.430	0.646	0.068
2	0.050	0.016	0.816	0.092	0.054	0.063	0.029	0.005	0.316
3	0.085	4.016	0.006	0.016	3.601	0.001	0.069	0.115	0.050
4	1.598	0.111	0.014	1.176	0.160	0.006	0.058	0.078	0.048
5	129.132	0.068	0.022	0.324	0.217	0.005	0.545	0.023	0.108
6	1.072	0.046	0.037	0.160	0.063	0.031	0.148	1.897	0.058
7	0.154	0.564	0.008	0.900	0.167	0.006	0.430	0.646	0.068
8	0.359	0.214	0.010	1.598	0.153	0.006	0.148	1.897	0.058
9	0.077	0.020	4.451	0.030	0.035	0.590	0.034	0.005	0.274
10	0.054	9.018	0.005	0.036	2.441	0.002	0.148	1.897	0.058

Table 1.47 Values of $f(z)=1/z^2$, calculated for the z-scores of Table 1.44 (Class B)

Feature Sample	Feature2 $f(z)$ values			Feature2*3 $f(z)$ values			Feature1/2 $f(z)$ values		
	$f(z_A)$	$f(z_B)$	$f(z_C)$	$f(z_A)$	$f(z_B)$	$f(z_C)$	$f(z_A)$	$f(z_B)$	$f(z_C)$
1	0.011	0.035	0.002	0.073	0.576	0.003	0.040	0.037	0.043
2	0.294	0.033	0.076	0.154	0.063	0.032	0.071	0.008	0.178
3	0.013	0.050	0.002	0.004	0.073	0.001	0.133	1.031	0.057
4	0.054	9.025	0.005	0.036	2.442	0.002	0.054	0.068	0.047
5	0.037	0.737	0.004	0.085	0.489	0.003	0.968	0.211	0.073
6	0.085	4.011	0.006	0.008	0.294	0.001	1.024	0.201	0.073
7	0.359	0.214	0.010	0.027	11.025	0.002	15.486	0.078	0.082
8	0.021	0.125	0.003	0.011	0.610	0.001	0.131	0.930	0.057
9	129.6	0.068	0.022	0.324	0.075	0.019	0.464	0.550	0.068
10	0.016	0.075	0.002	0.004	0.081	0.001	0.065	0.100	0.049

Table 1.48 Values of $f(z) = 1/z^2$, calculated for the z-scores of Table 1.45 (Class C)

Feature Sample	Feature2 f(z) values			Feature2*3 f(z) values			Feature1/2 f(z) values		
	$f(z_A)$	$f(z_B)$	$f(z_C)$	$f(z_A)$	$f(z_B)$	$f(z_C)$	$f(z_A)$	$f(z_B)$	$f(z_C)$
1	0.050	0.016	0.816	0.028	0.034	0.400	0.015	0.003	0.758
2	0.077	0.020	4.444	0.040	0.039	7.225	0.006	0.001	9.614
3	0.135	0.025	0.237	0.033	0.036	1.806	0.033	0.005	0.281
4	0.077	0.020	4.444	0.040	0.039	7.225	0.019	0.003	0.522
5	0.035	0.013	0.138	0.026	0.032	0.201	0.003	0.001	0.261
6	0.050	0.016	0.816	0.020	0.029	0.066	0.012	0.002	1.438
7	0.077	0.020	4.444	0.100	0.055	0.055	0.041	0.006	0.241
8	0.294	0.033	0.076	0.095	0.054	0.060	1.152	0.030	0.100
9	1.071	0.046	0.037	0.576	0.083	0.015	0.047	0.006	0.222
10	0.035	0.013	0.138	0.029	0.034	0.452	0.002	0.001	0.133

Table 1.49 Normalized $f(z)$ values for test samples for Class A as presented in Table 1.46

Feature	Feature2 normalized $f(z)$ values			Feature2*3 normalized $f(z)$ values			Feature1/2 normalized $f(z)$ values		
Sample	Weight (A)	Weight (B)	Weight (C)	Weight (A)	Weight (B)	Weight (C)	Weight (A)	Weight (B)	Weight (C)
1	0.730	0.082	0.188	0.052	0.047	0.901	0.376	0.565	0.059
2	0.057	0.018	0.925	0.440	0.258	0.302	0.083	0.014	0.903
3	0.021	0.978	0.001	0.005	0.995	0.000	0.295	0.491	0.214
4	0.928	0.064	0.008	0.876	0.119	0.005	0.315	0.424	0.261
5	0.999	0.001	0.000	0.593	0.398	0.009	0.806	0.034	0.160
6	0.928	0.040	0.032	0.630	0.248	0.122	0.070	0.902	0.028
7	0.212	0.777	0.011	0.839	0.156	0.005	0.376	0.565	0.059
8	0.616	0.367	0.017	0.910	0.087	0.003	0.070	0.902	0.028
9	0.017	0.004	0.979	0.046	0.053	0.901	0.109	0.016	0.875
10	0.006	0.993	0.001	0.015	0.985	0.001	0.070	0.902	0.028

After normalization, $f(z_A) + f(z_B) + f(z_C) = 1.0$ for every feature.

Table 1.50 Normalized *f*(z) values for test samples for Class B as presented in Table 1.47

Feature	Feature2 normalized *f*(z) values			Feature2*3 normalized *f*(z) values			Feature1/2 normalized *f*(z) values		
Sample	Weight (A)	Weight (B)	Weight (C)	Weight (A)	Weight (B)	Weight (C)	Weight (A)	Weight (B)	Weight (C)
1	0.229	0.729	0.042	0.112	0.883	0.005	0.333	0.308	0.358
2	0.730	0.082	0.189	0.618	0.253	0.129	0.276	0.031	0.693
3	0.200	0.769	0.031	0.051	0.936	0.013	0.109	0.844	0.047
4	0.006	0.994	0.001	0.015	0.985	0.001	0.320	0.402	0.278
5	0.048	0.947	0.005	0.147	0.847	0.005	0.773	0.169	0.058
6	0.021	0.978	0.001	0.026	0.970	0.003	0.789	0.155	0.056
7	0.616	0.367	0.017	0.002	0.997	0.000	0.990	0.005	0.005
8	0.141	0.839	0.020	0.018	0.981	0.002	0.117	0.832	0.051
9	0.998	0.001	0.000	0.775	0.179	0.045	0.429	0.508	0.063
10	0.172	0.806	0.022	0.047	0.942	0.012	0.304	0.467	0.229

After normalization, $f(z_A)+f(z_B)+f(z_C)=1.0$ *for every feature.*

Table 1.51 Normalized $f(z)$ values for test samples for Class C as presented in Table 1.47

Feature	Feature2 normalized $f(z)$ values			Feature2*3 normalized $f(z)$ values			Feature1/2 normalized $f(z)$ values		
Sample	Weight (A)	Weight (B)	Weight (C)	Weight (A)	Weight (B)	Weight (C)	Weight (A)	Weight (B)	Weight (C)
1	0.057	0.018	0.925	0.061	0.074	0.866	0.019	0.004	0.977
2	0.017	0.004	0.979	0.005	0.005	0.989	0.001	0.000	0.999
3	0.340	0.063	0.597	0.018	0.019	0.963	0.103	0.016	0.881
4	0.017	0.004	0.979	0.005	0.005	0.989	0.035	0.006	0.960
5	0.188	0.070	0.742	0.100	0.124	0.776	0.011	0.004	0.985
6	0.057	0.018	0.925	0.174	0.252	0.574	0.008	0.001	0.990
7	0.017	0.004	0.979	0.476	0.262	0.262	0.142	0.021	0.837
8	0.730	0.082	0.189	0.455	0.258	0.287	0.899	0.023	0.078
9	0.928	0.040	0.032	0.855	0.123	0.022	0.171	0.022	0.807
10	0.188	0.070	0.742	0.056	0.066	0.878	0.015	0.007	0.978

After normalization, $f(z_A) + f(z_B) + f(z_C) = 1.0$ for every feature.

Table 1.52 Normalized $f(z)$ values multiplied by the feature weights

Feature / Sample	Feature2 (total weight = 0.278)			Feature2*3 (total weight = 0.464)			Feature1/2 (total weight = 0.258)		
	Weight (A)	Weight (B)	Weight (C)	Weight (A)	Weight (B)	Weight (C)	Weight (A)	Weight (B)	Weight (C)
1	0.202	0.023	0.053	0.024	0.021	0.419	0.098	0.145	0.015
2	0.016	0.005	0.257	0.204	0.120	0.140	0.022	0.004	0.232
3	0.006	0.272	0.000	0.002	0.462	0.000	0.076	0.127	0.055
4	0.258	0.018	0.002	0.406	0.056	0.002	0.081	0.110	0.067
5	0.278	0.000	0.000	0.276	0.184	0.004	0.208	0.009	0.041
6	0.258	0.011	0.009	0.293	0.114	0.057	0.018	0.232	0.008
7	0.059	0.216	0.003	0.389	0.073	0.002	0.098	0.145	0.015
8	0.171	0.102	0.005	0.422	0.041	0.001	0.018	0.232	0.008
9	0.005	0.001	0.272	0.021	0.024	0.419	0.029	0.004	0.225
10	0.002	0.276	0.000	0.006	0.458	0.000	0.018	0.232	0.008

After this weighting, $f(z_A)+f(z_B)+f(z_C)=0.278$ for Feature2, $f(z_A)+f(z_B)+f(z_C)=0.464$ for Feature2*3, and $f(z_A)+f(z_B)+f(z_C)=0.258$ for Feature1/2. This table includes feature weight multiplied values from Table 1.49, for test data samples from Class A.

Table 1.53 Normalized $f(z)$ values multiplied by the feature weights

Feature	Feature2 (total weight = 0.278)			Feature2*3 (total weight = 0.464)			Feature1 /2 (total weight = 0.258)		
Sample	Weight (A)	Weight (B)	Weight (C)	Weight (A)	Weight (B)	Weight (C)	Weight (A)	Weight (B)	Weight (C)
1	0.063	0.204	0.011	0.051	0.411	0.002	0.086	0.079	0.093
2	0.203	0.023	0.052	0.287	0.117	0.060	0.071	0.008	0.179
3	0.056	0.213	0.009	0.023	0.435	0.006	0.028	0.218	0.012
4	0.002	0.276	0.000	0.006	0.458	0.000	0.082	0.105	0.071
5	0.013	0.263	0.002	0.069	0.393	0.002	0.198	0.044	0.016
6	0.006	0.272	0.000	0.012	0.451	0.001	0.206	0.038	0.014
7	0.171	0.102	0.005	0.001	0.463	0.000	0.256	0.001	0.001
8	0.038	0.234	0.006	0.008	0.455	0.001	0.030	0.217	0.011
9	0.278	0.000	0.000	0.359	0.084	0.021	0.111	0.131	0.016
10	0.048	0.224	0.006	0.021	0.438	0.005	0.078	0.121	0.059

After this weighting, $f(z_A) + f(z_B) + f(z_C) = 0.278$ for Feature2, $f(z_A) + f(z_B) + f(z_C) = 0.464$ for Feature2*3, and $f(z_A) + f(z_B) + f(z_C) = 0.258$ for Feature1/2. This table includes feature weight multiplied values from Table 1.50, for test data samples from Class B.

Table 1.54 Normalized f(z) values multiplied by the feature weights

Feature / Sample	Feature2 (total weight = 0.278)			Feature2*3 (total weight = 0.464)			Feature1/2 (total weight = 0.258)		
	Weight (A)	Weight (B)	Weight (C)	Weight (A)	Weight (B)	Weight (C)	Weight (A)	Weight (B)	Weight (C)
1	0.016	0.005	0.257	0.028	0.034	0.402	0.005	0.001	0.252
2	0.005	0.001	0.272	0.002	0.002	0.460	0.000	0.000	0.258
3	0.095	0.018	0.165	0.009	0.009	0.446	0.026	0.004	0.228
4	0.005	0.001	0.272	0.002	0.002	0.460	0.009	0.002	0.247
5	0.052	0.020	0.206	0.046	0.057	0.361	0.003	0.001	0.254
6	0.016	0.005	0.257	0.080	0.117	0.267	0.002	0.000	0.256
7	0.005	0.001	0.272	0.222	0.121	0.121	0.036	0.006	0.216
8	0.203	0.023	0.052	0.211	0.120	0.133	0.232	0.006	0.020
9	0.259	0.011	0.008	0.396	0.058	0.010	0.044	0.006	0.208
10	0.052	0.020	0.206	0.025	0.031	0.408	0.005	0.001	0.252

After this weighting, $f(z_A) + f(z_B) + f(z_C) = 0.278$ for Feature2, $f(z_A) + f(z_B) + f(z_C) = 0.464$ for Feature2*3, and $f(z_A) + f(z_B) + f(z_C) = 0.258$ for Feature1/2. This table includes feature weight multiplied values from Table 1.51, for test data samples from Class C.

Table 1.55 Sum of weights (from Table 1.52) for the assignment of test samples belonging to Class A for each of the possible classes: Classes A, B, and C

Sample	Sum weight (A)	Sum weight (B)	Sum weight (C)	Classification	Result
1	0.324	0.189	0.487	C	INCORRECT
2	0.242	0.129	0.629	C	INCORRECT
3	0.084	0.861	0.055	B	INCORRECT
4	0.745	0.184	0.071	A	CORRECT
5	0.762	0.193	0.045	A	CORRECT
6	0.569	0.357	0.074	A	CORRECT
7	0.546	0.434	0.020	A	CORRECT
8	0.611	0.375	0.014	A	CORRECT
9	0.055	0.029	0.916	C	INCORRECT
10	0.026	0.966	0.008	B	INCORRECT

The classification (column 5) is given to the class belonging to the maximum summed weight. The result (CORRECT or INCORRECT) is given in column 6. The accuracy is 50%, which is above the "random guessing" value of 33.3%.

Table 1.56 Sum of weights (from Table 1.53) for the assignment of test samples belonging to Class B for each of the possible classes: Classes A, B, and C

Sample	Sum weight (A)	Sum weight (B)	Sum weight (C)	Classification	Result
1	0.200	0.694	0.106	B	CORRECT
2	0.561	0.148	0.291	A	INCORRECT
3	0.107	0.866	0.027	B	CORRECT
4	0.090	0.839	0.071	B	CORRECT
5	0.280	0.700	0.020	B	CORRECT
6	0.224	0.761	0.015	B	CORRECT
7	0.428	0.566	0.006	B	CORRECT
8	0.076	0.906	0.108	B	CORRECT
9	0.748	0.215	0.037	A	INCORRECT
10	0.147	0.783	0.070	B	CORRECT

The classification (column 5) is given to the class belonging to the maximum summed weight. The result (CORRECT or INCORRECT) is given in column 6. The accuracy is 80%, well above the "random guessing" value of 33.3%.

third of the confusion between Classes A and C and less than a fourth of the confusion between Classes A and B.

As part of the analytic assessment, we then compare the testing and training accuracy across the three selected features. The confusion matrix results for the training

Table 1.57 Sum of weights (from Table 1.54) for the assignment of test samples belonging to Class C for each of the possible classes: Classes A, B, and C

Sample	Sum weight (A)	Sum weight (B)	Sum weight (C)	Classification	Result
1	0.049	0.040	0.911	C	CORRECT
2	0.007	0.003	0.990	C	CORRECT
3	0.130	0.031	0.839	C	CORRECT
4	0.016	0.005	0.979	C	CORRECT
5	0.101	0.078	0.821	C	CORRECT
6	0.098	0.122	0.780	C	CORRECT
7	0.263	0.128	0.609	C	CORRECT
8	0.646	0.149	0.205	A	INCORRECT
9	0.699	0.075	0.226	A	INCORRECT
10	0.082	0.052	0.866	C	CORRECT

The classification (column 5) is given to the class belonging to the maximum summed weight. The result (CORRECT or INCORRECT) is given in column 6. The accuracy is 80%, well above the "random guessing" value of 33.3%.

Table 1.58 Confusion matrix for the test results of this example

Normalized confusion matrix		Classifier output (computed classification) prediction		
		A	B	C
True class of the samples (input)	A	5	2	3
	B	2	8	0
	C	2	0	8

Recall is determined from the rows and precision from the columns. Class A has 50% recall, and Classes B and C have 80% recall. Class A has 56% precision, Class B has 80% precision, and Class C has 73% precision.

Table 1.59 Confusion matrix for the test results of this example, where instead of using the binary classification results, we are summing the weighted feature $f(z)$ values from Tables 1.55, 1.56, and 1.57 and normalizing (just dividing by 10)

Normalized confusion matrix		Classifier output (computed classification) prediction		
		A	B	C
True class of the samples (input)	A	0.396	0.372	0.232
	B	0.286	0.648	0.075
	C	0.209	0.068	0.723

Recall is determined from the rows and precision from the columns. Class A has 40% recall, Class B has 65% recall, and Class C has 72% recall. Class A has 44% precision, Class B has 60% precision, and Class C has 70% precision.

Table 1.60 Confusion matrix for Feature2 only, training data

Normalized confusion matrix		Classifier output (computed classification) prediction		
		A	B	C
True class of the samples (input)	A	3	4	3
	B	3	7	0
	C	3	0	7

Based on the diagonals, the accuracy is 57%.

Table 1.61 Confusion matrix for Feature2 only, testing data

Normalized confusion matrix		Classifier output (computed classification) prediction		
		A	B	C
True class of the samples (input)	A	5	3	2
	B	3	7	0
	C	2	0	8

Based on the diagonals, the accuracy is 67%.

Table 1.62 Confusion matrix for Feature2*3 only, training data

Normalized confusion matrix		Classifier output (computed classification) prediction		
		A	B	C
True class of the samples (input)	A	8	1	1
	B	3	7	0
	C	2	0	8

Based on the diagonals, the accuracy is 77%.

data (which is of course overfitting) and the testing data are shown for Feature2 in Tables 1.60 and 1.61, respectively. The accuracy on the training data is 57%, and on the testing data, it is 67%. This is an interesting result, as usually, the training data would outperform the testing data since the model is built from the training data.

The confusion matrix results for the training data (reported here just for comparative purposes) and the testing data are shown for Feature2*3 in Tables 1.62 and 1.63, respectively. The accuracy on the training data is 77%, and on the testing data, it is 70%. This result is consistent with expectations, with the training data outperforming the testing data.

Finally, the confusion matrix results for the training data (reported here just for comparative purposes) and the testing data are shown for Feature1/2 in Tables 1.64 and 1.65, respectively. The accuracy on the training data is 67%, and on the testing

Table 1.63 Confusion matrix for Feature2*3 only, testing data

Normalized confusion matrix		Classifier output (computed classification) prediction		
		A	B	C
True class of the samples (input)	A	6	2	2
	B	2	8	0
	C	3	0	7

Based on the diagonals, the accuracy is 70%.

Table 1.64 Confusion matrix for Feature1/2 only, training data

Normalized confusion matrix		Classifier output (computed classification) prediction		
		A	B	C
True class of the samples (input)	A	4	3	3
	B	3	7	0
	C	1	0	9

Based on the diagonals, the accuracy is 67%.

Table 1.65 Confusion matrix for Feature1/2 only, testing data

Normalized confusion matrix		Classifier output (computed classification) prediction		
		A	B	C
True class of the samples (input)	A	1	7	2
	B	3	5	2
	C	1	0	9

Based on the diagonals, the accuracy is 50%.

data, it is 50%. This result is consistent with expectations, with the training data out-performing the testing data.

With the data in Table 1.65, we see quite a change in the confusion matrix in comparison with any of the three "training" sets (Tables 1.60, 1.62, and 1.64) and the other two testing sets (Tables 1.61 and 1.63). This confusion matrix is very noisy, and for Class A, the recall is only 10%, and the precision is only 20%. Also, there are two "Class C for Class B" confusions, two more than in the other five confusion matrices combined. The mean accuracy of the three training sets is 67% (Table 1.66), and the mean accuracy of the testing sets is 62% (Table 1.67).

The overall classifier, using the three features together, had an accuracy of 70%, which outperformed the mean for the three features separately for both the testing

Table 1.66 Summed confusion matrix for all three features used separately, training data

Normalized confusion matrix		Classifier output (computed classification) prediction		
		A	**B**	**C**
True class of the samples (input)	A	15	8	7
	B	9	21	0
	C	6	0	24

The overall accuracy is the sum of the diagonals (60) divided by the sum of all matrix elements (90), or 67%.

Table 1.67 Summed confusion matrix for all three features used separately, testing data

Normalized confusion matrix		Classifier output (computed classification) prediction		
		A	**B**	**C**
True class of the samples (input)	A	12	12	6
	B	8	20	2
	C	6	0	24

The overall accuracy is the sum of the diagonals (56) divided by the sum of all matrix elements (90), or 62%.

and the training data. Outperforming the training data is unexpected but is definitely a feature of the model.

1.10.3 Comparing training and testing data set results

In the past section, we performed quick checking on each feature to determine if (a) the features performed better on the training than the testing data, (b) the set of features performed better than the mean performance of the features individually, and (c) the testing data performed better than the mean accuracy of the training features. Indeed, for (a), the mean accuracy of the features on the training data was 67%, compared with 62% on the testing data. This should be the case, since the size of the training data set was small and the training and testing data weren't cross validated. Also, the fact that the three features provided higher accuracy than any individual feature is encouraging. This is in spite of the fact that one (derived) feature provided much better accuracy than the other two surviving features and support the choice of the same number of features as are measured. The combination of three features applied to the testing data outperforming the individual features applied to the training data exemplifies the utility of the multifeature approach.

Overall, then, it is clear from Section 1.10 that there is a tremendous benefit from separating out training and testing. This benefit increases when the size of the testing set grows larger. Some of the principles learned in this section will be used to drive the overall meta-analytic approaches in the rest of the book: using multiple analytic techniques together generally provides more robust, more generalizable, and more accuracy analytic output.

1.11 Summary

This chapter provided a wide and occasionally deep overview of the field of analytics. Informatics and statistics were covered, as well as in particular the normalization of features, sample and population tests, and regression and estimation. One goal with estimation was to compare uncertainty in the independent and dependent variables, which is directly related to sensitivity analysis. The concept of residual entropy was introduced and applied to model definition sensitivity as model residual sensitivity. Next, k-means and k-nearest neighbor clustering are considered in enough detail to introduce the reader to these important processes for converting unstructured data into structured data. The addition of regularization approaches to clustering to "optimize" the clustering will be considered in a later chapter (Chapter 10). The counterintuitive concept of unclustering is introduced as a possible step in optimizing the cluster over time.

A four-state Markov model was introduced as a way of introducing how overall system optimization can be garnered from the behavior of individual states and their transitions. Machine learning approaches distinct from the more biologically inspired artificial intelligence (AI) approaches were overviewed. In particular, the concept of entropy was elaborated as a means of assessing how far in the path to optimal system design and/or behavior the system architect has proceeded. Support vector machines (SVMs) and the kernel were then described, and the salient elements of probability theory—specifically the Bayesian approaches—were reviewed. Dimensionality reduction was shown to be useful for assessing the order or complexity of a system (usually tied to information gain). Optimization was introduced, tied to search in this case, and the broader data mining and knowledge discovery approaches were at least superficially covered (more on them in later chapters).

Recognition was covered in greater depth because, like classification and clustering, it is an integrative analytic involving several types of algorithmic approaches. The example of image processing outlined important recognition approaches such as binarization, segmentation, key-point detection, classification, and the consideration of training data—all processes applicable to virtually any form of recognition. This latter point was supported by a brief consideration of 1D and 3D recognition in addition to the 2D image recognition. Next, the three main forms of ensemble learning (bagging, boosting, and stacking) were introduced, and a novel ensemble method, the spatial-continuity hybrid, was described. The artificial intelligence (AI) approaches covered in this chapter were genetic algorithms (GAs), artificial neural networks (ANNs), and immunologic approaches. For the GA discussion, only the simplest evolutionary approaches were covered, but the basics of populations, mutations, crossovers, and inversions were discussed in depth. For ANNs, multilayer perceptrons were used to illustrate the concepts of nodes, gains, back-propagation, and thresholding at each consecutive layer. Finally, for the immunology-inspired approaches, many potential research areas were identified.

The chapter concluded with an exhaustive coverage of a simple but very adaptable classifier approach. The degenerate binary case was covered first. Then, the general case was described, in which training and testing, weighting samples based on distances from all class populations, and the derivation of features from measured features are considered.

A wide array of introductory analytics books is available that can augment the content in this chapter [Negn04, Sewe08]. This chapter introduces, however, additional analytic approaches—which will be elaborated in the chapters to come—over that of existing publications on analytics, including the following:

(1) Design patterns and approaches for combining a multiplicity of analytic approaches
(2) Application to a wide range of fields
(3) Pragmatically, statistics-, and heuristic-driven evaluation approaches (such as for the ground-up classifier in Section 1.10)

Taken together, these approaches are intended to provide the means for all practitioners of data analytics—from the student to novice and from young engineer to system veteran—to build better systems. This chapter outlines some of the most important technologies used in intelligent systems. As can be seen from this material, this book is aimed at allowing one with a moderate understanding of statistics, calculus, logic, linear systems, and design patterns to be able to architect and deploy more intelligent systems than even the best individual intelligent algorithm designer can achieve—by using such a superior algorithm as the starting point, not the end point. This meta-architect must understand both the relative advantages and disadvantages and both the flexibility and the limitations of each of the component systems. The meta-architect need not understand these individual technologies well enough to improve them as they are; rather, she must understand how to make them more valuable within a larger system involving two or more intelligent components. Let us now consider the types of systems that will require these new system-based analysis skills. Let us move, then, from this lengthy introduction on analytics to the meta.

References

[Akba11] Akbari, R., Ziarati, K., 2011. A multilevel evolutionary algorithm for optimizing numerical functions. Int. J. Ind. Eng. Comput. 2, 419–430.

[Carr11] Carr, N., 2011. The Shallows: What the Internet is Doing to Our Brains. WW Norton & Co. 304 p.

[Hast09] Hastie, T., Tibshirani, R., Friedman, J., 2009. The Elements of Statistical Learning, second ed. Springer, pp. 337–387.

[Negn04] Negnevitsky M, "Artificial Intelligence: A Guide to Intelligent Systems," Addison-Wesley, ISBN 9780321204660, 415 p. 2004.

[Ott08] Ott, R.L., Longnecker, M.T., 2008. An Introduction to Statistical Methods and Data Analysis. Cengage Learning, ISBN 9780495017585. 1296 p.

[Poll10] Pollard, S.B., Simske, S.J., Adams, G.B., 2010. Model based print signature profile extraction for forensic analysis of individual text glyph. In: IEEE WIFS 2010, pp. 1–6.

[Sewe08] Sewell, M., 2008. Ensemble Learning. Department of Computer Science, University College London (revised August 2008), 16 p.

[Shan48] Shannon, C.E., 1948. A mathematical theory of communication. Bell Syst. Tech. J. 27 (3), 379–423.

[Sims10] Simske, S.J., Adams, G.B., 2010. High-resolution glyph-inspection based security system. In: IEEE ICASSP 2010, pp. 1794–1797.

[Sims13] Simske, S., 2013. Meta-Algorithmics: Patterns for Robust, Low-Cost, High-Quality Systems. IEEE Press and Wiley, Singapore.

[Walk98] Walker, K.N., Cootes, T.F., Taylor, C.J., 1998. Locating salient object features. In: Proceedings of the British Machine Vision Conference, pp. 557–566.

Further reading

Marsland, S., 2009. Machine Learning. Chapman & Hall/CRC, Boca Raton FL. 390 p.

Provost, F., Fawcett, T., 2013. Data Science for Business. O'Reilly Media, Inc., Sebastopol, CA.

Simske, S.J., Wright, D.W., Sturgill, M., 2006. Meta-algorithmic systems for document classification. In: ACM DocEng 2006, pp. 98–106.

Ground truthing

2

*Stories are the common ground that allow people to connect, despite all our
defences and all our differences*
Kate Forsyth (2014)
Truth is truth to the end of reckoning
William Shakespeare (1604)

2.1 Introduction

One of the key purposes of meta-analytics, at the algorithmic level, is to compare and
contrast two or more approaches. The *common ground* of multiple approaches to analytics is, of course, the story the data would tell if we had perfect insight into the
data's purpose, creation, sources of error, and future uses. The differences between
the analytic approaches, in fact, help explore the data's story more fully, allowing us
to more fully reckon the ground truth. Sometimes, reckoning is pruning from the
ground truth; other times, reckoning is amplifying or "boosting" some of the ground
truth. Such reckoning of ground truth is the subject of this chapter.

At the system level, however, a key purpose is to compare and contrast two or
more *frameworks* for approach. The latter consideration is the concern of this chapter, and this is not a small item of discussion. While flexibility at the algorithm level
is essential for machine learning and scalability, it is flexibility at the system (or,
roughly equivalently, at the architectural, design, and structural) level that affords
systems to be retroactively optimized for cost, robustness/adaptability, accuracy,
parallelism, etc. This assumes a perspective in which the algorithmic design is used
to allow the *current settings* to be optimized, whereas the system design is used to
allow the *future settings* to be optimized.

I make a further argument here, which one need not agree with to appreciate the
content of this chapter (though it wouldn't hurt). Consider security and privacy:
experts in these important technological areas share the mantra that "security and
privacy measures must be built into the original design." It is well known (and
reported by respected authorities such as the Institute of Electrical and Electronics
Engineers (IEEE)) that the costs of security breaches are several orders of magnitude
more than the costs of building security into the design in the first place. Now, consider meta-analytics. Analogous to security, I argue that the costs of trying to add
meta-analytic approaches after the fact will also be much more difficult (and thus
expensive) than building them in by design. There are several reasons for this.

Meta-Analytics. https://doi.org/10.1016/B978-0-12-814623-1.00002-2

Firstly, downstream uses of the meta-analytic output will already be in place, and many of these systems will, for a variety of reasons (cost, availability of software developers, product deadlines, market inertia, etc.), be relatively inflexible to changes in the type and structure of data created. Creation of a standard would add further intransigence. Secondly, algorithms and other machine learning processing—including how data are structured and pipelined—may be optimized for the current set of analytic output. Thirdly, there is a tendency among algorithm and artificial/machine intelligence (A/MI) system designers, including me, to feel that they have high sunk costs in the existing A/MI algorithms, software, and systems for them. One could argue that this third consideration could be readily overcome with a healthy change in attitude and that may well be the case. However, the first and second concerns are likely to remain irrespective of attitude adjustment. Therefore, providing a readily modifiable intelligent data structure—that is, the means to create information from the current and future data sets—is one of the key roles for the meta-analytic engineer. This is beyond analytics—it is analytics over time and scale.

Easier said than done, the approach outlined above requires upfront diligence, intelligence, and convergence. In this chapter, I provide a set of patterns for approaching "analytics around analytics," which comprises three separate considerations:

1. Prevalidation
2. Optimizing settings from training data
3. Learning how to learn

Each of these represents, in at least one way, a break with the traditional (training, validation, and testing) approach to specific analytics-related workflows (clustering, classification, etc.) and is meant to provide the same type of mixing of potential training data that meta-analytic approaches provide on the analysis end.

2.2 Pre-validation

An earlier version of this section was originally published and presented elsewhere [Sims17]. Here, it is extended to consider the broader use of prevalidation and put in content of degrees of freedom and other ensemble considerations.

In the world of analytics, the algorithms and intelligent systems employed are usually rated based on the accuracy of their output on test data. However, suppose you gave a history test to the world's top mathematicians, and whoever performed best on the Napoleonic Wars would be awarded the Fields Medal. Obviously, in this case, the wrong set of testing data is being used. In the related world of big data, it is not always this easy to discern what test data to use for validation—and which to ignore. Using k-fold cross validation, for example, may introduce redundancy or correlation within the data set, so that overtraining occurs. With large labeled data sets, certain events may occur with low frequency, resulting in class imbalance. We can address the former by keeping the training and validation sets separate from the test set. We address the latter by pruning the training and test sets so that they are uniform in size. But, what if, even after these approaches, certain data have significantly different clustering and/or classification behavior from the rest of the data. Surely, some amount of difference is acceptable. However, in some cases, the classes (irrespective of their labels) are simply of too poor quality to use in the validation process, that is, in relatively assessing which deployment classifier to employ [Mali11]. Alternatively, some classes may have dominant effects on overall measures like variance and entropy, and so, when ensemble methods (such as boosting) are used for classification, a small subset of classes will mislead the weak classifiers.

In such cases, an unbiased, automated, and efficient way of eliminating suspect classes from the validation set (and reintroducing them, of course, in the training set) is needed so that we can more reasonably assess the relative accuracies of the deployment classifier(s). This is particularly valuable when an ensemble of simple classifiers is to be used: We use a (majority) subset of the training data for validation of the deployment classifier *before* proceeding with training and testing; we employ validation→training→testing rather than the usual training→validation→testing. The "prevalidation" does not affect training; it simply determines what ensemble of simple classifiers will be used for the actual training.

For the example in this section, we focus on text classification based on the word statistics in the documents to be classified. That is, for every document and for all the documents in each class, we compute the term frequency (TF) for every word in the document/class. Term frequency times inverse document frequency, or TF*IDF [Salt88][Robe04], is commonly used in information retrieval and classification tasks [Kwok90][Ramo03] [Karb06]. We previously introduced a total of 112 TF*IDF methods for use as ensemble classifiers of text: 14 inverse document frequency methods for each of 8 term document frequency methods. This provides $14 + 8 - 2 = 20$ degrees of freedom in choosing the paired TF and IDF methods, which is a better estimate for the number of independent TF*IDF measurements than 112 for this set. That is, of the 112 TF*IDF approaches, there are an equivalent of approximately 20 independent approaches.

These TF*IDF measures were computed for a set of articles originally posted on the CNN.com website, each of which were manually assigned to one of 12 classes. Within each class, articles were assigned to two equally sized groups: one for training and one for testing. To avoid class imbalance, we were able to have 98 files per class: 49 for the validation and training steps and 49 for testing. To build a measure, we multiply one of the TF measures by one of the IDF equations, providing the aforementioned ensemble of 112 simple classifiers.

A validation or training experiment consists of preprocessing each document and creating a stream of tokens composed of individual words using the sharpNLP [Code13] C# open-source project. The token stream is then converted into a bag of words consisting of all nonstop words in each file. Stop words consist of common words that add no value to the calculation (e.g., "the," "of," and "but"). Once the TF*IDF measures are generated for each word in the file, a master list of words for all the files in a given class is created. We create this master list by summing all the TF*IDF values for each word and dividing this sum by the number of files in which the word is found (normalization). This gives us a single TF*IDF measure for each word found in a class that we can then use for classifying articles from the test set of document classes.

During testing, we first determine the TF*IDF measure values for all the words in a document. We then compare them with the normalized values for that word in each of the classes using the dot product of the TF*IDF value for the word in the test file with that of the normalized TF*IDF value for the word in each training class. The class that produces the highest dot product value sum with the file is then assigned as the class for that document. This procedure is used for all the test files in each class for each of the 112 TF*IDF measures.

A TF*IDF measure will classify a file or document set as one of the 12 CNN-provided classes (business, health, justice, living, opinion, politics, showbiz, sport, tech, travel, the United States, and world). The confusion matrix is constructed by creating a two-dimensional matrix in which the rows represent the "true" or "actual" class, while the columns represent the class assigned by the classification algorithm described above. To determine the accuracy of the TF*IDF measure, we divide the sum of values in the diagonal of the confusion matrix by the total number of files in all test files for all classes:

$$\text{Accuracy} = \sum (a_{1,1} \ldots a_{n,n}) \Big/ \sum_{i=1}^{n\text{Classes}} n\text{files} \qquad (2.1)$$

We then sort the TF*IDF measures by accuracy from highest to lowest accuracy and set a minimum accuracy to identify a subset of the 112 TF*IDF measures that best classify the files. We found that no single TF*IDF could classify all the documents with high accuracy [Vans17]. We did achieve relatively high-accuracy "validation" classifiers by combining the individual TF*IDF measures.

We defined a figure of merit metric to address the elimination of suspect or "outlier classes" during validation (i.e., before training). The CNN corpus [Lins12] consists of news texts extracted from the CNN website (www.cnn.com). This test corpus consists of articles written by professional news writers in English, reporting on 12 general interest classes. The set we used consisted of 1176 documents assigned equally to 12 classes (98 documents per class). The news articles obtained from the CNN website were carefully chosen in order to contain only text; thus, news articles with figures, videos, tables, and other multimedia elements were discarded (such articles may have unintentionally represented salient information in nontext form only). Sentence segmentation was performed by the Stanford CoreNLP [Stan17]. Stop words [Silv03] were removed although this had little effect on classification since TF*IDF methods were used. Word stemming [Frak92] converts each word into its root form, removing its prefix and suffix. After this stage, the text is structured in XML and included in the XML file that corresponds to the news article.

We used the 112 simple TF*IDF classifiers and weighted combinations of them (a form of boosting) for the weak and ensemble classification [Vans16]. On the training data, the poorest-performing classes are consistently those of the classes travel, living, opinion, the United States, and tech, in that order. We next used the top TF*IDF classifiers in weighted voting [Sims13]. The best classification results were generally obtained with six TF*IDF weak classifiers in combination. We devised a metric, the "figure of merit," to automatically determine when to stop removing classes from the validation set, defined in Eq. (2.2):

$$\text{Figure of merit} = \frac{\%\text{error\_reduction}}{\%\text{error}_{\text{remaining}}/df} \qquad (2.2)$$

The numerator is the amount of overall error reduced by removing the most suspect class. The denominator is the error remaining divided by the degrees of freedom (df) of the number of classes being compared, which is the (number of classes)-1. The denominator is the expected value of error reduction if all of the classes are equally useful. So, if the figure of merit is greater than unity, there is reason to believe that the current "suspect" class may be removed from the validation set (though of course reintroduced for the subsequent training set). It is an outlier for validation only (not for training).

Other novel, quantitative methods for providing sensitivity analysis on the confusion matrix during validation were computed. Imbalance in the confusion matrix during validation was determined using confusion matrix entropy [Sims13]:

$$e_1 = \frac{-\sum_i \sum_j \left[\left(\frac{c_{ij}}{c_{ij}+c_{ji}} \right) * \ln \left(\frac{c_{ij}}{c_{ij}+c_{ji}} \right) \right]}{N(N-1)} \text{ and}$$

$$e_2 = \frac{-\sum_i \sum_j \left[\left(\frac{c_{ji}}{c_{ij}+c_{ji}} \right) * \ln \left(\frac{c_{ji}}{c_{ij}+c_{ji}} \right) \right]}{N(N-1)} \text{ and } e = e_1 + e_2 \qquad (2.3)$$

Because many of the elements in the confusion matrix are 0 (i.e., the matrix is sparsely populated), two new metrics to describe nonuniformity in the confusion matrix were also introduced. These new metrics, taken together, should provide as much rigor as confusion matrix entropy and have the additional advantage of being appropriate for sparse matrices. The first metric is the Relative Absolute Transposition Difference (RATD), which is given by

$$RATD = \frac{\sum_{i=1}^{N} \sum_{j=i+1}^{N} |c_{ij} - c_{ji}|}{\sum_{i=1}^{N} \sum_{j=1, j\neq i}^{N} c_{ij}} \qquad (2.4)$$

where C_{ij}=confusion matrix element at position (i,j). This value gives a meaningful measure of how much variability is contained in erroneously assigning two classes with respect to each other. Higher values for RATD imply greater imbalance in classes, referred to as "attractor" and "repeller" classes [Sims13]. The RATD is further modified to have logarithmic behavior using

$$RATD = -\ln\left(\frac{\sum\limits_{i=1}^{N}\sum\limits_{j=i+1}^{N}\left|c_{ij}-c_{ji}\right|}{\sum\limits_{i=1}^{N}\sum\limits_{j=1,j\neq i}^{N}c_{ij}}\right) \tag{2.5}$$

The second new metric helps describe the overall variability in the confusion matrix, irrespective of the existence of attractor and/or repeller classes. The mean difference of off-diagonal expected values of elements, or MDODEV, is given by

$$MDODEV = \frac{\sum\limits_{i=1}^{N}\sum\limits_{j=1,j\neq i}^{N}\left|c_{ij}-\mu\right|}{\sum\limits_{i=1}^{N}\sum\limits_{j=1,j\neq i}^{N}c_{ij}} \tag{2.6}$$

This value uses the confusion matrix expected value, μ:

$$\mu = \frac{\sum\limits_{i=1}^{N}\sum\limits_{j=1,j\neq i}^{N}c_{ij}}{N(N-1)} \tag{2.7}$$

Validation and training, therefore, proceed as shown in Fig. 2.1. After training on all 12 classes, testing was performed on the remaining 50% of the articles. The accuracy of the best-performing individual TF*IDF was found to be 0.4473, while the accuracy of the worst-performing individual TF*IDF was found to be 0.1650. After this full-class-set training, we next performed training on 11, 10, 9, 8, and 7 classes after removing travel, living, opinion, the United States, and tech classes, respectively and cumulatively. Removing these classes was used to further evaluate the ground truth data (validation before training). The best and worst-performing individual TF*IDF measures were, in each case, similar to those with all 12 classes. Obviously, removing a class with poor accuracy should increase the overall classification accuracy, but more importantly, we established that the figure of merit is above unity for the removal of the first three suspect classes and then drops well below unity (Table 2.1).

Table 2.2 presents the measurements of RATD and MDODEV. These measures are much higher, as expected, for the confusion matrices corresponding to poor classification accuracy—the so-called (worst) examples. The higher values for RATD confirm the higher variability in comparing transposed values for poor classifiers. Similarly, the higher MDODEV values confirm the higher variability in confusion matrix misassignment for poor classifiers. However, for the purposes of validation before training, we are primarily concerned with how the elimination of the poor-quality classes affects RATD and MDODEV for good classifiers. Thus, we wish to mainly compare RATD and MDODEV for 12 (best) and 9 (best) classes. Here, RATD decreases by 46.3%, and MDODEV decreases by 26.0%, indicating that the removal of the classes results in more entropic intraclass behavior.

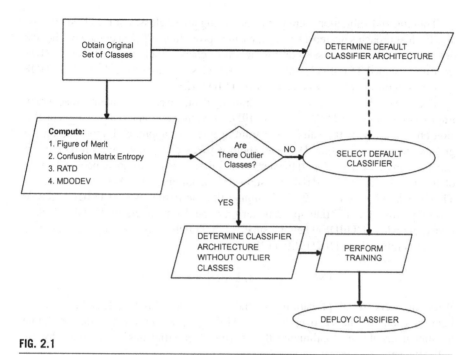

FIG. 2.1

Diagram of the validation→training→testing approach as outlined in Section 2.3.

Table 2.1 Figure of merit for sequential removal of five most suspect classes

Classes removed	Peak accuracy	Figure of merit
None	0.655	N/A
Travel	0.688	1.06
Travel, living	0.727	1.29
Travel, living, opinion	0.773	1.62
Travel, living, opinion, the United States	0.791	0.60
Travel, living, opinion, the United States, tech	0.808	0.53

Table 2.2 RATD (Eq. 2.5) and MDODEV (Eq. 2.6) for the best and worst TF*IDF classifiers with all 12 classes and the 9 classes remaining after pruning with the figure of merit (Eq. 2.1)

Number of classes (best/worst)	RATD (Eq. 2.5)	MDODEV (Eq. 2.6)
12 (best)	1.0832	0.9819
12 (worst)	3.5579	1.6366
9 (best)	0.5814	0.7267
9 (worst)	3.2016	1.5569

Training and validation were performed using all 12 classes or the "best" 9 classes. Each approach selected TF*IDF measures providing 100% accuracy on the 588 documents in the training set. For training on 12 classes, there were 10 such TF*IDF measures, named TFIDF-12; for training on 9 classes, there were 19 such TF*IDF measures, named TFIDF-9 (a superset of TFIDF-12).

Because of the 100% success on the training data, we achieved identical accuracy improvement for both TFIDF-12 and TFIDF-9 on the test data, making any conclusion on the utility of the validation→training→testing approach impossible on the grounds of accuracy alone. However, both degrees of freedom and probability of superset can be used to support the approach. Firstly, the minimum expected degrees of freedom for the 112 TF*IDF measures are the number of IDF-1+the number of TF-1, that is, $14 - 1 + 8 - 1 = 20$. This implies that the 19 members of TFIDF-9 almost certainly cover the TF*IDF space better than the 10 members of TFIDF-12. Secondly, the odds of TFIDF-9 being a superset of TFIDF-12 is given by the following ratio of combinations (102!19!/9!112!):

$$p(\text{superset}) = \binom{102}{9} / \binom{112}{19} = 1.767 \times 10^{-14} \tag{2.8}$$

With this very small probability of the extra nine TFIDF values in TFIDF-9 being chosen by chance over those in TFIDF-12, we may conclude that some additional insight into optimizing the ensemble classifier has been gained by the validation→training→testing approach.

The improved deployment accuracy justifies leaving out the three classes (living, opinion, and travel) from the training set per the figure of merit, RATD, and MDODEV. If we analyze the original confusion matrix (data not shown), we find that these three classes have a combined 6.1% accuracy, compared with the 57.6% accuracy for the other nine classes. These three classes distribute their errors similarly to the distribution of errors of the other classes, that is, sending most of their errors to the classes with highest recall (the so-called attractor classes [Sims13])—business, justice, showbiz, and world. The classes removed in the validation phase have both low recall and (relatively) high precision, meaning they are "repeller" classes and so distribute their error across other classes. Combined, these three classes had only three false-positive assignments compared with 222 false-positive assignments for the other nine classes: attracting false positives at 1/25 the rate of the other classes. These three "outlier" classes therefore act as an independent set of ground truth from the other nine classes. This means that subsequent evaluation of deployed ensemble classifiers determines how well the classifiers handle two relatively independent ground truth sets and not a continuum of ground truth. This may not preclude a deployment classifier from performing well on this more complex data set, but it does pose a different "pattern" of classification challenge, which in itself is of value for determining whether to use the methods shown herein. Table 2.2 provides another window on the improved cohesiveness of the nine classes after removing the living, opinion, and travel classes from the training set. The measurements of RATD and MDODEV decrease by 46.3% and 26.0%, respectively, for the best initial classifier after reducing the number of classes. The values of RATD and MDODEV do not change for the worst of the initial classifiers after validation, which emphasizes the assertion that the nine classes are a different type of class set from the 12 classes—not simply a reduction in the number of classes.

Training the deployment classifiers on a more cohesive ground truth set (nine classes) constitutes a different ensemble configuration from training the deployment classifiers on the original set of 12 classes. A different deployment classifier is recommended for these two cases (i.e., an ensemble of 19 rather than 10 simple classifiers). It may be that the 12-class deployment classifier better handles discontinuous data sets than they do continuous data sets. This may be disadvantageous when, after deployment, the amount of data to be handled is generally much more extensive than the training data and as such is likely to require a more robust classifier that can handle largely overlapping classes. The "validation before training" approach and its direct measurement through the figure of merit support what was observed for the confusion matrix, RATD, and MDODEV. We believe we ended up with a differently behaving 9-class training set than the original 12-class training set. Three suspect classes were culled from the training set, and the figure of merit sharply increased until the last of these was removed, after which it then sharply dropped below unity. Discontinuities such as these are generally rare and outline a means of determining when ground truth data contain discontinuities. Much remains to be established both theoretically and empirically, but the data presented in this section support the hypothesis that both validation-before-training classification accuracy and analytics of the validation-before-training confusion matrix can be used to provide a set of ground truthing data that may lead to enhanced ensemble classifier sets. Finally, the approach can be viewed as a specialized form of dimensionality reduction of the training set where the primary classes are pruned rather than using principal component analysis (PCA) or related methods. In the previous work [Sims17], noisy training data are removed from all labeled classes, rather than considering labeled classes as units to be inappropriate for training purposes. Future work will focus on comparing and contrasting these approaches.

This section proposes a new ordering for validation, training, and testing in classification. The approach is not about optimizing the classification accuracy, performance, or robustness per se; rather, it is about ensuring that the data used to later optimize the classification are not misdirecting or even contradicting that purpose. Therefore, it is about *optimizing the architecture* of the classifier to be deployed. Suppose that a minority subset of classes used in the training data have much higher variability than the majority remainder of the classes. These classes may make it difficult to assess how well the later-evaluated deployment classifiers will work on the other classes of data, but how do we decide which classes of ground truth are likely better to remove than keep? We propose that the figure of merit and the histogram, RATD, and MDODEV analytics give us a set of tools for deciding how to optimize an ensemble classifier on a reduced set of ground truth. Will this work on all data sets? That is unlikely, but it is likely to help in early learning in many cases. This is valuable, since a tenet of this book is that a learning algorithm is just the starting point. The real goal is a learning system, including its architecture.

2.3 Optimizing settings from training data

The use of validation→training→testing as an alternative to training→validation→testing is in some ways analogous to the use of boosting [Freu96][Scha99] as an ensemble method for classification. Boosting, in short, uses a panoply of weak classifiers in combination to create a strong classifier. This is generally done through the weighting strategy. Originally [Freu96], different weights were assigned to the training observations: those that were misclassified were weighted more heavily in the next iteration. Alternatively, after each iteration, a new classifier is added that focuses on the training observations that were incorrectly assigned in the iteration.

Fig. 2.2 outlines a system approach to boosting, in which the boosting approach is chosen as part of a predictive selection [Sims13] pattern. Predictive selection relies on a training phase in which an attribute of the training observation, or "training datum," is used to select the configuration of the machine intelligence thereafter used during deployment (or testing). The "prediction" is that one or more attributes of the datum allow the "selection" of a more custom machine intelligence approach than simply employing the same machine intelligence approach to all of the data. In classification, regression, and other machine learning processes, predictive selection is a powerful pattern. This is due to the "separability" of attributes: For example, some attributes are suited for assigning data to clusters, while others are more suitable for classification. As such, one set of attributes can be used to configure how the remaining attributes are used. For example, attributes A and B assign a training observation TO_1 to use attributes C, D, and E as input for classifier configuration CC_3, while the same attributes (with different values from those of TO_1) assign a training observation TO_1 to use attributes C, D, and E as input for classifier configuration CC_7. For the specific example of the boosting approach, the boosting approach category CC_3 may boost the weights of misclassified training observations using a logistic function, while the boosting approach category CC_7 may boost the weights of misclassified data using a staircase function (i.e., a step function with multiple thresholds). This innate degree of variation is, of course, a powerful motivation for a validation phase. However, it should be noted that the assignment of observations to boosting approach categories is in effect a form of run-time validation, as noted in Fig. 2.2.

The original boosting approaches focused on dynamically altering the weights of the training observations. In this way, the same ground truth data can be reused even as the set of weak classifiers grows in size. Another approach is for the number of weak classifiers to be relatively weighted based on their performance. In this approach, the relative value of each weak classifier is dynamically assigned based on one or more strategies. The number of weak classifiers can therefore be fixed beforehand, and the strategies tested for suitability for run-time assignment to boosting approach category ("strategy"). Here, the simplest strategy is for the weighting to be proportional to the accuracy or inversely proportional to the error rate of the weak classifier on training data. However, in some cases, the nature of the training

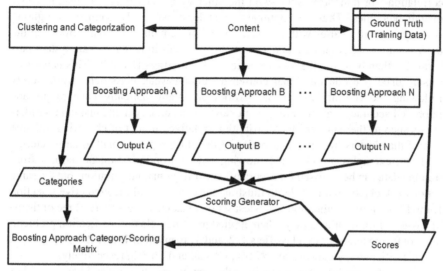

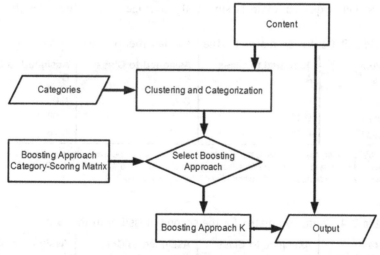

FIG. 2.2

Predictive selection as applied to boosting classification. The boosting approach can be based on weighting the training observations, weighting the weak classifiers, weighting both of these, and other methods.

(and later run-time) data is such that weighting according to the weak classifier's correlation—or noncorrelation—with the other weak classifiers may lead to better overall outcomes. Thus, the optimal—or at least ostensibly optimal—weighting strategy generally varies with the data set and/or domain of the data. Boosting the more accurate weak classifiers does not always result in better overall system performance than boosting the less accurate weak classifiers [Hast09]. This is not surprising once one considers that consensus among weak classifiers, while surely following the central limit theorem, does not mathematically have to provide improved accuracy; rather, it may come down to secondary mathematical considerations such as the nature of the distribution (relative amount of clustering, relative size of the clusters, relative distribution of the clusters from small to large, etc.).

Next, examples are provided showing how the optimization of settings from training data can be assessed for accuracy using different configurations but the same set of weak classifiers. In order to illustrate the extension of the predictive selection [Sims13] pattern to validation, a modest set of weak classifiers (here, three of them) are assessed for their accuracy when applied to a three-class classification problem. The confusion matrices for classifiers 1, 2, and 3 are given in Tables 2.3, 2.4, and 2.5. The classification accuracies are 77.0%, 68.7%, and 76.3%, respectively.

Next, we consider three predictive selection approaches or "architectures." For Table 2.6, we consider the simplest predictive selection approach, that is, where there is no actual selection, and we simply apply equal weighting to each of the weak classifiers. Our expected value is simply the average of the three classifiers. The

Table 2.3 Confusion matrix for the first classifier in the example

Actual class	Assigned to Class A	Assigned to Class B	Assigned to Class C
Class A	0.72	0.22	0.06
Class B	0.13	0.83	0.04
Class C	0.13	0.11	0.76

For this classifier, the misclassification, or "confusion," is highest between Classes A and B (mean=17.5%) and much lower for Classes A and C (mean=9.5%) and Classes B and C (mean=7.5%). For equal-sized classes, the overall accuracy is 0.770.

Table 2.4 Confusion matrix for the second classifier in the example

Actual class	Assigned to Class A	Assigned to Class B	Assigned to Class C
Class A	0.70	0.09	0.21
Class B	0.14	0.67	0.19
Class C	0.23	0.08	0.69

For this classifier, the misclassification, or "confusion," is highest between Classes A and C (mean=22%) and much lower for Classes A and B (mean=11.5%) and Classes B and C (mean=13.5%). For equal-sized classes, the overall accuracy is 0.687.

Table 2.5 Confusion matrix for the third classifier in the example

Actual class	Assigned to Class A	Assigned to Class B	Assigned to Class C
Class A	0.77	0.11	0.12
Class B	0.06	0.79	0.15
Class C	0.09	0.18	0.73

For this classifier, the misclassification, or "confusion," is highest between Classes B and C (mean = 16.5%) and much lower for Classes A and B (mean = 8.5%) and Classes A and C (mean = 10.5%). For equal-sized classes, the overall accuracy is 0.763.

Table 2.6 Confusion matrix for the equal weighting of the three classifiers of Tables 2.3, 2.4, and 2.5

Actual class	Assigned to Class A	Assigned to Class B	Assigned to Class C
Class A	0.73	0.14	0.13
Class B	0.11	0.763	0.127
Class C	0.15	0.123	0.727

This is simply the average of the confusion matrices for the three classifiers (linear addition). In most real-world combinations of classifiers, there will be nonlinear behavior (even though the mean accuracy will generally be the mean of the three classifiers). For equal-sized classes, the overall accuracy is 0.740.

weighted average of the three weak classifiers is shown in Table 2.6. With real-world data, there would be some deviation from the averages due to uncorrelated behavior of the three weak classifiers, but in general, the overall accuracy would be the mean of the three classifiers—that is, 74.0% accuracy—as obtained in Table 2.6.

Table 2.6 is an unsatisfying result, of course, as its accuracy is actually less than that of two of the three weak classifiers. This means that the equally weighted combination of several weak classifiers, the simplest "ensemble classifier," is often itself a weak classifier. The central limit theorem, of course, applies, so that even if the overall accuracy does not improve, the correct answer is likely to have a higher rank for this ensemble classifier than it does in the majority of the weak classifiers. This is a very important system aspect of using multiple analytic approaches simultaneously, since the time to verify the correct answer is often substantially reduced [Sims13]. However, for this section, we are more concerned with the accuracy, and so, we continue with more advanced predictive selection patterns.

Table 2.7 presents the expected results for a "perfect" predictive selection architecture, in which only the single best weak classifier is used to distinguish between each of the three binary classification pairs in the set, that is, between A and B, A and C, and B and C. The perfection of this architecture lies in its ability to select the best weak classifier for each pair from some attribute of the data, which is the same as being able to eliminate one of the three classes from consideration with 100% accuracy. Thus, it is an upper-end limit of the overall accuracy for predictive selection

Table 2.7 Confusion matrix for the "perfect" ensemble classifier where classifier 1 (Table 2.3) is chosen every time for comparing Classes A and C and for comparing Classes B and C and 3 (Table 2.5) is chosen every time for comparing Classes A and B. For equal-sized classes, the overall accuracy is 0.83

Actual class	Assigned to Class A	Assigned to Class B	Assigned to Class C
Class A	0.83	0.11	0.06
Class B	0.06	0.90	0.04
Class C	0.13	0.11	0.76

(ignoring for now emergence that is possible with extensive nonlinearity in the class domains). In Table 2.7, the overall accuracy is 83.0%, which corresponds to an error rate of 17.0%. This is an absolute reduction in error rate of 9.0% from the ensemble classifier of Table 2.6 and an absolute reduction of 6.0% in error rate from that of the best weak classifier (Table 2.3). The relative reduction in error rate is thus 34.6%, from 9.0%/(9.0%+17.0%), when compared with Table 2.6, and 26.1%, from 6.0%/(6.0%+17.0%), when compared with the best weak classifier. These are quite large reductions in error for most application domains. However, they are unrealistic, since being able to eliminate one class from consideration with 100% accuracy is a form of omniscience generally not possible.

A more realistic predictive selection situation is provided in Table 2.8. For this architecture, our predictive insight is simply to eliminate one of the weak classifiers from consideration for each of the binary classifications. This also is a form of "omniscience" but based on the central limit theorem that is likely to be far more robust than trying to find the single best weak classifier each time. The accuracy on training data (Table 2.8) is reduced to 79.7%. This is an absolute reduction in error rate of 5.7% from the ensemble classifier of Table 2.6 and an absolute reduction of 2.7% in error rate from that of the best weak classifier (Table 2.3). The relative reduction in error rate is thus 21.9% compared with Table 2.6 and 11.7% compared with the best weak classifier, computed as in the previous paragraph.

Table 2.8 Confusion matrix for the more realistic ensemble classifier where classifier 1 (Table 2.3) is left out from comparing Classes A and B, classifier 2 (Table 2.4) is left out from comparing Classes A and C, and classifier 3 (Table 2.5) is left out from comparing Classes B and C

Actual class	Assigned to Class A	Assigned to Class B	Assigned to Class C
Class A	0.81	0.10	0.09
Class B	0.10	0.785	0.115
Class C	0.11	0.095	0.795

For equal-sized classes, the overall accuracy is 0.797.

As discussed earlier in this chapter, the performance on training data is not enough to make the decision as to which architecture to deploy. A validation step is required: in the case of having three predictive selection approaches, the validation step consists of applying each approach to the "reserved" training data (or validation data) and selecting the one with the highest accuracy. Tables of validation data for Tables 2.6, 2.7, and 2.8 are shown in Tables 2.9, 2.10, and 2.11, respectively. These illustrate nicely the differences in how well validation (and later testing/deployment) does or does not follow the behavior of the training results.

Table 2.9 illustrates the averaging effect of combining the three classifiers (with equal weighting). The off-diagonal entries in the confusion matrix have much less variability than for the original data. However, the overall accuracy is not improved over Table 2.6. In fact, accuracy is reduced from 74.0% to 72.7%. Generally, such behavior is encouraging—if the accuracy of the validation set is as good as or better than the training set, there is a strong possibility that the algorithm is overtrained.

Table 2.9 Validation results for the equal weighting of the three classifiers of Tables 2.3, 2.4, and 2.5

Actual class	Assigned to Class A	Assigned to Class B	Assigned to Class C
Class A	0.71	0.15	0.14
Class B	0.12	0.75	0.13
Class C	0.14	0.14	0.72

For equal-sized classes, the overall accuracy is 0.727.

Table 2.10 Validation results for the "perfect" ensemble classifier of Table 2.7

Actual class	Assigned to Class A	Assigned to Class B	Assigned to Class C
Class A	0.78	0.13	0.09
Class B	0.10	0.82	0.08
Class C	0.15	0.16	0.69

Table 2.11 Validation results for the more realistic ensemble classifier of Table 2.8

Actual class	Assigned to Class A	Assigned to Class B	Assigned to Class C
Class A	0.79	0.11	0.10
Class B	0.09	0.79	0.12
Class C	0.13	0.10	0.77

For equal-sized classes, the overall accuracy is 0.783.

Table 2.10 shows the validation results for the "perfect" ensemble classifier. The accuracy drops from 83.0% to 76.3%, which indicates a lack of overtraining. The drop (6.7%) is greater than that in comparing Tables 2.6 and 2.9, consistent with the increased sensitivity of the algorithm to changes in the data set. Since the "perfect" ensemble selects only one classifier for each class, differences between the training and the validation classes will, generally, lead to greater differences in behavior for a select-single-classifier approach (Table 2.7) than for an averaging approach (Table 2.6), as illustrated by the 6.7% drop in accuracy for the former compared with a 1.3% drop for the latter.

For equal-sized classes, the overall accuracy is 0.763.

The final classifier architecture (Table 2.8) illustrated in this section is chosen to be more intelligent than the averaging classifier of Table 2.6 and less sensitive to changes in the data than the "perfect" ensemble classifier of Table 2.7. The accuracy results for the classifier are 79.7%, which is less than the "perfect" ensemble classifier (83.0%) but significantly better than the averaging classifier (74.0%). However, as illustrated in Table 2.11, the validation set results in nearly as high accuracy (78.3%), with only a 1.4% drop in accuracy compared with the training data. Thus, the ensemble architecture shares the high accuracy of the "perfect" ensemble classifier (and it actually tops it by 2.0% on validation data) along with the high robustness of the averaging classifier (dropping only 1.4% between Tables 2.8 and 2.11 compared with 1.3% between Tables 2.6 and 2.9 for the averaging classifier) on validation data.

What does this mean in practical terms? In this section, we set out to optimize the settings from training data. We did this by considering both a training set and a subsequent validation set, per the normal algorithmic machine learning approach. The validation set was not used, as it usually is, to determine the settings of the algorithm; rather, it was used to *select the architecture* for an ensemble classifier. In this example, the best validation results were obtained for the classifier that was both robust (each selected ensemble from the training phase consisted of two simple classifiers instead of just one) and accurate (the accuracy was much higher than the very robust but nondiscerning "equal weighting" classifier). In general, predictive selection approaches (Fig. 2.2) tend to identify an architecture that provides a good combination of robustness and accuracy, as shown here.

2.4 Learning how to Learn

Meta-analytic approaches are valuable for allowing us to learn how to learn, that is, in selecting the correct algorithm (or pattern of algorithms) therefore used for learning and, when deployed, solving the relevant analysis. Meta-algorithmic theory [Sims13] is also useful for intermediate analysis of the classes. Section 2.3 introduced several methods that allow suspect classes to be pruned from the prevalidation set for optimizing the architecture. In this section, we consider the attractor/repeller

Table 2.12 Example confusion matrix for a five-class problem, with the sums in each row and column given

↓Actual class \assigned class→	A	B	C	D	E	SUMS
A	0.65	0.13	0.09	0.07	0.06	1.00
B	0.17	0.57	0.13	0.05	0.08	1.00
C	0.06	0.11	0.78	0.02	0.03	1.00
D	0.13	0.08	0.12	0.42	0.25	1.00
E	0.06	0.03	0.08	0.22	0.61	1.00
SUMS	1.07	0.92	1.20	0.78	1.03	5.00
PRECISION p (e.g., 0.65/1.07)	0.607	0.620	0.650	0.538	0.592	0.601
$F\text{-score} = 2pr/(p+r)$	0.628	0.594	0.709	0.472	0.601	0.601

The columns sum the samples assigned to each class, and the diagonal elements divided by these sums are the precision values. The diagonal elements represent the recall values. The harmonic mean of precision and recall, or F-value, is shown in the lowest row.

theory from meta-algorithmics for its utility in validating the analytics architecture. We will consider the confusion matrix shown in Table 2.12.

The sums of the rows in Table 2.12 are all 1.00, because each sum represents 100% of the elements in a particular class. The columns, on the other hand, can deviate significantly from 1.00 depending on whether a class is an attractor (more samples than expected are assigned to this class) or a repeller (less samples than expected are assigned to this class). In this data set, Class C is the strongest net attractor, with 20% more than expected samples assigned to it. Class D is the strongest net repeller, with 22% less than expected samples assigned to it. The other three classes are much closer to unity, with no more than 8% deviation from expected value.

From this table, then, attractor/repeller theory suggests that Classes C and D are anomalous. To further discuss this thread, we consider the precision and F-score (harmonic mean of precision and recall), and specifically the variability in these scores, between the five classes. The mean±standard deviation of the precision is 0.601 ± 0.041, and the mean±standard deviation of the F-score is 0.601 ± 0.085. The two Classes C and D are thus 2.73 standard deviations apart in precision and 2.79 standard deviations apart in F-score. The corresponding two-tailed p-values are $p < 0.00633$ and $p < 0.00544$, respectively. This confusion matrix-driven analysis is not proof of any anomaly in the ground truth, but it is certainly a scent that needs to be tracked down.

Following the rules of Section 2.3, we may then decide to compute the figure of merit (Eq. 2.2), RATD (Eq. 2.5), and MDODEV (Eq. 2.6) metrics for the reduced set of classes with either or both of Classes C and D removed. In order to determine the figure of merit, we compute the accuracy of both confusion matrices, which is the mean of the diagonals. For Table 2.12, the accuracy is 0.606; for Table 2.13, the accuracy is 0.718. Thus, the figure of merit is $0.112/(0.282/3) = 1.19$. This is

Table 2.13 The confusion matrix of Table 2.12, example confusion matrix for a five-class problem, with the sums in each row and column given

↓ Actual class\assigned class→	A	B	C	E	SUMS
A	0.70	0.14	0.10	0.06	1.00
B	0.17	0.60	0.14	0.09	1.00
C	0.07	0.12	0.78	0.03	1.00
E	0.07	0.04	0.10	0.79	1.00
SUMS	1.01	0.90	1.12	0.97	4.00
PRECISION p (e.g., 0.70/1.01)	0.693	0.667	0.696	0.814	0.718
F-Score$=2pr/(p+r)$	0.696	0.632	0.735	0.802	0.716

The columns sum the samples assigned to each class, and the diagonal elements divided by these sums are the precision values. The diagonal elements represent the recall values. The harmonic mean of precision and recall, or F-value, is shown in the lowest row.

above 1.0 and so indicates that reducing the validation set to four classes is worth pursuing. We therefore compute RATD (Eq. 2.5) and MDODEV (Eq. 2.6) for both Tables 2.12 and 2.13. The values are more similar than for the example in Section 2.3: RATD changes from 1.57 to 1.68, and MDODEV changes from 4.72 to 3.42 in moving from five classes to four classes.

The figure of merit and MDODEV changes indicate that omitting Class D may provide a validation set that leads to an improved classifier architecture (the change in RATD is less promising). So, coming back to attractor/repeller theory, after dropping Class D, the new Table 2.13 represents only 80% of the ground truth data. Once again, we compute the variability in the precision and F-scores of these four classes. The mean±standard deviation of the precision is 0.718±0.066, and the mean-±standard deviation of the F-score is 0.716±0.071. The two Classes B and E are now the farthest apart: B and E are 2.23 standard deviations apart in precision and 2.39 standard deviations apart in F-score. The corresponding two-tailed p-values are $p<0.0257$ and $p<0.0168$, respectively. These p-values are statistically significant but with far less confidence than for the original Table 2.12. As expected (data not shown here), removing another class (in this case, Class B) results in a figure of merit below 1.0 and does not appear to provide a useful further pruning of the validation set.

Of course, the precision and F-score for Table 2.13 are higher than for Table 2.12 (0.718 and 0.716 for Table 2.13 while only 0.601 and 0.601 for Table 2.12); however, these results do not represent a better overall classifier; instead, they represent the possibility of using only those four classes (i.e., Classes A, B, C, and E) to determine the overall classifier settings before performing training and testing.

Table 2.14 represents a "best case" scenario for pruning the number of classes used for training. F-score improves from 60.1% to 61.8% and overall accuracy from 60.6% to 62.2%. Thus, attractor/repeller theory can be used to identify potential classes to omit for determining the architecture of the deployed classifier. Of course,

Table 2.14 Improved confusion matrix for a five-class problem, where the classifier was chosen based only on the behavior of a four-class problem (Classes A, B, C, and E)

↓Actual class \assigned class→	A	B	C	D	E	SUMS
A	0.66	0.12	0.08	0.08	0.06	1.00
B	0.15	0.58	0.12	0.06	0.09	1.00
C	0.07	0.09	0.77	0.03	0.04	1.00
D	0.13	0.09	0.10	0.46	0.22	1.00
E	0.06	0.04	0.07	0.19	0.64	1.00
SUMS	1.07	0.92	1.14	0.82	1.05	5.00
PRECISION p (e.g., 0.66/1.07)	0.617	0.630	0.675	0.561	0.610	0.619
F-Score $= 2pr/(p+r)$	0.638	0.604	0.719	0.506	0.625	0.618

The data shown are just as in Table 2.12. A modest improvement in overall classification precision and F-score is observed (from 0.601 to 0.619 for precision and from 0.601 to 0.618 in F-score).

pruning classes from the training set is not for the increased accuracy on a subset of the classes as evidenced in Table 2.13, since eventually all five classes have to be classified simultaneously. Rather, it is for improved training or "good meta-analytic citizenship."

However, meta-algorithmic theory affords a different type of "dimensionality reduction" when a highly accurate classifier for a subset of the classes exists. In Table 2.15, we have a very-high-accuracy binary classifier available for distinguishing between Class D and Class E. This classifier is 96% accurate, which is well above the mean accuracy for the five-class problem (Table 2.12), which implies that it is worth exploring the five-class classification problem as a four-class (three regular classes and one aggregate class), two-stage classification architecture: The first stage assigns the individual sample to one of the four classes, and the second stage assigns any sample assigned to the aggregate class to the correct original class.

As mentioned in Table 2.15 caption, Classes D and E originally introduced in Table 2.12 are combined into a single class because a very good binary classifier (96% accuracy) for distinguishing between these two classes exists. Classes D and E have "high internal confusion," that is, their misclassification rate within the five-class problem is high (confusion matrix entries are 0.22 and 0.25). So, an accurate binary classifier for these two classes has promise for the overall five-class problem. Indeed, the overall results (in which the accuracy of classification for Classes D and E is the product of the accuracy of aggregate and binary class accuracies) are a significant improvement over Table 2.12: precision improves from 60.1% to 67.9%, F-score from 60.1% to 68.2%, and overall accuracy from 60.6% to 68.0%.

As a quick note on the assessment of a "very good binary classifier," we summarize the confusion matrix techniques of the reference [Sims13], pp. 273–279.

Table 2.15 The confusion matrix of Table 2.12, using meta-algorithmic theory for aggregate classes, where Classes D and E are combined into a single class because a very good binary classifier for distinguishing between these two classes exists

↓Actual class\assigned class→	A	B	C	D+E	SUMS
A	0.65	0.13	0.09	0.13	1.00
B	0.17	0.57	0.13	0.13	1.00
C	0.06	0.11	0.78	0.05	1.00
D+E	0.095	0.055	0.10	0.72 (0.75)	1.00
SUMS	0.975	0.865	1.10	1.06	4.00
PRECISION p (e.g., 0.65/ 0.975)	0.667	0.659	0.709	0.679	0.679
F-Score $= 2pr/(p+r)$	0.658	0.611	0.743	0.699	0.682

The number of samples in D and E is normalized in the confusion matrix but must be remembered to be twice as large as the other classes in the final tally. The columns sum the samples assigned to each class, and the diagonal elements divided by these sums are the precision values. The diagonal elements represent the recall values. The harmonic mean of precision and recall, or F-value, is shown in the lowest row. Note that precision and F-score must be double-weighted for the aggregate class. Also, the 0.75 value for aggregate class D+E is corrected for the accuracy of the binary classifier, which in this case has 0.96 accuracy (percent correctly assigned). Since 0.96(0.75)=0.72, this is the value used for precision and F-score calculations for the aggregate class (before double weighting).

The accuracy of the two independent classes, D and E, is the mean of their individual accuracies, that is, $(46+64\%)/2 = 55\%$. Therefore, the accuracy, a_{binary}, of the binary classifier should provide a product, $0.75a_{binary} > 0.55$. Thus, so long as the binary classifier for Classes D and E has an accuracy of 0.733 or higher, it will provide overall improved accuracy for the hybrid classification system. Thus, in this case, a "very good" classifier is 73.3% accurate, which, while well above the 55% average for the two classes in the five-class problem, is probably not particularly difficult in most classification problems.

When meta-algorithmics [Sims13] is concerned, the most noticeable (statistically most probable) improvement was the mean number of ranked classification attempts until success, hereafter abbreviated $\mu(n_{RCAUS})$. Because consensus approaches generally follow the central limit theorem (some exceptions being poor cluster, class or taxonomic definition, or mislabeling), $\mu(n_{RCAUS})$ typically improves greatly as the number of algorithms providing the intelligence increases. Consensus, therefore, results in convergence toward correctness.

In this book, we are still concerned with $\mu(n_{RCAUS})$ but only where we need output in the form of assignment (classification, clustering, search relevance, etc.). Analytics, however, are concerned with more general tasks than just assignment. Analytics are concerned with arrangement (sorting), ranking, linking, relating (relevance, similarity, etc.), syntax, semantics, and/or proximity, with or without the need for assignment. For meta-analytics, then, the single best measurement may well be the uniformity of behavior in ground truth (training and validation) and testing. This can be assessed in several ways:

1. Entropy and other measures of randomness
2. Similarities in distribution
3. Functional means

Entropy is a powerful technique for assessing the randomness of a data set that can belong to one of N different discrete values. Entropy is defined by Eq. (2.9) as

$$e = -\sum_{i=0}^{N} p_i \log_B(p_i) \tag{2.9}$$

Note that if the base of the logarithm, B, is equal to 2, then the entropy, e, is in bits of information, per the large body of Claude Shannon's information theory work. The probabilities for each bin, p_i, are equal to each other and to $1/N$ when the distribution across the N discrete values has maximum entropy. A condition of maximum entropy does not prove randomness; for example, if the samples belong to bins $1, 2, 3, ..., N$ in sequence, then all $p_i = 1/N$, but the sequence is entirely predictable. This means that maximum entropy is a *necessary* but not *sufficient* condition for randomness in general.

Fortunately, when generating ground truth data, sequential randomness is usually not an issue. More importantly, the assignment of items to ground truth should result in an entropic distribution to the discrete values (bins, clusters, classes, etc.). Entropy can be used in other important stages of ground truthing and, more generally, analytics. For example, an excess of ground truth data can be pruned by iteratively removing the sample that most increases the entropy of the ground truth upon removal and continue until the entropy stops increasing or is below some small absolute difference, ε. Entropy can also be measured in a confusion matrix for classification problems, and ground truth data can be pruned by iteratively removing the sample that most increases the entropy of the confusion matrix upon removal, continuing in the same iterative fashion.

In addition to entropy measures, similarities in distributions can be used to determine if ground truth data are optimized for its purpose in assessing analytic approaches. One distribution that can be generated for an assignment-type analytic problem is the distribution of ranks for assignment. These are shown for a five-class assignment task in Table 2.16.

The results in Table 2.16 are shown graphically in Fig. 2.3. The ranking behavior for the incorrect Classes B, C, D, and E is highly correlated, as can be assessed by inspection. The relationship between these four classes can be assessed automatically using Pearson product-moment correlation. The relationship between the correct Class A and rank can be assessed by Spearman's rank correlation. The distribution of the ranks in the table for the incorrect classes is, a priori, expected to be evenly distributed across these classes. Of course, in most actual assignment

Table 2.16 Ranks of classes for assignment to Class A

Class	Rank 1	Rank 2	Rank 3	Rank 4	Rank 5
A	755	134	88	17	6
B	60	207	231	243	251
C	54	212	229	233	241
D	71	234	251	277	280
E	50	213	201	230	222

There are 1000 samples in Class A.

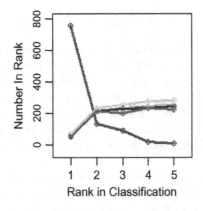

FIG. 2.3

Results for Table 2.16 shown graphically. Note the correlated ranking behavior of the four incorrect classes and the monotonic ranking behavior of the correct class (which has the highest value for rank in classification = 1).

problems, the ranks of the incorrect classes will not correlate well, and the entropy of the incorrect assignments will not be as high as shown. However, from the goal of having an even playing field from the ground truth data, we can prioritize the behavior of the ground truth with the following preference: if possible, all incorrect classes will have the same number of entries for the same rank, each of which is the number of samples minus the number of times the correct class is ranked for this rank, the remainder divided by the number of classes minus 1.

To the extent that the ground truth deviates from the preferred behavior just described, we may design a system to accommodate the desired behavior. We are also allowed to subsample reasonably from the ground truth to create individual instances of the analytic generator (whether it be a clustering algorithm, a classifier, an index generator, etc.) to create different intelligent systems geared for different purposes—for example, robustness, adaptiveness, accuracy, and consistency. Then, we may decide to have a final training performed with a different relative amount of, for example, robustness and accuracy. Interestingly, this approach generally comes along with robustness "for free." If, for example, a system is built to be both inexpensive and accurate, it will usually consist of several approaches with incomplete overlap in behavior, thus making it more robust (since the domain of the combined approaches will typically be greater than that of any single approach). Of course, with a large set of approaches, a system can be designed to have relatively uniform coverage of an entire domain, in effect normalizing for discrepancies in the density of ground truth.

The third means of assessing the uniformity of behavior in ground truth (training and validation) and testing are functional means. Functional assessment does not directly (e.g., mathematically) assess the ground truth, searching for differences in entropy or other nonrandom error behavior, as described above. Nor does it generally concern itself with the architecture and order of training and validation. Instead, it uses the behavior in the end application to feed back to the ground truth set. The simplest but still often useful functional means of pruning ground truth is the equalization algorithm, outlined here:

1. Perform analytic task (search assignment, clustering, classification, indexing, etc.).
2. Determine desired distribution of assignment to search, cluster, class, index, summarizations, etc.
3. Prune the overassigned groupings according to the strategy (e.g., remove the most redundant samples, remove the most borderline samples, and remove the sample most like others in the grouping) to match desired distribution.
4. Perform the analytic task and decide whether to roll back to the beginning of step 3, accept the pruning, or scale back pruning ambitiousness (e.g., reduce the amount pruned by a percentage and turn steps 3 and 4 into an iterative procedure).

This is a relatively simple procedure, but it allows a lot of approaches. If the desired distribution is to have search behavior that closely follows Zipf's Law [Mann99]—for example, document search—then the actual search behavior can be plotted and a maximum element Zipf curve fitted to the data such that it does not exceed the actual data meaningfully (error less than some small difference, ε). Then, documents can be subtracted to make the curve fit within ε of the desired Zipf curve.

A second example of functional means for assessing the value of a ground truthing set is determining how well the set performs in a task not used to assign the ground truth. An example of this is described in [Sims14], wherein the best translation engine is determined through measurement of which corpus of translated documents provides search behavior most closely matching that of the corpus of original (untranslated) documents. Ground truth documents for which search behavior in translation is poorest can be weighted more highly in the training phase (the feedback for weighting effectively comprises the validation phase), enriching the value of the translation by first selecting the best translation (based on the similarity of search) and then optimizing the search behavior by enhancing the weights of the documents for which search performed the most poorly.

Language-based analytics, in general, are rich grounds for the automated optimization of ground truth because they feature so many different analytic functions. Among these are summarization, indexing, translation, keyword generation, text clustering, text classification, most closely related document, search, tagging, and other linguistic tasks. These can be paired together as were translation and searching in the above example to optimize simultaneously the two (or more) analytic tasks for a corpus. Further examples of text-based analytics will be provided in the following chapters; for this chapter, suffice it to say that when one text analytic is used for ground truthing and another is used for functional measurement, a dual-task "system optimization" can emerge in a manner similar to expectation-maximization.

2.5 Deep learning to deep unlearning

Natural (i.e., real) biological intelligent systems are notoriously difficult to untrain, since development largely consists of the carving of neural pathways, that is, the removal of topically irrelevant connections to strengthen the particular set of pathways associated with a given memory, behavior, movement, etc. Further carving is engendered through the process of reentrancy, that is, when different clusters of information map content between themselves in a predictable temporal manner. Fine muscle tuning required for gymnastics, playing an instrument, or singing are good examples of this. Intuitively, it is easy to see the value of such "deep learning." Once training has occurred, a person can "chunk" trained activities and specialize even further, by adding esthetics, musicality, vibrato, etc. We have all had the experience of being able to recall trivial information from childhood with higher accuracy than names and events much more recently—this is the nature of neural training.

However, a possibility with machine learning that has not yet been taken full advantage of is the ability to do "deep unlearning," that is, being able to forget information in direct proportion to the age of the information. This "nonbiological" capability is most easily implemented on ground truth data, wherein the relative weighting given to training and validation sets diminishes over time. Effectively, a "time stamp" is placed on data, with weighting following an exponentially decreasing function. This is, intuitively, different from how humans learn, since they often remember "old facts" better than new facts, particularly as they age. However, in reality, a human brain is almost always storing a lot more recent information than it appears—it is just that this information is more distributed once the brain reaches adulthood. Thus, the "deep unlearning" concept for analytics is actually biologically inspired: it can be viewed as a means of internalizing the unlearning that we are generally not consciously aware of while we fit new experiences and ideas into our neural connections.

Generally speaking, the amount of deep unlearning is selected based on the desired trade-off between adaptiveness and robustness. When previous ground truth data are more aggressively "unlearned," the system is highly adaptive to new data. When previous ground truth data are only begrudgingly unlearned, the system is highly robust to data across the history of the system. In the next chapter, this topic will be taken up more under the consideration of "designs for pruning of aging data."

2.6 Summary

In this chapter, we operated under the assumption that ground truth data are *not sacred*. This does not mean that we get to prejudicially eliminate ground truth data and certainly not that we get to reduce the size of the problem space that the ground truth is being used to train an intelligent system to understand. Instead, we are employing a similar approach to boosting, wherein different weighting of the ground truth is used to better train and validate an intelligent system.

Why is this a concern? One reason is that many training instances use *k-fold* cross validation, wherein $\frac{(k-1)100\%}{k}$ of the ground truth is used for training, and the k subsets of the training data are used for testing. The k tests are then averaged to report the (usually over trained) test accuracy. Such a system may be very accurate, but it is usually not robust, since by definition the test set is much smaller than the training set except when $k<3$. Thus, k-fold systems are prebiased to being nonrobust but highly problem-focused systems.

Another aspect of ground truthing is that the ground truth set can be used for different system objectives. For example, the first round of training can be used for the optimization of accuracy, while the second round (or "validation") of training can be used for robustness. In Section 2.3, we used prevalidation such that pruning ground truth data led to a larger set of weak classifiers (improved robustness) and then reintroduced all of the ground truth for training to ensure accuracy across the entire data set.

A question to keep in mind as we explore meta-analytic approaches in the chapters to come is the following: "Does the sequential consideration of meta-analytic patterns on a ground truth set constitute a validation?" I will, unsurprisingly, argue that this is the case and that this approach is a new, more relevant form of "k-fold cross validation," where $k=$ the number of patterns explored on the training +validation set.

A second form of meta-analytics is when two or more meta-algorithmic approaches are used together for an analytic task. Here, the training sets are used to evaluate the individual meta-algorithmic patterns as described in the previous paragraph. The validation set is then used for evaluating paired meta-algorithmic behavior. The possibilities are many, but one thing is certain: meta-analytic patterns open the door for approaches other than the traditional (training, validation, and testing) sequence. For example, iterative training on multiple meta-algorithmic patterns can be followed by using the validation set for robustness rather than accuracy. Here, the mean number of ranked classification attempts until success, $\mu(n_{RCAUS})$, or the equivalent measure for clustering and other intelligent tasks can be optimized irrespective of the accuracy. Another optimization can be approached if the assignment is nonbinary, that is, assignment is weighted across many possible outcomes. Then, the validation set can be used for exploring which meta-analytics results in the most energy being assigned to the right outcome. This is often not the same as optimized accuracy. These approaches will be explored in more depth in later chapters.

References

[Code13] CodePlex. 2013. SharpNLP—Open Source Natural Language Processing Tools. Retrieved from https:/sharpnlp.codeplex.com/#.

[Frak92] Frakes, W., Baeza-Yates, R. (Eds.), 1992. Information Retrieval: Data Structures and Algorithms. Prentice Hall. 504 p.

[Freu96] Freund, Y., Schapire, E., 1996. Experiments with a new boosting algorithm. In: Proceedings of the 13th International Conference on Machine Learning (ICML '96), pp. 148–156.

[Hast09] Hastie, T., Tibshirani, R., Friedman, J., 2009. The Elements of Statistical Learning, second ed. Springer, pp. 337–387.

[Karb06] Karbasi, S., Boughanem, M., 2006. Effective level of term frequency impact on large-scale retrieval performance: by top-term ranking method. In: Proceedings of the 1st International Conference on Scalable Information Systems. vol. 37.

[Kwok90] Kwok, K.L., 1990. Experiments with a component theory of probabilistic informational retrieval based on single terms as document components. ACM Trans. Inf. Syst. 8 (4), 363–386.

[Lins12] Lins, R.D., Simske, S.J., Cabral, L.S., Silva, G.F.P., Lima, R.J., Mello, R.F., Favaro, L., 2012. A multi-tool scheme for summarizing textual documents. In: 11th IADIS International Conference WWW/INTERNET, Madrid, Spain.

[Mali11] Malik, H., Bhardwaj, V.S., 2011. Automatic training data cleaning for text classification. In: Data Mining Workshops (ICDMW), IEEE 11th International Conference on Data Mining, pp. 442–449.

[Mann99] Manning, C.D., Schütze, H., 1999. Foundations of Statistical Natural Language Processing. MIT Press, ISBN: 978-0-262-13360-9. 24 p.

[Ramo03] Ramos, J., 2003. Using tf-idf to determine word relevance in document queries. In: Proceedings of the First Instructional Conference on Machine Learning.

[Robe04] Robertson, S., 2004. Understanding inverse document frequency: on theoretical arguments for IDF. J. Doc. 60 (5), 503–520.

[Salt88] Salton, G., Buckley, C., 1988. Term-weighting approaches in automatic text retrieval. Inf. Process. Manag. 24 (5), 513–523.

[Scha99] Schapire, R.E., 1999. A brief introduction to boosting. In: Proceedings of the 16th International Joint Conference on Artificial Intelligence. vol. 2, pp. 1401–1406.

[Sims13] Simske, S., 2013. Meta-Algorithmics: Patterns for Robust, Low-Cost, High-Quality Systems. IEEE Press and Wiley, Singapore.

[Sims14] Simske, S.J., Boyko, I.M., Koutrika, G., 2014. Multi-engine search and language translation. In: EDBT/ICDT Workshops, pp. 188–190.

[Sims17] Simske, S.J., Vans, M., 2017. Learning before learning: reversing validation and training. In: ACM Document Engineering Symposium, pp. 74–77.

[Stan17] http:/nlp.stanford.edu/software/corenlp.shtml (Accessed 23 September 2017).

[Silv03] Silva, C., Ribeiro, B., 2003. The importance of stop word removal on recall values in text categorization. In: Proceedings of the International Joint Conference on Neural Networks. vol. 3.

[Vans16] Vans, M., Simske, S., 2016. Summarization and classification of CNN.com articles using the TF*IDF family of metrics. In: Archiving 2016, pp. 21–23.

[Vans17] Vans, A.M., Simske, S.J., 2017. Identifying top performing TF*IDF classifiers using the CNN corpus. In: Archiving 2017, pp. 105–115.

Experimental design

*Today's scientists have substituted mathematics for experiments, and they
wander off through equation after equation, and eventually build a structure
which has no relation to reality*
Nikola Tesla (1934)
All life is an experiment. The more experiments you make the better
Ralph Waldo Emerson (1844)

3.1 Introduction

As seen in the previous chapter, Nikola Tesla need not be concerned: meta-analytics
does not substitute mathematics for experiments. In fact, for ground truth data, meta-
analytics can be used to substitute experiments for the mathematics. Following
Emerson's advice, the more experiments, the better the meta-analytic system will
perform. Meta-analytic systems incorporate empirical data readily and avoid some
of the overtraining traps of many traditional approaches to the two broad areas of
clustering classification (learning or assignment) and prediction regression (estimation). Most importantly, however, meta-analytics allows two or more *experimental
designs* to be compatible within an overall system.

The resulting "system of systems" that can be considered a hybrid of these multiple system designs uses one or more—and preferably all—of the following as the
logical tools/processes for combining two or more systems:

1. Data normalization
2. Pruning of aging data
3. Interfaces
4. Gain
5. Domain normalization
6. Sensitivity analysis

System design as addressed by meta-analytics is a topic discussed in some depth in
Chapter 10, and in Chapter 4, we introduce the distinction between rank-biased systems and accuracy-biased systems, among others. In this chapter, we simply introduce
the means of combining multiple systems into what is designated a "system of systems," that is, a meta-analytic system. We start with data normalization and then consider data aging and data death. Finally, we borrow from linear system theory to
optimize data systems. Specifically, we define interfaces and gains, allowing data

Meta-Analytics. https://doi.org/10.1016/B978-0-12-814623-1.00003-4

systems to be combined in series and parallel. We then discuss domain normalization, allowing different sets of data to cooperate rather than compete. Finally, we consider the foundational topic of sensitivity analysis and system-of-system optimization.

3.2 Data normalization

3.2.1 Simple (unambiguous) normalization

At the simplest level, data normalization is concerned only with the treatment of the data as data (and not, e.g., the interrelationships among the data). For example, unit normalization is given by

$$\hat{d} = \frac{d}{|d|} \tag{3.1}$$

Here, $|d|$ is the Euclidean norm of the data vector, designated d.

Unit-normalized data are interesting when applied to estimation (i.e., regression) approaches. We consider one example comparison here. Data set one, D1, has five (x, y) pairs given by

$$D1 = \{(1, 1), (2, 2), (3, 3), (4, 4), (5, 5)\} \tag{3.2}$$

Meanwhile, data set D2 is given by

$$D2 = \{(1, 2), (2, 4), (3, 6), (4, 8), (5, 10)\} \tag{3.3}$$

When each set of y-values is normalized, we get

$$D1_{norm} = \left\{ \left(1, \frac{1}{\sqrt{55}}\right), \left(2, \frac{2}{\sqrt{55}}\right), \left(3, \frac{3}{\sqrt{55}}\right), \left(4, \frac{4}{\sqrt{55}}\right), \left(5, \frac{5}{\sqrt{55}}\right) \right\} \tag{3.4}$$

$$D2_{norm} = \left\{ \left(1, \frac{1}{\sqrt{55}}\right), \left(2, \frac{2}{\sqrt{55}}\right), \left(3, \frac{3}{\sqrt{55}}\right), \left(4, \frac{4}{\sqrt{55}}\right), \left(5, \frac{5}{\sqrt{55}}\right) \right\} \tag{3.5}$$

Thus, even though the original two sets of data had a linear regression equation of

$$\text{For } D1 \rightarrow y = x \tag{3.6}$$

$$\text{For } D2 \rightarrow y = 2x \tag{3.7}$$

we get the same normalized equation when they pass through the origin (and have the same discrete set of x-values).

Another means of normalizing data is to make two sets have the same mean. For a set of features, we can use zero-mean centering (ZMC) by computing the mean of each data set (or dimension in the case of clustering/classification features), and subtracting it from the original data set/dimension:

$$d' = d - \mu \tag{3.8}$$

For the original data sets D1 and D2, we get

$$D1_{ZMC} = \{(1, -2), (2, -1), (3, 0), (4, 1), (5, 2)\} \tag{3.9}$$

$$D2_{ZMC} = \{(1, -4), (2, -2), (3, 0), (4, 2), (5, 4)\} \tag{3.10}$$

For unit-normalized data,

$$\hat{d}' = \hat{d} - \mu \tag{3.11}$$

which for the original data sets gives

$$D1_{norm+ZMC} = D2_{norm+ZMC} = \left\{ \left(1, \frac{-2}{\sqrt{55}}\right), \left(2, \frac{-1}{\sqrt{55}}\right), (3, 0), \left(4, \frac{1}{\sqrt{55}}\right), \left(5, \frac{2}{\sqrt{55}}\right) \right\} \tag{3.12}$$

Finally, scaling, or standardizing data, involves zero-mean centering and then dividing the difference by the standard deviation:

$$d' = \frac{d - \mu}{\sigma} \tag{3.13}$$

For previously unit-normalized data,

$$\hat{d}' = \frac{\hat{d} - \mu}{\sigma} \tag{3.14}$$

After standardization, a data set has mean $= 0.0$ and standard deviation $= 1.0$. This is helpful so that one feature does not overwhelm another feature solely based on its scale.

3.2.2 Bias normalization

A more complicated, but perhaps more important, form of data normalization considers the interaction between the several data *sets*. The unit normalization, zero-mean centering, and standardization approaches above are unambiguous and are within a single data set. This *intra-set* form of normalization, which I term *bias normalization*, is not only ambiguous but also in some circumstances even contentious. I begin the exploration of bias normalization with an example.

Suppose you are interested in the outcome of an election and that you poll 100 people of which 1 is Black, 99 are non-Black, 35 are women, and 65 are men. Then, you wish to normalize the data to represent a population that is 13% black and 52% women. How do you normalize the votes? For the process, we define $B = 1$, $NB = 99$, $M = 65$, and $F = 35$. This simple two-parameter example will illustrate the ambiguity nicely. Suppose that we wish to bias normalize for gender. In this case, we use a multiplication factor M for the male data such that it normalizes to its proper representation, that is,

$$\overline{M} = k_1 M \text{ where } k_1 = 48/65 = 0.738 \tag{3.15}$$

With this bias normalization approach, we also adjust the female data using

$$\overline{F} = k_2 F \text{ where } k_2 = 52/35 = 1.486 \tag{3.16}$$

Table 3.1 Ideal distribution of people based on the example given, where 52% of the represented group are female and 13% are Black

	Male	Female
Black	6.24	6.76
Non-Black	41.76	45.24

Since there is only 1 Black person in the (poorly sampled) 100 interviewees, at least one table cell ("Black male" or "Black female") will be unrepresented.

Table 3.2 Actual distribution of people for the example given, representing a higher percentage of females for Black than for non-Black people

	Male	Female
Black	5.88	7.12
Non-Black	42.12	44.88

This is interaction, meaning deviation from dimensional independence.

This is all well and good for gender, but we clearly have a problem for Black individuals, since they are either 100% male or 100% female (one person!). If male, we have no way of representing Black females; if female, we have no way of representing Black males. This is indeed a worst-case scenario, as illustrated by Table 3.1, which shows that the expected values for "Black male" and "Black female," assuming that race and gender are independent, are 6.24 and 6.76, respectively. Both are nonzero, but one of them is certainly zero in our poll set.

In general, the expected entry for any element in an N-dimensional matrix will be the product of the category probabilities of each of the N-dimensions. This is simply based on independence of the individual dimensions. In Table 3.1, then, the expected percent of "Black females" is simply the product of the expected value of "Black" (i.e., 0.13) and the expected value of females (i.e., 0.52), which comes to 6.76 out of 100. In reality, there will often be interactions between one or more dimensions, and so, the individual cells of the table will not have the expected values for independent dimensions. For example, suppose there is a higher percentage of females among Black people than among non-Black people. We may then see an actual distribution as shown in Table 3.2.

We next consider four important aspects of experimental design as they relate to bias normalization. The higher the number of the design considerations, the better it is for data integrity and ultimately system robustness, but in some cases, collecting data is not possible due to cost, time, availability of representative data, and other reasons. Regardless, it is important to understand what *should* be done, even when it *cannot* be done, since this will help the data scientist to explain her results more fairly, credibly, and fully:

1. For the first design consideration, we need to ensure that each element in the N-dimensional matrix is represented by at least one sample. Depending on the

scarcity of the data, this may have to suffice, but in general—and particularly in the age of big data—we would want enough samples to have the data in the matrix element sufficiently represent the statistical distribution that all the data in this intersection of N-dimensions would follow. But, certainly, there needs to be at least one sample for any of the following (#2, #3, and #4) experimental design considerations to be addressed. In our example, we returned to polling and made sure at least 10 each of Black male and Black female individuals were interrogated. This augmented set is shown in Table 3.3.

2. For design consideration #2, we proportionately scale each matrix element based on the expected values for independent variables (or data-guided variable, if, e.g., a higher percentage of Blacks are women). With the addition of "Black male" and "Black female" individuals to their groups in Table 3.3, we are closer to proportional representation. Assuming that we have not the time, money, inclination, and/or opportunity to poll more people, however, we must still "weigh" the group "Black females" by 42.4% more than their numbers. That means we multiply each of their inputs by 1.424 in the final tally. The other three groups are weighted just under unity (from 0.957 to 0.997). This is illustrated in Table 3.4.

3. For design consideration #3, instead of using weighting coefficients to correct for underrepresented and overrepresented groups, we explicitly collect more data to make the experimental design matrix balance as it should for proportional representation. Effectively, we augment the matrix based on holding the most

Table 3.3 Augmented distribution where another 100 people were polled and a minimum of 10 people were included in each of the four matrix elements. Design consideration #1

	Male	Female
Black	12	10
Non-Black	88	90

Table 3.4 Scaling factor for Table 3.3 to achieve matrix elements correctly proportional to the distribution given in Table 3.2

	Male	Female
Black	0.98	1.424
Non-Black	0.957	0.997

All groups are now only slightly overrepresented (by 0.3%–4.3%) with the exception of Black females, who are still underrepresented by 42.4% compared with their relative percent of the overall population. Design consideration #2.

overrepresented group (MORG) to its current value and adding to each of the other groups until it has the right number in comparison with the MORG. The application of this design consideration to Table 3.4 is shown in Table 3.5. This is a "parsimonious" approach, requiring only nine samples to be added to the overall polling set to achieve balance. This number, divided by the size of the original matrix, is in fact an excellent indicator of the imbalance in the original data collection (designated IODC). Here, IODC=9/200=0.045. High values of IODC imply higher bias in the original data collection, and low values of IODC imply lower bias, or at least better effective balance, in the original data set.

4. If possible, this design consideration should be employed. For this consideration, we must also augment the MORG to ensure that we are not sampling from a statistically different set of data during the matrix augmentation (this is described in more detail in subsequent text and in Fig. 3.1). This is very important, since otherwise we cannot combine the new data with the old. Spatial (location), temporal (age and time of year), sensing (how collected), and storing (including filtering and compression) are among the many factors that could vary, drift, or even be intentionally changed from the original collection period to the augmented collection period. In our example, the "non-Black male" group is augmented by 16, and thus, each of the other groups needs to be augmented to provide a proportional final set of groups, as shown in Table 3.6.

Some discussion around how we arrived at the values for Table 3.6 will be helpful. As mentioned in the design consideration #4 text, we need to augment the MORG so that we are assured that the augmented data do not drift significantly from the original data. We meanwhile collect augmenting data for each of the other groups to bring the final (original+augmenting) table (Table 3.6) into proportion.

Fig. 3.1 shows the curve representing the augmentation termination protocol for the MORG. The termination occurs when the computed value for sample size is less than the number of samples in the augmentation group for two consecutive new sample additions to the augmentation set. The value for n is computed as follows, in Eq. (3.17), which repurposes a metric used for determining the sample size needed to show a given difference between two means (this is used for sample size calculations in [Ott84], pp. 166–167):

$$n = \frac{\left(z_{\alpha/2}\right)^2 \sigma_{aug}^2}{E^2} \tag{3.17}$$

Table 3.5 Desired number of people to poll for each group to match proportionally (per Table 3.2) with the most overrepresented group (rounded to nearest integer), which in this case is "non-Black male"

	Male	Female
Black	12	15
Non-Black	88	94

In this example, five extra "Black female" and four extra "non-Black female" individuals needed to be polled so that the proportions matched that of Table 3.3. Design consideration #3.

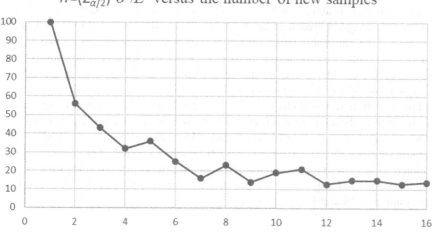

FIG. 3.1

Curve used to limit the number of new samples of the most overrepresented group (MORG) to add. The values for alpha ($\alpha=0.01$) and E and the acceptable difference between the means of the original and the augmented data sets are set beforehand based on acceptable probability of error and acceptable difference in the data, respectively. We set $z_{\alpha/2}=2.58$ since $\alpha=0.01$, and $E=0.5$ since this is "half a person" difference. The estimated sample size needed is given by $n=\frac{(z_{\alpha/2})^2 \sigma_{aug}^2}{E^2}$ [Ott84]. We are using this here differently than originally intended, that is, once enough samples have been added to the original set for the value of n in Eq. (3.17), we are confident that the two data sets can be combined without "temporal bias." We terminate the augmented data once the value for n is less than the number of augmented samples twice in a row (this happens for number of new samples $=15$ and 16).

Table 3.6 Desired number of people to poll for each group to match proportionally (per Table 3.2) with the most overrepresented group along with adding enough new individuals to the most overrepresented samples, which in this case is "non-Black male"

	Male	Female
Black	15	18
Non-Black	104	111

Values rounded off to integers. In this example, 16 "non-Black males" were added to ensure sufficiently small differences between the added and original data sets. This led to the addition of 3 extra "Black male," 8 extra "Black female," and 21 extra "Non-Black female" individuals so that the proportions matched that of Table 3.3. Design consideration #4.

The values for alpha ($\alpha=0.01$) and E, the acceptable difference between the means of the original and the augmented data sets are set beforehand. We wished to be 99.5% certain that the populations were statistically indistinguishable so that adding extra samples was worth the extra time, effort, and cost. We therefore set $z_{\alpha/2}=2.58$

since $\alpha=0.01$. Then, we needed to decide on E, the error in the means. Since the example problem is actually a discrete one, in which an integral number of individuals must be assigned to each group. Therefore, the smallest reasonable E is 0.5, "half a sample." We chose this value since it is "statistically conservative," that is, the smaller the value of E, the larger the augmentation set. We'd best be conservative here since it's our last chance to do what's proper statistically—we are, after all, on design consideration #4 of 4. So, we let $E=0.5$, which means that the estimated sample size needed is given by Eq. (3.17) and can be computed after each new sample is added to the augmentation set. Note that for the first augmentation value, we cannot compute the variance of the augmentation data, σ_{aug}, so we set it arbitrarily high (in this case to 100): so long as it is not less than 1, it does not initiate a termination test. We terminate the augmented data once the computed value for n is less than the number of augmented samples twice in a row (this happens for number of new samples $=15$ and 16, as shown in Fig. 3.1).

3.2.3 Normalization and experimental design tables

The normalization approaches above are focused on the data groups relative to one another. The data can also be looked at collectively. This is typically accomplished through entropy measurements. In a sense, shoring up underrepresented or unrepresented groups removes entropy that is viewed as a deviation from a proportional experimental design. In the discussion for design consideration #3, a single metric, the IODC, was used to indicate the relative imbalance of one experimental design compared with another. There, it was shown that IODC for Table 3.3 was 0.045. Computing the same value for the original data set, where Black males $=1$, Black females $=0$, non-Black males $=64$, and non-Black females $=35$ and where the distribution should be that of Table 3.2, yields a final set of Black males $=9$, Black females $=11$, non-Black males $=64$, and non-Black females $=68$. This means an additional 52 individuals must be polled, and IODC $=52/100=0.52$, more than ten times that of the IODC for Table 3.3. High values of IODC imply higher bias in the original data collection, and this is clearly the case for the very poorly balanced original design. Low values of IODC imply that the actual experimental design represents no additional error over the intended experimental design and so should have the same entropy.

In addition, direct measurements can be computed from the subtraction of two experimental design matrices. One example is given in Table 3.7, which represent the differences between Tables 3.2 and 3.1. The mean absolute value difference, or MAVD, is 0.36, wherein the mean value of a cell is 25.0, which yields a mean difference of $0.36/25.0=0.0144$, or 1.44%.

Low values of MAVD when comparing an experimental design to a matrix in which each dimension is assumed independent (such as Table 3.1) imply highly independent data dimensions, in which case the MAVD is a measure of deviation from independence.

Table 3.7 Differences between Tables 3.2 and 3.1. The sum of the cells in the original tables is 100.0, meaning the mean absolute value difference is 0.0144, or 1.44%

	Male	Female
Black	−0.36	0.36
Non-Black	0.36	−0.36

The experimental designs in this section are relatively simple: they are, after all, 2×2 matrices. In larger data systems, of course, the experimental design matrices will be larger—even much larger—in dimension. There, the differences between experimental design matrices will more properly be assigned to further analysis, such as histograms, which are more predisposed to direct entropy measurements. We will revisit entropy often in subsequent chapters.

3.3 Designs for the pruning of aging data

We've seen how to normalize data, for ensuring that different dimensions do not start off with either the advantage of scale or the advantage of numbers. In the latter case, we considered bias normalization as a means of preventing a MORG from hiding the rightly proportional input of other groups. We rightly corrected imbalance in the original data collection, or IODC. However, our discussion of bias normalization in Section 3.3 only scratched the surface of the temporal concerns we naturally have about any data set worth investigating, that is, any data set that is augmented over time. Bias normalization was shown to address some aspects of the *forward-in-time* (FIT) concerns of the data set. In this section, we are concerned with the *backward-in-time* (BIT) direction and the FIT. We might say that we are using a FIT-BIT to monitor the health of our data (we might not say that, either, as there may be some vaguely unpleasant trademark concerns!). We will start off here with the BIT and then come back to the FIT-BIT. BIT aging of data makes no assumptions about what type of data drift we will see in the future, while FIT-BIT aging of data projects into the future to more effectively hone the relevant data set in a real-time fashion.

Backward-in-time (BIT) aging of data in its simplest form uses the sample size calculation approach introduced in the previous section, culminating in Eq. (3.17) and Fig. 3.1. Here, we can consider this a form of temporal k-fold cross validation wherein the k-folds divide the relevant data set into k partitions of time, with the first partition being the oldest and the kth partition being the newest. Once so divided, the data can be evaluated using standard two-group statistical approaches, including at the onset the simple t-test:

$$t = \frac{\left|\mu_{oldest} - \mu_{(k-1)newest}\right|}{\sqrt{\frac{1}{n_{oldest}} + \frac{1}{n_{(k-1)newest}}}\sqrt{\left(\left(n_{oldest}-1\right)\sigma^2_{oldest} + \left(n_{(k-1)newest}-1\right)\sigma^2_{(k-1)newest}\right)/N-2}} \tag{3.18}$$

where here N is the total number of samples, n_{oldest} is the number in the first partition, and $n_{(k-1)newest}$ is the number in all of the other partitions. Thus, $n_{oldest}+n_{(k-1)newest}=N$. If the t-statistic is significant at the desired α, for example, with 99% certainty ($\alpha=0.01$), then we can conclude the oldest partition is significantly different from the $(k-1)$ partitions since and may decide to deprecate these data from the data set if, for example, it is to be used for training purposes.

Other approaches to BIT include matrix-based approaches and clustering-/classification-based approaches. With matrix-based approaches, we simply plot the mean and standard deviations for what we consider to be the most significant feature of an analytic task and then identify the outliers. If a large portion of the outliers belong to one or more of the data "partitions"—and in particular to the oldest partition of data—we may decide it is time to prune that data set. This is illustrated in the data presented in Table 3.8.

In Table 3.8, the simplest possible means of assessing the oldest partition is to perform a t-test for the oldest partition ($n=1$, first data row from the top) compared with the second oldest. For the four features (% road surface, no. of vehicles, no. of intersections, and road width), the t-statistics for comparing partitions 1 and 2 are 6.31, 3.50, 3.71, and 1.01, respectively, with respective two-tailed p-values of less than 10^{-5}, 5.93×10^{-4}, 2.8×10^{-4}, and 0.314. Since three of these are very highly significant for p-values of 0.01 or less, we can say that in the oldest image set, there was a lower percentage of road surface, less vehicles, and less intersections in the images. These changes, combined, may indicate that partition 1 is no longer relevant to the same set of traffic monitoring problems as the other partitions.

Table 3.8 Data sets (mean $\pm$ standard deviation) where $k=10$ (864 total images in original set) for a number of important features and boldface for the mean of the overall data set

n\Feature	% Road surface	No. of vehicles	No. of intersections	Road width (m)
1 (87 samples)	12.3±4.3	17.2±8.3	4.7±3.3	5.4±2.1
2 (87 samples)	15.7±2.6	22.2±10.4	6.5±3.1	5.7±1.8
3 (87 samples)	17.1±3.3	25.4±13.4	5.8±3.6	5.6±2.5
4 (87 samples)	17.9±2.9	25.6±11.3	6.5±3.9	6.2±3.1
5 (86 samples)	19.9±3.5	23.4±8.8	5.8±3.6	6.2±2.7
6 (86 samples)	19.3±4.5	32.1±9.7	6.7±2.8	6.1±2.3
7 (86 samples)	19.6±4.8	29.5±5.7	6.1±2.8	6.4±3.3
8 (86 samples)	20.7±5.3	30.1±7.7	6.9±3.9	6.5±2.9
9 (86 samples)	20.4±3.9	26.8±10.9	6.7±4.4	6.7±3.0
10 (86 samples)	22.5±6.0	33.1±9.7	7.3±2.9	6.8±2.8
Overall $\mu\pm\sigma$	**18.5**±5.2	**26.5**±10.7	**6.3**±3.7	**6.2**±2.4

The features here are for traffic monitoring.

As discussed in Chapter 1, analysis of variance (ANOVA) is a means of partition-ing the sources of variation in a particular variable. The simple ANOVA and a follow-on test such as Tukey's, Dunnett's, or Scheffé's method effectively general-ize the t-test to three or more groups, allowing paired group-group comparisons of statistical significance. Effectively, ANOVA is an on-ramp for clustering. In this sec-tion, we are concerned with partitioning in time and treating each partition as a single group for the $1 \times N$ ANOVA design. Effectively, we "force" the oldest partition to be a group and likewise either partition the remainder or perform k-means clustering on the rest using, for example, expectation-maximization approaches. The size of the partition can be varied somewhat based on refining approaches, for example, N-mean clustering using the partition centroids as the initial condition.

The transition from "BIT" to "FIT-BIT" is relatively straightforward. Regression or other predictive (e.g., Bayesian) techniques can be used to project current trends into the future. In Table 3.8, linear regression of each of the four features has a pos-itive slope with statistically significant Pearson correlation coefficient ($p < 0.001$ for each of the features). Thus, we can predict with high confidence that the percent of road surface in the images, the number of vehicles in the images, the number of inter-sections in the images, and the mean road width are likely to be higher than in the other groups. In general, groups two or more apart in partition number have two or more highly statistically significant differences among these four metrics. This indi-cates that noticeable changes occur over a period which is only a fraction of the total time that data is collected for the table. Given that, we can say with relatively high confidence that partition 11 is likely to have higher values than partition 9, partition 12 is likely to have higher value than partition 10, etc. In order to prove it, we can use the same ANOVA as cluster-analysis technique that we used for the BIT problem above.

3.4 Systems of systems

In this section, we borrow from linear system theory to optimize data systems in the manner of control systems, wherein the data analytics are the variable or variables controlled. To that end, we define interfaces and gains, allowing data systems to be combined in series and parallel. We then discuss domain normalization, allowing different sets of data to cooperate rather than compete together. Finally, we consider the foundational topic of sensitivity analysis and system-of-system optimization.

3.4.1 Systems

What is a system? The simplest definition is that a system is combination of multiple objects that in combination provide an overall set of behaviors or outputs that none of the components can provide alone. For our purposes, an analytic system is a combi-nation of two or more analytic components that leads to analytic output—that is, knowledge generation—that none of the individual analytic components are capable of providing by themselves. The reason for employing system theory is to give the reader a set of patterns, or "meta-analytics," for bringing analytic primitives together.

For a system to be valuable, it must provide the following three functionalities:

1. Componentization. Different elements, or components, of the system must be readily identifiable. Preferably, each element can act as either a black box (described only by its inputs and outputs—the transfer function is simply a mapping of the former to the latter) or a white box (full visibility into the internal structure of the component) as appropriate. This allows the system designer to be a relative novice (black box) or an expert (white box) on the individual component, as appropriate to her role in the overall system design and development task.
2. Modularity. Different components can, as reasonable, be swapped out with other components that provide the same functionality. For example, a convolutional neural network (CNN) used to classify images can be interchanged with a pattern matching system that is specifically geared for iris recognition when the task is specific to biometrics and not the more general image recognition for which the CNN was trained. Modularity is ensured by the adherence of the modules to interface (input and output) and gain (transfer function, including input and output "impedance"). An example of input impedance is the ratio of input terms to keywords generated in a text analytic task; in other words, the impedance is a ratio of two meaningful data streams in the module.
3. Series and parallel construction. This imposes a design constraint on the input and output of each module: the output provided is suitable to hand off to one (series) or multiple (parallel) modules as input. As such, the module cannot be tightly coupled to the subsequent module or modules, meaning the interfaces are clean and comprehensive. The possibility of having parallel uses of the output of the module also means that appropriate metadata useful for tagging any states, probabilities, or completed processes must be provided.

We now consider the application of these principles to systems that are adaptive in space (hybrid systems) and/or time (dynamically updated systems).

3.4.2 Hybrid systems

A hybrid system is simply a system composed of mixed elements. This includes the modular components introduced in the previous subsection. The simple mixing of elements, utilizing their input and output characteristics, is not enough to warrant the name "hybrid." Instead, hybrid systems engage the possibility of mixed design intentionally during training, validation, and in some cases testing, to continually optimize the system architecture—in light of the very real possibility of the pruning of irrelevant data and the anticipation of new data characteristics in the future.

The types of hybrid systems available depend on the quantity of interchangeable modules available for each component, the number of relevant components in the system, and the series/parallel design choices. While this set of tools for

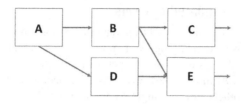

FIG. 3.2

Simple five-component (A, B, C, D, and E) hybrid system capable of modularity (n_A, n_B, n_C, n_D, and n_E) and different series-parallel pathways (ABC, ABE, ADE, ABE||ADE, ABC||ABE, ABC||ADE, and ABC||ABE||ADE). See text for details.

hybridization may seem somewhat limited, the number of possible system designs quickly becomes quite large. We consider this by example using Fig. 3.2. Suppose that we have a five-component system, for example, a security system in which one component is authentication (component A); one is biometric evaluation (component B), one is consumer downstream services (component C), one is contextual assessment (component D), and one is enterprise account access (component E). Furthermore, suppose that authentication is modular such that any of four authentication protocols can be used (LDAP, PKI, username/password, and access card); any one of four biometric protocols (e.g., face recognition, voice recognition, fingerprint recognition, and iris recognition, or four combinations) can be chosen; four different downstream consumer services can provide the user's needs; context can be selected in three ways (e.g., GPS, device ID, and proximity); and enterprise accounts can be accessed as restricted, confidential, private, or public (four versions).

Summing up the modularity possibilities by component, we have the following:

1. For A, there are four choices ($n_A = 4$).
2. For B, there are four choices ($n_B = 4$).
3. For C, there are four choices ($n_C = 4$).
4. For D, there are three choices ($n_D = 3$).
5. For E, there are four choices ($n_E = 4$).

The overall system combines series-parallel architecture with the modularity of components. There are three-component pathways to either consumer or enterprise services/accounts, as shown in Fig. 3.2. Assuming a user might wish to obtain consumer services and enterprise services together, there are seven different series-parallel paths through this system: ABC, ABE, ADE, ABE||ADE, ABC||ABE, ABC||ADE, and ABC||ABE||ADE, where || implies parallel. These have, respectively, 64, 64, 48, 192, 256, 768, and 768 different configurations, not including the crossover: both ABC||ADE and ABC||ABE||ADE have 768 configurations, but the latter has crossover from B to E. The inner details of how these pieces plug in together are not discussed here; however, the 2160 configurations are possible in even this relatively simple-looking five-component system.

3.4.3 Dynamically-updated systems

As discussed in Chapter 2, the ground truth data (used most importantly for training and validation purposes) in a "living" system are updated in real time. We are also concerned with how the system—and the pathways traversing the system—can be updated dynamically. At the simplest level, dynamic update of the system replaces one module with another within a single component, resulting in no change in the component-to-component pathway but perhaps significantly improving the system from one or more of the usual metrics of importance, that is, cost, accuracy, performance, robustness, or availability. If, for example, we are using the system of Fig. 3.2 described in the previous section, we may see an advancement in two biometrics such that their combination is far more accurate than any single biometric or combination. We then prune the single biometrics from consideration and dynamically update the component.

Other forms of dynamic updating include incorporating new analytics into a system where none were before (the addition of modules). Such a system may trigger a complete reconsideration of the training and validation data and approaches. Importantly, the new system can be directly compared initially to the individual modules already part of the component of interest without too much trouble, assuming that the same data is used for integrating the new analytic.

Another type of dynamic system is simply a "FIT-BIT" architected system, as described in Section 3.4. Here, the system's training data is projected into the future (FIT) and considered in partitions extending back to the oldest data (BIT). Dynamic update of the ground truth is a dynamic system.

The final type of dynamic system to outline in this section is one where the components themselves change. In the system of Fig. 3.2, for example, we may decide to add in a notification/approval component that can be invoked in parallel to the authentication. This would add many more possible configurations to the overall system and perhaps allow the system to be used in previously nonallowed situations (where auditing, certification, multifactor authentication, role-based access control, or specific approval is required).

3.4.4 Interfaces

Interfaces are the boundaries between two or more modules or components. Borrowing from software system design terminology, specifically for object-oriented programming (OOP) here [Gamm94], we declare that two modules are tightly coupled in a data analytic system when a group of classes are highly dependent on one another. In terms of data analysis, this means that the residual signal across any interface is not affected by the internals of the two modules themselves—the module-module differences are obfuscated at the interfacial level.

An example might help illustrate the value of the interface. Suppose that we have two different encryption algorithms that are used to convert unencrypted bit streams into secure bit streams. We can then collect histograms of the input (unencrypted) and output (encrypted) and compare both using normal methods, such as entropy of the digits in each byte, two byte, etc.; substring; and conditional entropy of sequential strings. If the input and output strings of two modules match for these measures, we can assume that the two modules can be interchanged without consequence, even if they implement greatly different internal processes such as Blowfish, AES, or RC6.

3.4.5 Gain

Gain is a relevant ratio of a measured output variable divided by a measured input variable. Based on the principles of interfaces—which in hardware are the electromagnetic/mechanical connections between modules and in software are the Interactive Data Language, or IDL, specifications—the parameters used for computing the gain should be part of the system specifications. However, this does not preclude there being multiple gains for a single module.

In electric circuits, for example, an amplifier has multiple gains—including at minimum a voltage, current, and power gain—based on the ratios of input and output parameters. If of interest, conductance, resistance, and impedance gains can also be defined. Overall, if there are N inputs and P outputs specified, there are $2NP$ simple gains that can be defined. More can be defined in some fields if products of more than one input or output are allowed in the numerator and/or denominator of the gains. For example, power gain is really the product of two other gains: voltage and current gain.

In addition to gains associated with ratios of input and output measurements, there are several other types of gain that are relevant to meta-analytics. These gains do not necessarily correspond with linear system gains but should be cataloged here for completeness. The first of these is information, which is normally associated with an increase in some measurable system entropy. If the information can be described using a histogram, with each element, i, in the histogram having probability $p(i)$, then the information gain is defined by Eq. (3.19):

$$\text{Information gain} = \sum_{final} p_i \ln(p_i) - \sum_{initial} p_i \ln(p_i) \qquad (3.19)$$

This is not the ratio of an output and input parameter, but it is certainly a relationship between them.

Functional gains are also of interest to the meta-analytic system designer. These are gains as they represent a functional relationship between some measurable content produced by the analytic system (output) and the content as entered into the system (input). Two simple examples, which are nonexhaustive and illustrative of a much larger set of functional gains, are *knowledge gain* and *efficiency gain*. Knowledge gain is a direct measurement of the product of an analytic system; for example, it can be the ratio of the number of terms or entries in a dictionary, taxonomy, or ontology after processing divided by the number of terms or entries before processing. Similar knowledge gains can be defined in terms of metadata entries, tags, search terms, translated words and phrases, etc.

A second functional gain of interest is efficiency gain, which is a gain in the system's ability to achieve its processing goals divided by the resources required for this achievement. This may seem to be the same as the performance of a system; however, it is rather more elaborate than a simple, singular measurement such as performance or for that matter accuracy, cost, or robustness. Efficiency from the perspective of meta-analytics may be viewed as parsimony of algorithm—the most efficient meta-analytic is the one with the most streamlined design. This could mean the minimum set of modules that performs the required analytic for system design, the minimum set of coefficients within the modules, the simplest approach to combining multiple analytics (e.g., weighted voting is a simpler approach than tessellation and recombination), etc.

The final types of gain to be considered here are discussed in greater depth in Chapter 10. We are speaking of gain in terms of successful bias of a system. That is, a system is biased toward one of seven design considerations. While there are undoubtedly more than seven, the ones focused on in Chapter 10 are (1) rank, (2) accuracy, (3) performance, (4) cost, (5) robustness, (6) modularity, and (7) scalability. The "gain" here is more broadly defined to compare a particular incarnation of a system design compared with the system it is intended to replace going forward. We consider gain and the seven types of system "biases" next:

(1)   In the case of rank-biased systems, the expected value of the rank of the actual correct answer provides the gain. If the previous analytic system provided the correct answer, on the mean, in 1.85 attempts, and the new system provides the correct answer, on the mean, in 1.51 attempts, then the "rank-biased gain" is $\frac{1/0.51}{1/0.85}$ or 1.667, since the reciprocal of rank is a measure of system performance. This implies a 66.7% improvement in finding the correct answer for this particular system upgrade (since perfect rank is 1.0, not 0.0).

(2)   When considering accuracy-biased systems, the gain is relatively straightforward: the gain can be simply defined as the accuracy of the new system divided by accuracy of the old system. However, the accuracy gain can be assigned to partitions of the input (leading to an array of gains), or the accuracies can be normalized; for example, the gain can be defined as the percent of possible improvement achieved. In this way, improving a system from 95 to 97% accuracy is more intuitively shown to have a gain of 1.40 (40% of the way to perfection) rather than 1.021 (the ratio of 0.97 to 0.95).

(3)   In the case of performance-biased systems, the gain is again the ratio of the reciprocals, here the reciprocal of the time for processing, usually of a large, diverse, and representative benchmark of tasks for the system. If, for example, a previous system could process the benchmark set in 21.75 h, and then a new system can process the benchmark in 18.23 hours, then the gain is $\frac{1/18.23}{1/21.75}$, or 1.193.

(4)   For cost-biased systems, the gain is also the ratio of the reciprocal of the cost of the new system divided by the reciprocal of the cost of the old system. Alternatively and equally, it can be defined by the throughput of the new system per X number of dollars, divided by the throughput of the former system per X number of dollars. Consider a voice recognition system in which for a 10% performance cost we are able to assign a voice transaction to freeware software 50% of the time and must use the full cost voice system the other 50% of the time. The performance is thus 0.10 of normal 50% of the time, and 1.10 of normal 50% of the time, or a mean of 0.60 of normal overall. The new throughput is thus 1/0.60 or 1.67 times the old throughout (per unit cost).

(5)   Next, we address robustness-biased systems. Here, the gain is based on the most important success criteria—be it performance, cost, accuracy, rank, or some linear combination thereof—as applied to data unfamiliar to the fully trained system. Thus, robustness-biased systems are measured using one or more of the other biases to measure the effectiveness of the system to "unsupervised" new data. Suppose, for example, we have two systems, A and B, which provide accuracies of 89.3% and 85.5%, respectively, on an existing set of training data. System A is overtrained compared with B but performs much better on downstream data for the next 6 months (88.4% compared with 84.1%). However, when a change in the environment leads to a change in the nature of the data, system A provides mean accuracy of 80.3% while system B provides mean accuracy of 82.3%. The robustness "gain" of system B over system A is based on the ratio of the reciprocals of lost accuracy of B over A, that is, 1/|85.5-82.3%| divided by 1/|89.3-80.3%|. The robustness gain here is a compelling 2.812, meaning B is 182% more robust to new data than A as assessed by accuracy.

(6)   For modularity-biased systems, there are several possibly meaningful gains that can be measured. The first is simply a ratio of the modules before and after a system redesign. This can be viewed as "module gain" since it reflects only the number of modules. A second, more qualitative, gain measurement, provides insight into the ability of different modules to substitute for each other. At the highest level, the mean number of modules available to perform a particular task "primitive" is compared before and after a system redesign, and the gain is the mean number of modules to perform tasks after/before. This can be viewed as the "modularity gain." A third type of gain is based on functionality. Within a larger ecosystem (many systems available for use within a larger organization), the mean reuse rate for modules before and after a system redesign can be compared. The "functional modularity gain" is the ratio of the use of the modules after/before the redesign. Presumably, a system that is well designed will provide more modules desired for reuse by other privileged users; therefore, these more usefully packaged modules will appear in more additional systems. This third form of modularity gain, obviously, will naturally creep upward as the number of systems or the size of the organization grows.

(7)   Finally, for scalability-biased systems, we are concerned with the relative use of the analytic techniques as the size of the problem space grows. A good example may be a binary classification algorithm—for example, a support vector machine or SVM—that falls out of utility as the number of classes grows beyond original design expectations and must be substituted for by other methods (Bayesian, neural, genetic, attribute-based, hybrid, etc.). Here, the gain is the relative use of an analytic approach after system scale increases to the relative use before scaling.

3.4.6 Domain normalization

We kicked off this chapter with an overview of data normalization. There, we focused on the measured data (i.e., the dependent variable) and how we could zero-mean center and/or standardize these data so that multiple dependent variables could be used together in such complicated systems as clustering and classification analytics. In this section, we are more concerned with the independent variables, ensuring that we can modify, or normalize, them sufficiently such that the dependent variable range behaves without bias when a plurality of outputs needs to collaborate for a task. In general, this involves remapping of the domain space such that range behavior is normalized.

Thus, one important means of domain normalization uses the measured attributes of the range to "back propagate" a (usually nonlinear) remapping of the input. Deemed *output space transformation* [Sims13], this approach normalizes the output of multiple algorithms or systems and in so doing performs a type of *empirical normalization*. Originally, it was noted that complicated analytic processes—which are often treated as black boxes—can provide rather idiosyncratic confidence values for the set of possible outputs. These confidence data may be as (a) a ranked set with no quantitative confidence values, as (b) relative confidence values, or even (in best case) as (c) actual probabilities. *Output space transformation* is the process used to enforce similar relative behavior among the processes when they are used together in a system of processes. This fundamentally requires converting any incomplete normalizations—such as approaches (a) and (b) mentioned just above—into "complete" normalizations involving the assignment of probabilities to all possible outcomes, ranged from 0.0 to 1.0.

In previous work [Sims13], output space transformation was shown to be both straightforward and useful in allowing three text classification processes to cooperate. The transformation investigated mapped an output probability p, to a new probability, p^{α}, prior to applying three sets of intelligent processes to the document classification task. This simple power law transformation was found to be advantageous for a 20% training set (on a 20,000 document system): transforming p to $p^{0.208}$, where p is the highest-accuracy engine probability output and removed 43 additional errors, that is, it reduced the overall system error rate by more than 8%. When the medium-accuracy process was independently transformed, the square root operator ($\alpha = 0.5$) removed the most (14) additional errors (another 3% reduction in error rate). Deploying these two transformations (with the output of the lowest-accuracy process left untransformed) provided an optimal 12,839 correct answers, 62 more than before the output space transformation: the error rate was relatively reduced by 11.3%.

Many other approaches to output space transformation exist. Perhaps, the simplest is relative curve alignment, which makes sure that the overall probability behavior of two different analytics behaves the same. This may simply involve subdomain expansion and compression to provide alignment, effectively a form of "dynamic time warping" applied to histograms, where "time" is simply the probability domain from 0.0 to 1.0.

3.4.7 Sensitivity analysis

Typical sensitivity analysis focuses on a matrix of partial derivatives and/or conditional partial derivatives. In general, sensitivity is the response of a system to an instantaneous change in a relevant part of its input. One area of particular interest for experimental design is the sensitivity analysis of data models. Suppose we have two models for fitting a set of data, and their residual signals (the behavior of the data after subtracting out the model) are effectively equivalent. The two models are

$$Model\,A,\ \hat{y} = -2.33x^2 + 8.67x + 4.78 \tag{3.20}$$

$$Model\,B, \hat{y} = 1.25\cos(3.45x + 0.54) - 1.11x^2 + 4.31x + 3.57 \tag{3.21}$$

We find the partial derivatives of these two simple models:

$$Model\,A,\ \frac{\partial \hat{y}}{\partial x} = -4.66x + 8.67 \tag{3.22}$$

$$Model\,B,\ \frac{\partial \hat{y}}{\partial x} = -4.31\sin(3.45x + 0.54) - 2.22x + 4.31 \tag{3.23}$$

We then set and compare the two partial derivatives and use Model A when

$$|-4.66x + 8.67| < |-4.31\sin(3.45x + 0.54) - 2.22x + 4.31| \tag{3.24}$$

And, we use Model B when

$$|-4.66x + 8.67| > |-4.31\sin(3.45x + 0.54) - 2.22x + 4.31| \tag{3.25}$$

This provides us with a means to select multiple models for a domain. We can modify the coefficients of models so that there is smoothness (continuity) at the subdomain boundaries if desired. Sensitivity analysis is an extremely important part of the analytic engineer's repertoire. Changes in the nature of data tell us about changes in the customer's behavior [Hays04] and point to the way in which all important aspects of analysis—what data to use for ground truth, what models to apply going forward, and what data to predict will follow—are changing or are about to change.

3.5 Summary

This chapter outlines important aspects of experimental design for analytics. The experimental design may occur after the data is collected, as it is about how to define the analysis of the data. In Section 3.3, the process of simple data normalization—unit normalization, zero-mean centering, and scaling—was outlined. This process allows different features or dimensions to contribute to an analytic task equally, before weighting is assigned. Bias normalization and four important design considerations corresponding to this form of normalization were then overviewed. Bias normalization is a means of preventing nonproportional data collection from distorting the conclusions of an analytic task. The design considerations find means of removing bias and are sensitive to the fact that real-world exigencies such as cost, time, availability and even ethics may prevent the analytics professional from always being able to employ the greatest rigor (i.e., design consideration #4). The application and interpretation of normalization are shown using simple matrix examples but are shown to scale with the size of the analytic task through the use of such metrics as the imbalance in the original data collection (IODC) and the mean absolute value difference (MAVD).

In Section 3.4, we considered the pruning of aging data, initially through the consideration of a backward-in-time (BIT) approach. We then progressed to a forward-in-time/backward-in-time approach (FIT-BIT) which allowed us to employ, effectively, an intelligent moving average to the data used to guide the experimental design.

In Section 3.5, we employed system theory to help frame the "engineering practice" around meta-analytics. The three necessary—and often sufficient—functionalities in a useful meta-analytics system are componentization, modularity, and the amenability to series and parallel construction. The advantages in providing a plethora of potential system designs using these three principles in conjunction were illustrated. The application of linear system theory—interfaces, gain, domain normalization, and sensitivity analysis—gives valuable insights into the design of the analytics. In particular, we show one perspective on sensitivity analysis as the partial derivative of a data model to changes in the domain. Given the choice of two models to fit the data, we argue that the one least sensitive to instantaneous changes in the input (domain) data is likely to be more useful in the future. Sensitivity analysis will be addressed in greater depth in later chapters, particularly Chapter 5.

Hopefully, the reader is now prepared to apply engineering principles to big data problems. In the next chapter, we overview the core meta-analytic approaches to make the application of these engineering principles more fruitful.

References

[Gamm94] Gamma, E., Helm, R., Johnson, R., Vlissides, J., 1994]. Design Patterns: Elements of Reusable Object-Oriented Software. Addison-Wesley. 416 p.

[Hays04] Hays CL, 2004. What They Know About You, The New York Times, 14 November 2004, also available on-line at http:/www.nytimes.com/2004/11/14/business/yourmoney/what-walmart-knows-about-customers-habits.html.

[Ott84] Ott, L., 1984]. An Introduction to Statistical Methods, second ed. Duxbury Press, Boston.

[Sims13] Simske, S., 2013]. Meta-Algorithmics: Patterns for Robust, Low-Cost, High-Quality Systems. IEEE Press and Wiley, Singapore.

Meta-analytic design patterns

4

A designer knows perfection has been achieved not when there is nothing left to add, but when there is nothing left to take away
Antoine de Saint-Exupéry (1939)
Patterns cannot be weighed or measured. Patterns must be mapped
Fritjof Capra (1996)

4.1 Introduction

Given the continually expanding scope of computing—in processing power, storage capacity, bandwidth, parallelism, and architecture—every day shifts the gauge of reasonable analysis closer to brute-force exhaustive search. Blockchain analysis is, for example, a driving force for the rapid improvement in blockchain mining hardware over the past several years. Image analysis has been a driving force in the improvement of graphics processing units. Artificial intelligence is a driving force for many types of computing hardware, the balance between general purpose processors and custom processors being dependent on the domain, and the size of the data problem.

Meta-analytics is a branch of analytics that allows a data scientist to move with the scope of computing, providing a set of patterns that can be readily gauged for appropriateness for the specific task. Appropriateness maps the resources (processing, storage, bandwidth, parallelism, etc.) with the specifications of the problem (amount of data, amount of metadata, number of floating point operations to be performed on each datum, etc.) and also with the relative expense—in terms of these same specifications—of each meta-analytic approach. The aforementioned blockchain mining has proved that given a strong enough (usually financial) motivation, hardware will quickly evolve to move certain data analysis problems ever closer to exhaustive search. In fact, as the number of leading zeroes (00000*...*) in a bitcoin nonce increases, the more exhaustive the blockchain hashing search becomes.

Regardless, meta-analytics are certainly timely. Learning the tools of meta-analytics—namely, the patterns, the steps in the patterns, and the algorithms required at each step—helps one to be prepared for migrating the analytics over time from one pattern to the other, rather than facing obsolescence of a particular approach. As Fritjof Capra notes, these patterns must be mapped—and this chapter will map a broad set of meta-analytic patterns. Contradicting Capra, however, these patterns will also be weighed and measured—that is, after all, the only way that they can cooperate to solve analytic problems.

Meta-Analytics. https://doi.org/10.1016/B978-0-12-814623-1.00004-6

Antoine de Saint-Exupéry provides a little princely insight into how meta-analytics work. They do not, in general, achieve their informational goals through adding to each other—simply adding analytic approaches tends to blur together information (central limit theorem), which can be valuable for classification problems but less so for data mining, search, summarization, regression, and many other analytic tasks. Rather, meta-analytic approaches generally focus on taking away the "personality" of remaining data, that is, extracting information until what remains is effectively indistinguishable from what remains for another data set upon which meta-analytics have been performed. This "equivalence of residual information" approach is what is meant by design perfection being achieved when there is "nothing left to take away." Once the residual data are without personality, all of the original personality has been digested into *information*.

4.2 Cumulative response patterns

A cumulative response curve [Prov13], also known as a lift curve or a cumulative gain chart, provides a particular set of insights for a predictive model. Typically, this represents the relative accuracy of classification, but it can be readily applied to regression, wherein the inverse of the distance from the actual value is the predictive model measured versus untrained regression. By lift is meant the relative effectiveness of a predictive model over random guessing. In this section, we use a simple binary classification example to illustrate how cumulative response curves and a new "conditional cumulative response curve" can be used to identify the samples most relevant to subsequent meta-analytic approaches.

The first cumulative response curve (hereafter "CRC") is shown in Fig. 4.1. We consider two points on the curve to illustrate the insight provided by a CRC. For example, the first point on the curve is (0.106, 0.50), which means that the 10.6% of samples most highly ranked (by Classifier A) belonging to Class 1 result in

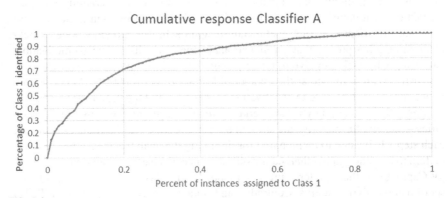

FIG. 4.1

Cumulative response curve for Classifier A.

50% of the samples that are actually from Class 1 are identified. The ratio is 0.500/0.106=4.72. Since this ratio is above 2.0, it is clear that the classification problem shown is imbalanced; that is, there are at least 4.72 times as many samples not belonging to Class 1 as there are samples belonging to Class 1. The peak ratio (in this case 14.3 when $x=0.01$ and $y=0.143$) usually corresponds to 100% accuracy—in this case, 7% of the overall set of samples belongs to Class 1, while 93% do not. Extending this, if the first Δx samples result in Δy percentage of a class (Class 1) being identified, then the percentage of the samples belonging to Class 1 is given by Eq. (4.1):

$$\text{Percentage in Class } 1 = (\Delta x/\Delta y)100\% \qquad (4.1)$$

For the example, $(0.01/0.143)100\%=7.0\%$ as noted above. This percentage in Class 1 can, of course, be directly measured from the ground truth data set, but we will use the following definition since it provides a good comparative value for the discussion to follow (Eq. 4.2):

$$EPC1 = Estimated_{Percent_{in_{Class1}}} = \left(\frac{\Delta x_{initial}}{\Delta y_{initial}}\right)100\% = \left(\frac{\partial x}{\partial y_{initial}}\right)100\% \qquad (4.2)$$

As mentioned, in most cases, EPC1 will be accurate since the initial few samples will be more or less 100% accurately assigned (especially for binary classification). Thereafter, the curve can be mined for any regions in which the slope $\Delta y/\Delta x$ approximates the slope 1/EPC1. These are areas of high interest to meta-analytics, as discussed below.

The second point of interest to our discussion on the curve in Fig. 4.1 is (0.2, 0.711). Here, 20% of the samples have been assigned to Class 1. We previously found EPC1 was 7%, and so, 0.711(7%) or 4.98% of the total number of samples actually belong to Class 1 and are assigned to Class 1. The accuracy is thus $(4.98\%)/(20\%)=0.249$. Note that this accuracy is also directly computed from $(\Delta y/\Delta x)$EPC1, which is $(0.711/0.20)(0.07)=0.249$.

4.2.1 Identifying zones of interest

One useful technique for identifying zones of interest is the use of a conditional cumulative response curve. Fig. 4.2 introduces this useful tool. As with any conditional expression, the joint probability of an event of interest, A, and an event known or assumed to have occurred, B, is dependent on having the events refer to the same partition of the overall probability space. Given any set of samples large enough to make the creation of a cumulative response curve feasible, there is a diminishingly small chance of any two analytic approaches having the same ranked order of samples. Therefore, in order to illustrate how the individual approaches are affected by the samples, we need to "pin" the sample ordering based on the ranked order of just one of the approaches. The approach (classifier, regression algorithm, clustering algorithm, etc.) that is used to pin the sample ordering is termed the "anchoring analytic." The manner in which to do this is illustrated by Fig. 4.2 and described next.

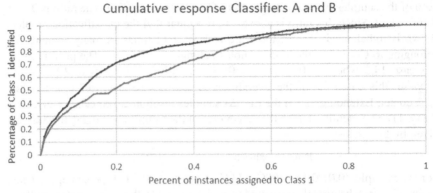

Cumulative response Classifiers A and B

Percentage of Class 1 identified (y-axis, values 0 to 1)

Percent of instances assigned to Class 1 (x-axis, values 0 to 1)

FIG. 4.2

Cumulative response curves for Classifier A (upper curve) and Classifier B (lower curve). The samples are chosen in the same order, based on the rankings for Classifier A. Thus, the curve for Classifier A is smoother than that for Classifier B, since the curve for Classifier B is actually a conditional cumulative response curve.

In Fig. 4.2, the cumulative response curve (hereafter "CRC") for Classifier A is used as the anchoring analytic (upper curve), as its performance is better than that of Classifier B (data not shown). This is because the area under the CRC is equal to 0.8256 for Classifier A but only 0.8078 for Classifier B. In general, when selecting the anchoring analytic for a conditional cumulative response curve (hereafter "CCRC"), select the analytic with the highest area under the CRC. When the ordering of anchoring analytic A is used, we see the CCRC for Classifier B as the lower curve in Fig. 4.2. This curve has a much lower area than the area under the CRC for Classifier B when Classifier B's sample ranking is used—it is 0.7512 instead of 0.8078. This means that there is a reduction in area under the curve of $0.8078 - 0.7512 = 0.0566$ in CCRC when compared with the CRC. This is a large difference, but more importantly, it is an opportunity.

Looking once more at Fig. 4.2, we see that the curve for Classifier A is smoother than that for Classifier B, since the curve for Classifier B is a CCRC and thus has some "disjointedness" where its ranking order of the samples deviates meaningfully from that of Classifier A.

Fig. 4.3 makes the relationship between the CRC for Classifier A, the anchoring analytic, and the CCRC for Classifier B, the dependent analytic, more explicit. The lowest of the three curves in Fig. 4.3 represents the difference CRC(A)−CCRC(B). If the sample ranking behavior of Classifiers A and B were closely related, we would expect this curve, CRC(A)−CCRC(B), to be rather smooth and to generally not rise very much above two times the difference in overall classifier accuracy (since the domain and range for that matter are 1.0, no normalization of this value is necessary). *Two smooth CRC curves will differ by a crescent moonlike sliver that is relatively well approximated by two triangles, and in such a case, the peak difference between*

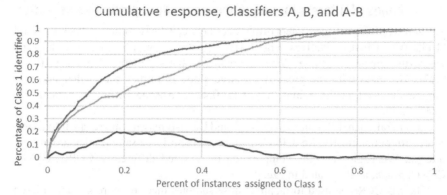

FIG. 4.3

Cumulative response curves for Classifier A (CRC) and Classifier B (CCRC, with A's CRC as the anchor analytic). The lowest curve is the difference between the two curves, CRC (A)−CCRC(B), which can be seen to have the greatest positive slope in the domain $x=(0.07, 0.17)$ and the greatest negative slope in the domain $x=(0.33, 0.58)$.

two CRC curves will be approximately twice the mean difference, and thus twice the difference in area since the domain is $(0, 1)$. For our example, this difference, CRC-Area(A) − CRC-Area(B), is $0.8256 - 0.8078 = 0.0178$. In reality (data not shown), the peak difference between CRC(A) and CRC(B) occurs when $x=0.20$ and is $0.694 - 0.643 = 0.051$, which is still far less than the observed peak difference between CRC(A) and CCRC(B), which is 0.203 when $x=0.18$.

In Fig. 4.4, the first derivatives (on intervals of $\Delta x=0.01$) of the two curves in Fig. 4.2 are plotted. The significance of these first derivatives is the topic of the next section.

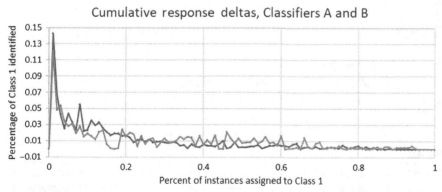

FIG. 4.4

Plot of the first derivatives of the cumulative response curves for Classifiers A and B.

4.2.2 **Zones of interest for sequence-dependent predictive selection**

The zones of relatively consistent differences between the two curves, "Delta-A" and "Delta-B", of first derivatives (Fig. 4.4) are given in Fig. 4.5. Zone A is the zone where the greatest positive slope is obtained, that is, in the domain $x=(0.07, 0.17)$. The zone with the greatest negative slope is further subdivided into two ranges: Zone B1 in the domain $x=(0.33, 0.42)$ and Zone B2 in the domain $x= (0.47, 0.58)$.

In general, such differences in Delta-A and Delta-B may not aggregate into zones. More programmatically, we define a pattern for identifying samples that are of high interest. We begin with the computation of a sorted differential-CCRC, or SD-CCRC, graph, as illustrated in Fig. 4.6.

The SD-CCRC is used to identify those samples that are more strongly biased toward one analytic approach versus the other, particularly in the context of augmenting the cumulative behavior of the curve. This is important, but it means that the values in Fig. 4.6—that is, Delta-A minus Delta-B values—are contextual to the changes in the cumulative behavior of the analytic approach. This sequentially relevant context distinguishes this SD-CCRC design pattern from the simpler, non-sequentially context-dependent meta-algorithmic pattern, predictive selection, as introduced elsewhere (Ref. [Sims13], pp. 189–192).

The steps involved in the SD-CCRC design pattern are recapitulated in Table 4.1. As described above, the first step is to compute the CRC for the anchoring analytic (this is the more accurate classifier, Classifier A, as shown in Fig. 4.1), designated CRC(A). In Step 2, the dependent analytic is referred to the anchoring analytic conditionally, and thus, its CCRC is computed (Fig. 4.2) as CCRC(B). Then, in Steps

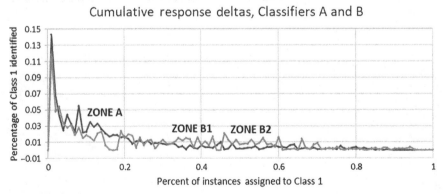

FIG. 4.5

Plot of the first derivatives of the cumulative response curves for Classifiers A and B. Three zones are identified. In Zone A, the derivative of Classifier A is higher than the derivative of Classifier B; in Zones B1 and B2, the derivative of Classifier B is higher than the derivative of Classifier A.

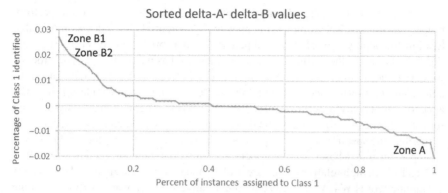

FIG. 4.6

Sorted differential-CCRC, or SD-CCRC, computed from Fig. 4.5, where the derivative of curve CRC(A), or Delta-A, has the derivative of curve CCRC(B), or Delta-B, subtracted. These values are then sorted from largest to smallest and various measurements performed as described in the text.

Table 4.1 Steps in the sorted differential-conditional cumulative response curve (SD-CCRC) design pattern, outlined in this section.

Sorted differential-conditional cumulative response curve (SD-CCRC) design pattern	
Step number	**Algorithm or process performed at this step**
1	Compute the CRC for anchoring analytic, A=CRC(A)
2	Compute the CCRC for dependent analytic, B, with reference to A=CCRC(B)
3	Compute the first derivative curve for CRC(A)=Delta-A
4	Compute the first derivative curve for CCRC=Delta-B
5	Compute the difference curve D-CCRC=Delta-A−Delta-B
6	Sort the SD-CCRC from largest (A favored) to smallest (B favored) samples
7	Mine the start and end zones of the SD-CCRC for predictors
8	Apply predictors to the meta-analytic deployment

3–4, the first derivative curve for both CRC(A) and CCRC(B) is computed (Figs. 4.4 and 4.5) as Delta-A and Delta-B, respectively. Step 5 computes the difference between CRC(A) and CCRC(B), designated D-CCRC=Delta-A − Delta-B. Step 6 involves sorting the individual values in D-CCRC and plotting in sorted order as SD-CCRC, shown in Fig. 4.6. All of these steps have been described in some detail already, and so, Steps 7–8 are of particular interest to us.

In Step 7, we now take advantage of the sorted samples in Fig. 4.6 to perform proper data mining. The mining is intended to find potential binary decisions of value to allow the deployment of advanced patterns such as predictive selection (see, e.g., Fig. 2.2). For all of the features, or metrics, measured as part of the analytic process, we determine whether the start and end ranges of the ground truthed data have reliable, consistent differences for the two analytics. If so, we can decide for that start zone to weight analytic A (in this case Classifier A) more heavily than analytic B and for the end zone to weight analytic B more heavily. These predictors are used, in Step 8, to select the specific analytic deployment for samples matching the predictor. For example, for a text-based analytic document, any document containing words W1, W2, and W3 in high relative frequency is likely to be in the start zone, and documents containing words W4, W5, and W6 in high relative frequency are likely to be in the end zone. Thus, when a sample not in the training set appears, it can be assigned to one of three deployments in this simple example:

1. W1, W2, and W3 occur with high frequency; deploy the analytic A favoring analytic.
2. W4, W5, and W6 occur with high frequency; deploy the analytic B favoring analytic.
3. Default analytic, favoring neither analytic A nor B. Here, {W1,W2,W3} and {W4,W5,W6} either both occur with high frequency or both occur with normal or low frequency.

4.2.3 Traditional cumulative gain curves, or lift curves

Cumulative response patterns, described in the previous few sections, are based on the cumulative gain curves (CGCs), also known as lift curves. These curves are a convenient way of evaluating a particular classifier, as so much information can be gleaned from a single curve.

Lift curves are simple in conception, and in this section, we show how to generate and analyze one. First, we collect all of our samples (or groups of samples with similar confidence) and rank order them based on the confidence values. The highest ranked samples are those we most confidently believe belong to the particular class to which we are assigning them. These samples have, for example, the highest confidence (relative or absolute) in their output probability for the specific assigned class. Next, we determine the accuracy of each sample (or sample set) and then the cumulative accuracy by summing the accuracies of the cumulative sets and dividing by the number of sets. We view the curve and look for when behavior noticeably changes—the change in behavior gives us insights into the limitations of the system and indicates where we may apply hybrid system approaches.

A data set used to generate a lift curve is presented in Table 4.2. Here, there are 10 sets of data, each with an accuracy between 0.75 and 0.99 for the class from which the data presumably come. The data sets are then rank ordered in order to ensure a monotonic lift cumulative gain curve. The cumulative gain curve with the set in rank

Table 4.2 Data set for a simple example of generating a cumulative gain curve, or lift curve.

Sample set	Confidence	Accuracy	Rank
1	0.68	0.91	6
2	0.56	0.77	10
3	0.78	0.95	3
4	0.84	0.98	2
5	0.66	0.86	7
6	0.57	0.75	9
7	0.77	0.96	4
8	0.91	0.99	1
9	0.63	0.82	8
10	0.69	0.89	5

This is a binary classifier, for which our engine reports confidences in the range of 0.56–0.91. The accuracies end up in the range of 0.75–0.99.

Table 4.3 Data set from Table 4.2 with the sample sets in order of confidence.

Sample set	Confidence	Accuracy	Cumulative accuracy	Rank
8	0.91	0.99	0.990	1
4	0.84	0.98	0.985	2
3	0.78	0.95	0.973	3
7	0.77	0.96	0.970	4
10	0.69	0.89	0.954	5
1	0.68	0.91	0.947	6
5	0.66	0.86	0.934	7
9	0.63	0.82	0.920	8
6	0.57	0.75	0.901	9
2	0.56	0.77	0.888	10

The cumulative accuracy sums to 88.8%, meaning selecting these 10 data sets results in overall accuracy of 88.8%. As we will shortly see, the CGC usually represents all sample sets at once, but these 10 sets are the beginning of the CGC, encompassing those samples for which confidence ≥0.56. The samples for which confidence <0.56 would create the rest of the CGC.

order based on the confidence values and accuracies is given in Table 4.3. The curve comprised of the data in Tables 4.2 and 4.3 itself is given in Fig. 4.7. Note that in this case, we only had classifier output where the class of interest is highest confidence (sample set 2 still has 56% confidence in A, which is above 50%). The confidence is highly correlated with the accuracy, as can be seen in the data in Table 4.3, but not entirely. The accuracy of sample set 1, with confidence 0.68, for example, is higher than the accuracy of sample set 10, with confidence 0.69. Overall, however, there is strong correlation between accuracy and confidence in Table 4.3, as given in Eq. (4.3):

$$\text{Accuracy} = 0.7153(\text{confidence}) + 0.3809 \qquad (4.3)$$

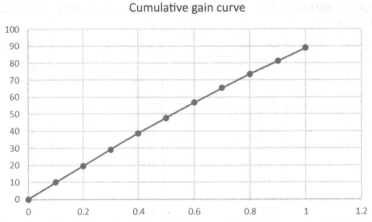

FIG. 4.7

Cumulative gain curve for Table 4.3 data. The curve has these attributes: (A) monotonic, (B) generally has decreasing slope as x-axis (percentage of samples assigned to the class) increases, and (C) asymptotically approaches 1.0 (or 100%).

For Eq. (4.3), the $R^2 = 0.902$. Table 4.3 also introduces the cumulative accuracy, which is the overall accuracy of the classification when the sample sets up to N sample sets are selected. By the time all the sample sets with confidence of 0.56 or higher are selected, the cumulative accuracy is 88.8%. Thus, eight out of nine samples have been classified correctly among all those reporting 56% or more confidence.

The CGC of Fig. 4.7 is extended in Fig. 4.8 to show a ray extending from the origin that illustrates perfect classification. The difference between the ray (straight line segment in Fig. 4.8) and the curved line is samples misclassified.

We next extend the concept of the CGC to a larger data set. In Table 4.4 are the first 20 entries in a larger example comprising 100 entries. In the data set of Table 4.4, there are 3000 samples, and therefore, the individual sample sets are 30 each in size. Table 4.4 is the cumulative accuracy of the samples with the highest calculated confidence belonging to Class A. Class A is one of three equally sized classes, each with 1000 samples (the other two being Class B and Class C, with 1000 samples each). A perfect classifier for Class A would therefore rank those 1000 samples that actually belong to Class A the highest, and by the time 33.3%, or 33 1/3 sample sets, of the samples are chosen, all of Class A is assigned correctly, and no samples from Class B or Class C are assigned to this set. However, we can see here that even assigning only 60% of this ideal number (600) results in 123 errors, for a 79.5% cumulative accuracy. A 100% cumulative accuracy for the last row in Table 4.4 would assign 600 samples to Class A, with no misclassifications.

Fig. 4.9 shows the lift curve for the data in Table 4.4 (which only covers the part of the curve for the x-axis going from 0.0 to 0.2) and the remaining 80% of the data

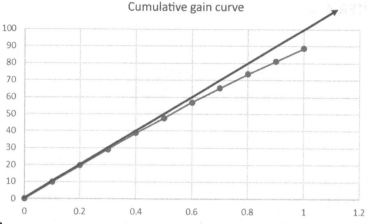

Cumulative gain curve

FIG. 4.8

Cumulative gain curve for the table data with the "perfect classification" indicated by the ray (line segment with an arrow at the end). The overall accuracy is nearly 100% until $x=0.4$ and thereafter diverges. The actual curve can never be above the ray. The intersection of the ray with $y=1.0$ (100%) is the percentage of samples actually in the class (here, 100%).

Table 4.4 Here are the first 20 entries (600 samples) in a larger example, where there are 3000 samples, and the individual sample sets are 30 each in size.

Percentage of instances	Percentage of positives targeted	Percentage targeted in perfect classification	Cumulative accuracy
0	0	0	1.000
0.01	0.03	0.03	1.0000
0.02	0.059	0.06	0.983
0.03	0.087	0.09	0.967
0.04	0.116	0.12	0.967
0.05	0.145	0.15	0.967
0.06	0.173	0.18	0.961
0.07	0.2	0.21	0.952
0.08	0.226	0.24	0.942
0.09	0.251	0.27	0.930
0.1	0.275	0.3	0.917
0.11	0.298	0.33	0.903
0.12	0.321	0.36	0.892
0.13	0.344	0.39	0.882
0.14	0.365	0.42	0.869
0.15	0.385	0.45	0.856
0.16	0.404	0.48	0.842
0.17	0.423	0.51	0.829
0.18	0.441	0.54	0.817
0.19	0.46	0.57	0.807
0.20	0.477	0.60	0.795

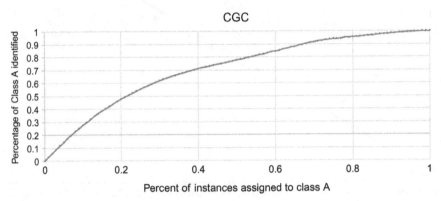

FIG. 4.9

Cumulative gain curve for Table 4.4 (0–0.2 pct) and the other 80% of the samples not shown in Table 4.4. This is the part of the curve included in Table 4.4 from 0 to 0.2 along the *x*-axis, "percentage of instances assigned to Class A."

set. We can see from the discussion to this point that the lift curve provides a particular set of insights for the predictive model. Typically, this represents the relative accuracy of classification, but it can be readily applied to regression, wherein the inverse of the distance from the actual value is the predictive model measured versus untrained regression. By lift is meant the relative effectiveness of a predictive model over random guessing.

Estimated percentage in Class A (EPCA), as defined in Eq. (4.4) (see also Eq. 4.2) will be accurate since the initial few samples will be more or less 100% accurately assigned (especially for binary classification).

$$EPC1 = Estimated_{Percent_{inClassA}} = \left(\frac{\Delta x_{initial}}{\Delta y_{initial}}\right)100\% = \left(\frac{\partial x}{\partial y_{initial}}\right)100\% \quad (4.4)$$

The overall percentage of samples in Class A is given by Eq. (4.5) (see also Eq. 4.1):

$$Percent_{inClassA} = \left(\frac{\Delta x}{\Delta y}\right)100\% \quad (4.5)$$

Finally, the accuracy of the curve at any point is determined by Eq. (4.6):

$$Accuracy = (\Delta y/\Delta x)^* EPC1 \quad (4.6)$$

Fig. 4.10 shows the curve of the CGC, or lift curve, running between the piecewise linear curve of perfect classification and the straight line segment, or ray, of random guessing. Of course, it is possible for the CGC to run BELOW the line of random guessing, in which case the CGC is a good predictor of failure (above expectation). We customarily show the CGC above the guessing line for either success or failure, since either is a form of information gain over purely guessing. Fig. 4.11 adds a number of significant labels to the three curves of Fig. 4.10 and deserves a closer evaluation to help glean the power of the CGC for determining key classification metrics.

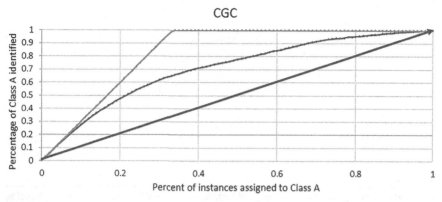

FIG. 4.10

Cumulative gain curve of Fig. 4.9 with additional line segments added. The lowest slope line segment is the CGC for random guessing, and the highest slope line segment is the CGC for 100% accuracy. The curve between these two line segments is the actual (measured) CGC.

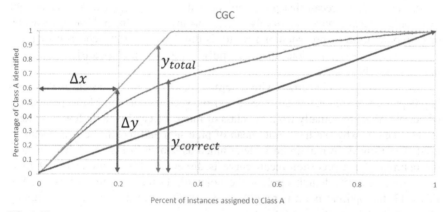

FIG. 4.11

Cumulative gain curve of Fig. 4.10 with additional labels to allow the computation of important classification metrics. Please see text for details.

In Fig. 4.11, the upper piecewise linear curve is the curve for perfect classification, and it reaches the $y=1.0$ mark in proportion to the number of samples in the class of interest divided by the total number of samples. In this case, that is 1/3 of the samples, since there are three equally sized classes. The lower curve, or ray, is the curve for random guessing. Precision at any point is the ratio of $y_{correct}$ to y_{total}. Early in the curve (i.e., when the "percentage of instances assigned to Class A" is just above 0.0), $y_{correct}$ is equal to (or nearly equal to) y_{total}, and so, the precision is approximately 1.0. Fig. 4.12 "unwraps" this relationship between $y_{correct}$ and y_{total}

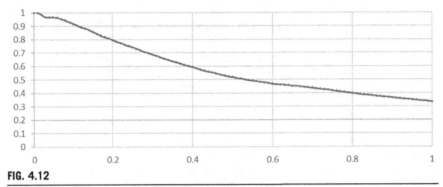

FIG. 4.12

Precision (y-axis) versus the percentage of instances assigned (x-axis)—note its asymptotes to the overall percentage in Class A, which in this example is 0.333.

to show that precision consistently decreases as the percentage of instances assigned to Class A increases—especially after this percentage is greater than the percentage of samples that actually are in Class A (i.e., 0.333).

In Fig. 4.12, we recall that precision is equal to $y_{correct}/y_{total}$. It is even simpler to calculate recall: recall is simply $y_{correct}$ at any value for x. The F-measure, or harmonic mean of precision and recall, is thus $2pr/(p+r)$, which in this case is $2y_{correct}/(y_{correct}+y_{total}^2)$. Note that generally, accuracy and precision are used interchangeably in a CGC.

We are typically concerned with determining an optimized system that is both highly precise (accurate, few false positives) and yet does not omit a large percentage of samples that are actually from the class of interest (recall is high, few false negatives). That is why the harmonic mean of precision and recall, the F-measure, is used. The F-measure maximum is determined as shown in Fig. 4.13. This is how the optimum for a precision-recall curve is discerned. The arrow in Fig. 4.13 is the minimum arrow length circling the point (0, 1) that hits the lift curve. For Fig. 4.13, the optimal point is roughly (0.32, 0.66), corresponding to an accuracy of approximately 0.69 (from 0.66/0.96).

In equation form, the optimum point $P_{optimum}$ is given by Eq. (4.7) and is the point on the lift curve where the Cartesian distance from upper left (0, 1) to the lift curve is minimum:

$$P_{optimum} = argmin(P \in CGC)\left\{(1-P_y)^2 + (P_x-0)^2\right\} = argmin(P \in CGC)\left\{(1-P_y)^2 + P_x^2\right\}$$

(4.7)

We have shown here that many useful analytics can be deduced just from the lift curve:

1. Percentage of samples in the class of interest from $\frac{\Delta x}{\Delta y}$
2. Percentage of samples from the class assigned at any value of x, from $y_{correct}$
3. Precision $= y_{correct}/y_{total}$
4. Recall $= y_{correct}$

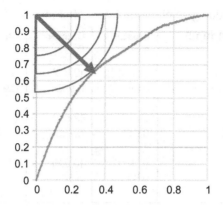

FIG. 4.13

The *F*-measure maximum is determined as shown here. Please see text for details.

5. F-measure $= 2y_{correct}/(y_{correct} + y_{total}^2)$
6. Optimum percentage of instances to assign to Class A and the recall and precision at that optimum, from Eq. (4.7)
7. Relative distance between actual precision and "perfect precision" and "random guessing precision," from the curves in Figs. 4.10 and 4.11

We now proceed to a consideration of the optimization of analytics.

4.3 Optimization of analytics

4.3.1 Decision trees

In some cases, a series of analytic steps either must be performed or are more effective when performed in a sequence. An example of this, familiar to many, is the decision tree, in which decisions can be based on specific attributes of the data set, for example, assigning to cluster A if the attribute is greater than threshold $T1$, assigning to cluster B if the attribute is in the range $(T1, T2)$, and assigning to cluster C if the attribute is less than threshold $T2$. The thresholds $T1$ and $T2$ can be determined using information gain as the decision approach: the values of $T1$ and $T2$ that most significantly reduce the entropy of the three new clusters A, B, and C in comparison with the original combination of the three clusters are chosen. Note that this is the opposite direction of entropy normally associated with decision trees (in which an increase in information gain is a measurable benefit of the right order of decisions). Table 4.5 illustrates three different distributions that provide a $(T1, T2)$ pair.

The information gain is the absolute value of the reduction of the entropy, shown here in Eq. (4.8):

$$\text{Information gain} = \left| \sum_{\substack{original \\ clusters}} p_i \ln(p_i) - \sum_{\substack{new \\ clusters}} p_i \ln(p_i) \right| \qquad (4.8)$$

Table 4.5 Information gain choosing three different values for $T1$ and $T2$.

Original cluster ={10,10,10} distribution	Cluster A	Cluster B	Cluster C	Sum of A, B,C
{a,b,c} Distribution 1	{6,2,1}	{2,6,3}	{2,2,6}	{10,10,10}
Entropy distribution 1, sum=2.793	0.848	0.995	0.950	2.793
{a,b,c} Distribution 2	{7,0,3}	{2,8,1}	{1,2,6}	{10,10,10}
Entropy distribution 2, sum=2.219	0.611	0.760	0.848	2.219
{a,b,c} Distribution 3	{8,1,1}	{0,9,3}	{2,0,6}	{10,10,10}
Entropy distribution 3, sum=1.765	0.639	0.563	0.563	1.765

The original cluster has 10 samples each from Classes A, B, and C, and so, the entropy of three such clusters=3.300. The information gain is thus 3.300-(entropy sum) or 0.507 for distribution 1, 1.081 for distribution 2, and 1.535 for distribution 3. Distribution 3 is thus chosen for maximum information gain in this example.

The original set has entropy=3.300 (entropy of a single cluster with {10,10,10} is 1.100, so we scale this to the three clusters we split into and make it 3.300), and distributions 1, 2, and 3 have information gains of $3.300-2.793=0.507$, $3.300-2.219=1.081$, and $3.300-1.765=1.535$, respectively. Thus, distribution 3 is a better choice (provides the best $T1$ and $T2$ of the three choices shown) than distribution 1 or 2.

The decisions in decision trees, of course, need not be determined by information gain, though it is an approach I favor since I view meta-analytics as a process by which multiple analytic approaches are used to "scrub the personality" from a set of data. Regardless, the approach of information gain can be extended to customized patterns for an individual. This is the subject of the next section.

4.3.2 Putative-identity triggered patterns

An important outcome of Table 4.5 is the understanding that the possible information gain is a function of the particular downstream analytics (in the case of Table 4.5, the accuracy). Similarly, it is a function of the type of task that is being addressed. In this section, this point is illustrated through the example of a specific approach to biometrics that is designated "putative-identity-based biometrics." This in turn introduces an analysis approach termed "putative-identity triggering." This is a helpful pattern when we can subpartition a larger analysis space based on real-time context.

Suppose that we wish to identify an individual based on a small but relatively accurate set of biometric measurements. For example, these biometrics can be voice recognition, iris recognition, facial recognition, keyboard dynamics, and fingerprint recognition. The biometrics can be continuous and/or challenge-based (e.g., where the user is asked to perform a task like speaking a specific set of words), so we may have a total of 10 effective biometrics from this set of five recognition approaches ($N_B = 10$).

The number of ways these N_B individual biometrics can be used to create a personalized biometric is astonishing. The number of permutations of these biometrics is $N_B!$, which for $N_B = 10$ is 3.63×10^6. And this is just for different orderings of the N_B biometrics. If a subset of $N_S \leq N_B$ biometrics are also allowed, then the number of biometrics possible is given by Eq. (4.9):

$$\sum_{k=1}^{N_B} k!$$
(4.9)

For $N_B = 10$, this sum is 4.04×10^6. In addition to the sequencing, we can also consider combinations of the N_B biometrics (meaning all $k \leq N_B$ biometrics are required, but their order doesn't matter), which is given by Eq. (4.10):

$$\sum_{k=1}^{N_B} \frac{N_B!}{k!(N_B - k)!}$$
(4.10)

For $N_B = 10$, this is equal to $2^N - 1 = 1023$, since the empty set is not useful. The set of combinations is of course a subset of the permutations, and so, we have not yet generated any new biometric identification patterns. But when we allow the weighting of the combinations to vary over a reasonable range of values, we suddenly have N_R possible values (i.e., coefficients for weighted combinations) across the range. Assuming N_R is the same for every biometric, the number of weighted combinations is now given by Eq. (4.11):

$$\sum_{k=1}^{N_B} (N_R)^k \frac{N_B!}{k!(N_B - k)!}$$
(4.11)

Let us suppose that we can divide each biometric into a range of 10 relative weights. Then, $N_R = 10$, and the above sum is 2.59×10^{10}. All of the combinations (1.02×10^4 for $N_B = 10$) where the weighting of the coefficients is identical are degenerate cases to the permutations, but this still leaves the relevant number of weighted combinations at 2.59×10^{10}.

In addition to the permutations and weighted combinations described, there are other, advanced, patterns based on meta-algorithmics (such as predictive selection). Clearly, then, the number of patterns possible is higher—generally much higher—than the number of individual biometrics that can be efficiently collected, even in today's age of relatively ubiquitous distribution of sensors (cameras, microphones, accelerometers, etc.). As such, a specific pattern personalized to an individual is generally more effective for biometric identification—using an individualized pattern, in general, reduces the false identification of people other than the legitimate individual. The change in false positives can be used as a measurement for *information gain* for the individual versus the nonindividuals in the set. This measurement will be different from the information gain defined for clustering above but still presents a valuable comparative metric for the effectiveness of a given analytic approach.

Suppose that for one combination of three biometrics, an individual moved from the 73rd ranked identity to the 21st ranked identity with a weighted combination. The information gain here is (73/21)=3.48. Measurements of information gain can be used to rate the relative value of each personalized pattern—and in combination with measurements of performance, cost and robustness, among other factors, can be used as input to optimize an overall system (e.g., if one expensive biometric does not consistently appear in the personalized patterns, it can be left out of the overall system with cost savings and relatively minor impact on accuracy, performance, etc.).

4.3.3 Expectation-maximization and maximum-minimum patterns

Expectation-maximization (EM), or perhaps better-named expectation-optimization, is an effective means of playing two processes off against each other to provide an optimized result for the system comprising these and perhaps additional processes. In the most commonplace form, expectation-maximization cycles between assigning samples to clusters defined by a single value (after the first iteration, this is the current cluster centroid) and then defining the centroids of clusters from the values assigned: rinse and repeat. The two processes traded off are (1) defining clusters based on all the assigned samples and (2) assigning samples to the closest defined cluster centroid.

Other trade-offs can be used for an EM (or at least EM-inspired) process. As one example, we can switch the set of features used to cluster iteratively in the two halves of the EM algorithm. The example provided here is for text clustering. Suppose that we determine the number of features—in the case of text clustering, this might be the number of keywords or key phrases used to describe a cluster—for optimal clustering is N. Then, we decide to cluster based on $N+M$ and $N-M$ keywords and iteratively hone in on an optimization. This can be done by leaving out terms not occurring in both clusters from the redefinition of the clusters. This form of EM thus performs "omission of terms" for (re)definition of cluster centroid between iterations. Termination conditions for iteration do not have to change in comparison with the normal EM algorithms, however.

The complexity of EM algorithms includes the definition of even further elaboration, designated the extended expectation-maximization pattern (EEMP), as illustrated in Figs. 4.14 and 4.15. This EEMP is actually a hybrid pattern, incorporating principles of evolutionary algorithms in an effort to avoid local optimization sometimes accompanying EM approaches.

In Fig. 4.14, the approach for advanced text clustering is extended to a series of three EM-like steps incorporated as a sequence within a relatively more protracted and elaborated iteration. The clusters are initiated along any usual preferred means

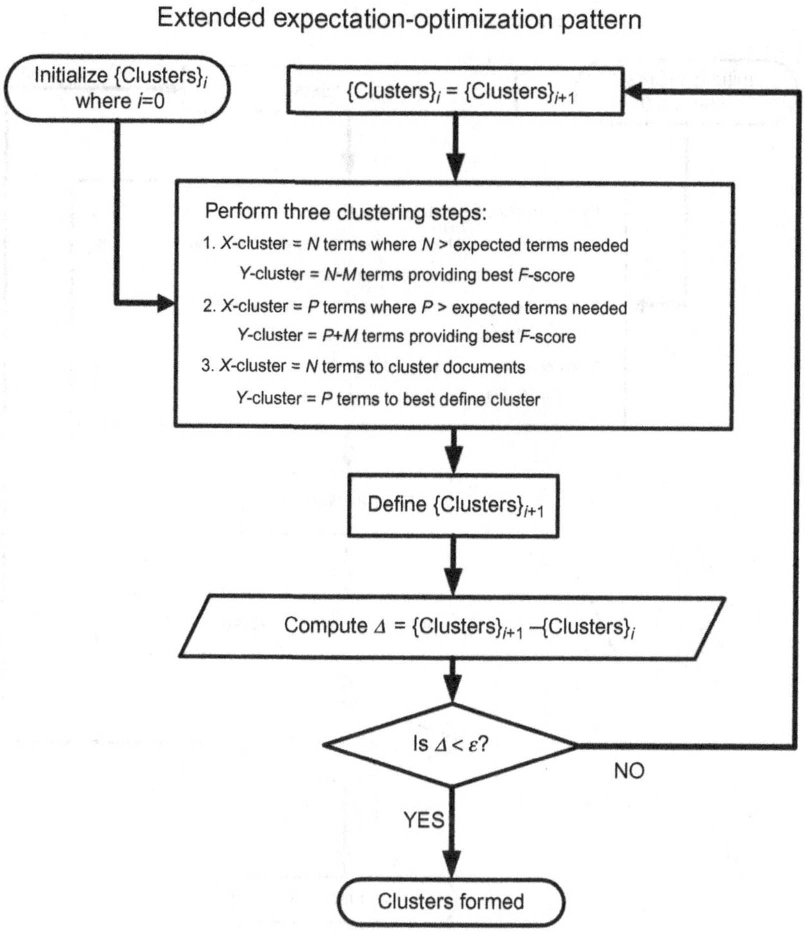

Extended expectation-optimization pattern

FIG. 4.14

Applied (specific) version of the extended expectation-maximization pattern applied to text clustering (e.g., for taxonomy definition, search, document sequencing, and related tasks). Note the sequential set of three operations used to define two simultaneous clusters that are milled to create the accepted cluster definitions.

(e.g., randomly), and then, the iteration continues unless the difference, Δ, between the current and previous iteration is less than a threshold, ε. In the EM portion of the algorithm, instead of one juxtaposed pair of operations, there are three:

(1) First, the X cluster is formed from a surfeit of text features (terms that are keywords and/or key phrases, chosen through methods such as $TF*IDF$ [Vans17]), while the Y cluster is formed from a scarcity of text features. That is, the number of terms, N, used to create the "X" clusters is M more than that used

Extended expectation-optimization pattern

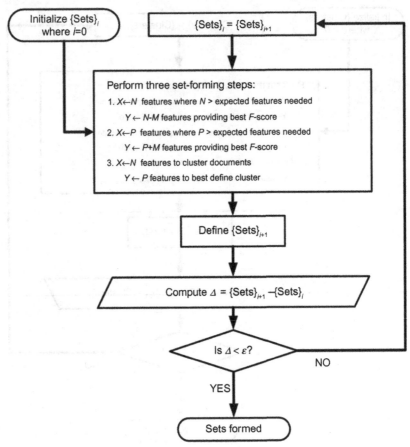

FIG. 4.15

Generic version of the extended expectation-maximization pattern. Note the sequential set of three operations used to define two simultaneous "sets of sets" that are milled to create the accepted set of sets definition. Features are available both manually (expert features) and automatically.

to create the "Y" clusters. The values for N and M can be determined a number of ways experimentally, including empirically or historically (e.g., from similar sized and composed document sets). In the pattern shown in Fig. 4.14, the F-score approach is suggested. That is, after selecting N terms, we subtract $1 \ldots N/2$ terms from N and select the value that provides the highest cluster F-score, that is, the cluster set with the highest value of between-cluster variance divided by within-cluster variance. The value of M is then determined, and the Y cluster is presumed to be optimized along this vector.

(2) In the second step, we define a new "X" cluster based on P terms, where P is less than the expected (empirically, historically, etc.) number of terms. Then, we add 1 … P terms onto the "X" cluster to define a new "Y" cluster, the optimal value of which is also selected using the F-score measurement above. Note that information gain of the added terms could also be used instead of the F-score.

(3) In the third step, the "X" and "Y" clusters are defined of precisely N and P terms. We now have three sets of "X" and "Y" clusters, which allow us to define a final set of clusters using meta-analytic means. For example, for each of the steps, we can define clusters solely based on the interaction of the "X" and "Y" clusters and then assign unassigned samples to the clusters based on distance. The definition of the clusters dictates the key terms for the next iteration. We can then vote on the cluster assignment of the samples based on the cluster assignments of these three steps.

Fig. 4.15 generalizes the approach of Fig. 4.14 (and the previous paragraph) and extends it to other application areas. The basic principal is to perform the following three steps:

1. Select the expected number of features and form the first set using these. Allow a second set to exceed this number of features by up to two times (or other relevant multiplier, depending on the nature of the problem space) and optimize based on a domain-independent measurement such as F-score or information gain.
2. Select a set of features less than the expected value (e.g., 2/3 the expected value for the most balanced situation) and form the first set using these. Allow a second set to exceed this number of features by up to two times (or other relevant multiplier, depending on the nature of the problem space) and optimize based on a domain-independent measurement such as F-score or information gain.
3. Select clusters from two preselected values without F-score, information gain, and optimization.

After these three steps, a plethora of potential combination approaches can be followed, including erosion and recombination (prune the regions and combine the resulting pruned clusters, along the lines used for the text clustering above), voting, weighted voting, and expert system decisions (comparing the terms in the clusters to the keywords in the downstream classes, etc.).

One example of employing the extended expectation-maximization pattern is given in Table 4.6. A linear combination of 10 *TF*IDF* equations was applied to a 588-document test set comprising 12 document classes as described elsewhere [Vans17], with these classes being the 12 CNN-provided classes (business, health, justice, living, opinion, politics, showbiz, sport, tech, travel, the United States, and world). Clustering accuracy is determined based on finding the 12 clusters that correspond to the 12 classes and counting only those correctly assigned to these 12 clusters as being "accurate." Attachments to the wrong cluster, extra clusters, and unclustered documents are considered "inaccurate." For this test, the three steps

Table 4.6 Twenty iterations of the extended expectation-optimization pattern as illustrated in Fig. 4.14, applied to the database described in Ref. [Vans17].

Iteration	Accuracy of clustering	Iteration	Accuracy of clustering
1	230/588=0.391	11	373/588=0.634
2	267/588=0.454	12	370/588=0.629
3	273/588=0.464	13	375/588=0.638
4	303/588=0.515	14	371/588=0.631
5	338/588=0.575	15	375/588=0.638
6	345/588=0.587	16	371/588=0.631
7	352/588=0.599	17	375/588=0.638
8	367/588=0.624	18	371/588=0.631
9	365/588=0.621	19	375/588=0.638
10	368/588=0.626	20	371/588=0.631

For a small positive ε, it is clear that the iterations terminate at 9. Note that the iterations oscillate between accuracy=0.631 and 0.638 after iteration 13.

in Fig. 4.14 are performed in sequence; then, clusters are pruned to the intersection of at least two of the three "X" and "Y" cluster sets. The initial *TF*IDF* weightings and initial clusters are computed from the equal-sized training set (588 documents). During testing, the *TF*IDF* key terms are taken for the next iteration as the terms weighted from 0.01 to 1.00 times the highest weighted *TF*IDF* term in the cluster (typically ~50 terms used). Interestingly and perhaps a consequence of the relatively small size of the document test set (49 documents/class, total of 588 documents), the accuracy of the clustering drops slightly by iteration 9 and oscillates by iteration 13. The convergence is rapid.

A question worth asking about Table 4.6 is, "why does this work?" Part of the answer, certainly, is that the three steps in each iteration offset each other nicely. In forcing the hybrid "X"+"Y" cluster in Step 1 to be larger than expected and the converse for Step 2, there is an aspect of evolutionary algorithm to forcing one cluster to be larger than expected and the other to be smaller than expected. This ensures that a diverse population exists after the three steps, leaving creativity for combining these to form the clusters for the next iteration.

4.4 Model agreement patterns

In this section, the nature of defining models for the data will be assumed. For more information on techniques for modeling and model fitting, you the reader are kindly referred to Chapter 7. This section addresses how to assess agreement among models through an approach designated "equivalence of residual data monotony."

Among the models of interest to us are the various regression approaches (elastic net, lasso, linear, logistic, polynomial, ridge, and stepwise being perhaps the most common seven regressions), decision trees and random forests (which can also be based on regression), Bayesian methods, neural networks, and other piecewise models (which can take on many forms, including the incorporation of expert information/human observation).

In this section, we consider hybrid regression and model fitting as two examples of how to find agreement with a proposed model. In hybrid regression, we provide an alternative viewpoint in which we are more concerned with what we *do not* model. In modeling and model fitting, we are concerned with the stability of our model, in particular, its temporal, scale, distribution, and reliability stability. We begin with hybrid regression.

4.4.1 **Hybrid regression**

Regression techniques are used to provide predictive output for input across a large range of values. Linear, polynomial, and logistic regressions match curve descriptors for the relationship between independent (covariate) and dependent variables. Ridge regression, also known as weight decay, adds a regularization term, effectively acting like a Lagrange multiplier, to incorporate one or more constraints to a regression equation. Least absolute shrinkage and selection operator (lasso) and stepwise selection perform both feature selection (a form of dimensionality reduction, in which only a subset of the provided covariates are used in the final model, rather than the entire set of them) and regularization (which allows the regression to avoid overfitting by introducing, e.g., interpolated information). Advanced forms of lasso alter the coefficients of the regression rather than setting some to zero as in stepwise selection. Finally, the elastic net adds penalty terms to extend lasso and provides a combination of lasso and ridge functionality. Regression approaches, therefore, have grown more complex over the past several decades in order to be able to more closely fit the covariates (independent variables)—this is the purpose of the variable weighting of the covariate coefficients—and also prevent overfitting and incorporate constraints, which is the purpose of the regularization approaches. However, the perspective on the covariates here is one of being able to model the data as best as possible.

An alternative approach, which has distinct meta-analytic advantages, is to be more concerned with what we **do not** model, that is, to fit a plurality of regression models—and their corresponding coefficients and weightings—to the data until the residual data behave in a desired way. Without any other motivation, the residual data should behave such that its entropy is maximized. This means that the data itself have no further information to be extracted. This sounds relatively easy: define the objective function to be a general regression model (e.g., a weighted average combination of the seven regression models described herein), subtract the entropy, and minimize. However, the nonmodel variability (i.e., the "randomness" of the residual data) itself may also need to be normalized over the domain of the data. This means we have both *raw* and *normalized* forms of *residual data*. Raw residual data are simple, and a simple measure of its randomness is given in Eq. (4.12):

$$\text{Residual entropy} = \sum_{i=1}^{i=N} p_{residual(i)} \ \ln p_{residual(i)} \qquad (4.12)$$

It becomes slightly more complicated when we consider normalized residual data. Since by definition the data are nonuniform across the domain, normalization is a means of correcting the baseline for this situation. This means we interpret the data using system theory as signal+noise and assume that the noise is nonuniform. Uniform, or white, noise is of course modeled by raw residual data.

Thus, residual entropy simply requires a definition of the noise or a *noise model*. Common noise models include Gaussian noise, Laplacian noise, and proportional noise. The latter simply assumes that the energy (magnitude) of the noise is proportional to the magnitude of the signal. Cohesive noise, therefore, can be added into a regression equation along the lines of a regularizing term described above. The cohesiveness of a noise model is considered discovered when the residual of the data after the regression model and the cohesive noise model have been removed is truly random; that is, it follows the entropy behavior of a random signal.

4.4.2 Modeling and model fitting

From the perspective of meta-analytics, modeling and model fitting are the process of describing all but the randomness of the data and then simplifying this description to its minimum summary, respectively. An example of the former is to compute the model residual entropy, which is the same basic equation as Eq. (4.12), replicated here in Eq. (4.13):

$$\text{Model residual entropy} = \sum_{i=1}^{i=N} p_{model\_residual(i)} \ \ln p_{model\_residual(i)} \qquad (4.13)$$

Effectively, modeling and model fitting are a further generalization of regression, discussed in the previous section. Significant work [Hast09][Mars09] has been focused on regression and, separately, optimization processes. It is clear that optimization processes can be brought to bear on both the modeling and the model fitting. The data model and the coherent noise model can be posited, and then, the least squares fit between the models and the actual data used to determine the coefficients. As an example, suppose that we use a lasso regression analysis and assume that the error is proportional to the square of the covariates. Then, our optimization process will be to minimize over β_0 the intercept, the vector β of the covariate coefficients, and the error coefficient η, using the following objective function (Eq. 4.14):

$$J = \min_{\beta_0, \beta, \eta} \left\{ \frac{1}{N_s} \sum_{i=1}^{N_s} \left(y_i - \beta_0 - x_i^T \beta - (x_i^T)^2 \eta \right)^2 \right\} \text{subject to } \|\beta\|_1 < threshold \qquad (4.14)$$

In addition to optimization concerns, we are also concerned with the stability of our model. In Chapter 2, we consider the sensitivity of the models to variations of the training data, including the prevalidation step and ignoring some of the classes to be supported when determining the configuration of the model. However, models are also sensitive to some pragmatic concerns, including its utility over time (a form of "robustness"), its utility when scale-up occurs, its utility when the algorithm is distributed (including to other languages and hardware platforms), and its reliability or its ability to make reasonable predictions even when exposed to data far from the training data (a second form of "robustness"). How are these four concerns addressed?

1. Utility over time can be addressed by assessing the drift in the data that the process/analytic system is meant to handle. This requires ground truth data to be organized based on time of creation, and a predictive model of when the data will drift far enough for the current system to satisfactorily handle the data can be gleaned. This is "introspective prediction" on the system itself.
2. Utility by scale is best addressed by "undertraining" the data. Ideally, this means using as small of a percentage of ground truth as possible (e.g., 2.5%–20% as in Ref. [Sims06]), so that a much larger percentage of the ground truth can be used for validation and/or testing. This generally leads to greater robustness to scaling.
3. Utility by distribution is a measure of how modular an approach is. For nearly any algorithmic task, there is domain specificity—for example, text algorithms are generally quite different from those used for extracting information from images, sensor information, etc. Domain specificity is not, therefore, a sign of a nonmodular approach. However, high sensitivity to context shifts (such as moving to a different but related language or moving from one camera to another) is indicators that an analytic approach is overfitted to its task. This may be acceptable for a high-value, high-security, etc. process, but it should be understood that the approach is likely not generalizable.
4. Utility by reliability can be tested by specific apportionment of training data. Training and validation sets that are not highly correlated can be used to test the reliability of the analytic approach. This type of robustness is almost certainly not garnered when a k-fold cross validation is used to train and test the analytic approach.

4.5 Co-occurrence and similarity patterns

In natural language processing and other linguistic applications, *co-occurrence* refers to an above expected value of two terms occurring in a given sequence. Usually, this means an idiomatic expression along the lines of "sharp wit" or "meteoric rise," but it can also mean semantic proximity of the sequencing is a part of a list (e.g., the two terms are separated by commas). Similarity, on the other hand, is generally related to some form of distance metric, with more similar items being closer together. Similarity is, in this sense, a form of sharing, or mutual information. In the context of cluster analysis, similarity can be defined as the negative squared Euclidean distance [Frey07] or the familiar cosine of the angle between the vector representation of two items. Perhaps, the easiest measurement of similarity is the Jaccard similarity coefficient, which is the sum of the ratios of minimum(x_i, y_i)/maximum(x_i, y_i) for all (x_i, y_i) pairs over the domain of i.

Analytic patterns focused on co-occurrence, and similarity is, not surprisingly, useful for relatively mature analytic problems when consensus rather than discovery is needed. Voting and weighted voting patterns use similarity among analytic approaches and the central limit theorem to help ensure that the correct answer is sufficiently highly ranked. In a search, this might be advantageous to ensure that the best URL to send the querying person to is generally present in a small subset of possible outcomes.

I provide one example of this in Table 4.7, which is based on the same data set as in Table 4.6 (12 classes of 49 test samples each). Here, the broad impact of combining analytics that are based on co-occurrence (in this case, the co-occurrence of relatively rare terms) and similarity (here, smaller cosines for vectors of the relatively rare terms) is shown: the impact of additional analytics in a weighted voting scheme has a larger effect on ranking than on accuracy.

In Table 4.7, accuracy is the percentage of documents assigned to the correct class, while ranking is the mean rank of the correct class. For example, if three documents belonging to the "travel" class had "travel" as their first, fourth, and third highest weighted classes, then the mean rank is $(1+4+3)/3 = 2.67$. Thus, ensemble methods and particularly those based on co-occurrence and/or similarity tend to move the correct answer higher in the overall ranked list (*rank*) more so than simply moving the correct result to the top of the list (*accuracy*). In terms of system design theory (see Chapter 10 for more on this and related topics), this means co-occurrence and similarity-based ensemble approaches are *rank-biased systems*, not *accuracy-biased systems*.

Table 4.7 Accuracy and rank of correct answer when 1, 2, 3, 4, or 5 algorithms are used in a 12-class document classification problem [Vans17], using weighted voting for overall consensus. Note the relatively much larger impact on rank compared with accuracy.

Number of analytics combined	1	2	3	4	5
Accuracy	0.391	0.464	0.505	0.526	0.534
Mean rank of correct class	3.54	2.67	2.36	2.07	1.78
Percentage accuracy improvement (percentage of error reduced from 1 analytic)	N/A	0.120	0.187	0.222	0.235
Percentage rank improvement (percentage of distance to 1.0 from 1 analytic)	N/A	0.343	0.465	0.579	0.693

With five analytics combined, the rank has improved by 69.3%, and the accuracy has improved by 23.5% (i.e., the error rate is reduced 23.5%) when compared with the original, highest-accuracy analytic.

4.6 **Sensitivity analysis patterns**

Sensitivity analysis is an underappreciated part of any analytics—let alone meta-analytics—project. Without sensitivity analysis, we generally resort to less satisfying means of gauging the robustness of a system, such as k-fold cross validation and other methods that may result in overtraining. In addition to avoiding such mistakes, sensitivity analysis provides significant positive advantages. One of these is that sensitivity analysis allows us to more carefully define the metrology necessary for inspecting the interfaces between components of a modular, large-scale system.

The simplest sensitivity analysis pattern is the sensitivity-driven ensemble selection pattern, which consists of the following steps:

1. Identify and, as possible, rank the factors in the system based on the relative magnitude of the partial derivatives of the factors in the region of interest, that is, $\left\|\frac{\partial y}{\partial x}\right\| / \|y\|$.
2. Determine the appropriate coefficients of determination for the behavior of these factors in the region of interest.
3. Multiply the outputs of (1) and (2) to get a weighted significance coefficient for each factor.
4. Create a pool of algorithms for the ensemble with the representation of factors in the algorithms proportional to the relative weighted significance coefficient of each factor.
5. Deploy the ensemble and perform ensemble operations (boosting, bagging, etc.).

The sensitivity-driven ensemble selection pattern, therefore, proceeds with traditional ensemble techniques once the factors are identified, ranked, and relatively weighted.

A second sensitivity analysis pattern worth noting in this brief section is the sensitivity-driven dimensionality reduction pattern. Fundamentally, this is a feature selection, not a feature extraction, form of dimensionality reduction. Up front, we evaluate the relative sensitivity of each feature, y, to variation in the input, as above given by $\left\|\frac{\partial y}{\partial x}\right\| / \|y\|$. Alternatively, we can use the magnitude of the range of y or the standard deviation of y rather than the norm $\|y\|$. Since this is a book on meta-analytics, why not try all three—norm of y, range of y, and standard deviation of y—and combine the results using weighted voting? Regardless, the features are then ranked in order, and we can remove the lowest-weighted features in order up to 5%, 10%, 20%, etc. of the overall sum of $\left\|\frac{\partial y}{\partial x}\right\| / \|y\|$ when computed for all dependent variables y.

4.7 **Confusion matrix patterns**

Confusion matrices are extremely powerful shorthand mechanisms for what I call "analytic triage." As described in Chapter 2, confusion matrices illustrate how samples belonging to a single topic, cluster, or class (rows in the matrix) are assigned to the plurality of possible topics, clusters, or classes.

My preferred use of confusion matrices is in *balanced* and *normalized* form. The "balanced" term means that each class, cluster, or topic has the same number of

Table 4.8 Example confusion matrix for a five-class problem, with the sums in each row and column given.

↓Actual class \assigned class→	A	B	C	D	E	SUMS
A	0.54	0.06	0.21	0.09	0.10	1.00
B	0.05	0.62	0.12	0.18	0.03	1.00
C	0.17	0.04	0.55	0.11	0.13	1.00
D	0.08	0.22	0.03	0.63	0.04	1.00
E	0.07	0.05	0.09	0.05	0.74	1.00
SUMS	0.91	0.99	1.00	1.06	1.04	5.00
PRECISION p (e.g., 0.54/0.91)	0.593	0.626	0.550	0.594	0.712	0.615
F-score$=2pr/(p+r)$	0.565	0.623	0.550	0.611	0.726	0.615

The columns sum the samples assigned to each class, and the diagonal elements divided by these sums are the precision values. The diagonal elements represent the recall values. The harmonic mean of precision and recall, or F-value, is shown in the lowest row. The mean recall is 0.616, and the mean precision and F-score are 0.615 each.

samples. The "normalized" term means that each of these groupings is represented as having 1.00 samples. Thus, the sum of each row in a balanced and normalized confusion matrix is 1.00, because each row sum represents 100% of the elements in a particular topic, cluster, or class. The column sums may deviate appreciably from 1.00 depending on whether a topic, cluster, or class is an attractor (more samples than expected are assigned to this class) or a repeller (less samples than expected are assigned to this class), as described in Chapter 2.

In Table 4.8, a data set for distinguishing between five different spoken vowel sounds using an automatic speech recognition (ASR) engine is shown in balanced, normalized form.

In this data set, there are no strong attractors or repellers, though Class D is the strongest net attractor with 6% above expected value of samples assigned to it, and Class A is the strongest repeller with 9% less samples assigned to it than expected. There are other important insights that come from exploring Table 4.8. For example, based on the off-diagonal elements of the matrix, we can see that the pairs (A, C) and (B, D) are more closely related to each other than the other three classes. For example, Classes A and C have greater "within pair" confusion (0.21 and 0.17, mean=0.19) than "outside pair" confusion (0.06, 0.09, 0.10, 0.04, 0.11, and 0.13, mean=0.09), meaning this pair is a good candidate to be "pulled out" from the larger set of classes and focused on for a binary classifier. A similar recommendation can be made for the pair of Classes B and D, for which "within pair" confusion has a mean of 0.20 and the "outside pair" confusion has a mean of only 0.06. The ratio of (within pair)/(outside pair) is a good metric for deciding which binary classifier to pursue first. The 3.3 ratio for B and D is the highest one for the confusion matrix of Table 4.8.

This section gives a flavor of how confusion matrices can be used to evaluate large topic identification, clustering, and classification training sets and recommends system deployment attributes. More on how confusion matrices can be employed for triage will be covered in later chapters and in particular with respect to multipath predictive selection in Chapter 6.

4.8 **Entropy patterns**

Entropy is such an important topic that is discussed in many sections, including Section 4.3.1 (decision trees and information gain), Section 4.4.1 (hybrid regression), and Section 4.4.2 (modeling and model fitting). Entropy-based patterns thus are not as specific as many of the other pattern types discussed in this book. Entropy is, rather, another tool like the confusion matrix (see the previous section) that should be used whenever possible to validate that an analytic approach is indeed "removing the personality" from a set of data.

In Chapter 11, a deeper consideration of both "aleatory" and "expert system" techniques is tendered. Here, the two related approaches are introduced and the meta-analytic patterns associated with them considered in shallow depth. I begin with "aleatory" techniques, which mean, according to the definition of the term, techniques that depend on one or more contingencies, that is, techniques that depend on luck (usually bad luck).

Therefore, an aleatory pattern is one that is immune to or at least relatively buffered from random events. Aleatory approaches are designed to be optimized for robustness to the failure of individual parts. In the context of meta-analytics, this means *optimized insensitivity* to the removal of a single element of a multicomponent system or ensemble. Conceptually, this is the converse of typical "forward optimization," wherein we add more and more algorithms (e.g., in an ensemble approach such as bagging or boosting) until no further addition improves the metric for the analytic. For aleatory techniques, metrics are *removed* until significant sensitivity to further removal is encountered.

In order to assess optimized insensitivity, we perform the following tasks, which when combined designate the *sequential removal of feature aleatory pattern*:

1. Identify the elements—for example, features or labels—which are candidates for removal.
2. Construct the appropriate instrument for analysis.
3. Complete the fields in the instrument.
4. Make the final recommendation and deploy the recommended analytic system.

One simple example is given here, taken from an image authentication application I wrote to distinguish authentic from counterfeit images. Originally, 12 image features—red, green, blue, cyan, yellow, and magenta saturation and, separately, intensity—were used as image features. These are abbreviated RS, GS, BS, CS, YS, MS, RI, GI, BI, CI, YI, and MI in the discussion that follows. Each of these features is used individually for binary classification of an image as coming from an authentic versus counterfeit product. The classification accuracies range from 0.55 for blue saturation (BS, just above "guessing" value of 0.50) to 0.90 for green intensity (GI, 9 out of 10 samples correctly classified). These values are cataloged in Table 4.9.

Table 4.9 Twelve image features (R=red, G=green, B=blue, C=cyan, M=magenta, Y=yellow, S=saturation, and I=intensity) and the accuracy when each image features is the sole feature used in the binary classification problem (authentic vs. counterfeit).

Image feature	RS	GS	BS	CS	MS	YS	RI	GI	BI	CI	MI	YI
Accuracy	0.71	0.77	0.55	0.62	0.76	0.87	0.83	0.90	0.67	0.65	0.74	0.78

Based on the results of Table 4.9, there are four values (BS, CS, CI, and BI) that are lower than the other eight values and are good candidates for removal. Regardless, the features can now be individually ranked, and so, Step (1) is complete. The appropriate instrument for analysis (Step 2) is to then sequentially remove the features and observe the behavior (Step 3). This is shown in Table 4.10.

In Table 4.10, a simple linear analytic instrument (sequential removal of the lowest-ranked remaining feature) is used. In this case, removing the four lowest-accuracy features did result in peak accuracy when the features are combined using weighted voting, in this case with the weighting of feature j proportional to the inverse of the error, that is, $1.0 - a_j$ where a_j is the accuracy of feature j by itself, as shown in Eq. (4.15):

$$W_j = \frac{1.0 / (1.0 - a_j)}{\sum_{i=1}^{nclasses} 1.0 / (1.0 - a_j)} \tag{4.15}$$

The final recommendation (Step 4) is to deploy the binary classification system with only 8 of the 12 features, namely, RS, GS, YS, MS, RI, GI, YI, and MI. This example is incredibly simple, and in general, multiple sequences for removal would be

Table 4.10 Results when the least accurate features are removed in reverse-ranked order.

Features removed	Overall accuracy (weighted voting)
BS	0.954
BS+CS	0.957
BS+CS+CI	0.962
BS+CS+CI+BI	0.963
BS+CS+CI+BI+RS	0.960
BS+CS+CI+BI+RS+MI	0.951
BS+CS+CI+BI+RS+MI+MS	0.941

The overall accuracy peaks when the four lowest-accuracy features (BS+CS+CI+BI) are removed. After that, accuracy decreases when additional features are removed.

attempted, especially around the peak accuracy; four reasonable candidates are the following (with their accuracies in parentheses):

1. BS+CS+BI (0.963)
2. BS+CS+BI+RS (0.962)
3. BS+CS+CI+RS (0.964)
4. BS+CS+CI+BI+MI (0.961)

Note that in this example, removing the combination "BS+CS+CI+RS" gives the highest overall accuracy. In reality, the training results are not very sensitive after the removal of BS and CS to the next four lowest-ranked features in accuracy. More on the sensitivity to features, including noting discrepancies in ordering when comparing individual with aggregate results, is covered in Chapter 11.

A second aleatory pattern is also of interest here. This second aleatory pattern is designated the *sequential variation of feature output aleatory pattern*. Applying this pattern, the results of each of the features are varied by a predetermined amount and the effect on overall accuracy (aggregated or broken out into a confusion matrix or other comprehensive analysis instrument) cataloged. The features with larger impact on the overall accuracy may be increased in relative rank, especially if the ranking is used subsequently on a pattern such as the *sequential removal of feature aleatory pattern*. The output of the *sequential variation of feature output aleatory pattern* is a table of sensitivities.

Turning now to expert system techniques, our concern is on validating the domain expertise by calculating the effect of applying it on overall system measurements such as entropy, accuracy, robustness, cost, performance, and other system optimizations of interest. Importantly, for expert system patterns—just as with sensitivity analysis and aleatory patterns described earlier in this chapter—the underlying assumption is that there is considerable value to be gained by keeping the descriptive original variables or "observations" as part of the final deployment. That is, we use feature selection, not feature extraction, for dimensionality reduction.

The primary concern of an expert system is internalizing the decision-making algorithm, which usually includes an inference engine and a knowledge base or rule engine. For meta-analytics, one important concern is in properly considering the input from multiple analyses. For expert systems—and in particular when these expert systems include domain expertise distilled as a set of rules—how do we best incorporate the natural "interrupts" that are immediate and natural for a human expert? I argue that perhaps the easiest way to implement this is to use John Rawls' "veil of ignorance" [Rawl71], based on John Locke's state of nature, as applied to the algorithms we have available.

With a veil of ignorance, all algorithms are considered equal until they prove themselves otherwise. A good meta-analytic pattern for this "agnostic" approach to algorithms is the predictive selection pattern, a variant of which is given in Fig. 2.2. The predictive selection pattern assigns a particular observation to one or more categories from a set of categories on which data are trained. One drawback of the predictive selection algorithm is that the categories are defined in advance (i.e., before the training phase). For an expert system, however, the interrupt may occur under a context that is not anticipated by the training. For example, the image classification example described in this section involves identifying counterfeit samples. A rule defining a counterfeit sample is quite likely to be discovered after training; for example, a counterfeiter may misspell a word (or, more typically, spell a word correctly that the brand owner had intentionally misspelled on the legitimate product label). Then, this rule is an "interrupt" or "override" to the system, irrespective of the training set. However, from the veil of ignorance standpoint, this rule can be readily brought into the system if in fact it is highly accurate. The veil of ignorance therefore equates training with posttraining interrupt, allowing only the accuracy of a decision to drive its future relevance. Such a system is therefore a *continually learning system*. Given this perspective, expert system pattern is therefore one in which training and interrupting are both relevant to the system decision.

4.9 Independence pattern

Closely related to entropy patterns, independence patterns are concerned with "scrubbing away" the personality of data until all of the paths through the data are independent. From a statistical standpoint, independence is given by the formula Eq. (4.16):

$$p\left(\bigcap_{n=1}^{N_P} E_n\right) = \prod_{n=1}^{N_P} p(E_n) \tag{4.16}$$

where N_P is the number of possible events, E_n is event n of the N_P possible events, and $p(E_n)$ is the probability that event n occurs. Thus, the probability that any number of events will occur simultaneously is simply the individual event probabilities multiplied together. Let us now consider the total probabilities when there are three events and four events, generalize this to N_P events, and then consider this in light of confusion matrices.

Three events: Here, we consider three events, A, B, and C. The set of probabilities for an event A with probability of occurring $p(A)=0.6$, an event B with probability of occurring $p(B)=0.7$, and an event C with probability of occurring $p(C)=0.8$ is given by the following set, where $p(\overline{X})$ means the probability of event X not occurring:

$$p(A) = p(A)p(B)p(C) + p(A)p(B)p(\overline{C}) + p(A)p(\overline{B})p(C) + p(A)p(\overline{B})p(\overline{C})$$

$$p(B) = p(A)p(B)p(C) + p(A)p(B)p(\overline{C}) + p(\overline{A})p(B)p(C) + p(\overline{A})p(B)p(\overline{C})$$

$$p(C) = p(A)p(B)p(C) + p(A)p(\overline{B})p(C) + p(\overline{A})p(B)p(C) + p(\overline{A})p(\overline{B})p(C)$$

The total probability $p(A)+p(B)+p(C)$, therefore, is given by the following:

$$p(A)+p(B)+p(C) = 3p(A)p(B)p(C)+2p(A)p(B)p(\overline{C})+2p(A)p(\overline{B})p(C)$$

$$+2p(\overline{A})p(B)p(C)+p(A)p(\overline{B})p(\overline{C})+p(\overline{A})p(B)p(\overline{C})+p(\overline{A})p(\overline{B})p(C) \qquad (4.17)$$

Plugging in $p(A)=0.6$, $p(B)=0.7$, and $p(C)=0.8$, we get the following:

$$p(A)+p(B)+p(C) = 3(0.6)(0.7)(0.8)+2(0.4)(0.7)(0.2)+2(0.6)(0.3)(0.8)$$

$$+2(0.4)(0.7)(0.8)+(0.6)(0.3)(0.2)+(0.4)(0.7)(0.2)+(0.4)(0.3)(0.8)=2.1, \text{as it must}$$

Four events: Here, we consider four events, A, B, C, and D. As for the three event case above, the value $p(\overline{X})$ means the probability of event X not occurring:

$$p(A) = p(A)p(B)p(C)p(D)+p(A)p(B)p(C)p(\overline{D})+p(A)p(B)p(\overline{C})p(D)$$

$$+p(A)p(\overline{B})p(C)p(D)+p(A)p(B)p(\overline{C})p(\overline{D})+p(A)p(\overline{B})p(C)p(\overline{D})$$

$$+p(A)p(\overline{B})p(\overline{C})p(D)+p(A)p(\overline{B})p(\overline{C})p(\overline{D})$$

$$p(B) = p(A)p(B)p(C)p(D)+p(A)p(B)p(C)p(\overline{D})+p(A)p(B)p(\overline{C})p(D)$$

$$+p(\overline{A})p(B)p(C)p(D)+p(A)p(B)p(\overline{C})p(\overline{D})+p(\overline{A})p(B)p(C)p(\overline{D})$$

$$+p(\overline{A})p(B)p(\overline{C})p(D)+p(\overline{A})p(B)p(\overline{C})p(\overline{D})$$

$$p(C) = p(A)p(B)p(C)p(D)+p(A)p(B)p(C)p(\overline{D})+p(A)p(\overline{B})p(C)p(D)$$

$$+p(\overline{A})p(B)p(C)p(D)+p(A)p(\overline{B})p(C)p(\overline{D})+p(\overline{A})p(B)p(C)p(\overline{D})$$

$$+p(\overline{A})p(\overline{B})p(C)p(D)+p(\overline{A})p(\overline{B})p(C)p(\overline{D})$$

$$p(D) = p(A)p(B)p(C)p(D)+p(A)p(B)p(\overline{C})p(D)+p(A)p(\overline{B})p(C)p(D)$$

$$+p(\overline{A})p(B)p(C)p(D)+p(A)p(\overline{B})p(\overline{C})p(D)+p(\overline{A})p(B)p(\overline{C})p(D)$$

$$+p(\overline{A})p(\overline{B})p(C)p(D)+p(\overline{A})p(\overline{B})p(\overline{C})p(D)$$

The total probability $p(A)+p(B)+p(C)+p(D)$, therefore, is given by the following:

$$p(A)+p(B)+p(C)+p(D) = 4p(A)p(B)p(C)p(D)+3p(A)p(B)p(C)p(\overline{D})$$

$$+3p(A)p(B)p(\overline{C})p(D)+3p(A)p(\overline{B})p(C)p(D)+3p(\overline{A})p(B)p(C)p(D)$$

$$+2p(A)p(B)p(\overline{C})p(\overline{D})+2p(A)p(\overline{B})p(C)p(\overline{D})+2p(A)p(\overline{B})p(\overline{C})p(D)$$

$$+2p(\overline{A})p(B)p(C)p(\overline{D})+2p(\overline{A})p(B)p(\overline{C})p(D)+2p(\overline{A})p(\overline{B})p(C)p(D)$$

$$+p(A)p(\overline{B})p(\overline{C})p(\overline{D})+p(\overline{A})p(B)p(\overline{C})p(\overline{D})+p(\overline{A})p(\overline{B})p(C)p(\overline{D})+p(\overline{A})p(\overline{B})p(\overline{C})p(D)$$

$$(4.18)$$

Any number of events: Here, we consider N events. Interestingly, for N events, the sum of all individual probabilities $\sum_{n=1}^{N_P} p(i)$ is equal to Eq. (4.19):

$$N_P \prod_{n=1}^{N_P} p(i) + (N_P - 1) \sum_* \prod_{n=1}^{N_P} [(N_P - 1)p(*) + (1)\overline{p}(*)] + \ldots + (2) \sum \prod_{n=1}^{N_P} [(2)p(*)$$

$$+ (N_P - 2)\overline{p}(*)] + (1) \sum \prod_{n=1}^{N_P} [(1)p(*) + (N_P - 1)\overline{p}(*)] \tag{4.19}$$

where (*) indicates any set of $1 \ldots N_P$ combinations that gives the current iteration n a total of $(N_P - n)$ probabilities of occurring $p(*)$ and, simultaneously, n probabilities of not occurring $\overline{p}(*)$—for example, $(N_P - n)=1$ and $n=3$ for a term such as $p(A)p(\overline{B})p(\overline{C})p(\overline{D})$ or $p(\overline{A})p(B)p(\overline{C})p(\overline{D})$.

Application to Confusion Matrices: This sum (Eq. 4.19) gives us the overall system accuracy if the probabilities $p(*)$ are the accuracies of individual classes, rather than events. That is, the sums in Eqs. (4.17), (4.18), and (4.19), when applied to confusion matrices, are actually the sum of the diagonal of the confusion matrix. The overall classification accuracy is then simply this sum divided by the number of events. To provide an example, a 3×3 confusion matrix is given in Table 4.11. The accuracies for the three classes are $p(A)=0.6$, $p(B)=0.7$, and $p(C)=0.8$.

For Table 4.11, the off-diagonal elements are similar when comparing Classes A and B and Classes B and C. The two elements for comparing Classes A and C, however, differ largely (0.18 and 0.06).

Using independence theory, we provide the initial off-diagonal values for this confusion matrix in Table 4.12. Moving across row X, the probability for the

Table 4.11 Sample 3×3 confusion matrix to illustrate the application of probabilistic independence concepts to overall system accuracy.

↓Actual class\assigned class→	A	B	C	SUMS
A	0.60	0.22	0.18	1.00
B	0.19	0.70	0.11	1.00
C	0.06	0.14	0.80	1.00
SUMS	0.85	1.06	1.09	3.00

Table 4.12 Sample confusion matrix of Table 4.11 with initial off-diagonals per the accuracy of the individual Classifiers A, B, and C. See text for mathematical details.

↓Actual class\assigned class→	A	B	C
A	$p(A)$	$p(\overline{A})p(B)$	$p(\overline{A})p(C)$
B	$p(A)p(\overline{B})$	$p(B)$	$p(\overline{B})p(C)$
C	$p(A)p(\overline{C})$	$p(B)p(\overline{C})$	$p(C)$

diagonal element is $p(X)$, and for every other element, it is $p(\bar{X})$ multiplied by the probability of the corresponding column's diagonal element. The numerical values corresponding to Tables 4.11 and 4.12 are given in Table 4.13.

However, the values in Table 4.13 are not correct, since the rows do not sum to 1.00. Thus, we normalize every row Y by the following normalization factor, Eq. (4.20):

$$CME_{Y \neq X}[X, Y] = p(\bar{Y}) \left[\frac{p(\bar{Y})p(X)}{\sum_{i=1, i \neq Y}^{N_{classes}} p(\bar{Y})p(i)} \right] \qquad (4.20)$$

The CME is the confusion matrix entry (X, Y) anywhere but along the diagonal (thus, $Y \neq X$). Essentially, every off-diagonal element is initially (1.0-the accuracy of the row's class, or $(\bar{Y})$) multiplied by the accuracy of the column's class as in Table 4.12 (theory) and Table 4.13 (example). Then, the sums of the off-diagonal elements are used to normalize these values, and the normalized values are multiplied by $p(\bar{Y})$ so that the sum of the off-diagonals plus the row's class accuracy—that is, $p(Y)$—sum to 1.0 as must be the case for a normalized confusion matrix. The results of this normalization are shown in Table 4.14.

The actual and independence-optimal off-diagonal elements are compared in Table 4.15. The mean difference is 0.042 in magnitude, which is 28% of the mean

Table 4.13 Sample confusion matrix of Table 4.11 with initial off-diagonals per the accuracy of the individual Classes A, B, and C.

↓Actual class\assigned class→	A	B	C	SUMS
A	0.60	0.28	0.32	1.20
B	0.18	0.70	0.24	1.12
C	0.12	0.14	0.80	1.06
SUMS	0.90	1.12	1.36	3.38

See text for mathematical details

Table 4.14 Sample confusion matrix of Table 4.11 with independence-optimal off-diagonals per the accuracy of the individual Classifiers A, B, and C.

↓Actual class\assigned class→	A	B	C	SUMS
A	0.600	0.187	0.213	1.000
B	0.129	0.700	0.171	1.000
C	0.092	0.108	0.800	1.000
SUMS	0.821	0.995	1.184	3.000

See text for mathematical details.

Table 4.15 Actual confusion matrix elements (Table 4.11) minus the independence-optimal elements of Table 4.14 and their value as a percentage of the optimal value (in parentheses).

↓Actual class\assigned class→	A	B	C
A	0	0.033 (17.6%)	−0.033 (−15.5%)
B	0.061 (47.3%)	0	−0.061 (−35.7%)
C	−0.032 (−34.8%)	0.032 (29.6%)	0

off-diagonal element. This means that 28% of the maximum possible personality in the confusion matrices is still present.

Thus, we have seen how to use the independence-optimized confusion matrix in comparison with the empirical confusion matrix for purposes of determining how much "personality" is left to extract from the confusion matrix. The mean of the off-diagonal magnitudes is, of course, a reflection of the overall error rate of the confusion matrix. The mean percentage "personality" remaining (difference between empirical and independence-optimal confusion matrix) is a reflection of how much more information can be extracted from the overall classification approach. Once all the personality is removed (and the empirical and independence-optimal confusion matrices are nearly equivalent), the overall system has reached its maximum accuracy.

4.10 Functional NLP patterns (macro-feedback)

Functional natural language processing (NLP) is based on linear system theory. At the simplest level, we feedback success in one process to optimize a related but usually largely independent process. One tangible example of this was given in an earlier report, albeit on a small scale rather than large scale [Sims14]. There, the best translation approach was considered the one that provided search behavior most closely matching that of the corpus of original (untranslated) documents, as mentioned in Chapter 2. More generally, one NLP task—be it summarization, indexing, translation, keyword generation, text clustering, text classification, most closely related document, search, or tagging—can be optimized by using another one of these (or other or multiple) analytic tasks as the validation set.

Chapter 8 considers a different class of functional NLP patterns (synonym-antonym and reinforce-void), which are based on term occurrence statistics. The feedback for these patterns is the relative occurrence of the terms before and after specific operations are performed on the documents containing the terms. The names are included here for "list of patterns" completeness in this largely overview chapter.

4.11 Summary

This chapter introduces the main themes of the meta-analytic approaches, which will be elaborated in greater detail in the remaining 10 chapters. Stepping back for a broader perspective, this chapter focuses on the process of removing what is informally termed "personality" from data—be it raw data or cumulative data such as represented by a confusion matrix.

For cumulative response curves (CRCs), our focus was on aligning two or more CRCs to enable identification of specific zones of interest for sequence-dependent predictive selection, which relies on sorted differential-conditional CRCs, or SD-CCRCs. It is shown that the start and end zones of the SD-CCRC are especially useful to mine for predictors. We then saw that the traditional cumulative gain curve (CGC), or lift curve, is a highly convenient means of illustrating classification error, precision, recall, and accuracy with any percentage of the samples assigned to a particular class.

Optimization of decision trees was driven by the maximum information gain (Eq. 4.8), and an optimization application focused on biometrics was used to illustrate the approach. The number of possible biometrics is relatively small, but the number of meta-analytic approaches that can use these biometrics is shown to be very large. Sequencing, weighted linear combinations, and predictive selection pre-clustering approaches are shown to provide the possibility for billions of customized analytics, even when only 10 biometrics are used. This underpins a different type of information gain, where we measure the relative ability of a custom pattern compared with a generic pattern at identifying an individual from a (potentially quite large) set of nonindividuals. Here, the custom biometric approach and weighting can be thought of as the individual's public key and their response to it a form of private key. Next, expectation-maximization (or expectation-optimization) approaches were considered. Principles of evolutionary approaches were incorporated into an iterative optimization approach (Fig. 4.15), and its applicability to text clustering is described. Rapid convergence on a set of relatively difficult to classify text classes was shown.

Next, model agreement patterns were discussed. Residual entropy was discussed in context of removing the personality from a data set, and adding a noise model was used to extend the value—and universality—of regression approaches such as lasso (Eq. 4.14). Robustness through the utility of a regression approach to temporal, scaling, distribution, and reliability parameters was discussed.

Co-occurrence and similarity algorithms, like meta-algorithms [Sims13], are expected in general to have a more pronounced effect on ranking of the correct class than on accuracy of classification. An example illustrating this was given in Table 4.7. This introduced the topic of system design theory, to be elaborated later in the book (and in particular in Chapter 10), and co-occurrence and similarity-based ensemble approaches are described as *rank-biased systems*, not *accuracy-biased systems*.

Sensitivity analysis started with the relatively rudimentary sensitivity-driven ensemble selection pattern, which uses the partial derivative and a confidence weighting for each factor to create a weighted significance coefficient for each factor. These coefficients are used to drive ensemble methods such as boosting, bagging, or even weighted voting. A second pattern, the sensitivity-driven dimensionality reduction pattern, is shown to be a feature selection, not a feature extraction, form of dimensionality reduction: the features are ranked from first to last and can be pruned with high confidence that the order matches the order of linear combination of features typical of a feature extraction dimensionality reduction approach.

Confusion matrix approaches are revisited briefly, summing up attractor/repeller theory and comparing "within pair" and "outside pair" confusion to be able to target dimensionality reduction through the replacement of two classes with a binary classifier that follows a one-dimensional reduced classification.

Entropy is an important topic throughout analytics, but in Section 4.9, we introduce aleatory approaches—that is, approaches that are as insensitive as possible to errors in individual parts of the analysis. We term this *optimized insensitivity* and provide sequential removal of features by two different means, allowing us to perform a reasonable level of dimensionality reduction while also identifying likely correlations among features. A second aleatory approach, the *sequential variation of feature output aleatory pattern*, purposely introduces error to see what the system insensitivity to errors of each feature is. An expert system approach using a "veil of ignorance" to weight both features and rules together without knowledge of their origin is introduced.

The chapter concludes with a description of independence in probability theory and its direct application to confusion matrices (Eq. 4.20). This section shows that the end point in using confusion matrices is not necessarily to maximize overall accuracy, but rather to minimize the difference between the off-diagonal elements from their independence-optimal values (i.e., those values predicted by independence).

Finally, functional natural language processing (NLP) techniques are introduced to show how broad domains can be used to create separate functional gains (e.g., search and translation) to be used together to optimize over analytic performance. This approach can be thought of as a form of expectation-optimization at the macro level.

With this important framing chapter completed, we now turn our attention to sensitivity analysis and big systems engineering, which frames the use of meta-analytics in deployed systems.

References

[Frey07] Frey, B.J., Dueck, D., 2007. Clustering by passing messages between data points. Science 315 (5814), 972–976.

[Hast09] Hastie, T., Tibshirani, R., Friedman, J., 2009. The Elements of Statistical Learning, ed. Springer, pp. 337–387.

[Mars09] Marsland, S., 2009. Machine Learning. Chapman & Hall/CRC, Boca Raton FL 390 p.

[Prov13] Provost, F., Fawcett, T., 2013. Data Science for Business. O'Reilly Media, Inc., Sebastopol, CA.

[Rawl71] Rawls, J., 1971. A Theory of Justice. Belknap (Harvard University Press), Cambridge MA 560 p.

[Sims06] Simske, S.J., Wright, D.W., Sturgill, M., 2006. Meta-algorithmic systems for document classification. In: ACM DocEng 2006, pp. 98–106.

[Sims13] Simske, S., 2013. Meta-Algorithmics: Patterns for Robust, Low-Cost, High-Quality Systems. IEEE Press and Wiley, Singapore.

[Sims14] Simske, S.J., Boyko, I.M., Koutrika, G., 2014. Multi-engine search and language translation. In: EDBT/ICDT Workshops, pp. 188–190.

[Vans17] Vans, A.M., Simske, S.J., 2017. Identifying top performing TF*IDF classifiers using the CNN corpus. In: Society for Imaging Science and Technology Archiving 2017 Final Program and Proceedings, pp. 105–115.

Sensitivity analysis and big system engineering

Beauty of whatever kind, in its supreme development, invariably excites the sensitive soul to tears
Edgar Allan Poe (1846)
Manhood coerced into sensitivity is no manhood at all
Camille Paglia (1992)

5.1 Introduction

If you've made it this far and have been reading from the beginning, there is some good news. You've now covered enough to be confident, conversant, and even congruent when speaking to other analytic experts. The first four chapters were, in effect, the first half of the book and were intended to get the fundamentals of analytics across, albeit hopefully in a novel and more expansive manner than do comparative analytics texts.

The "second half" of this book focuses on incorporating important system level and/or novel approaches to the field of analytics. In so doing, meta-analytic systems are created. Another key focus in this chapter and Chapters 6–14 is their applications. We begin this half of the book with a consideration of how sensitivity analysis approaches can be employed for analytics. Building on two patterns for incorporating sensitivity analysis techniques, we then extend them to a number of important areas in meta-analytics; specifically, settings for individual algorithms and for hybrid systems of multiple algorithms. In line with Edgar Allan Poe, we are hoping the beauty of hybrid systems will not only move the sensitive soul to tears but also move the system architect to consider employing sensitivity techniques more robustly in their analysis. In line with Camille Paglia, we feel that the system designer need not be coerced into using sensitivity analysis; however, it probably wouldn't hurt to appropriately justify it. As far as building analytics into the system from the ground up, then, "sensitivity analysis is considered … as a prerequisite for model building in any setting, be it diagnostic or prognostic, and in any field where models are used" [Salt04]. In Ref. [Salt04], they show that sensitivity analysis can and should be applied to a wide variety of analytic models and specifically to decomposing the variance of the output, in diagnostic modeling and in simulations.

In Chapter 4, we mentioned that sensitivity analysis is an underappreciated part of any analytics project. Sensitivity analysis can be applied directly to any of the "variables" in a system design, allowing a multilayered approach to assessing the

Meta-Analytics. https://doi.org/10.1016/B978-0-12-814623-1.00005-8

robustness of a system and avoiding such "overtraining" traps as k-fold cross validation, which is effectively testing on the training data. In k-fold validation, the training set is often 90% of the available data for training and testing ($k=10$), and the
testing results are reported on 10% of the data at a time. Unless the training and testing data are highly uncorrelated—and even if they were, why would they be for a
majority of the $k=10$-folds?—this is effectively reporting testing results on training
data (see Sections 1.10 and 1.11 for more on why this is not a good strategy).

This is the stick, but there is also a carrot: sensitivity analysis provides significant
positive advantages. Sensitivity analysis is one of the best ways to determine how
well a system comes together as a compound of its modules, by affording a mean
of assessing the interfaces between components of a modular, large-scale system.
In Chapter 4, we introduced the sensitivity-driven ensemble selection pattern, recapitulated here in light of the sensitivity:

1. First and foremost, sensitivity analysis is an assessment of the partial derivatives
   of the factors in the region of interest, that is, $\left\|\frac{\partial y}{\partial x}\right\|/\|y\|$, or the relative magnitude
   of the partial derivative compared with the norm of the dependent variable in a
   region. After computing these, we rank the factors in the system based on their
   relative magnitudes. Dividing the partial derivative by the norm of the variable
   removes the need to normalize each variable in the region.
2. Next, we determine the appropriate coefficients for the behavior of these factors
   in the region of interest. This means that we can weight each of the values
   $\left\|\frac{\partial y}{\partial x}\right\|/\|y\|$ by their contribution to error. This can be done by separately
   considering each factor as outlined in Section 1.11.
3. We can then multiply the outputs of (1) and (2) to get a weighted significance
   coefficient for each factor, implying this is the relative contribution of the factor
   to the overall (measured) system behavior.
4. Create a pool of algorithms for the ensemble with the overall coefficient for the
   algorithms proportional to the relatively weighted significance coefficient of
   each factor.
5. Deploy the ensemble and perform ensemble operations (boosting, bagging, etc.).
   In this way, the sensitivity-driven ensemble selection pattern proceeds with
   traditional ensemble techniques once the factors are identified, ranked, and
   relatively weighted.

A second sensitivity analysis pattern introduced in Chapter 4 was the sensitivity-
driven dimensionality reduction pattern. Here, the relative sensitivity of each feature,
y, to variation in the input, as above given by $\left\|\frac{\partial y}{\partial x}\right\|/\|y\|$, is evaluated first. Other
means of assessing the relative sensitivity are to use the magnitude of the range
of y, or the standard deviation of y, rather than the norm $\|y\|$. As mentioned previ-
ously, simultaneously employing the norm of y, the range of y, and the standard deviation of y and then combining the results using weighted voting are another way of
adding potential robustness to the solution. However weighted, the features are then
ranked in order, and we can remove the lowest-weighted features in order up to 5%,
10%, 20%, etc. of the overall sum of $\left\|\frac{\partial y}{\partial x}\right\|/\|y\|$ over all y. This last filtering step

allows us to remove any irrelevant attempts to add robustness, anyway. Thus, the combination of using a large array of features and then filtering is a useful design approach, in general.

In Chapter 3, we noted that sensitivity analysis typically focuses on a matrix of partial derivatives and/or conditional partial derivatives. We defined the "sensitivity" as the response of a system to an instantaneous change in a relevant part of its input. In particular, the sensitivity analysis of any model for the data is essential in modern system design (and should not be omitted). Suppose we have two models for fitting a set of data and their residual signals (the behavior of the data after subtracting out the model) are effectively equivalent. The two models are

$$\text{Model A, } \hat{y} = -4.68x^2 + 3.45x + 1.23 \tag{5.1}$$

$$\text{Model B, } \hat{y} = 7.45x^2 - 8.68x + 1.23 \tag{5.2}$$

Quick inspection shows that both models have the points (0.0, 1.23) and (1.0, 0.0) in common.

For sensitivity analysis, we find the partial derivatives (slopes) of these two simple models:

$$\text{Model A, } \frac{\partial \hat{y}}{\partial x} = -9.36x + 3.45 \tag{5.3}$$

$$\text{Model B, } \frac{\partial \hat{y}}{\partial x} = 14.90x - 8.68 \tag{5.4}$$

We see that Model A has a slope of 0 when $x = 0.369$ and Model B has a slope of 0 when $x = 0.583$. In general, though, we use a hybrid model, using Model A when

$$|-9.36x + 3.45| < |14.90x - 8.68| \tag{5.5}$$

This becomes three equations, based on the ranges in x:

$$-9.36x + 3.45 < 8.68 - 14.90x \; ; \; x = (-\infty, 0.369) \tag{5.6}$$

$$9.36x - 3.45 < 8.68 - 14.90x \; ; \; x = (0.369, 0.583) \tag{5.7}$$

$$9.36x - 3.45 < 14.90x - 8.68 \; ; \; x = (0.583, +\infty) \tag{5.8}$$

Rearranged, each of Eqs. (5.6), (5.7), and (5.8) becomes Eq. (5.9):

$$5.54x < 5.23 \text{ or } x < 0.944 \tag{5.9}$$

So, we use Model A whenever $x < 0.944$ and Model B whenever $x > 0.944$. As mentioned with a different example in Chapter 3, this provides us with a means to select multiple models for a domain. We can modify the coefficients of models so that there is smoothness (continuity) at the subdomain boundaries if desired. For example, we see that Model A has the value $y = 0.316$ when $x = 0.944$ and Model B has the value $y = -0.325$ when $x = 0.944$, and so, switching from Model A to Model B at $x = 0.944$ would result in a large discontinuity at $x = 0.944$. Therefore, we may provide some moving average of the two models, ending at $x = 1.0$ where they are equal and, due to symmetry, starting the same distance in front of $x = 0.944$ (i.e., at $x = 0.888$). This is a totally acceptable strategy, called "blending," and it reminds us that the goal to keep the sensitivity of the models to a minimum is only one aspect of the overall model. For example, if Eqs. (5.1) and (5.2) describe the cost of the system, we would be more concerned with accuracy than sensitivity per se.

5.2 Sensitivity analysis of the data set itself

In Section 3.4, the aging of data and statistical approaches to this important topic were overviewed. In this section, we address additional approaches to monitoring, augmenting, pruning, and otherwise maintaining throughout its life cycle the data that we use to define the model and its settings. We start off with a discussion of performing sensitivity analysis on the critical points for a classification feature selection procedure.

In Section 1.10, the concept of "critical points" between the means of two populations to be compared (for categorization, labeling, classification, and the like) was introduced. In that section, we simply rank ordered the means of the distributions and then computed the critical points to be between the consecutive means at the point that is the same number of standard deviations (usually a different value for each of the two populations) from the pair of means. If all populations have the same variance, then the critical points are simply the midpoints between the means. If there are N populations, this method defines $N-1$ critical points. This approach, however, is readily generalized to cover any additional comparisons. If, for example, critical points are defined between a population and the two closest populations to either side of it in ranked order, then there are $N-1$ critical points for the nearest neighbors and an additional $N-2$ critical points for the second-nearest neighbors. In the extreme, where critical points of all possible lengths up to $N-1$ are computed, there are a total of $N(N-1)/2$ critical points, or $\frac{1}{2}(N^2-N)$ critical points. This is Order(N^2) instead of the original Order(N).

So, in general, how do we decide how many critical points to define? One quantitative means of determining how many neighbors in each direction to compute critical points for is determinable by the ratio of the range of a single population to that of the set of all populations. Suppose that we have the following eight classes of training data, here defined by their means and standard deviations:

1. 45.7 ± 5.4
2. 56.8 ± 11.6
3. 65.4 ± 9.9
4. 66.9 ± 8.4
5. 72.7 ± 11.1
6. 73.4 ± 8.8
7. 81.6 ± 7.7
8. 83.2 ± 5.6

We see from this that the geometric mean of the standard deviation is the eighth root of the product $(5.4 \times 11.6 \times 9.9 \times 8.4 \times 11.1 \times 8.8 \times 7.7 \times 5.6) = 8.2$. The samples themselves span the range 40.3–89.3 (the total range being $89.3 - 40.3 = 49.0$) for mean $\pm$ standard deviation (note that the upper end is set by population 7 and not population 8, even though population 8 has a higher mean). The ratio is thus $8.2/49.0=0.167$, and so, the range of all the populations is roughly six times that of a single population. Note that we could have just as simply made this the ratio of 1.96 standard deviations (alpha=0.05), and the ratio would have been substantially different, that is, $16.1/(96.7-34.1)=0.257$. Here, the range of all populations is roughly four times that of a single population. In general, then, we set the number of neighbors for which to compute critical points based on the alpha level and the following algorithm:

1. Find the upper level of the combined set of populations as the maximum value of the (population mean)$+n_{alpha}\times$(population standard deviation) across all populations, where n_{alpha} is the number of standard deviations from the mean to obtain the desired alpha level of confidence in the mean, and this is 1.645 for alpha=0.10, 1.96 for alpha=0.05, 2.33 for alpha=0.02, and 2.58 for alpha=0.01 (two-tailed test). This is designated $Population_{UPPER}$.
2. Find the lower level of the combined set of populations as the minimum value of the (population mean)$-n_{alpha}\times$(population standard deviation) across all populations, where n_{alpha} is the number of standard deviations from the mean to obtain the desired alpha level of confidence in the mean, and this is 1.645 for alpha=0.10, 1.96 for alpha=0.05, 2.33 for alpha=0.02, and 2.58 for alpha=0.01 (two-tailed test). This is designated $Population_{LOWER}$.
3. Find the range of the overall set of populations$=Population_{UPPER}-Population_{LOWER}$.
4. Find the geometric mean of the range of the individual classes using the same probability alpha. This is simply n_{alpha} multiplied by the $N_{Classes}$-root of the product of all the class standard deviations. The value $N_{Classes}$ is the number of classes. For example, if n_{alpha} is 8, as in our example, then it is the eighth root of the product. This is the geometric mean of the standard deviation of the classes, or $GM(\sigma_{Classes})$.
5. Find the mean range of the classes$=2*GM(\sigma_{Classes})$.
6. Calculate the mean overlap ratio$=MOR=(Population_{UPPER}-Population_{LOWER})/2*GM(\sigma_{Classes})$.
7. Set the number of neighbors to either side as $N_{Classes}/MOR$. Round up to the nearest integer.

In the example given, MOR is the inverse of the 0.257 value computed for alpha=0.05. Thus, $MOR=3.89$, and the ratio of $8/3.89=2.06$. We could round this up to three, in which case we define $7+6+5=18$ critical points. However, using 2 instead of 3 neighbors, we have $7+6=13$ critical points, which would probably work just as well. The main utility of the critical points, of course, is to comparatively assess features, and so, we can also adjust the number of nearest neighbors based on the size of the data set, the absolute number of classes, and the percentage of overlap between classes. Regardless, the seven-step algorithm given here will work well. We now turn our attention to other aspects of data set sensitivity analysis.

Characterizing the critical points gives us some preliminary insight into the nature of the ground truth, or training data, at hand. One aspect of meta-analytics is to go beyond the normal treatment of ground truth associated with regular analytics. The cumulative data set should be used to determine if data should be retired (age-based pruning), augmented (underrepresentation imputation of ground truth), or destabilized. Age-based pruning was covered in Section 3.4. Augmentation is simple enough. Underrepresented clusters, categories, or classes of data can have additional samples added directly (through the targeted collection of more samples) or indirectly (through simulation). Destabilization, however, merits a slightly deeper discussion.

Why do we want to "destabilize" data in the first place? Isn't stability good? Not when the rest of the world is unstable. In data science as in politics, it is often risky and even ill-advised to be stable when all of your peers are unstable. Making sure that each subgroup of data has similar overall variability ensures similar robustness and "educational opportunity." Often, stability in data sets is the data science equivalent of "teaching to the exams" in human education: the process of reducing the gamut of input, intentionally or unintentionally, generally makes the student or system less robust to new input [Kohn00]. Destabilization then is data "open-mindedness."

Destabilization can legitimately be performed in several situations, including (a) when one set of ground truth has statistically significantly different entropy than the other sets, (b) when one set of ground truth is more or less qualitative/quantitative than the other sets, and (c) when one set of ground truth is created by different means than the other sets. A fourth, slightly different form of destabilization is (d) when the grouped behavior of the data is too similar by analytic evaluation. We address each of these in order.

One form of stabilization, (a) above, is also one of the easiest to discover, if you are looking. Data sets differing in entropy are likely examples of "selective oversampling," wherein specific subgroups within a larger class are overrepresented. In many cases, such overrepresentation is all but inevitable, unless the experimentalist has an unlimited budget. Admittedly, in many of the examples in this book, data "stabilization" occurs, simply because I have access to a limited number/variety of sensing, recording, or other analysis equipment—not to mention conscious and/or subconscious bias to collect data suitable to illustrate the point(s) I intend to make in a given section of the text. Any time there is a bias, spoken or unspoken, in how data are captured, there is a risk of data stabilization. This occurs when one device is the adopted norm, due to ubiquity, cost, standards of practice, etc. It can also occur when the population available is not representative; for example, differences in ancestry vary greatly in comparing on campus to off campus, urban to suburban to rural, etc. Finally, it can occur due to differences in "setting bias" wherein one photographer prefers a different f-stop (aperture), shutter speed, ISO, focal length, and the like, and this set is different from that preferred by another photographer. This may lead to subtle differences in the data sets that are exposed once analytics are generated. To "destabilize" such data, we need to define a measure of entropy that partitions (or "discretizes") one or more feature ranges and allows for a statistical comparison among the clusters, categories, or classes. In the case of a setting, the "bins" that are used to compute the individual probabilities from which the entropy (please see Eqs. (1.14) and (1.15) in Section 1.8.1) is computed may be derived directly from the menu options (e.g., only a discrete set of f-stops, shutter speeds, etc. are available). For other features, a reasonable histogram that partitions the space "fairly" should suffice.

The second type of destabilization occurs when the ground truth sets differ in their qualitative and/or quantitative nature. Using the example of camera settings, one camera may have only discrete settings, and another may have an analog dial that allows a continuum of settings. Another, say less expensive camera, may have a lot less f-stops altogether. It is not immediately clear how to impute values between discrete settings to have the same variety of behavior as those coming from a continuum. One means of destabilizing data coming from a less diverse environment is to add noise stochastically to match the spread of the more diverse environment. For example, a discrete setting can be treated as the mean of a distribution and a distribution fitted to it so that it covers the range between its two nearest critical points with the same amount of variance as in the other group taken from a continuum. This is another use of the critical points described earlier in this section.

A third setting for destabilization is when one set of ground truth (whether for training, validation, and/or testing) is created by a different process than the other sets. This can result in data artifacts that are indistinguishable from actual differences between groups but may change the nature of the differences and so remain hidden—unless the analytic expert is aware of the context (or metadata) for the data collection. Often, this form of stability occurs through imbalances in data collection, using referred to as inequalities of scale. These inequalities can include time, time of day, location, and demographic differences that may be compounded across groups. They may even be hidden by statistical tests. For example, features 1 and 2 for groups A and B may have had statistically nonsignificant differences for location, but when an ANOVA (analysis of variance) is performed, we see a statistically significant difference in comparing feature 2 for group B to feature 1 for group A. This interaction may strongly affect any group-to-group differences later reported. For this reason, ANOVA should be used for any multifactor feature set, if possible. When there are known to be inequalities of scale in comparing two or more data sets, data deletion, data augmentation, or data imputation should be considered. The latter can be performed as described above using the critical points between data groups.

A fourth form of destabilization is applicable when all groups have highly correlated analytic evaluation behavior. Functional outputs such as accuracy, cost, robustness, and other system behavior can be plotted against the amount of data used or the percentage of data used from the ground truth set. The different groups are then assessed based on the nature of these data graphs (or other visualizations). These assessments can be based on relative behavior of the different groups or on their pruning behavior (i.e., when removing the same percent of oldest, most suspect, lowest confidence, etc. training data) data. Sensitivity to pruning data may undercover some patterns in the data over time (e.g., unreported imputation and attempts to obscure highly correlated data)

5.3 Sensitivity analysis of the solution model

Solution models are broader than data models. Solution models generally describe the manner in which an input is converted into an output. The ratio of output to input is the transfer function, and it is often modeled as the ratio of two polynomials, which provides both convenience and generalizability (not to mention ease of building individual modules). We describe the system behavior as

$$I(t)*[a_0 + a_1(t) + a_2(t-\Delta) + a_3(t-2\Delta) + \ldots + a_n(t-(n-1)\Delta)] =$$
$$O(t)*[b_0 + b_1(t) + b_2(t-\Delta) + b_3(t-2\Delta) + \ldots + b_n(t-(n-1)\Delta)] \qquad (5.10)$$

In Eq. (5.10), sensitivity analysis is rather straightforward. Given no *a priori* knowledge about the behavior of the input, $I(t)$, or the output, $O(t)$, we can determine the sensitivity of the equations from the variability in each of the coefficients $\{a_0, a_1, \ldots, a_n, b_0, b_1, \ldots, b_n\}$. For example, if in running multiple training sets we find that a_0 is 54.6 ± 7.7, a_1 is 22.4 ± 12.1, a_n is 13.6 ± 3.5, b_0 is 123.4 ± 2.3, b_1 is 37.9 ± 6.1, and b_n is 15.9 ± 4.4, then we can safely assert that the overall transfer function, $O(t)/I(t) = a(t, t-\Delta, \ldots, t-(n-1)\Delta)/b(t, t-\Delta, \ldots, t-(n-1)\Delta)$, is most sensitive to a_1 in the numerator (since the variability as standard deviation, not as coefficient of variation, has the highest expected impact) and most sensitive to b_1 in the denominator. The relative effect of numerator and denominator is affected by the sum of coefficients.

Regardless, in this section, we are not as concerned with transfer functions as we are with sequences in a solution. We are interested in analyzing a solution to find where the uncertainty is highest. We consider a process such that we want to know the next value of $\mathbf{x}$ when we have the current value of $\mathbf{x}$ and a set of boundary conditions:

$$\mathbf{x}(n+1) = \mathbf{A}\mathbf{x}(n) + \mathbf{b} \qquad (5.11)$$

Since $\mathbf{x}(n)$ and $\mathbf{x}(n+1)$ are vectors, our sensitivity is distributed across a set of linear equations in $\mathbf{x}$. However, the relative sensitivity of each element of $\mathbf{x}(n+1)$ is now predicted by the matrix element value, assuming $\mathbf{x}(n)$ values have uniform means.

5.4 Sensitivity analysis of the individual algorithms

Most algorithms have a number of settings, which are often coefficients for weighting different factors, either in isolation or in combination with other algorithms. The relative weights are often determined once (either on a single set of training data or on a k-fold set of training data), which precludes understanding the sensitivity of the setting. This is unfortunate, since clearly the k-fold evaluation allows a modest sensitivity analysis to be performed—the resulting mean and standard deviation of both the training and test data can be used as the sensitivity, which provides a sort of validation for the data.

As an example, suppose that we wish to employ a weighted voting algorithm, where, for example, the overall weight given to each algorithm is determined by the inverses of the error rate, the accuracy, or any of several other reasonable approaches, as outlined in Ref. [Sims13]. For this example, we combined three simple image classifiers (A, B, and C) with their weights set proportional to the inverse of their error rates (highest for C and lowest for B). These normalized (summing to 1.0) weights are A=0.32, B=0.45, and C=0.23, as shown for the "default" row in Table 5.1. We are interested in determining the effect of varying the weights for A, B, and C, both positively and negatively, to determine the absolute, relative, and directional sensitivity of the weights for each classifier. This helps us in at least two ways: (1) It tests the model for combination, which is in this case inverse error-dependent weighted voting, and (2) it may help us optimize the settings if we get consistent results.

The results for these +10 and −10% changes in the weightings of the three Classifiers A, B, and C are shown in Table 5.1. The values are calculated as follows: The weight of the classifier that is to be changed is increased by 10% or decreased by 10%, and the remaining weights are then adjusted, so the sum of weights is still 1.0 (normalized). So, when the A weight moves from 0.32 to 0.35 (+10%), B weight decreases to 0.43, and C weight decreases to 0.22, so the sum of 0.35+0.43+0.22=1.0. For B weight, 0.45 is replaced by 0.45/(0.45+0.23) multiplied by 0.65, which comes to 0.43.

The sensitivity to a +10% change in A is −0.7%, and to a −10% change in A, it is −0.4%; to a +10% change in B, it is +0.08%, and to a −10% change in B, it is −1.6%; and to a +10% change in C, it is −0.1%, and to a −10% change in C, it is −0.3%. The *mean sensitivity* is the percentage change in accuracy divided by the percentage change in the weight, which is therefore −0.07 and −0.04 for A, +0.08 and −0.16 for B, and −0.03 and −0.01 for C. From this, we see that the magnitude of the mean

Table 5.1 Sensitivity matrix for weighting of three classifiers that are combined together in a weighted voting classification pattern

Situation	A weight	B weight	C weight	Hybrid accuracy
Default	0.32	0.45	0.23	0.895
A+10%	0.35	0.43	0.22	0.888
A−10%	0.29	0.47	0.24	0.891
B+10%	0.29	0.50	0.21	0.903
B−10%	0.35	0.40	0.25	0.879
C+10%	0.31	0.44	0.25	0.894
C−10%	0.33	0.46	0.21	0.892

The sensitivity to a ±10% change in A is −0.7% and −0.4%; to a ±10% change in B, it is +0.08% and −1.6%; and to a ±10% change in C, it is −0.1% and −0.3%. Please see text for details.

sensitivity to B is more than twice that of A and is six times that of C. So, the overall accuracy is most sensitive to the weighting of Classifier B, and there only the positive direction results in a positive effect on the weighted voting combination accuracy. In this simple example, then, the system can be optimized by changing the relative weighting of Classifier B positively.

The next step is to test various positive shifts of the weighting of B and assess the hybrid accuracy. For some new sets of {A,B,C} weighting based on continuing in the directions of "positive effects on accuracy," we chose these weighting triples = {0.32,0.45,0.23}, {0.31,0.46,0.23}, {0.31,0.47,0.22}, {0.30,0.48,0.22}, {0.30,0.49,0.21}, {0.29,0.50,0.21}, {0.28,0.51,0.21}, and {0.28,0.52,0.20}. For these eight combinations, we measured that the hybrid accuracy was, respectively, 0.895, 0.896, 0.898, 0.904, *0.906*, 0.903, 0.0903, and 0.901. Thus, the peak is accuracy = 0.906 for the weights {0.30,0.49,0.21}. Since this is the only positive direction for sensitivity, we have almost certainly found a better set of weights than the original set of {0.32, 0.45, 0.23}. Note that this optimization simultaneously considered the absolute, relative, and directional sensitivities of the coefficients.

5.5 Sensitivity analysis of the hybrid algorithmics

Moving up a level, from the level of individual algorithms cooperating for a solution to adding more meta-algorithmic (e.g., ensemble, hybrid, and combinatorial approaches) systems to an existing hybrid system, our sensitivity is now focused on the overall change in system behavior when a new meta-algorithm is added to the system.

In Table 5.2, we are looking at the sensitivity of a hybrid system to each of its components. The components could be individual algorithms along the lines of the example covered in the previous Section 5.5; however, the approach is generalizable to any combination of meta-algorithms in addition to any combination of algorithms.

Table 5.2 Sensitivity matrix for adding a meta-algorithmic pattern to an existing hybrid system

		Meta-algorithmic number				
		1	2	3	...	N
Meta-algorithmic number	1	—	NA	NA	NA	NA
	2	1+2	—	NA	NA	NA
	3	1+3	2+3	—	NA	NA
	...	...	...	...	—	NA
	N	1+N	2+N	3+N	...	—

The comparisons made are indicated by "1+2," "1+3," etc., in the table. There are N(N−1)/2 total comparisons to be made. Please see text for details.

Table 5.3 Sensitivity matrix for adding a meta-algorithmic pattern to an existing hybrid system

	Meta-algorithmic number				
	A (0.822)	B (0.833)	C (0.755)	D (0.734)	E (0.714)
Meta-algorithmic number A (0.822)	—	NA	NA	NA	NA
B (0.833)	0.833	—	NA	NA	NA
C (0.755)	0.838	0.844	—	NA	NA
D (0.734)	0.844	0.829	0.812	—	NA
E (0.714)	0.825	0.855	0.811	0.777	—

There are N(N − 1)/2 total comparisons to be made. Please see text for details. The values in parenthesis are the accuracies for each of the individual classifiers, while the table entries are the accuracies for the paired set of classifiers

We start with algorithms first. If, for example, we wished to explore adding another classifier, say Classifier E, to four classifiers already employed in a weighted voting pattern, then we might get the specific incarnation shown in Table 5.3. The table does not simply show what the weighted voting output is for Classifiers A+B+C+D and then A+B+C+D+E, which is important, but does not give a complete picture of the value of adding Classifier E. In the case of Table 5.3, it so happens that adding Classifier E improved the overall accuracy from 0.855 to 0.868, which is a 9.0% reduction in the error rate. But, more importantly, Table 5.3 can be used to assess the relative value of adding Classifier E to any of the other classifiers in the problem in several interesting ways. The first is to compute the peak sensitivity according to Eq. (5.12):

$$\text{Peak Sensitivity} = \max \left(f(i, M) - f(M) \right) \qquad (5.12)$$

In order to determine the peak sensitivity, we find the maximum difference between functions (accuracy being the "function" in this case) of two variables, subtracting the original function (accuracy) of one variable; for example, $f(i,M) - f(M)$. For A, the peak sensitivity is for (D), since accuracy(A,D)−accuracy(A)=0.022. For B, the peak sensitivity is for (E), since accuracy(B,E)−accuracy(B)=0.022. For C, the peak sensitivity is for (B), since accuracy(B,C)−accuracy(C)=0.089. For D, the peak sensitivity is for (A), since accuracy(A,D)−accuracy(D)=0.110. Finally, for E, the peak sensitivity is for (B), since accuracy(B,E)−accuracy(E)=0.141. This is indeed the highest overall sensitivity, and importantly, the mean sensitivity of B and E is (0.022+0.141)/2=0.82. This is the highest overall sensitivity, implying that Classifiers B and E complement each other nicely. Thus, we have two methods for sensitivity analysis. The first is finding the classifier that best complements each classifier (this is peak sensitivity, or Eq. 5.12), and for {A,B,C,D,E}, this is {D,E,B,A,B}. We see that Classifier C is the only classifier that does not provide a peak sensitivity for any other classifier. Also, B and E provide the highest single (0.141) complement and the highest mean (0.82) complement pair. The mean complement by pair is thus the second sensitivity analysis metric from the table.

A third sensitivity analysis from the data in Table 5.3 is to find the mean and range of each classifier for complementing the other ones. For Classifier A, the mean is 0.76 (of 0.00, 0.083, 0.110, and 0.111), and the range is {0.00, 0.111}. The mean is thus the sum of the differences in the matrix for A with B, C, D, and E compared with the accuracy of B, C, D, or E alone and then divided by 4. For Classifier B, the mean is 0.84, and the range is {0.11, 0.141}. For Classifier C, the mean is 0.51, and the range is {0.11, 0.97}. For Classifier D, the mean is 0.35, and the range is {−0.04, 0.63}—the negative value is because when D is added to B, it pulls the classification accuracy from B's 0.833 to a combined 0.829. In general, this happens quite frequently, especially as our systems approach optimization. Finally, for Classifier E, the mean is 0.31, and the range is {0.03, 0.56}. Based on the means, the classifiers with the strongest "pull" (mean increase in accuracy when paired with another classifier) are, in order, B (pull=0.79), A (pull=0.76), C (pull=0.51), D (pull=0.35), and E (pull=0.31). This happens to be the exact order of the individual classifiers for accuracy, which implies a generally correlated set of classifiers. However, we see that adding Classifier E, in spite of its relatively low accuracy, has a positive impact on each pairing with another classifier. This implies it should prove a robust addition to the overall classification.

Thus, we see how to use Table 5.1 for combining classifiers, each of which may by itself a meta-algorithm. For "pure" meta-algorithms, peak sensitivity is given by Eq. (5.12). Whether algorithms or meta-algorithms are being assessed, the number of comparisons to be made for the sensitivity analysis is $N(N-1)/2$ where $N=$ the number of meta-algorithmic patterns being considered for adding into the system.

5.6 Sensitivity analysis of the path to the current state

The final topic in sensitivity analysis to be covered here is related to path. This has a lot of applications, particularly in its use in Markov models and Bayesian networks. We start off considering its application to the Markov model originally presented in Section 1.7.3. In Table 5.4, we see all of the transition probabilities for the four-state system. In specific, we will be interested in the "no change" state-state transitions, that is, A→A, B→B, C→C, and D→D, with probabilities 0.33, 0.12, 0.26, and 0.22, respectively.

Table 5.4 Table (subset of the data in Table 1.3) for the Markov model with four states of Fig. 1.11, with all state-state transition probabilities

		State n			
		A	B	C	D
	A	0.33	0.25	0.22	0.20
State $n-1$	B	0.33	0.12	0.23	0.32
	C	0.28	0.24	0.26	0.22
	D	0.39	0.19	0.19	0.23

This is the starting point for the sensitivity analysis shown in Table 5.5 and described in the text.

In Table 5.4, note that each row sums to 1.0, as it must since the next state is always either A, B, C, or D. The columns do not have to sum to 1.0, and rarely do, but do give us a relative estimate of what percentage of time the system spends in each state. A closed-form solution of the Markov model is not available, so for the data of Table 5.4 (and later Table 5.5), the percentages are the means of three separate trials with 10^7 consecutive states.

In Table 5.5, we carry out the sensitivity analysis using the "steady-state" situations of having state $n-1$ and state n be the same. We could have used any other variation, for example, changing any of the 16 transition probabilities in Table 5.4 in both a positive and negative direction. For the purposes of illustration, though, we will simply change the four probabilities AA, BB, CC, and DD (steady-state staying at states A, B, C, and D, respectively) by +3% and separately by −3%. When this occurs, we must adjust the other probabilities downward, and so, for example, we decrease each of AB, AC, and AD probabilities by −1% when AA is increased 3% and increase each of AB, AC, and AD probabilities by +1% when AA is decreased 3%.

The results of each of these +3% and −3% variations are shown in Table 5.5. Sensitivity is measured based on the effect of adding or subtracting 3% of the times

Table 5.5 Table with eight simple sensitivity analyses performed

Condition of the test	A pct (delta)	B pct (delta)	C pct (delta)	D pct (delta)
Original (see Table 5.4)	0.3331	0.2067	0.2239	0.2363
AA=0.36, AB=0.24, AC=0.21, AD=0.19	0.3433 (+0.0102)	0.2039 (−0.0028)	0.2203 (−0.0036)	0.3433 (+0.0102)
AA=0.30, AB=0.26, AC=0.23, AD=0.21	0.3233 (−0.0098)	0.2094 (+0.0027)	0.2272 (+0.0033)	0.2401 (+0.0038)
BB=0.15, BA=0.32, BC=0.22, BD=0.31	0.3311 (−0.0020)	0.2124 (+0.0057)	0.2218 (−0.0021)	0.2348 (−0.0015)
BB=0.09, BA=0.34, BC=0.24, BD=0.33	0.3349 (+0.0018)	0.2013 (−0.0054)	0.2261 (+0.0022)	0.2377 (+0.0014)
CC=0.29, CA=0.27, CB=0.23, CD=0.21	0.3302 (−0.0029)	0.2048 (−0.0019)	0.2311 (+0.0072)	0.2339 (−0.0024)
CC=0.23, CA=0.29, CB=0.25, CD=0.23	0.3357 (+0.0026)	0.2085 (+0.0018)	0.2170 (−0.0069)	0.2387 (+0.0024)
DD=0.26, DA=0.38, DB=0.18, DD=0.180	0.3312 (−0.0019)	0.2044 (−0.0023)	0.2210 (−0.0029)	0.2433 (+0.0070)
DD=0.20, DA=0.40, DB=0.20, DD=0.20	0.3348 (+0.0017)	0.2091 (+0.0024)	0.2265 (+0.0026)	0.2296 (−0.0067)

The tests performed were to add and subtract the margin of error (1.96 standard deviations, or 0.03) to the "steady-state" values of AA, BB, CC, and DD, respectively and distribute the delta evenly across the remaining three state-state transitions, as shown in the first column. The effects on the overall time spent in each state are shown in parentheses. Please see text for more details.

a state remains in state for the next iteration. The expected impact of the sensitivity is the variation added multiplied by the percentage of time spent in a given state. Since the variation is $\pm 3\%$ and the percentage of time spent in the states A, B, C, and D (from the first data row in Table 5.5) is 0.3331, 0.2067, 0.2239, and 0.2363, respectively, then we expect the change on percent time spent at A, B, C, and D to be 0.0100, 0.0062, 0.0067, and 0.0071, respectively. As we see in Table 5.5, the mean effects on state A are 0.0100 (exactly as expected), the mean effects on state B are 0.0056 (lower than expected), the mean effects on state C are 0.0071 (higher than expected), and the mean effects on state D are 0.0069 (roughly as expected). Sensitivity is defined as the mean effect on the state (of the + and the − variability added divided by 2), divided by the percent of the time in the particular state, per Eq. (5.13):

$$\text{Sensitivity} = \frac{|+Effect\,on\,State| + |-Effect\,on\,State|}{2 \times Percent\,of\,Time\,in\,State} \tag{5.13}$$

From Eq. (5.13), the sensitivity of AA=(0.0102+0.0098)/(2*0.3331)=0.0300, the sensitivity of BB=(0.0057+0.0054)/(2*0.2067)=0.0268, the sensitivity of CC=(0.0072+0.0069)/(2*0.2239)=0.0315, and the sensitivity of DD= (0.0070+0.0067)/(2*0.2363)=0.0290. Values above 0.03 (the $\pm$variability added) are higher than predicted (this is true of CC), and values below 0.03 are lower than predicted (this is true of BB). We see from this set of results that state C is the one upon which the output is most sensitive. It makes sense for us, then, to focus on making sure that state C is made as predictable as possible (for cost, throughput, performance, accuracy, or whatever else is being measured or managed at each state) to best improve the predictive power of the overall system.

Markov chains are also readily amenable to path sensitivity analysis. Suppose we have a Markov chain A→B→C and we wish to calculate the probability of this path. The probability is $p(A|BC) \times p(B|C) \times p(C)$. The overall sensitivity of the chain's probability is therefore a function of the uncertainly of $p(A|BC)$, $p(B|C)$, and $p(C)$. We use this to compare two close results, for example, $p(ABC)$ and $p(ACB)$. Suppose $p(A|BC)$ is $20 \pm 4\%$, $p(B|C)$ is $40 \pm 10\%$, and $p(C)$ is $30 \pm 6\%$. Then, suppose $p(A|CB)$ is $19 \pm 3\%$, $p(C|B)$ is $38 \pm 5\%$, and $p(B)$ is $31 \pm 3\%$. We see that $p(ABC)=0.0240 \pm 0.0192$ and $p(ACB)=0.0224 \pm 0.0098$. Clearly, we see that $p(ABC) > p(ACB)$, but $p(ABC)$ could be as low as 0.0048, and $p(ACB)$ is never lower than 0.0126. If it is catastrophic from a process standpoint (quality control, risk assessment, etc.) to be below a certain value, for example, 0.0075 or 0.0100, then we may choose $p(ACB)$ as the best path or sequence.

5.7 Summary

This chapter began with a review of sensitivity analysis approaches overviewed in this chapter and Chapters 6–14, elaborating further on the use of sensitivity analysis to assign individual models to portions of the domain for hybrid models. A deeper consideration of how many critical points to use for feature selection (initially introduced in Sections 1.10 and 1.11) was provided and later shown to be useful for destabilizing data groups with less entropy than other groups with which it will be analyzed. Destabilization was discussed for four situations: (a) when one set of ground truth has largely different entropy than the other sets, (b) when one set of ground truth is more or less discretized than the other sets, (c) when one set of ground truth is created by different means than the other sets, and (d) when the grouped behavior of the data is too similar by analytic evaluation.

Sensitivity analysis was then applied to a solution model. In linear system theory, the coefficients of the transfer function can be monitored for their variability over time directly, since the numerator and denominator both have linear equations. Sensitivity for a system of multiple equations is determined from the $\mathbf{A}$ matrix elements in the equation $\mathbf{x}(n+1)=\mathbf{A}\mathbf{x}(n)+\mathbf{b}$.

Sensitivity analysis of individual algorithms in an ensemble, combinatorial, or other hybrid system was considered in Table 5.1. By varying the weights in a weighted voting system, we could compute absolute, relative, and directional effects. In our example, only one direction of sensitivity resulted in improved overall accuracy. This allowed us to focus on this direction for optimizing the overall system, in the end achieving an additional 1.1% in accuracy and reducing the error by 10.5% of its initial value.

A matrix approach to sensitivity analysis was used to determine if adding another algorithm or meta-algorithm is as effective as the combinations that have already been performed in a hybrid design. Three types of sensitivity—peak sensitivity of the combinations or maximum complement pairing, mean complement by pair, and mean and range of complementing—are computed for each of the multiple algorithms/meta-algorithms, and any anomalous behavior can be discerned.

Finally, sensitivity analysis of path was overviewed. This approach was shown to be particularly applicable to Markov models and Bayesian networks. We revisited the Markov model from Chapter 1 and showed how sensitivity analysis can point us to focus on the measurements upon which the final outputs are most sensitive.

References

[Kohn00] Kohn, A., 2000. The Case Against Standardized Testing: Raising the Scores, Ruining the Schools. Heinemann, Portsmouth, NH. ISBN 0-325-00325-4. 104 p.

[Salt04] Saltelli, A., Tarantola, S., Campolongo, F., Ratto, M., 2004. Sensitivity Analysis in Practice: A Guide to Assessing Scientific Models. John Wiley & Sons Ltd. 219 p.

[Sims13] Simske, S., 2013. Meta-Algorithmics: Patterns for Robust, Low-Cost, High-Quality Systems. IEEE Press and Wiley, Singapore.

Multipatch predictive selection

6

Those who have knowledge, don't predict. Those who predict, don't have knowledge
Lao Tzu
If the path be beautiful, let us not ask where it leads
Anatole France

6.1 Introduction

The predictive selection pattern for meta-algorithmics was introduced in Ref. [Sims13] and comprises a statistical learning phase along with the run-time phase. During statistical learning, each possible configuration of the algorithm, analytics, or system to be deployed is considered along with each logical partition of the data space. In this way, we can determine the precision of each decision and always employ the algorithm, analytics, or system with the highest precision for the partition to which a run-time sample belongs. Predictive selection was therefore shown to reduce to the rule of selecting the option with the highest precision in a specific predictor test. The predictive selection approach is innately rational, as its most rudimentary form is simply conditional probability: maximizing the utility (cost, accuracy, performance, robustness, etc.) of the selected algorithm, analytics, or system given a specific event has occurred. Although wise, the founder of Taoism did not anticipate the power of predictive selection. With predictive selection, knowledge and prediction interplay as part of the process. Knowledge of the partitioning includes understanding what partitions to make as much as which downstream system to employ for each partition. And, the prediction is directly related to the knowledge of the precision of each system (or analytics or algorithm) for each partition. So long as the partitions are consistent over time, knowledge and prediction are used simultaneously, making predictive selection a Tao of analytics.

Nor do we stop with Lao Tzu. Anatole France quipped that "if the path be beautiful, let us not ask where it leads," but with predictive selection, we see both the beauty and the direction at the same time. The beauty lies in the ability to partition, repartition, and layer the predictive elements for the downstream algorithm, analytics, or systems, and where it leads is guided by the better estimate provided by the optimized predictive steps. We begin our discussion with the baseline predictive selection pattern.

Meta-Analytics. https://doi.org/10.1016/B978-0-12-814623-1.00006-X

6.2　Predictive selection

First and foremost, predictive selection is about collecting data. The predictive part of the design pattern is focused on categorization. Data that are collected need to be partitioned so that each partition can be used to optimize the downstream algorithm, analytics, or system that provides the particular machine intelligence output required of the problem. Partitioning involves assigning input data to clusters (generally partitioned by their location along ranges of specific content measurements, called features or metrics), to conditions (which can include contextual information, such as metadata or thresholds), and to expert rules (which can be internalized from domain expertise garnered from experience or can be imposed directly in the case of regulations, standards, and auditable levels of quality).

Importantly, data can be used to assign content to more than one category at a time. This affords a level of complexity for the overall system design that is analogous to the connections in an artificial neural network. Data used for prediction can assign the output to two or more categories, and based on the precision of the training data for those categories, we can choose to select the optimum system design based on as few as one of the categories and as many as all of the categories. As an example, suppose a data set is analyzed and found to belong to categories A, B, C, and D. The precision associated with those categories are, from the training data, 0.89, 0.87, 0.84, and 0.76. Depending on the circumstances, we may find better overall behavior by considering A only (the highest precision); A and B (e.g., within 5%); A, B, and C (e.g., within 10%), or all four (throwing away no categories identified, assuming they are all accurately assigned). Which of these is the "best" strategy? There is no a priori "right" answer; instead, deciding how multiple categories will be used for selecting the algorithm, analytics, or system to employ should be the task of the validation stage of the algorithm. With this in mind, we now cover some more of the specific of predictive selection, starting with the means of prediction.

6.3　Means of predicting

Prediction is a broad topic. From the simplicity of correlation, to the relative sophistication of conditional probabilities such as Markov and Bayesian approaches, to the esoteric nature of deep learning and meta-algorithmic patterns, we have several options for training a system to understand how to configure itself. In this chapter, our primary focus is on using partitions of the input data as a means of assigning differential categories to the subsequent analysis in order to improve the overall measured behavior of the system. Usually, the measurement is of accuracy, but predictive selection can be used to optimize any objective function, which could be concerned with cost, throughput performance, robustness, modularity, sensitivity, scalability, etc., in addition or in place of accuracy. We will default with classification as the presumed subsequent analysis here unless indicated otherwise.

The core decision for prediction is to decide how the input should be partitioned and how the data within each partition should be interpreted for the selection process that follows. Six prediction approaches are outlined here, which combined are nonexhaustive but certainly very helpful to get the gist of the process across:

1. The simplest partition is a yes/no or pass/fail decision. For this prediction approach, if "A" is contained in the data, we then use the data in one way to select the downstream process. If "A" is absent, we then use another. This approach is analogous to a decision tree if we "chain" yes/no or pass/fail decisions conditionally on the output of previous decisions. For example, if "yes" to A, then we select pass/fail on "B"; otherwise, we select pass/fail on "C."

2. The next simplest partition is a threshold. This is a binary decision and so is similar in concept to yes/no or pass/fail. Data above the threshold are assigned to one partition, and data below the threshold are assigned to another partition. Suppose that we are looking at images in a database taken from within a downtown area. We may then decide that if there are more than five moving objects of a large size, we will use one particular image understanding algorithms; if less than five, we will use another. This selection method works well when our objective function is cost, throughput performance, choosing the degree of parallelism, etc.

3. The next partition method is subrange-based partitioning. At its simplest, this is a multiple threshold approach, where we subdivide a range into consecutive subranges that comprise the partition. Subrange-based partitioning is the starting point for two more complicated forms of partitioning, described next.

4. Conditional partitioning is based on a Boolean expression, the simplest of which is AND. Here, the partition may be based on an appropriate subrange for each of two or more features. Even more complexity can be supported if a function of two or more features is also partitioned by subrange.

5. Sequential partitions are partitions applied to data that are collected in a time series, such as ECGs, EEGs, and temperatures, or as video, for example, surveillance information. Because the sequential events are related, we may anticipate different subranges, even for the same type of data, over time. A good example is if an object is accelerating in a video or if heart rate is changing during an exercise stress test.

6. Finally, consensus partitioning is a specialized type of conditional partitioning where the partition is defined based on the data and the metadata (or contextual) information associated with the data. For example, if two different sensors are used but have different sensitivities or calibration, then a different subrange may be used for each sensor based on the metadata identifying the manufacturer and settings of the sensor.

We now continue with the broader, and in some ways more interesting, process of selection.

6.4 Means of selecting

The means of selecting is based on maximizing the precision of the particular approach. The concept of precision is straightforward and is illustrated here (Table 6.1) for a simple three-class classification problem, which may be the behavior of the classifier selected based on a partitioning, as described in the previous section. In Table 6.1, we have a total of 100 normalized samples that belong (as ground truth training data) to one of three classes: A, B, and C. However, as is true of any nonideal classifier, there are some classification errors. For Class A, 64.2% of the samples actually coming from Class A are assigned (correctly) to Class A; however, 14.7% of the samples from Class A are (incorrectly) assigned to Class B, and 21.1% of the samples from Class A are (incorrectly) assigned to Class B. A similar interpretation can be garnered for the Class B and Class C "true class" rows in Table 6.1.

We see, therefore, that recall for each class is readily determined. Recall is the number of samples that actually belong to the class that are in fact assigned to the class divided by the number of samples that actually belong to the class. Since the denominator is 100.0 for each class in Table 6.1, we see that the recall for Classes A, B, and C are 0.642, 0.596, and 0.714, respectively. However, it is precision, not recall, that gives us the most confidence in an assigned class. Precision is determined in Table 6.1 from the columns, rather than the rows. Precision is the ratio of the number of samples assigned to a class correctly divided by the number of samples assigned to the class overall. So, for Class A, this ratio is $(64.2)/(64.2+16.7+14.8)=0.671$. Similarly, for Class B, this is $59.6/88.1=0.677$, and for Class C, this is $71.4/116.2=0.614$. So, the recall is highest for Class C, but the precision is lowest. It is precision that tells us what the probability of an assignment being correct is, though, making this the basis of predictive selection. If the classifier of Table 6.1 tells us that a sample belongs to Classes A or B, we are roughly 6% more likely to have the right classification than if it tells us a sample belongs to Class C.

Having this understanding, we can now compare this with the confusion matrix for a different classifier. This second classifier produces the confusion matrix shown in Table 6.2, which using the same approach as for Table 6.1 yields precisions of 0.557, 0.713, and 0.696 for Classes A, B, and C, respectively.

Table 6.1 Simple confusion matrix to illustrate the concept of precision.

Normalized confusion matrix		Classifier output (computed classification) prediction		
		A	B	C
True class of the samples (input)	A	64.2	14.7	21.1
	B	16.7	59.6	23.7
	C	14.8	13.8	71.4

Precisions of Classes A, B, and C are 0.671, 0.677, and 0.614, respectively. Please see text for details.

Table 6.2 Second confusion matrix for a classifier distinct from that of Table 6.1.

Normalized confusion matrix		Classifier output (computed classification) prediction		
		A	B	C
True class of the samples (input)	A	55.8	20.9	23.3
	B	19.8	74.6	5.6
	C	24.5	9.2	66.3

Precisions of Classes A, B, and C are 0.557, 0.713, and 0.696, respectively. Please see text for discussion.

Table 6.3 Precision values for the classifiers of Tables 6.1 and 6.2.

Class for precision	A	B	C
(1) Classifier of Table 6.1	0.671	0.677	0.614
(2) Classifier of Table 6.2	0.557	0.713	0.696

In Table 6.2, we see lower recall for Classes A and C in comparison with Table 6.1. Additionally, the precision values are different, being higher for Classes B and C, and lower for Class A. These values are captured in Table 6.3. The overall accuracy of both classifiers is similar (the mean of the diagonal elements of the confusion matrices): 0.651 for Table 6.1 and 0.656 for Table 6.2. This means that either classifier used by itself will provide between 65 and 66% accuracy on the three-class problem. However, using predictive selection, we should be able to use the differential precisions of the two classifiers to our advantage.

From Table 6.3, our maximum precision is the situation in which Classifier (2) reports that the sample belongs to Class B. In order, Table 6.3 suggests we adopt the following strategy to classifying samples obtained during the run-time, or deployment, phase:

1. If Classifier (2) classifies the sample as being from Class B, assign the sample to Class B.
2. Else, if Classifier (2) classifies the sample as being from Class C, assign the sample to Class C.
3. Else, if Classifier (1) classifies the sample as being from Class B, assign the sample to Class B.
4. Else, if Classifier (1) classifies the sample as being from Class A, assign the sample to Class A.
5. Else, if Classifier (1) classifies the sample as being from Class C, assign the sample to Class C.
6. Otherwise, Classifier (2) classifies the sample as being from Class A, but we cannot ever reach this step unless Classifier (1) provides no classification whatsoever, since this is the lowest precision of any of the size options.

Taken together, this list results in a relatively simple rule. If Classifier (2) classifies the sample as being from Class B or C, then assign the sample to the classification of Classifier (2); otherwise, assign it to the class that Classifier (1) identifies.

In this example, because each classifier is used when it provides the higher precision for the class, we might expect the combined accuracy to be approximately the mean of the three higher precisions for the classes; that is, 0.671, 0.713, and 0.696 for Classes A, B, and C, respectively. If so, this would be 0.693 or an error rate reduction of 10.8% in comparison with the accuracy of 0.656 for the (slightly) better classifier (0.307 is 10.8% less than 0.344), Classifier (2), and a 12.0% reduction in error (from 0.349 to 0.307) in comparison with the accuracy of Classifier (1). Note that error rate is 1.0 minus the accuracy. The actual results for such a problem depend on how the precision of the classifier varies for the samples classified as being from Class A for the classifier not used, that is, Classifier (2). We see that for Classifier (2), 55.8/(55.8 +19.8+24.5)=0.5574 of the samples classified as being from Class A actually is from Class A. For these samples, the classifier we actually use is Classifier (1), for which the precision is 0.671. Similarly, 19.8/(55.8+19.8+24.5)=0.1978 of the samples classified as being from Class A actually is from Class B. For these samples, Classifier (1) has a precision of 0.677. Finally, 24.5/(55.8+19.8+24.5)=0.2448 of the samples classified as being from Class A actually is from Class C, and Classifier (1) has a precision of 0.614 for these. The overall precision of Classifier (1) for samples that Classifier (2) assigns to Class A is thus the sum:

$$(0.671 \times 0.5574) + (0.677 \times 0.1978) + (0.614 \times 0.2448) = 0.658 \qquad (6.1)$$

This means that the overall accuracy of the two-classifier system is the mean of 0.658, 0.713, and 0.696 for Classes A, B, and C, respectively, or 0.689. This is a reduction in error rate of 9.6% compared with Classifier (2) and a higher (of course) reduction in error rate of 10.9% compared with Classifier (1).

This example illustrates how using the principle of "selecting the option with highest precision" leads to better overall system performance. But precision is not the only tool we have at our avail. The entity selected by a predictive selection approach need not be a single category or class as in the above example; instead, it can select an entire system with the specifics (settings, weights, etc.) of the system design selected by the predictive measurements. Selecting a different system for deployment for each partition in the predictor is associated with the regional optimization pattern [Sims13]. The so-called predictive selection with secondary engines approach [Sims13] may be more concerned with *ranking* the selected choices than in dictating that a specific choice be adopted. This is because in most real-world systems, the output of the system is analyzed just as carefully—if not more so—as the training data. The output can be considered to see if it passes a certain criterium, and if so, there is no need to select the next choice from the ranked list. Note that the criterium can be any quality metric germane to the task, for example, mechanical strength, surface finish smoothness, electric insulation, and density. The criterium can also be analytic rather than a material or physical property. For example, if accuracy or performance requirements are not met, a new system design might be chosen.

Another important approach within the predictive selection repertoire is the "separation of task" for prediction and selection. Here, one particular variable is analyzed by subrange, and each of its subranges triggers a different configuration for the prediction. These configurations can include different system architecture patterns and different weightings for the multiple components.

Related but alternative to the separation of task, we can use an effectively infinitely scalable system to use as many features as we possibly can to obtain multiple estimates for the output from this ensemble. The features themselves are defined by subranges, and for each subrange, we apply the output of the classifier with the highest precision to the ensemble overall decision. This might sound difficult, but it is fortunately very easy to elucidate with the help of a table. So, using a table as our crutch (and who reading this hasn't used a table once in their life to rise off the floor?), we can see from Table 6.4 that each of the features can be defined by 2 or more subranges. In Table 6.4, we show four features with a variable number (3, 4, or 5) of subranges.

In Table 6.4, each of the subranges is of the same size. Thus, for Feature 1, each subrange comprises 33.3% of the samples; for Features 2 and 3, each subrange comprises 25% of the samples, and for Feature 4, each subrange comprises 20% of the samples. Also, in Table 6.4, the precision of each of three algorithms for each

Table 6.4 Table used for illustrating the multirange, multifeature predictive selection approach.

Feature	Subrange	Precision, algorithm A	Precision, algorithm B	Precision, algorithm C
Feature 1	Subrange 1	0.655	0.677	0.699
	Subrange 2	0.669	0.674	0.681
	Subrange 3	0.683	0.669	0.658
Feature 2	Subrange 1	0.734	0.804	0.777
	Subrange 2	0.744	0.755	0.813
	Subrange 3	0.766	0.711	0.783
	Subrange 4	0.779	0.667	0.753
Feature 3	Subrange 1	0.555	0.599	0.634
	Subrange 2	0.563	0.588	0.613
	Subrange 3	0.571	0.597	0.580
	Subrange 4	0.557	0.614	0.603
Feature 4	Subrange 1	0.665	0.707	0.645
	Subrange 2	0.634	0.745	0.662
	Subrange 3	0.651	0.696	0.684
	Subrange 4	0.689	0.689	0.704
	Subrange 5	0.745	0.694	0.723

Values shown are the precision values for each of Algorithms A, B, and C. In each row, the underlined value is the one with the highest precision. Please see text for details.

Table 6.5 Overall precision of each algorithm for each feature, irrespective of subrange, for Table 6.4 values.

Feature	Precision, Algorithm A	Precision, Algorithm B	Precision, Algorithm C
1	0.669	0.673	0.679
2	0.756	0.734	0.782
3	0.562	0.600	0.608
4	0.677	0.706	0.684

Please see text for details.

subrange is given. The highest precision of each triplet (row) is underlined. There is an appreciable variability in precision among the triplets and among the algorithms for the same subranges—up to 0.112 difference for the three algorithms—and among the subranges for the same algorithm, up to 0.137 difference among the subranges for the same algorithm, in Table 6.4. By subrange, the rows of Table 6.4 have a mean range of 0.050.

Table 6.5 highlights the differences in the algorithms by feature, and Table 6.6 highlights the differences in the subranges (mean of all three algorithms). In Table 6.5, the mean range across the rows is 0.033 or a third lower than that of Table 6.4. This shows the efficacy of breaking the features up into their subranges, since greater variability allows us to select algorithms with differential precision.

Table 6.6 Mean precision of each subrange for the three algorithms.

Feature	Subrange	Mean precision, algorithms A, B, and C
Feature 1	Subrange 1	0.677
	Subrange 2	0.675
	Subrange 3	0.670
Feature 2	Subrange 1	0.772
	Subrange 2	0.771
	Subrange 3	0.753
	Subrange 4	0.733
Feature 3	Subrange 1	0.596
	Subrange 2	0.588
	Subrange 3	0.583
	Subrange 4	0.591
Feature 4	Subrange 1	0.672
	Subrange 2	0.680
	Subrange 3	0.677
	Subrange 4	0.694
	Subrange 5	0.721

Column 3 is the mean of columns 3, 4, and 5 in Table 6.4. Please see text for details.

The 50% relative increase in range of precision should help provide higher overall precision in the predictive selection approach eventually implemented. The mean precision values of Table 6.6 also hide a much larger subrange-algorithm interaction that is so evident in Table 6.4. For the four features, the range over the set of sub-ranges is 0.007, 0.058, 0.013, and 0.049, respectively, for Features 1, 2, 3, and 4. The mean of these is only 0.032, virtually the same as for Table 6.5. In short, Tables 6.5 and 6.6 justify breaking the features into subranges and using multiple algorithms, as depicted in Table 6.4.

Next, we determine the impact of this subrange-algorithm interaction in Table 6.7. Selecting the highest precision algorithm for each subrange results in between 1.8 and 6.0% lower error rate (1.0—precision) compared with the single best algorithm by features in Table 6.4. The improvement is obtained at the expense of adding the subranges, which may have the unanticipated side effect of overtraining the data. If, however, the subranges are likely to continue throughout the (deployment) lifetime of the system, the added advantages of improving the overall precision of the selected algorithm are likely to remain.

In this simple example, we do not actually see how the subrange-partitioning predictive selection approach affects the overall accuracy of the classification. In order to perform that assessment, we would need to provide a full multifeature classification along the lines of the process outlined in Sections 1.10 and 1.11. Most important for improving the overall classification accuracy is how independent the features are in their behavior. Also, the features will be weighted differently based on our confidence in each of them—from Table 6.7, we expect Feature 2 to be weighted the most heavily, and Feature 3 to be weighted the least heavily. For the particular data used to create these Tables, the classifiers were used for text classification, and indeed, the overall accuracy of the system was improved from 0.886 to 0.902, a reduction of the error rate from 0.114 to 0.098 (14% reduction in error). Interestingly, this was almost as much as the summed improvement of all four features in Table 6.7 But, of course, "results may vary."

Table 6.7 Overall precision of each subrange-optimized selection from Table 6.4, with improvement over best single algorithm from Table 6.5 in parenthesis.

Feature	Precision, subrange-optimized selection (pct improvement over Table 6.5)
1	0.688 (2.8% lower error rate)
2	0.795 (6.0% lower error rate)
3	0.615 (1.8% lower error rate)
4	0.719 (4.4% lower error rate)

Percent improvement is in error rate, not accuracy. Please see text for details. These precisions are the means of the best for each subrange (3, 4, or 5 in number) in a feature.

6.5 Multi-path approach

Everything up to this point in this chapter was meant to illustrate the power of using precision to guide predictive selection algorithms, and so with just a few minor twists, this has been a hopefully interesting but certainly not revolutionary extension of the predictive selection examples in [Sims13]. In this section, however, we get to explore the application of predictive selection process to path analytics. We begin with a consideration of how the partitioning associated with the process can be used to find an optimal decision tree.

In the previous section and specifically in Table 6.4, the ranges of the features were broken up and assigned to subranges of equal size and then treated as different conditionals within the overall selection phase. However, the subranges were made of equal size (i.e., the same number of training samples) simply for convenience of calculation and thus illustration in the tables. In practice, we may wish to refine these subranges in order to maximize the variance in the ranges. We perform this in a manner analogous to that employed by decision trees. The first decision is to determine a subrange and then determine a figure of merit for the subrange and any additional subranges it automatically creates (above and below it). If the figure of merit for any above or below it is low enough, then another subrange definition can occur. All subrange definitions in our simple example here were splits, and the decision tree formed by iterative splitting that resulted in the highest mean range in the subranges (across the three classifiers—this value was 0.050 in Table 6.4) was kept. This was chosen in place of a variable such as highest cumulative difference in precision among all the subranges, as this approach led to the definition of as many subranges as possible (in this case, 20 per feature since subrange boundaries were limited to multiples of 5% of the samples). By the subranges so formed, the rows of Table 6.8 have a mean range of 0.064, substantially higher than the "uniform" subranges in Table 6.4. The final "multipath predictive selection" output is given in Table 6.8, which offers the largest observed improved in precision ranges across subranges when subranges have step by 0.05 boundaries. Each "path" is the set of splits occurring in the overall range.

In Table 6.8, several results stand out in comparison with Table 6.4. First off, the peak precision values are higher in the mean than those of Table 6.4. This is because the multipath approach leads to subranges with higher variability, and so, half of that additional variability is expected by normal statistical laws to be on the high end, that is, the change in range should be half above and half below the mean. Secondly, less subranges were chosen. This is good news, as it means we probably had more subranges than needed for Table 6.4, so at least, we don't feel that Table 6.4 "underpartitioned" the range. It also means that the changes in which classifier should be used for the analysis only occur once or twice per feature: this implies that the features chosen are generally "stable" and thus generally useful. Thirdly, we see that the subranges are not uniform in size in Table 6.8. Instead of dividing the ranges evenly into thirds or halves, we see two ranges divided into (0.45 and 0.55) partitions, another into nearly equal thirds (0.30, 0.40, and 0.30), and the last into half and two quarters (0.50, 0.025, and 0.025).

Table 6.8 Table used for illustrating the multipath approach to subrange optimization.

Feature	Subrange (pct)	Precision, algorithm A	Precision, algorithm B	Precision, algorithm C
Feature 1	Subrange 1 (0.55)	0.657	0.677	0.702
	Subrange 2 (0.45)	0.684	0.668	0.651
Feature 2	Subrange 1 (0.30)	0.735	0.807	0.779
	Subrange 2 (0.40)	0.752	0.727	0.824
	Subrange 3 (0.30)	0.782	0.670	0.729
Feature 3	Subrange 1 (0.45)	0.558	0.593	0.627
	Subrange 2 (0.55)	0.565	0.606	0.592
Feature 4	Subrange 1 (0.50)	0.650	0.730	0.666
	Subrange 2 (0.25)	0.668	0.672	0.712
	Subrange 3 (0.25)	0.740	0.692	0.692

Here, there are 10 subranges, rather than 16, among the 4 features, and the mean range of the subranges (rows) for the 3 algorithms is 0.064.

The new set of subrange partitions do lead to better overall precision, of course. Otherwise, simply slicing the ranges into equal pieces would have had some strange magic to it. However, with full disclosure, it should be noted that the "equal" subranges in Table 6.4 were like the pigs in Orwell's "Animal Farm," that is, more equal than others. If you were paying careful attention to Table 6.4, you noticed that there were three subgroups for Feature 1, four subgroups for Features 2 and 3, and five subgroups for Feature 4. These were of course not selected randomly, but instead were the output of a clustering estimate for the Features—which not coincidentally were 3, 4, 4, and 5, respectively. Regardless, even with the number of partitions "intelligently" picked based on clusters for Table 6.4, the multipath predictive selection approach outlined in this section affords even higher precision, as shown by the underlined precision values in Table 6.8 and the mean precisions shown in Table 6.9.

In Table 6.9, the total error rate lowering across the four features is 25.0% (mean=6.3%), two-thirds again more than the 15.0% total (mean=3.8%) for Table 6.7. Based on this, we may expect that when these improved subranges are deployed for text classification as above (where we use all four features together with weight), we might see a significant additional improvement in overall accuracy

Table 6.9 Overall precision of each subrange-optimized selection from Table 6.8, with improvement over best single algorithm from Table 6.5 in parenthesis.

Feature	Precision, subrange-optimized selection (pct improvement over Table 6.5)
1	0.694 (4.7% lower error rate)
2	0.806 (11.0% lower error rate)
3	0.615 (1.8% lower error rate)
4	0.728 (7.5% lower error rate)

Percent improvement is in error rate, not accuracy. Note that the percentage of samples falling into each subrange is accounted for in the final precision. Please see text for details.

(which for the classifier of Section 6.6 improved from 0.886 to 0.902), perhaps to 0.913 if the same "two-thirds again more accurate" results are obtained on the testing data. However, we measure only a slight improvement in classification accuracy on testing data, from 0.886 to 0.907, in comparison with selecting the best classifier for each feature (0.886) or compared with selecting uniform-size subranges (0.902). This is, nevertheless, an appreciable reduction of the error rate from 0.114 to 0.093 (18.4% reduction in error). The trade-off here is that having less overall subrange partitions (10 instead of 16) removes some sources of overtraining in comparison with the earlier example, but the addition of optimal ranges leads to some overtraining, since any minor shift in the optimal range from training to testing data will affect accuracy. Overall, though, the combination of multipath with multiple subrange predictive selection, in combination with a weighted voting approach to combining the four features, leads to an impressive reduction in error rate.

One more type of multipath predictive selection can be used, which is more analogous to a Markov chain than to a decision tree. Here, the predictive selection is used to select a distinct set of features for each classifier, and then, each classifier (in an ensemble of classifiers) only bases its decision on those features. In the example of this section and Section 6.4, Classifiers A and B are very likely to omit Feature 3 using this approach.

6.6 Applications

An interesting application for predictive selection that is not immediately apparent from the above examples is to allow the algorithms to feed back their results and accept the output tied to the results with the highest precision. We are not "selecting" which algorithm or system to use, but rather which outcome to most trust. A good example is scene recognition, where we are trying to figure out the context of a location. One image recognition engine may report there are three chairs, one sink, one table, and three appliances in a room and so report with precision=0.856 that it is a kitchen. Another image recognition engine may report four stools, one sink, one table, two drink dispensers, and one appliance in a room and report with precision$=0.843$ that it is a bar. We accept the classification as kitchen, but not with high confidence.

Other applications of predictive-selection-based approaches will be used in later chapters, particularly Chapters 12 and 13. However, it is readily seen from the generic nature of the discussion in this chapter that predictive selection approaches are excellent choices for any type of system involved in discriminating two or more classes, clusters, categories, or contexts. The real question to ask as a system design engineer is, "where can and should I use predictive selection in this project?" The answer of whether to use is almost invariably "yes."

6.7 Sensitivity analysis

Many of the predictive selection approaches overviewed in this chapter are effectively "introspective" to sensitivity analysis. In Section 6.6, for example, the multipath predictive selection approach innately provides a measure of sensitivity analysis since we are recording the range in precision for each of the partitions as we consider all of the possible paths to the final partition configuration. Likewise, we see that nearly all predictive selection approaches provide the equivalence of sensitivity analysis during the training, or category-generating, stage. This is because we are highly interested in ensuring that the categories we use for selection are indeed the most reliable. A good part of the discussion in Section 6.5, then, is focused on how our partitioning affects the sensitivity of the predictive selection process to the features used for the analysis. In this case, the most sensitive partitions can be viewed as the "optimal" partitions, because they provide a higher discriminatory power for each partition (subrange) and feature. We must always be careful to ensure that, in our eagerness to find partitioning with higher overall system precision, we do not overtrain the system. It makes good sense to try several different predictive selection approaches and select the one that provides good overall performance and robustness to validation and testing data.

6.8 Summary

This chapter describes the broad set of ways in which the predictive selection pattern can be used to improve the performance of intelligent systems. The primary focus of the predictive selection pattern is on improving decision-making accuracy, although the approach of intelligent partitioning and differential deployment of selection tasks based on maximizing precision is broadly useful in optimizing any system objective function.

After describing the assignment of data to categories, we next overview six different approaches to partitioning. These are (1) yes/no or pass/fail; (2) threshold-based partitioning; (3) subrange-based partitioning; (4) conditional partitioning, which supports any Boolean relationship between two or more features; (5) sequential partitioning, which may result in changing subrange definitions even for the exact same type and range of data, over time; and (6) consensus partitioning, which is a particular type of conditional partitioning based on both the data and the metadata (or contextual) information associated with the data.

We then discussed how an ensemble of classifiers (or any other analytics) can be used together based on accepting the output of the one with the highest precision. Calculating the overall precision is possible after the overall strategy has been reduced to a set of rules. Generally, an appreciably more precise system is obtained through this approach. The risk is, of course, that the system may be overtrained.

Next, we considered means of selection based on the partitioning. Partitioning of the input can use a "separation of task" approach, wherein an auxiliary data feature is used to assign the sample to one of a plurality of partitions. Then, the precision of each of the algorithms, analytics, or systems for each of the subranges and for each of the features is considered. The overall improvement in system behavior will depend on how the features interact together, but this is a meta-algorithmic [Sims13] consideration downstream from the predictive selection. For this section, the precision of the individual features was highlighted.

Finally, we considered multipath predictive selection, in which we allowed a number of possible decisions to be made and computed a figure of merit score to each path that not only is robust to the utility of the output but also does not quickly devolve into creating as many partitions as possible (or no additional partitions, for that matter). Using a functional measurement such as the range of precisions for the entire ensemble of algorithms, analytics, or systems in each partition was shown to work well.

Reference

[Sims13] Simske, S., 2013. Meta-Algorithmics: Patterns for Robust, Low-Cost, High-Quality Systems. IEEE Press and Wiley, Singapore.

Modeling and model fitting

7

You never change things by fighting the existing reality. To change something, build a new model that makes the existing model obsolete
Buckminster Fuller

If we are to achieve a richer culture, rich in contrasting values, we must recognize the whole gamut of human potentialities, and so weave a less arbitrary social fabric, one in which each diverse human gift will find a fitting place
Margaret Mead (1935)

7.1 Introduction

The value of modeling to the analytics scientist can hardly be exaggerated. Modeling is getting our head around the data, not only predicting what the future of the data will bring but also predicting how the future data will be best analyzed. As Buckminster Fuller, the scientist now eponymous with the C_{60} soot molecules buckminsterfullerene, notes, "To change something, build a new model that makes the existing model obsolete." Easier said than done, of course, because as another wise man once said, "It's tough to make predictions, especially about the future." That sage was Yogi Berra. So, it is agreed that in order to make sense of the future before it is the present, we must be ready to earn our predictive license. The road test for this license is being able to create a new and better model when new and better data arrive. Two key sets of tools to do so are (1) a broad set of approaches that borrow from other areas of successful human learning and (2) a set of evaluation analytics that help us to optimize the settings of the model we've chosen.

Margaret Mead notes that "we must recognize the whole gamut of human potentialities, and so weave a less arbitrary social fabric, one in which each diverse human gift will find a fitting place." This is a call for meta-analytics if there ever was one. Let us simply replace "human" with "analytic" and "social fabric" with "system architecture" and we obtain the following: "we must recognize the whole gamut of analytic potentialities, and so weave a less arbitrary system architecture, one in which each diverse analytic gift will find a fitting place." And Margaret's always keen insights are complimented by her skepticism toward unsupported analytics, such as testing for racial differences in intelligence. Margaret, in addition, was the researcher who used cultural anthropology analysis to show how diverse cultural patterns, as an ensemble or hybrid, contribute to a fundamental unity in

Meta-Analytics. https://doi.org/10.1016/B978-0-12-814623-1.00007-1

human behavior and cultural propensities. Using cultural anthropology to derive meaningful analytics? What an example for model generation and model fitting! With Margaret's cross discipline approach in mind, we look to chemistry and biology for design inspiration in the following three sections.

7.2 Chemistry analogues for analytics

The main point of this and the following two sections is to help "expand the mind" of the analytic engineer by showing how strong analytic ideas can come from a wide range of fields of study. In this section, among the many candidates for analogy, we consider the five fundamental types of chemical reactions, the percent yield of reactions, and the concept of limiting reagents.

The five fundamental (simplest) chemical reactions are readily described in mathematical expressions, as captured in Eqs. (7.1)–(7.5):

$$A + B \rightarrow AB \text{ (composition reaction)} \tag{7.1}$$

$$AB \rightarrow A + B \text{ (decomposition reaction)} \tag{7.2}$$

$$AB + 0 \rightarrow A0 + B0 \text{ (combustion reaction)} \tag{7.3}$$

$$AB + C \rightarrow AC + B \text{ (single replacement reaction)} \tag{7.4}$$

$$AB + CD \rightarrow AD + BC \text{ (double replacement reaction)} \tag{7.5}$$

The composition and decomposition reactions are straightforward. In composition, two elements are brought together into a single compound. This is akin to joining, or merging, two clusters, classes, categories, or indexes (collectively "group"). The decomposition is the reverse: a compound is split into two components. This is obviously analogous to splitting two groups. The combustion reaction is subtler than composition or decomposition reaction. In the chemical combustion reaction, oxygen in the form of O_2 is used to "burn" the compound AB and reduced it to its elements. The compound AB may be a carbohydrate, for example, $C_6H_{12}O_6$, and thus, $6O_2$ is used to "burn" this into $6H_2O$ and $6CO_2$. In analytics, a second group is added to an existing group, revealing a formerly hidden "merged" grouping, resulting in two new groups A and B, each augmented by part of the new data set O. A good example of this is when there is noticeable bimodality to a class, with the new samples falling largely below the lower mode's mean or above the upper mode's mean. The new data thus exacerbate the bimodality of the overall data set, making it easier to see the original compound group AB as existing as two groups A and B augmented by portions of the new data set O. The new data thus combust the (presumable inappropriate) merging of data sets A and B.

The final two elementary reactions are the single and double replacement reactions. The first one replaces an aggregate of A and B with an aggregate of A and C, allowing B to stand as its own group. This is, from an analytics perspective, similar to combustion, except that all of the new data C are more closely related to A than to B. This means that the overall data are drifting toward the A side of the aggregate and statistically isolating the B data. The regrouping is driven by the appropriate clustering, classification, and/or categorization algorithms. The double substitution reaction is essentially the same as combustion, except that the portion of the O group pulling A away from B is here designated D and the portion of the O group pulling B away from A is here designated C. We also see that originally, C and D were associated with each other. So, the two groups are essentially splitting and then recombining into novel aggregates. This might happen when new measurements, analysis, or relative significance of the features is associated with the data.

This set of five simple chemical equations should be applied to any existing data sets throughout their life cycle and evaluated statistically. This approach will be used to ensure that the current groupings (clusters, classes, categories, and indexed sets) are not contraindicated. This is tantamount to cluster optimization using regularization, which is covered in detail in Section 10.3. For now, it is worth noting that we can determine candidate elements A, B, C, D, and O in the five Eqs. (7.1)–(7.5) above and then test the representation on either side of the arrow→for goodness of fit with the data (along the lines of the methods described in Section 7.6).

Extending the chemistry analogues, the statistical analysis of the groupings is akin to the determination of the percent yield in a chemical reaction. In chemistry, the percent yield is the ratio of product obtained over the theoretical maximum (which is determined by the limiting reagent). In analytics, the percent yield is the ratio of the amount of information that is actually and measurably extracted from a data set divided from the theoretical maximum of information that can be extracted from a data set. A simple example illustrates the analytics relevant part of this. Suppose that we have three categorization engines participating in categorizing a large set of data. We know these three engines to have categorization accuracies of 0.7, 0.8, and 0.9, respectively. In order to calculate the theoretical maximum of the ensemble system, we use the difference between the theoretical performance of the three engines in independent voting and the performance of the best engine (0.9) as our percent yield. For the latter, we have 2^N possible voting outcomes, where $N=3$:

1. Engines 1, 2, and 3 correct with probability$=0.7*0.8*0.9=0.504$
2. Engines 1 and 2 correct, 3 incorrect with probability$=0.7*0.8*0.1=0.056$
3. Engines 1 and 3 correct, 2 incorrect with probability$=0.7*0.2*0.9=0.126$
4. Engines 2 and 3 correct, 1 incorrect with probability$=0.3*0.8*0.9=0.216$
5. Engine 1 correct, 2 and 3 incorrect with probability$=0.7*0.2*0.1=0.014$
6. Engine 2 correct, 1 and 3 incorrect with probability$=0.3*0.8*0.1=0.024$
7. Engine 3 correct, 1 and 2 incorrect with probability$=0.3*0.2*0.9=0.054$
8. Engines 1, 2, and 3 incorrect with probability$=0.3*0.2*0.1=0.006$

Adding the majority voting correct cases (1.), (2.), (3.), and (4.), we see that if the three engines are independent, we will expect 0.902 accuracy ($0.902=0.504+0.056+0.126+0.216$), only slightly above the best single engine of 0.900.

Thus, our theoretical peak accuracy is 0.902, and our theoretical yield is a paltry 0.902–0.900, or 0.002. If in combining the three engines we observe 0.907 accuracy, then our yield is $(0.007/0.002) \times 100\% = 350\%$. If, however, it is a similar but lower value of 0.897 (just 1% less, after all), then our yield is $(-0.003/0.002) \times 100\% = -150\%$. In the latter case, we would be better off using just the single engine with 90% accuracy.

Extending this example further, suppose we recrafted the low-accuracy engine to yield 80% accuracy. The engine accuracies are now 0.8, 0.8, and 0.9. Repeating the analysis above, this yields a theoretical peak accuracy of 0.928 for the three engines if they are independent and a now more appreciable theoretical yield of 0.028. If in combining the three engines we observe 0.919 accuracy, then our yield is $(0.019/0.028) \times 100\% = 68\%$. If, however, we use a meta-algorithmic pattern [Sims13] and are able to exploit uncorrelated behavior between the three engines and now achieve a similar but higher value of 0.929 (just 1% more, after all), then our yield is $(0.029/0.028) \times 100\% = 104\%$. How can a yield be above 100%? The answer is that the assumption for the theoretical maximum (independence of the three engines) wasn't entirely correct.

The last concept from chemistry we'll cover in this brief section is that of limiting reagent. In chemistry, the limiting reagent is the reactant that "runs out" first in a reaction, allowing no further product to be formed. Let's explain this with chemistry we all know about—recipes. If you are making pancakes where the recipe calls for 2 eggs for every cup of flour and you have 3 eggs and 1.75 cups of flour in the kitchen, then the eggs are the limiting factor. This is because 3 eggs are the flour equivalent of 1.5 cups, which you have in excess, and 1.75 cups of flour are the egg equivalent of 3.5 eggs, which you cannot use. You will run out of eggs in the recipe with 0.25 cups of flour leftover.

In analytics, the limiting reagent can range from the simple to the subtle. In the three-engine categorization example above, the limiting reagent was the categorizer with the lowest accuracy. By improving it to be just as accurate as the poorer of the other two categorizers, we increase the range for the percent yield 14-fold (from 0.002 to 0.028). Effectively, then, as applied to this classification ensemble, the limiting reagent approach is a form of sensitivity analysis. There is value in taking this sort of perspective to the field of analytics. The limiting reagent approach is a means of assessing (1) where to take more data, (2) what the key relationships between input and output are, and (3) how to build a model that is robust to the nature of the data in the components (reactants and products, in chemistry). We now turn to a specialized branch of chemistry, organic chemistry, for further insight. Interestingly enough, I am not using analytical chemistry for analogy with analytics.

7.3 Organic chemistry analogues for analytics

One of the more relevant areas in organic chemistry for exploring meaningful analytic approaches is sequential, or chained, oxidation-reduction reactions, such as occur with polymerization. Like the "cell differentiation" analogy in the following section, we can use this process as insight for design approaches for dynamic systems.

We begin with the oxidative processes (leading to a more positive oxidation number on the carbon) of converting methane to a chain of products [Holm09]. The forward reaction produces methanol, formaldehyde, formic acid, and carbon dioxide. The reverse reaction (the Sabatier reaction, see Ref. [Wilb09] for more on the general chemistry in this section) can use carbon dioxide to regenerate (through a series of reduction reactions, leading to a more negative oxidation number on the carbon atom), give, or take a few oxygen atoms and water molecules in either direction. We will mainly focus on the oxidation process, as it is illustrative. Methane (CH_4), an alkane, is oxidized to become methanol (CH_3OH), an alcohol (here, due to the gain of an oxygen atom). This is in turn oxidized (here, through the loss of a hydrogen molecule, H_2) to become methanal (common name "formaldehyde"), CH_2O. Another oxygen atom can be gained, oxidizing methanal to become HCOOH, or methanoic acid (common name "formic acid"). Then, methanoic acid can be further oxidized, again by the loss of hydrogen H_2, to become carbon dioxide CO_2.

So, if you've read to this point, you may be scratching your head and wondering what the full oxidation of methane has to do with analytics. Quite a bit, if you keep an open mind here, especially since the analytic system, architect should have a creative approach to the life cycle of analysis. In this reaction, oxidation creates the future data, and reduction looks back at the past state of the data. Several important themes emerge. First off, there are multiple means of refining the categorization. In the case of the oxidative reaction, we can proceed to the next product through the addition of an oxygen atom or through the subtraction of a hydrogen molecule. These amount to the same net effect on the carbon, changing its oxidation by +1 for each hydrogen (total +2) or by subtracting a −2 (total +2). This is an important point for analytics. We can add categorization value to a sample or an entire set of data, by adding information or by subtracting noninformation. Think of homing in on the description of a "ball." At one stage, we may have the tags "round," "hollow," "light weight," and "orange" associated with the object. This seems like it might be a basketball or a street hockey ball. We add content by tagging it with "prolate spheroid" and "brown" and subtract content by removing the imprecise terms "round" and "orange." The remaining descriptors are now "hollow," "light weight," "prolate spheroid," and "brown." Most of us would now (rightly in this case) think this is a football.

The second theme of this oxidation-reduction analogy is that differentiation is not a simple, linear-in-time evolution. Analytics are an evolution in time and space. A current analytics is living in the present, and from the standpoint of the pragmatic use of the analytics, we wish to add any and all tagging that helps differentiate the data and remove any and all of the tagging that helps confuse the data with other data.

The third theme of the oxidation-reduction discussion is that each subsequent (or antecedent) reaction is reversible and there is energy involved in moving from either direction. We could really push this analogy and start talking about spontaneous, exothermic, and endothermic reactions—not to mention catalysts—but the point is already made. As analytic engineers, we should be setting up our data analysis systems to have the same type of robust bidirectionality as nature provides with oxidation-reduction reaction sequences.

7.4 Immunological and biological analogues for analytics

In Section 1.8.3, immunologic algorithms were introduced. There, we noted that immunologic algorithms are based on the *distributed, recognition-based, layered* system of memory that is your immune system. This hybrid system includes innate memory, collaborative or "distributed" memory, and learned memory, meaning that there are several layers of information contained. This remarkable system provides as rich a set of memories in many ways as the central nervous system, but without the consciousness. These layers readily intercommunicate, allowing information to be shared and so reinforced or downgraded based on consensus or the lack of consensus. This means that the immune system is capable of both deep learning and *deep unlearning*. Deep unlearning is a very important concept and was earlier described as based on the real immune system concept of clonal deletion, which is the process by which the immune system learns not to attack the self. More broadly, deep unlearning is connected to the need for machine intelligence to know when previous material—and rules of behavior based on them—is no longer relevant. This means that deep learning is really only revolutionary when it is dynamic.

In Section 1.8.3, key concepts in immunologic algorithms were covered, which of course will only be touched on lightly here (see Ref. [Delv17] or other general immunology texts for more in depth on these topics). The main goal of this section is to provide helpful modeling approaches to the would-be system architect. A few—antigens, antibodies, and hybrid design—are reexplored here because of their significance.

The concept of antigens—fragments of information that can be recognized by the antigen-binding site on the antibody—is repurposable to system design. In the context of machine learning, an antigen is a specific element or combination of elements that trigger a downstream set of activities by the machine learning system. This may mean the occurrence of a rare event triggers a different response—for example, a different analytics algorithm or design pattern—to be applied. One example is a "trigger" word that indicates switching from monolingual to bilingual analysis of text or speech. Another example is the recognition of a certain object that requires attention by specific algorithms; for example, a speeding automobile in a school zone triggers an expanded range of sensors and tracking algorithms.

In the immune system, these antigens trigger the antibodies, which are molecules with the ability to recognize antigen and, after the recognition occurs, moderate the behavior, location, and scalability of the response to antigen. Antibodies are molecules with different sections or sites, which enable them to participate in different chemical reactions or "binding." In machine learning, the analogue to antibodies may be the detection of a specific pattern of data in a sample, which then binds downstream analytics. The antigen binding thus triggers relevant analytics, which are used to further validate that the antigen-antibody complex is a correct match. This is a feedback approach requiring full completion of a specified set of process checks. The receptor binding site then attaches the antibody to its category, cluster, and/or class set and adds its analytics to those of the set. An example of antigen-antibody binding in text analytics is term frequency times inverse document frequency (tf^*idf). This "binds" terms with high frequency in a given set of text (antigen) to much lower frequency in a larger corpus of text (antibody). The concept of tf^*idf, or relative rarity of occurrence, can obviously be extended to nontext applications as well.

The use of multiple tf^*idf terms is an example of multiple model hypotheses. The other "antigens" or fragments of information generated as part of the data mining process can be combined with the tf^*idf to identify a particular immune system challenge. In a sense, the logic behind a decision tree can be extended to model formation, wherein multiple models are created and the goodness of fit of all of the models together represents our ability to understand the context of the threat.

Not discussed in Chapter 1, but meriting a brief overview here, is the analogy between immune cell differentiation and increasingly refined analytics. In the differentiation of cells, a stem cell is the starting point. As we know from the appreciable attention that stem cells currently get in the media, stem cells are unspecialized, or undifferentiated, and thus can "grow up" to be any of a wide range of differentiation cells. We can think of the stem cell as an infant or toddler and the differentiated cell as an adult with a career. Perhaps, the fact that most adults are expected to hold 10 or more jobs is the analogy to scientists being able to manipulate stem cells, but we will shelve that discussion for this book. The important point is that a stem cell is expected to progress to a more differentiated pluripotent progenitor cell and then to an even more differentiated progenitor cell. Next, in an analogue to choosing a university, apprenticeship, or internship, the pluripotent cell specializes into a committed lineage cell, which now effectively knows the general nature of its adult "career." Finally, the cell completes its development, finishing life as a somatic differentiated cell ("somatic" distinguishing it from "germ" cells, or reproductive system cells). Note that many of the cells, such as neurons or muscle fibers, may live as long as the individual, while others, such as epidermal cells and erythrocytes, will only live a few weeks to months.

This provides two important and rich analogies that can be used in the definition of an analytic system. The first is the stage of differentiation. The stage of maturation corresponds to an increasing precision of classification and thus a larger descriptive vocabulary for the samples so differentiated. A simple example provides insight here. The stem cell equivalent might be distinguishing between a vehicle and an animal in a video. The pluripotent progenitor equivalent might be then classifying the vehicle as a car, truck, motorcycle, etc. and classifying the animal as a cat, dog, human, escaped primate, etc. The pluripotent cell may provide make, model, year, and color of the car and height, build, and gender of the human. The committed lineage cell analogue might be a candidate set of license plate numbers for the car and a "lineup" of potential individuals for the human. Finally, the somatic differentiated cell analogue might be the specific car (including license plate and vehicle identification number (VIN)) or the specific individual, including name, Social Security number (SSN), and address. At each stage of differentiation, a more descriptive categorization of the vehicle and person is garnered. At the price of specificity, however, can come "commitment" to a mistaken category if there is no manner in which to validate the categorization.

This concern is addressed by the second important rich analogy, which is the ability of the categorization to "rewind" a level (or more) and be recommitted to an alternate path. This is analogous to the ability to split and reform classes (e.g., from subgroups of two or more previously defined classes), form new categories, recluster data samples as the size of the database scales, etc. As classes become more specialized, we may not wish for them to become more intransigent. Thus, the degree of specialization and the degree of mutability can be controlled separately. Interestingly, we have seen these two factors—specialization and mutability—be separated in cell biology. Even in the early 2000s, cell differentiation was viewed as a one-way function: once differentiated, a cell could not be "undifferentiated." A specialized cell was designated a "terminally differentiated" cell and was seen as being permanently specialized until natural or programmed (apoptosis) cell death. Then, in 2006, scientists showed that they could turn a differentiated cell back into a stem cell with its pluripotentiality restored [Taka06]. In a biological system, stem cells have their DNA loosely arranged and ready to transcribe their messages (e.g., create RNA). As signal molecules trigger differentiation, the process of specialization involves turning off unneeded genes. Genes that are required in the mature cell's functionality remain active. As an aside, this mechanism is not dissimilar from how different neural pathways are carved in the developing brain. It is the subtraction of unnecessary neural connections, a process termed *synaptic pruning* [Chec98], that leads to learning and other mental specialization associated with the maturation of the brain. Regardless, for cell development, researchers [Taka06] noticed that there were a small subset of genes that are expressed in stem cells but not in differentiated cells. Thus, differentiation is associated with—at least in part—*genetic pruning*. By reintroducing a set of four genes from this subset into specialized cells, they were made to act like stem cells. These genes were shown to remodel the DNA of the cells, and genes that had been shut down during differentiation were now turned on. The scientists, now understandably Nobel laureates, designated these cells *induced pluripotent stem cells*, or iPS cells. The name is very descriptive: these cells have turned back the clock on specialization and become less specialized. They have reversed the pruning.

How do we, as analytic system designers, use these concepts to our advantage? We can complement the specialization that goes with fine-tuning the categorization, classification, and clustering with a separately controlled adaptability continuum. As a categorization or other data tagging/description process matures, we expect to see the adaptability of the categorization to diminish. But by how much? This is another opportunity for the system architect to ingest domain expertise, as we would naturally expect this "plasticity" to vary from one domain to the next. The amount of plasticity—and not the decision of whether to have plasticity—is therefore the key parameter for training.

7.5 Anonymization analogues for model design and fitting

Few concepts are more important from an application standpoint than anonymization of data. Also known as deidentification, this is an approach in which the identity, but not the utility, of data has been tokenized, obfuscated, or removed. In anticipation of the following section, which covers the basics of determining goodness of fit for a model, anonymization is tightly associated with entropy. That is, we presume that the best analytic model for the system will be the model with the highest residual entropy. This is the entropy of the data remaining when the model is subtracted out. Importantly, this approach can be extended to both system and error models, by feeding back validation information to the model training data. The process is as follows. To initialize, assign your ground truthing data to a training and validation set, preferably equally sized. Then, perform the following steps in iteration until a maximum number of iterations are reached, the same results are obtained for two iterations in a row, the (least squared) error is less than some minimum value, the variance of the linear absolute errors is less than some minimum value, and/or the entropy of the error is above some threshold indicating "cryptographic" level of entropy:

1. Use the training data to create a model of the data.
2. Use the validation data to subtract the model from and characterize the error.
3. Add the error model to the model of the data.
4. Swap half of the training and validation sets, so each represents 50% of the previous training and validation set.

As an example of the approach outlined, imagine that you would like to use your voice as a biometric, but you do not wish someone recording your voice to do the same. In this circumstance, you can provide an algorithm to turn your voice into custom speech, such that an automatic speech recognition (ASR) engine not only will be able to recognize the voice if and only if it has the correct algorithm to anonymize the voice but also make the voice quite different from other voices. The training set determines the model for anonymizing the voice, while the validation set ensures it has an acceptably small number of false positives for other primary or secondary (also anonymized) voices in the database. As a particular feature, you can also use an affected accent to make spoofing your voice that much harder.

7.6 LSE, error variance, and entropy: Goodness of fit

To rank data models for goodness of fit, we need some easy-to-compute, unambiguous, and robust analytics. While there are more complicated means of assessing models, the three provided in this section, together with their weighted combinations, provide a broad and highly adaptable means of ensuring the model has no systemic residual error. Closely tied to the anonymization process described in the previous section, let us explore these three metrics and then discuss how they can be used together and even used to optimize the analytic system architecture.

Least squared error, hereafter LSE, is simply defined by Eq. (7.6):

$$LSE = \min\nolimits_{models} \left(\sum_{i=1}^{n_{samples}} (sample_i - model_i)^2 \right) \tag{7.6}$$

Here, the least squared error is the one with the minimum sum of squared differences between each of the sample points and the predicted value of the sample points based on the model. Recall from Chapter 1 that linear regression is a simple model for data and it used the LSE to optimize the slope and intercept of the regression line. The LSE, also known as the L2-norm, is often a better metric than error variance because it is disproportionately sensitive to larger deviations from the model than the absolute deviations, or absolute errors, from which the error variance is computed. The error variance is the variability in the L1-norms, as shown in Eq. (7.7):

$$Error\ variance = \frac{\sum_{i=1}^{n_{samples}} \left(|sample_i - model_i| - \frac{\sum_{i=1}^{n_{samples}} |sample_i - model_i|}{n_{samples}} \right)^2}{n_{samples} - 1} \tag{7.7}$$

Error variance is a useful metric providing a different type of analysis than LSE because it is looking at the distribution of the error, not just the magnitude of the error. For that reason, the error variance is also usefully computed as the error coefficient of variance, as defined in Eq. (7.8), which even more represents the relative variability in the error (irrespective of the error magnitude):

$$Error\ coefficient\ of\ variance = \frac{\sqrt{Error\ variance}}{\frac{\sum_{i=1}^{n_{samples}} |sample_i - model_i|}{n_{samples}}} \tag{7.8}$$

The third metric of interest is the entropy of the error. Here, the error is broken up into bins across the range of the error magnitude and the normal entropy of the bins computed as described in Section 1.7.1, Eqs. (1.14) and (1.15). Care is taken to break up the range into uniform subrange spans such that a large number of samples are in each subrange. If the subranges are taken to be a power of 2, usually 2^8, then the maximum entropy per Eq. (1.15) is 8.00. Entropy is another measure of uniformity of distribution but imposes a different rule set on the distribution than error variance.

Combined, these three measures—LSE, error variance, and entropy—provide a "you can run but you can't hide" analysis to expose irregularities in the error data. Other histogram approaches along the lines of those presented in Ref. [Stur16] and its referenced publications can also be employed if further assurance of model goodness of fit is required. However, insofar as showing model goodness of fit, entropy is probably the cleanest method. All three metrics require a threshold value, and in general, a combination of the three, weighting entropy 3 parts and LSE 2 parts to error coefficient of variance 1 part, seems to work well for optimizing the model using the iterative process of the previous section.

7.7 Make mine multiple models!

Alliterative and yet appropriate, we conclude with a "make mine multiple models Margaret Mead meme." Paraphrasing Mademoiselle Mead, we know the advantages of a system in which each diverse analytic gift will find a fitting place. This is why we simultaneously consider LSE, error variance, and entropy. This is why we try to find relevant analogies from across the fields of science (even if only chemistry and biology are touched on deeply here). This is why we are, in this chapter and in this book as a whole, looking for as many approaches as possible. The richness of analogy is tremendous, even if we cannot directly apply the analogues to our own idiosyncratic analytic problem. This is because it gets us to think outside of our normal comfort zone, to think outside of the expected approaches to a problem space, and to deconstruct the problem we are addressing both critically and creatively. If nothing else, applying many different approaches to a particular analytic challenge will get us to probe more of the assumptions that we are making as we proceed. It will also help us to break down the barriers between different types of analytic problems and help us to apply lessons learned from one domain to another. Collaboration among widely diverse algorithms is our final analogy in this chapter—it provides the same breath of fresh air and robustness to problem solving than diversity of thought and experience brings to any team. Ms. Mead and I both recommend you use this to your advantage.

7.8 **Summary**

This chapter provides a different view of modeling and model fitting than will be found in any other text on analytics. The basic premise of this chapter is that virtually any advanced field of science, engineering, or technology can be employed for defining data system models of utility in dynamic, scalable, modular, and robust systems. Particular attention is paid to chemistry, organic chemistry, and immunology approaches, but the ability to pull from other fields is also made clear. The use of anonymization as a way of testing the optimization of a model is then put forth, followed by a discussion of some important metrology for the modeling.

Chemistry analogues used for analytics begin with a discussion of the five simplest chemical reactions. Composition, decomposition, combustion, single substitution, and double substitution are shown to be analogous to a wide range of regrouping approaches in analytics. All five equations should be applied to data sets, along with the associated statistical evaluations, to ensure that the current groupings are not contraindicated. Following these reactions, the concept of percent yield is applied to analytics, as the percent of the theoretical improvement in the analytic output that is gained. This section concludes with a discussion of limiting reagents, which provide a sort of sensitivity analysis for the overall analytic model.

Next, we considered the analogy between a sequence of reversible/bidirectional organic chemistry reactions (oxidation-reduction) and the need for robust analytics. We noted that there are multiple means of refining the categorization, including the addition of new tagging information and the removal of ectopic tagging information. We noted that data specialization (categorization, classification, clustering, indexing, etc.) is not a simple, linear-in-time evolution. We also noted that data analytics should be bidirectional in a sequence, even if more energy is required to go in one direction when compared with the other.

Next, we reviewed some of the immunologic analogues from Chapter 1 in light of the chemistry analogues. We extended the concept of deep unlearning, with both an immune and neural system allusion. We discussed the analogy between immune cell differentiation and the continual refinement of analytics. The stage of differentiation, or maturation, corresponds to an increasing precision of classification or indexing and thus a larger descriptive vocabulary for the associated data tagging. We also described the ability of data categorization to "rewind" a level (or more) and be recommitted to an alternate path—a process very much analogous to the oxidation-reduction discussion.

Next, anonymization of data is shown to be consistent with the measurements of system error entropy, least squared error (LSE), and variance. Training data is used to define a model and validation data to characterize the error in the model. The next iteration uses the data model plus the error model as the defining model. Anonymization's utility in providing both secure and reliable voice biometry is briefly discussed. Next, the model error metrics of LSE, variance, and entropy are defined, and their employment for determining model goodness of fit is provided.

The chapter finishes with what one might call a "make mine multiple models Margaret Mead meme." We next proceed to a chapter focused on meta-analytic patterns and in specific synonym-antonym and reinforce-void patterns.

References

[Chec98] Chechik, G., Meilijson, I., Ruppin, E., 1998. Synaptic pruning in development: a computational account. Neural Comput. 10 (7), 1759–1777.

[Holm09] Holmen, A., 2009. Direct conversion of methane to fuels and chemicals. Catal. Today 142, 2–8.

[Delv17] Delves, P.J., Martin, S.J., Burton, D.R., Roitt, I.M., 2017. Roitt's Essential Immunology, thirteenth ed. Wiley-Blackwell, ISBN: 978-1-118-41577-1. 576 p.

[Sims13] Simske, S., 2013. Meta-Algorithmics: Patterns for Robust, Low-Cost, High-Quality Systems. IEEE Press and Wiley, Singapore.

[Stur16] Sturgill, M., Simske, S., 2016. Mass serialization method for document encryption policy enforcement. In: ACM DocEng Symposium, pp. 193–196.

[Taka06] Takahashi, K., Yamanaka, S., 2006. Induction of pluripotent stem cells from mouse embryonic and adult fibroblast cultures by defined factors. Cell 126 (4), 663–676.

[Wilb09] Wilbraham, A., Staley, D., Matta, M., Waterman, E., 2009. Prentice Hall Chemistry, first ed. Pearson Education. 971 p.

Synonym-antonym and reinforce-void patterns

Greatness is so often a courteous synonym for great success
Philip Guedalla (1930)
We must reinforce arguments with results
Booker T Washington (1903-4)
Percibimos el vacío, llenándolo
Antonio Porchia (1943)
There is an abundance of scarcity
Steve Simske (2018)

8.1 Introduction

Powerful patterns from other fields of science can be readily and successfully brought to bear on data analysis. In the previous chapter, the fields of chemistry, biology, and immunology were the source of analytic approaches. In this chapter, we continue with patterns inspired by some of the great ideas in philosophy and logic to create rich methods for extracting rules and information from data. As Philip Guedalla notes, we are predisposed to use greatness and success synonymously. In the next section, we will turn this phrase sideways, by using synonyms to generate successful—and hopefully also great—analytic approaches.

The second major pattern type described here is the reinforce-void pattern, which can be viewed as a broad extension of the synonym-antonym patterns, where the synonyms are a form of reinforcement and the antonyms at least somewhat analogous to voids. The entire approach shares much with the famous Hegelian dialectic, which consists of three elements: (1) a thesis, which is, for example, the proposed tags, categories, and/or classes to assign data; (2) an antithesis, which undermines or opposes the thesis; and (3) a synthesis, which resolves the opposition of thesis and antithesis. A good example of this is the use of term rareness to identify keywords in a set of texts. The synthesis might be the words occurring with anomalous high frequency in the text, and the antithesis might be the words occurring with anomalous low frequency in the text. The synthesis is more sophisticated than the traditional tf^*idf, or term frequency times inverse document frequency, which only accounts for the commonality of an individual term. Instead, the synthesis is the ratio of the common term tf^*idf divided by the uncommon term tf^*idf and highlights the relative difference in two or more terms. This synthesizes both the differential high frequency of

Meta-Analytics. https://doi.org/10.1016/B978-0-12-814623-1.00008-3

some terms and the differential low frequency of the other terms. This approach can be applied to nontext data as well.

This type of reinforcement provides results that can be directly applied to separating true positives from false positives. For example, articles on Seattle, the city, and George, the first president of the United States, may both contain a differential high frequency of the term "Washington," but the former will have a much higher "Washington" to "Virginia" ratio than the latter and the latter a much higher "Washington" to "Seattle" ratio. And note that both will have a much higher "Washington" to "Booker" ratio than the author this chapter's second lead-in quote (showing the scalability of the approach!).

The reinforce-void pattern indeed fills a much-needed void, and as Antonio Porchia noted (in my translation), "we perceive the void when we fill it." This is not only a nice play on words but also an indication of why the synthesis approach works well for scalability. When we wish to distinguish two samples by category or indexing, the easiest way to look for those high ratios is to understand where the voids are. If we only have the categories on "Seattle" and "First US President," it may not occur to us that the term "Booker" might be a good differentiating term. Once the "Booker T Washington" class enters into the training data/categorization, though, we notice this former void by filling it.

The final quote to kick off this introduction is by the author himself. It is a play on words, but it speaks to the fact that we must always be cautious not to "perceive voids" as something far more important than they might be. For example, what if the cloud-based management software company Booker opened a new office in Washington, DC? It's rather easy to see how this categorization might go awry. This is just an example of why we need an abundance of scarcity, not just a single scarcity, to perform scalable clustering, categorizing, indexing, and classification—collectively "perceptual analytics."

8.2 Synonym-antonym patterns

The easiest pattern with which to introduce the Hegelian dialectic-inspired patterns of this chapter is the synonym-antonym. This is a simple trade-off in which the terms that support a given theme—tag, category, class, and index—are collectively added and the terms that contradict the given theme are collectively subtracted. These approaches are readily applied to a variety of text analytics, including search behavior and term rareness. The discussion here is based on the term frequency times inverse document frequency approach [Salt88], which formalized a method for relatively weighting terms that occur disproportionately in one category, as suggested earlier [Levi83]. Such methods are excellent for extracting key phrases [Turn00], which are in turn used to provide accurate extractive summarization [Ferr15].

For the synonyms, we can define the $tf*idf$ to be the sum over a set of synonymic terms of the products $w(i)*tf(i)*idf(i)$, where $w(i)$ is the synonymic weight given based on proximity to the categorization term of interest. The range of $w(i)$ is [0.0, 1.0], and in general, we use only $w(i) > 0.5$. The weights can be calculated based on a variety of lexicographical methods or acquired from a lexical database such as WordNet [Word18]. For the antonyms, we can define the tf^*idf to be the sum over a set of antonyms of the products of Eq. (8.1):

$$SAT = [1 - w(i)]^* tf(i)^* idf(i) \tag{8.1}$$

where $w(i)$ is the *synonymic weight* of the antonym, making $1 - w(i)$ the *antonymic weight* of the antonym. Antonymic weights can be computed using the same methodologies as the synonyms, and the range of antonyms is therefore also [0.0, 1.0]. In general, we use only $w(i) < 0.25$. Antonyms are generally less correlated negatively with key terms of a category than synonyms are correlated positively.

There are several ways of applying the synonymic and antonymic metrics as calculated. The simplest is a single-factor decision of category. For each category (or tag, index, etc.) we consider, the terms having synonymic weighting in the document are scored as in Eq. (8.2):

$$SST = w(i)^* tf(i)^* idf(i) \tag{8.2}$$

where the sum of all such synonymic terms is computed and designated the SST. Then, the terms having antonymic weighting in the document are scored as in Eq. (8.1), and the sum of all such antonymic terms computed and designated SAT. The difference, SST-SAT, is then compared for each category, and the category (or categories, if multiple categories are allowed) with the maximum value of SST-SAT is the one assigned to the document.

In addition, the synonymic and antonymic weightings can be used to create relative rareness products such as SST/SAT or disassembled into individual ratios of the terms. Alternatively, the term $w(i)^*tf(i)^*idf(i)$ scores can be compared with the category training document $w(i)^*tf(i)^*idf(i)$ scores using the inner product and the document assigned to the class with the highest SST-SAT inner product.

8.3 Reinforce-void patterns

The second pattern family is that of reinforce-void, which is shown to provide an interesting balance between consensus-driven approaches and rule-based approaches. We start off with a discussion of how tf^*idf can be brought to bear on reinforce-void approaches, but we continue with the broader set of applications possible using this method, best described as "adding by summing positives and by subtracting negatives."

In terms of reinforcement, when the calculated value of tf^*idf for a given term is much greater than the mean tf^*idf values of all terms, designated $\mu(tf^*idf)$, then a term is declared *reinforced*. We generally learn a threshold coefficient C_1 such that we can simply declare all terms with $tf^*idf > C_1^*\mu(tf^*idf)$ as the reinforced terms. Note that the system behavior should not be overly sensitive to the value of the threshold coefficient, since we will also be concerned with void terms below. In terms of void, when the value of tf^*idf for a term is $\ll \mu(tf^*idf)$, a term is declared *void*. It need not have any thematic relationship to any of the reinforced terms, although the most valuable reinforce-void pairs can be used for discriminating distinct groups of data. As an alternative to tf^*idf, reinforcement can be declared for any term for which, when it is removed from the remaining set of nonreinforced terms, it leads to an increase in overall entropy of the remaining terms greater than some minimum value.

The contrasting component of this pattern, void, can be determined by using the following:

1. Remaining entropy, which, as for reinforcement, when removed from the remaining set of nonreinforced terms, leads to an increase in overall entropy of the remaining terms greater than some minimum value. Entropy increases with either anomalously overrepresented terms (reinforced terms) or underrepresented terms (void).

2. Expectation-maximization (EM) inspired approaches. The inspiration here comes from using one approach to "shuffle" the data and then a second approach to "assign" the data. In traditional EM, we iteratively define the representative value of a cluster, usually the centroid, and then assign samples to it based on a particular measurement of proximity, usually the Euclidean distance. Once the assignment has occurred, we redefine the representative value as the shuffle step. We repeat this until convergence. Expanding on this, we are interested in defining a representative sample and then assigning samples based on their goodness of fit to the representative. Once the assignments have completed, we then redefine the representative of the group based on the attributes. It is here that the reinforce-void trade-off becomes so valuable. Once we have the new groupings, we compare the relative reinforcements and voids in each of the groupings and then redefine the groupings based on the reinforce-void combinations and start the next iteration. An example of this process is given later in this section.

3. Different coefficients of each sample tf^*idf and $C_1^*\mu(tf^*idf)$. Here, we allow the value of C_1 to vary among the terms based on the relative value of the terms to the problem space. A good example of this is to determine whether specific terms are tagging, indexing, or categorization terms, in which case we may decide to be more lenient with C_1, that is, allow C_1 to have a lower relative magnitude so that it is more likely to be considered a reinforced term or allow C_1 to have a higher relative magnitude so that it is more likely to be considered a void term. The tagged, indexed, and/or categorized terms can be obtained from the document metadata (e.g., author-provided or repository-provided). Suppose we see the term "gluten" listed as a tag for a considerable percentage of the documents. We may then decide to let $C_1=2.0$ (instead of a normal value of 5.0 or 10.0), and any document with more than twice the normal occurrence frequency of "gluten" in the text reinforces the term. We also rarely see the term "lecithin" in the database in spite of its normal high correlation with the term "gluten" elsewhere and so decide it is a good void candidate for this categorization problem. Thus, we assign $C_1=0.5$ (instead of a normal value of 0.2 or 0.1), and any document with less than half the normal occurrence frequency of "lecithin" voids the term.

Here, we follow up with an expectation-maximization example: suppose that we have three main topics in a large set of documents that we wish to recognize, tag, and repurpose. These topics are (1) skateboarding, (2) surfing, and (3) concert-going. In the first iteration, we simply take all of the documents with author keywords (lemmatized versions thereof, usually) "skateboard," "surf," and "concert" and assign these to the three categories of interest. We can then use the synonym-antonym matching of the remaining documents to assign them to one of the three classes or go "bigger" and perform a vector space model [Salt75] assignment of the unassigned documents even in this first iteration. After the documents are assigned, we generate the text statistics about the documents and then perform the next iteration with the vector space model or other suitable assignment means. This is repeated until no further changes (or diminishingly minor changes) occur in two consecutive iterations. The synonym-antonym matching can be thresholded, so only the highest differentially rated terms between classes would be used. We might see a cutoff in relevant terms after "wheels," "waves," and "woodwinds" and before "amped," "ramped," and "cramped."

As noted above, conceptually, this family of approaches is related to the Hegelian dialectic, which consists of the thesis and antithesis used together in some manner to produce a synthesis. Above, we discussed the use of the *tf*idf*; however, we could just as readily have chosen any other term-rareness-based mechanism, such as the Helmholtz-inspired approach [Bali10]. The key is that the reinforced terms are those occurring with disproportionately high frequencies and the voided terms are those occurring with disproportionately low frequencies. In the discussion above, thesis was reinforcement, and antithesis was void. Important, then, was the claim of the *ratios* of the high frequencies to the low frequencies being the synthesis. But this is not necessarily a good synthesis. Consider, for example, frequencies with relatively low coefficients of variance of 0.10. Let us suppose that we use $C_1 = 5.0$ for the reinforce and $C_1 = 0.2$ for the void. Let us also suppose for the sake of simplicity that all samples fall within two standard deviations of the mean. From the coefficient of variance (COV), that means all samples are between [4.0, 6.0] for the lowest reinforced samples and between [0.16, 0.24] for the highest void samples. The maximum ratio is therefore $6.0/0.16 = 37.5$, and the minimum ratio is $4.0/0.24 = 16.7$. This is a pretty wide range of ratios even for two populations with low COV. Thus, we may confine our synthesis to those ratios whose means are higher than the predicted means, which are the ratios of the means of the reinforced and void terms (in our example, $5.0/0.2 = 25.0$). Note that the ratio of two Gaussian curves will exceed the ratio of the means, which is a nice result and indicates that well-behaved Gaussian behavior will be rewarded by being used as "synthesis features." It is worth noting how readily such an approach can be applied to nontext data. For example, if we are classifying video images as "urban" versus "rural" based on the presence of buses (a reinforcement for "urban" and a void for "rural") and the presence of stock animals (a void for "urban" except for Pamplona in midsummer and a reinforcement for "rural") and we obtain a mean ratio of 41.4 for "urban" and a (reverse) mean ratio of 13.6 for "rural," with the anticipated ratios being 30 and 15, respectively, then we can decide to keep bus/stock as a reinforce-void for "urban." We may decide to drop stock/bus as a reinforce-void for "rural." This simple example outlines how the behavior and not just the absolute values, of the reinforcement/void ratios, can be employed as criteria for feature selection.

We are particularly interested in using reinforce-void to true positives from false positives. In classification/categorization lingo, this means we wish to drive higher precision. Please read (or reread) Chapter 6 if you are wondering why we would focus on precision! As an additional example to the "Washington" one above, let us add a third category onto the "urban" and "rural" categorization example of this section. This one will be "agricultural," and for this category, we see even higher values for "stock." In adding this category on, we also add recognition algorithms to find "borders" that include fences, walls, and barbed wires. We compute the reinforce-void ratios for each of these three categories in comparison with a large set of images including many other categories. These values are tabulated in Table 8.1. The reinforce-void ratios for "buses" come to 20.0 for the urban images and 0.05 and 0.045 for "rural" and "agricultural," respectively. Computing for "stock," the reinforce-void ratios are 0.01, 2.3, and 45.5, respectively, for "urban," "rural," and "agricultural." Finally, for the new object, "borders," the ratios are 1.1, 1.4, and 21.5, respectively.

Once these values are tabulated, we can determine which of them are reinforce and which are void features. In our example, we are looking for occurrence or non-occurrence of greater than or equal to 5 times the normal for reinforcement and less than or equal to 1/5 the normal for void. For "urban" images, then, buses are rein-forcers, and stock is voiders. For "rural," buses are voiders. For "agricultural," buses are voiders and both stock and borders and reinforcers. The other three sets of data are neither reinforcers nor voiders. So, from this, we look for high stock/bus and high border/bus ratios as indicators of the category "agricultural" and high bus/stock ratios as indicators of the category "urban." We have no "self-contained" way to look for "rural," but must instead differentiate it by having a void amount for buses and a normal value for stock and borders.

Table 8.1 Three objects recognized and counted for images belonging to three categories: "urban," "rural," and "agricultural"

Value computed	Urban	Rural	Agricultural
Buses	20.0 (reinforce)	0.05 (void)	0.045 (void)
Stock	0.01 (void)	2.3 (neither)	45.5 (reinforce)
Borders	1.1 (neither)	1.4 (neither)	21.5 (reinforce)
Buses versus stock	2000	246	1011
Buses versus borders	18.2	28	478
Stock versus borders	110	1.64	2.116

The values provided are the ratio of the occurrences in the images compared with the expected occurrences in a large set of images involving many more classes than just the three shown here. The ratios are the ratios of the means in the same column, and the higher ratio is given, and "reinforce," "void," or "neither" is indicated in parentheses. Please see text for details.

As noted in the introduction to this chapter, in order to distinguish, or "discriminate" two samples by category or indexing, we truly need an abundance of scarcity, not just a single scarcity. The "perceptual analytics" we wish to perform use reinforce-void and as such benefit from the ability of reinforce-void approaches to generate a plain text set of rules to apply. For the example of Table 8.1, we can provide a set of "domain expertise rules" for "urban," "rural," and "agricultural" as follows:

1. For "urban," we expect reinforcement of buses and void of stock. The ratio of buses to stock will be very high. The ratio of borders to stock will generally be large.
2. For "rural," we expect void of buses and intermediate values of stock and borders. The ratio of stock and borders to buses will generally be large.
3. For "agricultural," we expect void of buses and reinforce of stock and borders. The ratio of stock/bus and borders/buses will be very high. The ratio of stock and borders will not be expected to have categorization relevance.

8.4 Broader applicability of these patterns

The two interrelated patterns described above can be used together or in conjunction with other patterns, to drive further understanding. As described above, the trade-off between synonym and antonym and between reinforcement and voiding allows the analytics architect to perform an expectation-maximization inspired design, which is highly advantageous for scalability, robustness, and adaptability.

Collectively, these patterns and the expectation-maximization inspired system designs incorporating them are termed multiphase counterbalanced approaches. The multiple phases may be as straightforward as expectation and maximization. In the example above, the "representative" sample of a category is defined based on the most relevant (e.g., synonym) and least relevant (e.g., antonym) terms, and once samples are assigned to each category, the category is redefined based on its overall cosine vector model (i.e., all text, not just the category-specific text). This approach is effective and quite generalizable. By using a subset of what describes the class to assign samples to the class, there is a trade-off in the specificity of the class for the two parts of the iteration, which provides a more robust solution.

The approach can be extended to three phases in the iteration. In the first phase, the representative sample of the class is defined. In the second phase, all samples are assigned to one or more categorizations based on their affinity (e.g., Euclidean distance and cosine of the angle between the sample and representative sample). Then, samples that are anomalous for a subset of the terms used, for example, are outliers using the same set of most relevant and least relevant terms used to define the representative sample, for example, are pruned before beginning the next iteration. The threshold on this refinement (akin to a form of validation) phase should be different than that used for the definition of the category definition in the first phase, so that phases two and three do not simply add and subtract identical subsets of samples.

This three-step approach has an alliterative mnemonic, *"define, assign,* and *refine,"* and provides an additional phase to expectation-maximization (we may call it expectation-maximization-elimination in the content of E-M).

8.5 Summary

This chapter provides insight into the use of two different, though related approaches to categorization analytics. The first, synonym-antonym, focuses on the weighting of synonyms and antonyms based on their similarity or dissimilarity to categorization terms, multiplied by the relative rareness of the terms. The overall weight is $w(i)*tf(i)*idf(i)$ per term, and the summed weights of synonymic and antonymic behavior can be used for assignment purposes.

Next, the broader reinforce-void pattern family is discussed. In this section, we described how residual entropy, expectation-maximization (EM), and varying the coefficients for the ratio of occurrences to nonoccurrences can be used to generate effective features. The analogy to the Hegelian dialectic is highlighted. The behavior of reinforcement/void ratios compared with their expected values can be used as a criterion for feature selection. The use of reinforce and void for multicategory discrimination is shown by example.

We conclude the chapter with a discussion of an extension of the familiar expectation-maximization (E-M) algorithm. Here, we designate this multiphase counterbalanced approach "define, assign, and refine," but it could also be termed expectation-maximization-elimination, or E-M-E.

References

[Bali10] Balinsky, A.A., Balinsky, H., Simske, S.J., 2010. On Helmholtz's principle for documents processing. In: ACM Symposium on Document Engineering. vol. 10, pp. 283–286.

[Ferr15] Ferreira, R., Lins, R.D., Cabral, L.S., Freitas, F., Simske, S.J., Riss, M., 2015. Automatic document classification using summarization strategies. In: ACM DocEng 2015, pp. 69–72.

[Levi83] Levinson, S., 1983. Pragmatics. Cambridge University Press, New York, NY.

[Salt75] Salton, G., Wong, A., Yang, C.S.A., 1975. A vector space model for automatic indexing. Commun. ACM 18 (11), 613–620.

[Salt88] Salton, G., Buckley, C., 1988. Term-weighting approaches in automatic text retrieval. Inf. Process. Manag. 24 (5), 513–523.

[Turn00] Turney, P.D., 2000. Learning algorithms for keyphrase extraction. Inf. Retr. 2 (4), 303–336.

[Word18] WordNet. 2018. A Lexical Database for English, https://wordnet.princeton.edu/ (Accessed 19 July 2018).

Further reading

Simske, S., 2013. Meta-Algorithmics: Patterns for Robust, Low-Cost, High-Quality Systems. IEEE Press and Wiley, Singapore.

CHAPTER

Analytics around analytics

9

For the things we have to learn before we can do them, we learn by doing
Aristotle
As areas of knowledge grow, so too do the perimeters of ignorance
Neil deGrasse Tyson (2012)

9.1 Introduction

A book on meta-analytics is clearly going to focus on design patterns to bring multiple analytics to bear on a problem. The past few chapters have focused on precisely these—predictive selection, chemistry- and biology-inspired algorithms, and reinforcement-void being the exemplars. In this chapter, we consider another definition of "meta," the "more comprehensive and transcending" one. Going beyond simple analytics, we are focused on several introspective analytics about the analytics we are capturing. Next, we describe how to optimize the settings for analytics from the training data (a form of introspective validation). We then overview how to use expectation-maximization analytics to optimize systems and system settings (not just the algorithms or analytics). We conclude with ways to integrate analytics into the very fiber of system life cycle: functional measurements of the effectiveness of analytics in their purported roles.

The quote from Aristotle is at first read bizarre, because its opposite is "the thing we don't have to learn before we can do" it—that is, an innate ability. It also strikes me as sententious, since Aristotle was the guy too lazy to throw a heavy and a light object down a drop at the same time, and so, a decent understanding of gravity had to wait for Galileo and the leaning tower of Pisa, at least apocryphally. Certainly, Aristotle is guilty of believing that objects fall at a speed that is proportional to their weight (hint for nonphysics folks: they don't). But I still like the quote by Aristotle for its relevance to meta-analytics: the thing we have to learn before we can do it is to accept the fact that no single analytic approach is going to provide the best results for a given problem, problem space, or system all of the time. We learn this by doing meta-analytic design and seeing the advantages that a meta-analytic approach provides for a wide range of important system design concerns, including but not limited to (a) performance; (b) robustness; (c) accuracy; (d) cost; (e) modularity and repurposability; (f) testing, measurement, and validation; (g) scalability; and (h) reliability. This book should provide the encouragement and hopefully the means to do the thing we need to do to learn. Ouch, that hurt just to write, but I'll blame Aristotle.

237

Meta-Analytics. https://doi.org/10.1016/B978-0-12-814623-1.00009-5

Newton often acknowledged that his advancements were because he was standing on the shoulders of giants, among which Aristotle is certainly found. I feel in this book that I am trying to *understand* on the shoulders of giants. The giants I allude to are those who paved the way for analytics and "big data" to fill the role they do in today's world. And meta-analytic approaches are a knowing nod to the fact that there are quite likely two (or more!) brilliant analytics that can be implemented at any "knowledge opportunity" in a system design. A wise system designer doesn't usually try to outdo the genius that came before; instead, the designer tries to use this genius to advantage in a meta-approach, that is, in a system.

The quote by Neil deGrasse Tyson is even more relevant to this chapter. The price we pay for gaining knowledge stems from the double-sided nature of knowledge. There is a reinforcement-void quality to knowledge: when we learn something more in a subject (reinforcement), we recognize something else that we have yet to know (void). This void is part of the perimeter of ignorance. Awareness of this void certainly helps us focus our subsequent learning, attempting to fill the void with understanding. But every time we do, we make the body of knowledge larger and thus increase its perimeter (or surface area). Envisioning knowledge as being surrounded on all boundaries by ignorance, this naturally means that ignorance grows every time we add to knowledge. It's a good time to be a data scientist, because it means the more you learn, the more you're needed. Let's go grow that perimeter.

9.2 Analytics around analytics

To start the consideration of "meta-" in "meta-analytics" where we mean "more comprehensive and transcending," all we need to do is make the "meta-" sequentially broader, each "meta-" encapsulating the previous. The first meta- is the meta-analytic concerned with employing two or more analytics (prediction and selection, reinforcement and void, etc.) in an intelligent hybrid pattern. The second meta- is the meta-analytics concerned with going beyond the hybrid analytics and taking an analytic approach to evaluating the already potentially meta-analytic system that we are using to generate information and intelligence from data sets. In this section, we consider the topics of entropy and occurrence vectors, functional metrics, and expectation-maximization approaches, before concluding with a brief discussion of system design concerns.

9.2.1 Entropy and occurrence vectors

If you've read the previous chapters, then you've already seen the value of entropy for determining how much information is contained in a system or system design and for determining the goodness of fit of a system model. The mantra for the latter is "the better the model fits the data, the higher the entropy of the residual error between the system and model." From this perspective, entropy is particularly valuable for determining the randomness of a particular distribution. The magnitude of random noise in a system is certainly a concern, but the nature of random noise is such that we, as system designers, feel that we have done all we can to prevent a structured, or systematic, noise from being missed or ignored.

Entropy as a means of assessing uniformity of distribution can be used on a variety of distributions. One of the more subtle uses is in difference sets. The superficial application of this is in comparing data sets over time. We can assign entire data sets, subdomains of the data sets, or even subsets of the data associated with a specific metadata label (time/date, location, person collecting the data, device collecting the data, etc.) to the compared groups (among other options). Changes in entropy are used solely as a data "triage," indicating the need for follow-up evaluation. A simple use of entropy change is to monitor repositories for encryption compliance. We have been able to distinguish compression and encryption, as well as different encryption processes, in past work [Stur16]. Applying entropy assessment to subsets of data is an extremely automated process, which means it is effectively infinitely scalable, and can be run as an "idle-time process" to any desired level of thoroughness.

Entropy measurements can also be used to correlate descriptive distributions such as histogram of occurrences of different terms (in documents) or items (in videos), among other "sortable" data. Such data can of course be compared also with a model for the data. Suppose that we are looking at a histogram of word occurrences in a corpus, irrespective of the document assignments. Zipf's law, which propounds that the occurrence frequency of any word is inversely proportional to its relative rank in occurrences, can be used to model the actual frequencies. Corpora can be directly compared with each other and with the ideal Zipf distribution using entropy of the residuals as a metric. This is shown through the sequential data sets of Tables 9.1, 9.2, 9.3, and 9.4, described next.

In Table 9.1, we provide the residual entropy as a ratio of the maximum residual entropy for comparing any two of four word frequency distributions. For simplicity, no alignment of the terms between the compared pairs of distributions is performed; thus, the entropy value represents only differences in the shape of the distribution of ranked terms, not the actual terms across the distributions. In Table 9.1, we see that

Table 9.1 Percent of maximum entropy in residual distribution for comparing any pair of the three word frequency distributions A, B, and C or in comparing any of the three with the ideal Zipf's law distribution, first data set

Corpus	A	B	C	Zipf ideal
A	1.000	0.956	0.878	0.794
B	0.956	1.000	0.812	0.899
C	0.878	0.812	1.000	0.957
Zipf ideal	0.794	0.899	0.957	1.000

Comparison of the same sets results in maximum entropy (all values=0.000) by definition. Please see text for details.

Table 9.2 Percent of maximum entropy in residual distribution for comparing any pair of the three word frequency distributions A, B, and C or in comparing any of the three with the ideal Zipf's law distribution, second (cumulative) data set

Corpus	A	B	C	Zipf ideal
A	1.000	0.943	0.856	0.803
B	0.943	1.000	0.826	0.897
C	0.856	0.826	1.000	0.949
Zipf ideal	0.803	0.897	0.949	1.000

Comparison of the same sets results in maximum entropy (all values=0.000) by definition. Please see text for details.

Table 9.3 Percent of maximum entropy in residual distribution for comparing any pair of the three word frequency distributions A, B, and C or in comparing any of the three with the ideal Zipf's law distribution, difference between second (cumulative) and first data sets (values of Table 9.1 subtracted from values of Table 9.2)

Corpus	A	B	C	Zipf ideal
A	0.000	−0.013	−0.022	0.009
B	−0.013	0.000	0.014	−0.002
C	−0.022	0.014	0.000	−0.008
Zipf ideal	0.009	−0.002	−0.008	0.000

Please see text for details.

Table 9.4 Percent of maximum entropy in residual distribution for comparing any pair of the three word frequency distributions A, B, and C or in comparing any of the three with the ideal Zipf's law distribution, difference between eleventh and tenth, tenth and ninth, ..., second and first data set (mean ± standard deviation of the 10 sequential comparisons)

Corpus	A	B	C	Zipf ideal
A	0.000±0.000	−0.006±0.012	−0.002±0.011	0.011±0.003*
B	−0.006±0.012	0.000±0.000	0.013±0.005*	0.003±0.002*
C	−0.002±0.011	0.013±0.005*	0.000±0.000	0.001±0.001*
Zipf ideal	0.011±0.003*	0.003±0.002*	0.001±0.001*	0.000±0.000

*Data sets are cumulative, meaning data set 11 has 11 times the data as data set 1. Statistics that are statistically significantly different from 0.000 at two-tailed z-test of a<0.05 are indicated by *. Please see text for details.*

distributions A and B have highly entropic differences between them and that distribution C has a highly entropic difference distribution in comparison with an idealized Zipf distribution. This means that there are no predictable differences between A and B, not C from a Zipf distribution.

In Table 9.2, another equally sized set of data for corpora A, B, and C are added to the original data set (cumulative data set twice the original size), and these are pair-wise compared or compared with the ideal Zipf distribution. While the values are similar to Table 9.2, we can see that there is some variance in the entropy in comparing the two sets. These differences are captured in Table 9.3.

In order to see if any trends observed for single differences in Table 9.3 continue for additional sets of data, we accumulate 10 difference entropies from samples taken over time (for cumulative data sets 2, 3, 4, ..., 11 times the size of the first data set). The means and standard deviations of these samples are shown in Table 9.4, along with the statistically significant trends, as determined by two-tailed z-tests of the means (compared with the expected values of 0.0).

In Table 9.4, four statistically significant trends are observed (don't be fooled by the eight asterisks—the matrix is symmetrical, and so, each pairwise comparison shows up twice in the matrix). For all three distributions—A, B, and C—the trend is for newer data sets to have higher entropy when differenced from the ideal Zipf's law. This is likely a result of larger values of data more closely approximating a Zipf distribution, but this was never a guarantee unless the actual complete distribution really did follow a Zipf. The other trend is for entropy in comparing B and C to increase, meaning these two populations start to have no structured differences as they accumulate in size.

Note that the approach taken here, evaluating entropy as the cumulative data set increases in size, can behave differently from evaluating the correlation of the two sets. With correlation, the terms would usually be aligned, and so, the differences calculated would be for comparing terms that are not usually ranked the same in each distribution (and the ranking of an individual word in each distribution would also likely vary). Thus, we are looking for the correlation of frequency of words such as "because" and "market," but these words might be ranked 675 and 1423 in corpus 1 and ranked 423 and 2431 in corpus 2. With the entropy measurement described above, we are comparing the frequency of terms 675, 423, 1423, and 2431, which might match "had" and "because," "because" and "take," "market" and "consider," and "form" and "market," respectively, for the two distributions. The key is that entropy evaluates differences in the shape of the distribution, whereas correlation evaluates differences in the occurrence frequency of the same terms.

The third example use of entropy as a means of assessing uniformity of distribution is to directly compare vector representations of the term frequencies. The comparison is done by multiplying the frequencies of the like terms together and summing them, a process called the inner product. This approach combines the entropy and correlation approaches as described above. A word vector is simply the set of occurrences of the words, divided by the total number of words. For the example here, we might see the first corpus has frequencies for "had," "because," "market," and "form" of 0.000122, 0.000087, 0.000043, and 0.000029, respectively. If the form of the second distribution is exactly the same as the form for the first distribution, then the frequencies for "because," "take," "consider," and "market" would be exactly 0.000122, 0.000087, 0.000043, and 0.000029, respectively. Of course, this doesn't often happen with real data, and so, our measured values are a similar but not identical 0.000108, 0.000091, 0.000053, and 0.000031 for "because," "take," "consider," and "market," respectively. The vector model then multiplies together all of the values for the same terms in the two distributions and sums them. We only have the values for "because" (0.000087 and 0.000108 in the two distributions) and "market" (0.000043 and 0.000031 in the two distributions), for which the "inner products" are $87 \times 108 \times 10^{-12}$ and $43 \times 31 \times 10^{-12}$. Suppose we had a simple distribution with four terms with frequencies 0.4, 0.3, 0.2, and 0.1. The inner product of these two exactly equal distributions is therefore $(0.4)^2+(0.3)^2+(0.2)^2+(0.1)^2=0.16+0.09+0.04+0.01=0.30$. The maximum sum is clearly dependent on the nature of the distribution and in particular the frequency of the most common terms. We can always predict the maximum possible inner product from Eq. (9.1):

$$\text{Max inner product} = \sum_{n=1}^{N_{terms}} \max\left((p_A(term_n))^2, (p_B(term_n))^2 \right) \tag{9.1}$$

In Eq. (9.1), $p_A(term_n)$ is the relative frequency of term n in distribution A, and $p_B(term_n)$ is the relative frequency of term n in distribution B. This maximum possible inner product can be used to normalize the sums of inner products so they can be compared across corpora. For the simple two-term results, we obtained for "because" and "market," the maximum possible inner product is $(108)^2 \times 10^{-12}$ for "because" and $(43)^2 \times 10^{-12}$ for "market." The percent of the maximum that we actually obtained is thus $(87+31)/(108+43)=0.781$. Note that this value is a very useful metric for determining document similarity (and for recommending the next document to read while learning a topic).

The vector model is akin to correlation in that it finds the relative amount of shared term frequency and akin to entropy in that it exposes differences in the distribution (if, e.g., we use it for subdomains of the terms, i.e., the first 1000 terms and then next 1000 terms). Regardless, with entropy, correlation, and occurrence vectors, we have a strong set of analytics to recognize potential differences in distributions before in-depth analytics have been applied.

9.2.2 Functional metrics

The fundamental rule on functional metrics is "if you can find one, please use it." There are many advantages to functional metrics, including the reduced (often to zero) need to create ground truth (human labeled) data and the ability often to catch two birds with one worm (to rewrite a less pleasant idiomatic expression). First, though, we'll describe what is meant by "functional," and then, a few examples will naturally follow.

Functional metrics are measurable processes that in their normal working, or "functioning," give us insight into other analytics. A familiar functional measurement is the behavior of a set of search queries such as mentioned in Section 2.4 and described in Ref. [Sims14]. Here, we are interested in being able to rate a set of translation engines without having to request a bilingual speaker/reader to perform the evaluation. Instead, we use an automatic index generator to generate a set of indexing terms, which are then used for search queries. In order to gauge which translation engine performs best, the translation engines are used to simultaneously translate the corpora and the search terms. The corpus/search query set that provides the search behavior most closely matching that of the original (untranslated) document set is deemed the best translator. The reason this works is that the search terms are almost certainly translated with a different accuracy, tactic, etc., than the documents themselves—the search terms are generally just single or compound words rather than full sentences. The functional measurement (search behavior) is used to rank the analytics (in this case text translator) in the correct order.

Another example is the use of a functional measurement (classification) to functionally test another analytics (summarization). For a document corpus, different classification engines are used to assign the documents to their correct classes. The 20 newsgroups data set [Lang95] is a standard classification set, and if these 20,000 newsletters are summarized, we would expect the accuracy of classification to drop from peak values as high as 82% [Sims06]. However, the summarization engine whose output provides the highest overall accuracy on the 20,000 summarized newsletters (assuming each summarizer is allowed the same amount of compression, e.g., to 20% of original length) is identified as the best summarizer. The classification accuracy is the automatically computed functional metric that is used to assess the best analytics (in this case, summarization engine).

A third example is the use of a functional metric (face recognition accuracy) to identify the best face detection algorithm. This example is a bit different from the one above and hopefully illustrates some of the craftsmanship that can be involved to avoid the dreaded extra work of human tagging (and interference!). At first glance, this might appear contradictory—how can we rate face detection accuracy based on face recognition, since face recognition is a precursor step to it? By analogy, this is like using object recognition accuracy to rate the binarization (thresholding) algorithm—see Section 1.7.7 for more on this subject. Since binarization is upstream from object recognition, we know that the relative accuracy of a binarization algorithm—for this type of problem, at least—can be inferred with relatively high confidence based on the object recognition accuracy. The same can be said for face recognition downstream from face detection (segmentation). What is needed in both cases is a good labeled object repository. Fortunately, there are many of them [Fish18], not only for face recognition but also for many other biometrics. These repositories allow us to use an already-labeled data set to test another. The key to applying this type of approach is modularity of system design. So long as the only difference in the system is the analytics of interest, we can infer the differences in the downstream measured behavior as resulting from differences in the attributes of the modularized analytics. Interestingly, the follow-up on this approach is also very palatable from an automation standpoint. We can readily subdivide the outcomes (face recognition categories) and so perform an "inverse predictive selection" algorithm on the categories. That is, we can assign the images for the face recognition to categories *a posteriori* and then find attributes from these categories that could be fed forward to subdivide the input space in case a different face detection algorithm might be indicated for two or more subgroups.

Another example of a functional metric worth overviewing here is one in which the functional measurement is more derived than the analytic it is optimizing. For this example, consider a speech recognition engine being used for GPS guidance. The best speech recognition engine is deemed the one that provides the shortest time in directed navigation tasks. There are a number of ways of aligning the data sets, including comparing like paths and computing the number of backtracks and reversals, which don't need in-depth discussion here. The key is that the function is giving good driving directions, while the functional measurement is an attribute (time, distance, number of backtracks, etc.) of the primary function. Thus, this example represents a class of functional measurements in which *secondary functions*—not just primary functions—are used to score the different candidate analytics. This motif could in theory be extended further—for example, to tertiary functions like the miles per hour (distance/time)—but the further from primary functional measurements we get in our assessment metrics, the less likely the evaluation is to be robust to changes in the inputs to the system over time. The recommendation is to use primary functions *wherever possible*.

Before leaving this section, an analogy might be worth considering. The difference between direct measurement of a new analytic for optimization and using functional metrics as illustrated here is analogous to the difference between anatomy and physiology. The anatomy of an organism is its structure, the way it comes together. The physiology of an organism is the way it works. Ideally, we match form and function for an optimized system, the premise being that the best architecture for the system is the one that functions the best. In this way, the method of functional metrics illustrated by the examples here innately *makes sense* to the system designer. That being said, never be fooled by the beauty of an algorithm, analytic, or architecture. Beauty may only be skin—I mean interface—deep. A beautiful design married to a healthy skepticism is the ideal union: a system for analyzing data is also a system to which data analysis can be applied for its betterment.

9.2.3 E-M (expectation-maximization) approaches

Expectation-maximization (EM)-inspired approaches were considered for their analogous nature to reinforce-void patterns in Section 8.4. In the traditional implementation, originally formalized in Ref. [Demp77], we iteratively define the representative value of a cluster, which is usually the centroid, and then assign candidate samples to it based on a proximity measurement (often the Euclidean distance). Once the assignment has occurred, we redefine the representative value from the assigned candidate samples and repeat the process until convergence is indicated.

For this section, we are more concerned with the analytics around the E-M as an analytic. Two types of analytics immediately come to mind when applying E-M or E-M-inspired approaches: (1) analytics on the speed of convergence of the algorithm and (2) analytics on the entropy of convergence of the algorithm. One means of gathering these analytics without loss of statistical power—that is, cheating on the actual degrees of freedom available—is to use multiple initial representative values (starting points). We should always be allowed initial assignments equal to the number of samples minus the number of classes minus 1, based on degrees of freedom alone. For (1), we may wish to use a directionally proportional (including Cartesian coordinate and angular variability) distance computation for convergence. The angle can be assessed using a Hough transform, and the rough aspect ratios of the clusters can be garnered from a set of nearest neighbor connections, using the largest connected components to estimate any directional bias (e.g., ovoid vs. circular) in the shapes of the "cluster estimates." For (2), the entropy approaches of the previous Section 9.2.2 can be brought to bear on the cluster differences between two iterations. The direction of the changes of the points from their cluster centroids can be accumulated in a histogram, for example, one varying from 0 to 360 degrees in 5-degree increments. The entropy of this 72-bin histogram can then be assessed, with the assumption that it will approach its maximum of 6.17 bits of information—since $\log_2(72) = 6.17$—as the convergence occurs.

9.2.4 System design concerns

When choosing among even the relatively small set of design options for the analytics around analytics, we must consider a large range of important system design concerns, including but not limited to (a) performance; (b) robustness; (c) accuracy; (d) cost; (e) modularity and repurposability; (f) testing, measurement, and validation; (g) scalability; and (h) reliability. At first glance, this might seem like a very open-ended problem, but when looked at from the right angle, it is a simple design strategy. For each of these design concerns, before beginning any implementation, plan an "analytics strategy" for each of them, and implement it from the ground up. This design should also preferably occur before—or at least concurrently—to the designing of other system-wide concerns such as security, manufacturing process, sourcing and procurement, EMI/RFI remediation, and the like.

A simple example for each of these is given here. For performance, a simple analytic is the difference entropy when the system is benchmarked on the same data set before and after each new module is functionalized. For robustness, a vector model of the behavior of two versions on a broad array of input will help to determine areas of focus for system improvement—domains with inner products substantially lower than maximum are indicative of instability to input and thus nonrobustness. For accuracy, functional output such as classification is a good system analytic approach. For cost, the entropy of system behavior (in performance, robustness, accuracy, etc.) for different changes in system design, each with the same impact on cost, can be used to identify the subsystems most sensitive to cost. For modularity and repurposability, the coefficient of variance methods is useful for qualifying the changes when modules are substituted with stubs or other nonfunctionality (or the inverse, when stubs are replaced with functionality or when different functionalities performing the same task are substituted). Scalability can be tested by vector modeling of the behavior attributes across new samples: the behavior of existing samples does not need to be calculated, making this an O(N) calculation. Finally, reliability can generally be tested along the lines of robustness.

I have focused on entropy in this chapter, because it can be applied to subsets of the data, and it can be fitted to the expected error distributions readily (e.g., Gaussian or the difference between two Gaussians). In most cases, though, entropy could be substituted reasonably by variance or coefficient of variation measurements, even though they have a slightly different interpretation. My preference is to calculate all three for the different insights that they may provide.

9.3 Optimizing settings from training data

Next, we describe how to optimize the settings for analytics from the training data (a form of introspective validation). Considerable detail around ground truthing and optimizing the use and life cycle of training data was given in Chapter 2 and will not be repeated here. Instead, here, we consider how to optimize the settings for the analysis of the analytics from the training data. We do this in part by viewing training data pruning as an analogue for information extraction. This is an area of considerable interest to analytics presently. In Ref. [Zend17], for example, two key questions are asked of the test data: (1) "What should be part of the test data set to ensure that the required level of robustness is achieved?," and (2) "How can redundancies be reduced (to save time and remove bias due to repeated elements)?" The first question considers the breadth of the training (or testing) data, while the second question considers the depth of the training set in specific areas. Sounds a little familiar in this chapter but suffice it to say that it might make sense to check the training/test set for entropy of representation across the sample input domain. This handles the (too much) depth (in one subdomain) problem and allows us to address the breadth so long as we know what *should* be in the distribution.

Optimizing settings goes deeper than simply ensuring that the training and testing data represent the entire input domain and do not overrepresent any subdomain. We have learned about the "representative sample" of a cluster, category, or class, particularly in the application of expectation-maximization analytics. But another type of representative sample may be required. For example, which samples from a population are best able to highlight the deviation from other populations? One approach that has some success in certain applications is in separating data into bands based on standard deviations apart from the mean for different features. Usually, the best features for this approach are the ones that best distinguish a certain population from another. Samples falling within a standard deviation of the mean for this feature may be more representative of the underlying population than those more than a standard deviation away. There are two potential advantages to this approach: (1) We use the central limit theorem to find more representative samples for distinguishing classes by including all samples within a standard deviation (or other multiples of standard deviations) rather than just the mean, and (2) we allow the samples outside of the central zone to be mined for the creation of new categories. We can think of these "outliers" as potentially benefitting from the analytics equivalent of "reproductive isolation," which leads to speciation by preventing two subpopulations from interacting. Our "data isolation" can be used to consider splitting classes into subclasses, the outlier subclasses of which are then encouraged/allowed to interact with splintered subpopulations from other populations.

9.4 Hybrid methods

We start off this section showing how to use expectation-maximization (shorthand E-M and we call them expectation-optimization, or E-O, since this is a broader range of applications than just maximization) analytics to optimize systems and system settings (not just the algorithms or analytics). We have covered E-M/E-O algorithms in some detail in Sections 8.4 and 9.2.3 above. Here, we are concerned with using the E-O approach as part of a larger analytic system. One means of employing E-M is by adding a third step to expectation and optimization, here called regularization but used in an even broader sense than the regularization applied to clustering, for example, in Chapter 10.

As first mentioned in Section 1.7.8, clustering outcomes can be attained using a kNN (k-nearest neighbor) approach for sample assignment to clusters. The kNN algorithm is a classic approach to aggregating data, going back at least 50 years [Cove67]. Adding a third step in each iteration, regularization, creates an E-O-R, or "Eeyore," algorithm that hopefully builds a sturdier structure for analytics than might the eponymous donkey. Regardless, the regularization step is straightforward, in its rudimentary form involving no more than an F-score (please see Section 1.6.2 for more on F-scores). The F-score is the ratio of between-cluster and within-cluster variance and is calculated for each value of k in the reasonable range of k values for the data. For large numbers of clusters (medium to large data sets), we may choose to provide a moving average of F-score versus k in order to choose the true optimum for k, especially where each cluster may correspond to a distinct set of follow-on analytics.

As mentioned, the F-score is used in analysis of variance (ANOVA) and other statistical comparisons. The F-score is defined as in Eq. (9.2):

$$F = \frac{MSE_b}{MSE_w} \tag{9.2}$$

In Eq. (9.2), the numerator, MSE_b, is the mean-squared error between the groups, and MSE_w is the mean-squared error within the groups. The ratio of MSE_b/MSE_w—that is, the F-score—can be used to optimize clustering. The highest F-score corresponding to an acceptable/valid value of k indicates the naive best clustering for the data. We will add regularization onto this approach in Chapter 10, but for now, it is worth noting that this method is scalable to any size data space and any number of clusters. The range of acceptable k can be obtained in several ways: domain expertise, estimated cluster size from histogram of distances from each sample to all other samples, metadata differences in the data labeling, etc.

Other hybrid methods for analysis include computing more traditional distance metrics, like the Jaccard similarity coefficient, given by Eq. (9.3):

$$Jaccard(A, B) = \frac{|A \cap B|}{|A \cup B|} = \frac{|A \cap B|}{|A| + |B| - |A \cap B|} \tag{9.3}$$

The Jaccard distance, which represents the dissimilarity between two sets of data, is given by Eq. (9.4):

$$Distance_{Jaccard} = 1 - Jaccard(A, B) = \frac{|A \cup B| - |A \cap B|}{|A \cup B|} = \frac{|A| + |B| - 2|A \cap B|}{|A| + |B| - |A \cap B|} \tag{9.4}$$

Other forms of the Jaccard approach can be attempted as well. Jaccard[n] variants are shown in Eq. (9.5):

$$Jaccard[n](A, B) = \frac{|A|^n |B|^n}{|A|^n + |B|^n} \tag{9.5}$$

As many of the Jaccard equations can be used as desired, and they can be evaluated precisely along the lines of any other feature for classification, categorization, or clustering.

In Section 7.7, least squared error (LSE), variance of the error, and entropy measurements were used to determine the goodness of fit of a data model. These three metrics were chosen as they are easy to compute, unambiguous, and robust to the range of data input. A weighted combination of these three metrics can be used to evaluate the different Jaccard metrics, for example, to see which of them tracks best with error in the model. Also, like the Jaccard methods, the weighted combination of these can be used for the regularization step in the Eeyore algorithm.

A final type of regularization will complete this section. Up to this point, we have been concerned with quantitative regularization, that is, regularization based on a computed regularization term, which is then optimized across a range of values to suggest an optimum configuration of the incremental expectation-optimization results (E-O-R). However, qualitative regularization is also possible. By qualitative, we mean that the regularization is performed *in situ* rather than being evaluative across a range. Regularization of the boundary points in a support vector, or *in situ* reclustering, can both be regularized by the following methods:

(a) Use only those points that are closer to a boundary at some point than ANY other member of their cluster. This deselects points that have "line of sight" to another cluster (or class in the case of SVM). This qualitative rule is adaptable; for example, we may wish to include points that only have one, two, or other points that are closer to the nearest boundary point (thus, this scales with the size of the data sets in the clusters/classes).

(b) Reseed clusters based on the inverse of their distance from the representative sample (e.g., centroid) of the cluster. The closer to a boundary, the more likely such a point can be used to reseed a new cluster. This is a qualitative variant of the approach outlined in Section 9.4.

9.5 Other areas for investigation around the analytics

Analytics are the algorithms, processes, and systems into which we input raw data and from which we extricate information, knowledge, recommendations, and estimations. The simplest analytics are descriptive outputs such as mean, standard deviation, and z-score. Analytic processes include the more sophisticated patterns—predictive selection, inverse predictive selection, reinforce-void, weighted voting, sensitivity analysis, cumulative response, extended expectation-optimization, among others—which can be employed for a wide variety of analytic problems with very little domain customization necessary. Systems for analytics include the classification approach of Chapter 1 and the clustering approach of Chapter 10, and these tools provide a means of structuring and organizing the information generated by the algorithms and processes. Analytics around these analytics include assessing, simultaneously, which of these provide the best desired output for the analytic system. This can be assessed along the lines of any/all of the system concerns of Section 9.2.4 and provide a means of optimizing the analytics strategy for the system in deployment.

Analytics about analytics, more generally, are functional measurements of the effectiveness of analytics in their purported roles. This is a broad area of meta-analytics in which any insight into how the analytic processes being applied to a system are being (or not being) effective can be collected for evaluation not of the primary data, but of the effectiveness with which the data is being evaluated. This is increasingly important as a larger amount of data is collected each day. Without this form of data "introspection," we can only hope that data are being analyzed effectively and appropriately. With the widespread implementation of Internet-connected sensors, there is the ability to augment other collected sensor data when additional clarity is required. An increasingly important part of meta-analytics will indeed be knowing when and how to augment data already being analyzed with data that has not yet been analyzed, but may add understanding.

9.6 Summary

In this chapter, we went beyond the meta-analytic approach of bringing two or more analytics together to improve the overall analytic behavior (cost, accuracy, robustness, etc.). We measured the analytics themselves. The analytics around analytics include applying methods based on entropy, including the application of entropy to difference sets; the application of entropy to descriptive distributions such as histograms (with discussion of the relationship to correlation); and the use of occurrence vectors, which allow inner products to be calculated that merge the best of Jaccard and correlative approaches. The manner in which to calculate the maximum inner product is given.

Next, functional metrics in which one or more measurable processes that in their normal working, or "functioning," give us insight into other analytics we wish to evaluate were considered. The examples given helped illustrate some of the art in the process, while the recommendation to use primary functional metrics where possible and to use existing databases of labeled functional metrics helped illustrate the science in the process. One particular functional metric design pattern mentioned, the "inverse predictive selection," has been used by the author in numerous applications to provide better forward estimation as part of optimizing the analytics.

We briefly revisited expectation-maximization approaches covered in a different light in Section 8.4. Here, we are focused on the analytics around the E-M analytic, namely, the speed of convergence and the entropy of the convergence. Next, we reinforced the value of connecting analytics around important system design concerns of (a) performance; (b) robustness; (c) accuracy; (d) cost; (e) modularity and repurposability; (f) testing, measurement, and validation; (g) scalability; and (h) reliability.

Optimizing settings from training data is first concerned with ensuring that the data set used for training or testing is both as broad and as uniformly deep as needed to ensure optimal system robustness. Training data are also useful for defining representative samples and, as appropriate, for defining new categories from outlier data.

Finally, hybrid methods are covered. Expectation-maximization, or as described here "expectation-optimization," approaches are augmented with regularization to create an expectation-optimization-regulation, or E-O-R ("Eeyore"), algorithm. The Eeyore algorithm affords a two-factor optimization based on iterative assignment to representative samples (E-O) and optimization of the number of clusters with an F-score calculation. Jaccard similarity, distance, and variants are covered, and we complete the chapter's new material with a consideration of qualitative regularization and a big picture view of meta-analytics as "analytics about analytics."

References

[Cove67] Cover, T.M., Hart, P.E., 1967. Nearest neighbor pattern classification. IEEE Trans. Inf. Theory 13 (1), 21–27.

[Demp77] Dempster, A.P., Laird, N.M., Rubin, D.B., 1977. Maximum likelihood from incomplete data via the EM algorithm. J. R. Stat. Soc. Ser. B 39 (1), 1–38.

[Fish18] Fisher RB, 2018. CVonline: Image Databases, School of Informatics, University of Edinburgh, http://homepages.inf.ed.ac.uk/rbf/CVonline/Imagedbase.htm (Accessed 25 July 2018).

[Lang95] Lang, K., 1995. NewsWeeder: learning to filter netnews. In: Proceedings of the Twelfth International Conference on Machine Learning, pp. 331–339.

[Sims06] Simske, S.J., Wright, D.W., Sturgill, M., 2006. Meta-algorithmic systems for document classification. In: ACM Symposium on Document Engineering, pp. 98–106.

[Sims14] Simske, S.J., Boyko, I.M., Koutrika, G., 2014. Multi-engine search and language translation. In: EDBT/ICDT Workshops, pp. 188–190.

[Stur16] Sturgill, M., Simske, S., 2016. Mass serialization method for document encryption policy enforcement. In: ACM DocEng Symposium, pp. 193–196.

[Zend17] Zendel, O., Murschitz, M., Humenberger, M., Herzner, W., 2017. How good is my test data? Introducing safety analysis for computer vision. Int. J. Comput. Vis. 125 (1–3), 95–109.

Further reading

Simske, S., 2013. Meta-Algorithmics: Patterns for Robust, Low-Cost, High-Quality Systems. IEEE Press and Wiley, Singapore.

System design optimization

10

As to methods, there may be a million and then some, but principles are few. The man who grasps principles can successfully select his own methods. The man who tries methods, ignoring principles, is sure to have trouble
Harrington Emerson (1911)
Insanity: doing the same thing over and over again and expecting different results
various sources
Have no fear of perfection—you'll never reach it
Salvador Dalí

10.1 Introduction

Often attributed to the other Emerson (Ralph Waldo, that is—please see quotes for Chapter 3), Harrington Emerson clearly understood the role of a system architect: she who approaches system design by trying one method after the other is doomed to inefficiency. She may be successful in the end—tenacity overcomes a lot misdirection—but she is likely to enjoy the process a lot more if the methods are applied to a principled architecture and if the methods themselves are understood from a larger perspective than the individual—perhaps custom and perhaps idiosyncratic—system being designed. For this reason, we focus on the principles of analytics and meta-analytics and show how a core set of principles apply to the methods used for analyzing both the data and the system using the data.

Another quote often attributed to a very famous person (Albert Einstein, you've probably heard of him) is that insanity is "doing the same thing over and over again and expecting different results." This is the flip side of a core tenet of meta-analytics. With a wide variety of meta-analytic approaches—from the patterns for hybrid analytics to the use of analytics on the analytics themselves and on system design—the analytic system designer need never do the same thing over and over. The principles of meta-analytics allow the designer to employ a "virtual infinity" of approaches without a huge change in methodology, system design, or test plan. One goal in system design is to get as much as you can with as little redesign as possible. But another, perhaps equally important, goal is to be able to react to situations that are clearly going awry without losing your previous investment in design, your previously collected data and information, and indeed your cool.

Meta-Analytics. https://doi.org/10.1016/B978-0-12-814623-1.00010-1

Salvador Dalí's advice is another encouragement to stay cool in the face of data inundation. Unless you are a perfect expert in an area, there will always be more that you can extract, or should I say extricate, from the data. We strive for perfection, but if we could reach it, we wouldn't need measurements like recall, precision, accuracy, F-score, z-score, t-score, and the like. With that humbling fact in mind, let's continue to explore tools to move us closer to perfection.

10.1.1 System considerations—Revisiting the system gains

In Chapter 3, we described how ensemble methods, such as those described in Ref. [Sims13], tend to move the correct answer higher in the overall ranked list (*rank*) more so than simply moving the correct result to the top of the list (*accuracy*). In terms of system design theory, the co-occurrence and similarity-based ensemble approaches of previous chapters are designated as *rank-biased systems*, not *accuracy-biased systems*. This is a well-known benefit of meta-algorithmic approaches, and it has a huge positive impact on overall system cost models, since the highest costs are often associated with recovering from errors. Rank-biased systems make less errors over time, even if they make (slightly) more primary errors (have slightly lower rank=1 accuracy). This is because intelligently designed ensemble systems generally have higher percentages of rank=2 and rank=3 results than individual algorithms.

System gain is a ratio of a measured output variable of interest to the system users, divided by a measured input variable also of interest to the system users. Because module-to-module interfaces should be fully specified as part of the system design, the two parameters used in the gain formula should be explicitly listed and explained in the system specifications. This is especially important where there are multiple relevant gains for a single module and its input and output interfaces. For example, an instrumentational amplifier, which is often used for medical applications because of its very high input impedance, excellent common-mode rejection ratio (CMRR), and stable voltage gain, has multiple gains that are of interest to the electronic system designer, including voltage, current, and power gain. These ratios are based on two inputs and two outputs (input and output current and voltage), and CMRR is effectively the same except that the input voltage is that across the positive and negative terminals of the operational amplifier. From these same input and output values, impedance, admittance, resistance, and conductance gain can also be computed. As mentioned in Chapter 4, if there are N inputs and P outputs specified, there are 2NP simple gains for the module. More can be defined if more composite inputs and outputs can be used; for example, power gain is really the product of two other gains: voltage and current gain.

The gains mentioned above are based on the direct measurements at the interfaces. In the field of analytics, the input and output are data and/or information, and so, the system gains can be defined based on the data (content gains) or based on attributes of the data (context gains). Information gain was earlier defined as an attribute/context gain, as it was associated with an increase in some measurable system entropy (information being extracted increases entropy). If the system information is written to a histogram, with each element, i, in the histogram having probability $p(i)$, then its information gain is determined from the change in the entropy (Eq. 3.19, rephrased in Eq. 10.1) from input to output, a familiar motif now for anyone who has read these chapters consecutively:

$$\text{Information gain} = \sum_{output} p_i \ln(p_i) - \sum_{input} p_i \ln(p_i) \qquad (10.1)$$

Eq. (10.1) provides a relationship between input and output and if negative indicates the loss of information (meaning we overreached on our modeling, modularization, etc.). This equation is a gain, but is obviously no longer a ratio.

Extending the concept of a gain to that of differences in information allows us to create a category designated earlier as functional gains. Functional gains represented an upgrade in the value of data in some problem space and so embody a functional relationship between measurable content produced by the analytic system (output) and the content as entered into the system (input). In Chapter 3, two functional gains discussed are *knowledge gain* and *efficiency gain*. We revisit these in context of all that we have explored in the intervening five chapters.

Knowledge gain is a direct measurement of the product of an analytic system or else a measurement comparing it with alternative products. In text analytics, the knowledge gained can be assessed, among other ways, by comparing the entropy and coverage the analytics have to a specific, salient text reference such as a dictionary, taxonomy, or ontology. Similar knowledge gains can be defined in terms of metadata entries, tags, meaningful coverage of a set of search queries, inclusion of foreign words and phrases, etc. Knowledge gain can also be qualitative—increased use of a system, increased downloading from a mirror site, etc. may indicate that its knowledge base has improved in value.

A second functional gain of interest is efficiency gain, which is indicative of improved ability of an information system to achieve its processing goals, normalized by the resources required for this achievement. This is not the same as the performance, or throughput, of a system, although it certainly relates to it. Efficiency in most cases more closely correlates with the rank efficiency of a system, that is, its ability to yield the correct answer more quickly. Efficiency can come from simple improvement in indexing or in adding contextual information (user and her historical behavior, GPS location, time of day, etc.). Efficiency from the perspective of applying meta-analytic approaches may be viewed as parsimony of algorithm—the most efficient meta-analytic is the one with the most streamlined design or the design that can be conveyed with the shortest amount of description. This could also be efficiency in terms of the number and complexity of modules that are required to design the analytic, the minimum set of coefficients and other wildcard expressions within the modules, the simplest meta-analytic pattern (e.g., weighted voting is a simpler approach than reinforcement-void), etc. Discussed in Chapter 4, we can now look at these gains in light of the design choice we made for the system.

A third functional gain of interest, not previously introduced, is *robustness gain*. We are ready to explore this gain based on what we learned from the synonym-antonym and reinforcement-void patterns explored in Chapter 8 and the analytics around analytics in Chapter 9. A gain in robustness is an improvement in a system architecture that allows the system to respond better to changing input, including changes in the nature (depth and breadth) of the input, the scale of the input, and the context of the input. In previous chapters, we have discussed several ways in which to improve robustness. The simplest conceptually is to employ hybrid analytics by design, benefitting from the factor that ensemble analytics, meta-analytics, and other combinatorial approaches tend to cover the input spaces more completely, and with entropy and variance measurements to support this, more evenly. Straightforward ways of representing system robustness include data indicating the worst-case through-put, the worst-case accuracy, the worst-case costs, etc. The most robust systems are generally the most reliable, and thus, the variability in response to input is lowest.

10.1.2 System gains—Revisiting and expanding the system biases

The reason to measure gain in the first place is to quantify the return on investment that we get from a system. As system designers, we are generally motivated to put a certain priority—or more usually set of priorities—on a system. In the product design and deliver world, the priorities are features, time, and resources, which means teams naturally measure product testing, schedule, and staffing quite closely. In the world of analytics, the measured factors are tied to the information that the analytic system purports to deliver. As such, we will typically see an analytic system bias to one or more of the following key measurables: (1) rank, (2) accuracy, (3) performance, (4) cost, (5) robustness, (6) modularity, and (7) scalability. If we emphasize one of these factors more than another, we need to show the end users or at least the boss whose approval is needed to continue the exciting analytic work that this factor indeed shows "gain" after implementation of our analytic design. The "gain" of an analytic system priority is of course broadly defined to allow comparison of a particular incarnation of a system design compared with the system it is intended to replace going forward. Not a problem, so long as the gain we show is (a) quantitative, (b) repeatable, (c) meaningful, and (d) significant enough to meet the requirement(s). We reconsider the gain of these seven types of system "priorities" or "biases" in this section.

In the case of rank-biased systems, the relative improvement in the calculated mean value of the rank of the actual correct answer provides the gain. Suppose that we are using a classifier for text data, and the previous classifier provided 78% accuracy, but the mean rank of the correct classification was 2.19. That is, the previous analytic system provided the correct answer, on the mean, in 2.19 attempts, and the new system provides the correct answer, on the mean, in 1.65 attempts, albeit with a lower accuracy of the primary classification of 76%. Since we are concerned with the "rank-biased gain" of this system, we note that it is $\frac{1/1.65}{1/2.19}$, or 1.327, as we know that the reciprocal of the rank is a measure of system performance. This implies a 32.7% improvement in finding the correct answer for this particular system upgrade. Interesting, the reduction in accuracy is 2.6%. So, unless the cost of a primary classification mistake is more than 12.5 times the cost of never getting the right classification, this system is justifiable rank-biased rather than accuracy-biased.

This leads right in to accuracy-biased systems. Here, we can also compute a gain in a rather straightforward fashion. Earlier, we defined the gain as the accuracy of the new system divided by the accuracy of the old system, which is very much in line with traditional gains like voltage, current, or power gain. This is a broad brush, though, and the accuracy gain will usually be calculated on partitions of the input (leading to an array of gains), which is very much in line with the training phase of a predictive selection approach. The gains are often transformed; for example, the gain can be defined as the percentage of possible improvement achieved, which is another way of saying how much the error percentage has been reduced. I generally prefer error percentage over accuracy myself, because it is what I am trying to change. Improving a system from 78% to 87% accuracy, as example, has a gain of 1.409 (40.9% of the way to perfection) when we consider what we're trying to change with our algorithm. Simply presenting the gain as 1.115 (the ratio of 0.87 to 0.78) does not really capture a "feel" for what we have accomplished.

For performance-biased systems, the simplest gain—that of throughput—is again the ratio of the reciprocals, in this case the reciprocal of the time for processing. Performance gains are an exception to rule of applying k-fold training and generally benefit from an averaging. The k-fold also ensures that any real "back breakers" for performance are counted k times in the performance data. So, performance is the system concern that most benefits from k-fold evaluation, and not accuracy. Computing the performance gain is undemanding: if, for example, a previous system could process the benchmark set in a k-fold mean time of 56.3 h and then new system can process the benchmark in 47.4 h, then the gain is $\dfrac{1/47.4}{1/56.3}$, or 1.188.

For cost-based systems, the gain is also the ratio of reciprocal of the cost of the new system divided by the reciprocal of the cost of the old system. Nothing particularly exciting about this, but the real value of a cost model is when it is tied to risk. If, for example, we look at the cost gain as throughput of the new system per N number of dollars, divided by the throughput of the former system per N number of dollars, then the cost gain is really a function of the variability in the throughput. For example, we reconsider the voice recognition system in which for a 10% performance cost (tied to preanalysis of the voice and the decision on whether to use freeware or for-pay software), we are able to assign a voice transaction to freeware software 50% of the time, and must use the full cost voice system the other 50% of the time. This means that we only have to pay 50% as much overall for the high-robustness, for-pay software. The performance is thus 0.10 of normal 50% of the time and 1.10 of normal 50% of the time or a mean of 0.60 of normal overall. The improved throughput is 1.67 times the old throughput when using the means. However, suppose that a penalty is paid whenever we have to use the for-pay system more than estimated and the payment is three times the normal pay. What is the new risk to the system? Let us check the algebra:

(a) P = percentage of the time above 50% we have to use the for-pay software.
(b)   Throughput/1.10 = throughput with the up-front predictor to use freeware or for-pay software.

(c) $(0.50+3P)=$ payment for the for-pay software.
(d) $(0.50+3P)=1.0/1.10$ at breakeven.
(e) $P=0.136$ at breakeven.

This could be a little concerning. If we ever use the for-pay service 13.6% of the time more than expected, we will not make money. As such, our validation testing for the system should simulate multiple pay periods and find out how much "3X" costs will be involved, as this will surely reduce our cost gain, since we get no rebate when we use the for-pay software less than 50% of the time.

Our next gain is robustness gain. Robustness-biased systems are systems for which we are encouraged to split our training and validation sets up into multiple units and vary the training and validation percentages. One means of performing this is to provide a 2-to-k enumerated training plus validation design, as shown in Table 10.1. This means we allow the k in the k-fold training+validation design to vary from 2 to k (in the case of Table 10.1, the maximum $k_{max}=10$) and use validation data with a percentage from $1/k_{max}$ to 0.5. The variability in the results for the 2-to-k-fold training gives a good idea of the robustness of the system. Ideally, the results are uniform across the range of k.

Note that we did not specify on what robustness was measured. It could be performance, accuracy, rank, scalability (e.g., where we apply Table 10.1 to different sized data sets), or some linear combination thereof in a cost model or other derived objective function. Robustness-biased systems are measured using one or more of the other biases to measure the effectiveness of the system to "unsupervised" new data. Suppose for example we have two systems, A and B, which have associated costs of $14.5M and $17.8M, respectively, on an existing set of training data. Based on a 2-to-10 enumeration, we see that system A is overtrained compared with B (has higher variance in the validation) and performs much better on downstream data

Table 10.1 k-fold-based training and validation for a robustness-biased system (2-to-k enumeration), with $k_{max}=10$

k	Number of training sets	Percentage of validation sets
10	10	0.100
9	9	0.111
8	8	0.125
7	7	0.143
6	6	0.167
5	5	0.200
4	4	0.250
3	3	0.333
2	2	0.500
1	N/A	N/A
Total	54	0.167

The mean percent validation is 0.167, although the percent validation is across the range [0.10, 0.50].

for the next 6 months ($14.5M compared with $17.8M). However, when a change in the environment leads to a change in the nature of the data, system A has a new cost of $19.6M, while system B has a new cost of only $18.3M. The robustness "gain" of system B over system A is based on the ratio of the reciprocals of changes in cost of B over A, that is, $1/|$18.3M - $17.8M|$ divided by $1/|$19.6M - $14.5M|$. The robustness gain here is a compelling 10.2, meaning system B is more than 10 times as robust in its system cost to new data when compared with system A.

For modularity-biased systems, we have some options in our definition of gain, and some understanding of how you are writing, testing, and approving new functionality is necessary to test and make the final decision on the reporting of gain. Certainly, the simplest and most obvious gain is the ratio of the modules before and after a system redesign. This can be viewed as "module gain" since it reflects only the number of modules. This is a problematic ratio, however, since the ratio will be strikingly different for the same degree of product maturity in comparing, among others, a waterfall and agile/scrum approach software development. Another reasonable—and in this case more quantitative—modularity gain assesses the interchangeability of different modules. The mean number of modules to perform a particular process or action after dividing by the mean number before a system redesign is the modularity gain for a system of analytics, algorithmics, and intelligent processes. This gain can be qualified by the aggregate number of processes accumulated in each module, to ensure that the change from one iteration to the next of the architecture is not simply due to module splitting or merging. A third type of modularity gain is based on the functionality of the modules and is therefore more "tightly coupled" to the actual implementation details of the modules than the other two modularity gains. Within a larger ecosystem (e.g., a software repository with multiuser check-in/checkout), the mean implementation rate for specific modules before and after a system redesign can be calculated. This "functional modularity gain" is the ratio of the use of the modules after/before the redesign, again qualified where necessary to account for module splitting or merging. A well-designed system will presumably end up with a single (though perhaps overloaded) method for each individual task, and so, reuse rates of good modules will climb. This modularity gain might be used to identify the modules most crucial for early functionality testing, based on their relative popularity of adoption.

The last gain we reconsider here is scalability gain. This type of gain may be confused with robustness because, of course, as more data are flooded into the system, the potential for input previously unencountered increases. Here, however, we are more concerned with how the number of categories, clusters, and/or classes grows irrespective of the domain of the input (e.g., what had previously thought to be classes are shown to be multiple classes after the number of samples grows, etc.). As such, we may see the need to switch algorithms or even the architecture around the algorithms from using an individual algorithm (Bayesian, ANN, etc.) to using a hybrid or combinatorial approach. The scalability gain, then, is not about the system attributes but instead has an algorithm's eye view of the data. The scalability gain is the relative use (adoption rate, number of uses rate, etc.) of a particular analytic approach after system scale increases.

10.1.3 **Nothing ventured, nothing gained**

Without measurement, there are no analytics. Without analytics, there are no system gains. Without system gains, it is potentially difficult to convince your customers, your manager, and/or your government to continue investing in a system that already "works well enough." Improving the quality of a system is the goal of every engineer; improving the return on investment is the goal of every savvy businessperson. Therefore, it should be the goal of every analytic designer to support both parties in their pathways to success. If you want to be an analytics systems engineer, you must design system processes to be measurable throughout their lifecycle.

The final system gain we should certainly consider here is the gain based on the ratio of "increased system value" to "cost of investment in analytics." This is not a trivial calculation. Investing in the front end for analytics may mean purchasing, placing, calibrating, wireless connecting, and maintaining a previously unbudgeted array of sensors. It may mean having to change the database size, distribution, and costs, not to mention the plan for data archiving and deprecation. Additional software, recycling/disposal, auditing, safety, privacy, and security concerns will need to be addressed. Offsetting these costs must be a positive return on investment. This is where data analytics can be tied to marketing, among other concerns. If, for example, the additional sensors provide better product safety, this is something that can be used to differentiate a product. The data themselves may have value; for example, a reliable and distributed set of image sensors may be useful for surveillance, traffic monitoring, and other imaging applications. Repurposing (selling) of the data may be a positive entry in this particular gain equation.

10.2 **Module optimization**

As systems become more complex, it becomes more passé—or at least less necessary—to talk about the need to modularize the design. An important part of system design optimization is to determine whether the modular implementation is efficient. Among the often huge set of design choices, how is a particular design selected? The raw analytics for design optimization will come as no surprise: measures of relative values of entropy, error variance, and sensitivity. These data need to be actively analyzed and used to trade off what are hopefully a diminishing set of design options as more of the system is rolled through testing, measurement, validation, quality assurance, and other best manufacturing practices during development. Choices to make include whether to split a subsystem or module into two or more parts, whether to join two or more modules, or whether to extricate commonalities in two or more modules and pull them into a separate subsystem or modules, changing the familial (parent-child) relationships between these functionalities. The reduction of tight coupling should be reflected in the amount of communication between modules, discussed next.

An important criterion in the decision process, aside from the error measurement and evaluation, is the communication/messaging between subcomponents. It is not necessarily the total amount of messaging that we may wish to minimize; instead, we may wish to minimize the amount of messaging that must be channeled through one module unused (pass-through messaging) or the amount of message processing as a percentage of the overall processing time. In the pass-through case, we may consider any messaging that passes through a module without being used by the module as too tightly coupled; here, we would likely employ a software design pattern such as a message factory.

Another approach to optimizing the messaging is to optimize the ratio of within-module messaging to between-module messaging. The optimal design is accomplished when this ratio of traffic(within modules)/traffic(between modules) is a maximum. Designing the system from the perspective of messaging is an interesting "hybrid" approach to some of the other ones adventured previously (cost, accuracy, robustness, rank, etc.) and affords a relatively independent means of "shuffling and reorganizing" the elements. Speaking of shuffling and reorganizing, we next return to clustering but dive much deeper than in Chapter 1.

10.3 **Clustering and regularization**

Clustering using k-means and k-nearest neighbor approaches was introduced in Section 1.6.1. Regularization of regression and estimation approaches was overviewed in Section 1.5.3. In this section, we bring these two great approaches together, not unlike the peanut butter and chocolate aficionados in the vintage Reese's advertisements of the 1980s. While the approaches in this section are straightforward to compute and effective, it should be noted that there is existing literature in this area that also applies local and global regularization [Wang09], albeit through different methods. The goal in this section is not to be exhaustive, but instead to show how relatively easy it is to check a fitness value with a reasonable regularization penalty.

For regularization of regression, there are generally two competing forces at work. In the first place, we are trying to minimize the squared error distance between the regression curve and the empirical data. This is called the least squared error (LSE) and is defined from $LSE = \min \sum_{i=1}^{n_{samples}} (y_i - \hat{y}_i)^2$ where $\hat{y}$ is the regression value and y is the empirical value. If we fit a curve of order $N-1$ to N samples, however, we can guarantee no error, but the curve fitting the points will almost certainly be far more complex than necessary (and will not represent a real relationship between independent and dependent variables). To prevent this overfitting, we add a penalty to the error function, usually in the form of $\frac{\lambda}{2}\|w\|$, where $\|w\|$ is the norm of the weights (coefficients) of the regression equation where $\hat{y} = \sum_{j=0} w_j x^j$. Because the weights of the coefficients are penalized during optimization, they are prevented from growing to fill in all the degrees of freedom.

More generally, regularization penalizes behavior that leads to optimization with overfitting. For example, we can fit 10 points exactly with a ninth-order regression, but the coefficients of the linear regression are likely to expand very significantly. Thus, we optimize a positive term, the fitness of the model to the data, from which another positive term, the "penalty" or regularization term, is subtracted. For a regression curve, the form may be given by Eq. (10.2), equivalently Eq. (10.3):

$$J = Fitness - Penalty \tag{10.2}$$

$$J = \frac{1}{\left(\sum (predictedpoint - actualpoint)^2\right)} - \lambda \sum \|coefficient\| \tag{10.3}$$

where $\|coefficient\|$ is its L2-norm (square of the coefficient weight). The penalty term should be geared to keeping the approach reasonable: (1) too low of a value for λ, and the data are highly overfit; and (2) too high of a value for λ, and the subtleties of the fit are lost (e.g., a curve is fit by a line).

Obviously, this process can be extended to other areas of machine learning. We have previously covered k-means and related clustering approaches, which use an iterative method of assigning samples to clusters: (1) assign all samples to the nearest representative sample (initially k random points and after the first iteration of the k representative points of the clusters) and (2) redefine the representative sample of the cluster (usually as the centroid of all the points now belonging). This is a tidy optimization process, often referred to as expectation-maximization (I prefer expectation-optimization), but it does not provide us with the optimum value for k.

Thus, we need to determine k through an optimization process of its own. Recalling that our objective function, J, is the fitness-penalty, we are already familiar with the definition of fitness as an F-score (Eq. 10.4):

$$Fitness = F - score = \frac{(mean\ squared\ error\ between\ clusters)}{(mean\ squared\ error\ within\ clusters)} \tag{10.4}$$

To complete the definition of J, we need a penalty term such that k doesn't just automatically become equal to the number of samples when fitness starts out greater than 1.0 and so that $k=1$ doesn't happen when fitness starts out less than 1.0. The means to prevent these extremes (unless they really are the rare case when they're optimal) is regularization, and this will be shown through example.

In Fig. 10.1, the simple set of 12 points in (x,y) that we will use for clustering and for illustrating the regularization processes is given. When I eyeball it, there seem to be three clusters:

1. Points (1,6), (1,7), (2.5, 7), (3,8), and (4,7)
2. Points (1,3), (1,4), (2,2), and (3,1)
3. Points (4,4), (5,3), and (5,5)

Other folks looking at it break up the first cluster into points {(1,6), (1,7)} and {(2.5, 7), (3,8), (4,7)}. And running expectation-maximization algorithms, still other

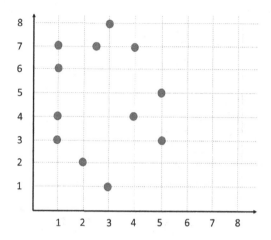

FIG. 10.1

Simple set of points for clustering and for illustrating the regularization processes.

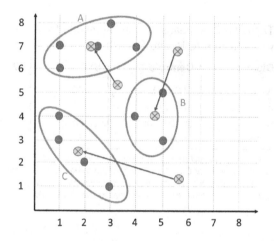

FIG. 10.2

Example $k=3$ clustering.

clusters emerge, but for illustration, I will just compare the two clustering results shown in Figs. 10.2 and 10.3.

For the k-means clustering example where $k=3$ (Fig. 10.2), the arrows indicate the direction the representative value (initial point and thereafter centroid) of the three clusters that might have moved overall during the iterations. Once those three clusters have been defined (as shown by the ovals in Fig. 10.2), we calculate the sum squared error of differences (just the sum of L2 distances here) around the centroids of the clusters (rows 2, 3, and 4 of Table 10.2, SSE column). The SSE of the clusters themselves is compared with the centroid of the clusters and is given in Table 10.2,

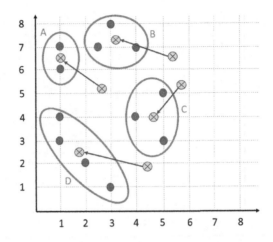

FIG. 10.3

Example $k=4$ clustering.

Table 10.2 k-means clustering results for $k=3$, with clusters A, B, and C as shown in Fig. 10.2

Cluster	Centroid	SSE	df
A	(2.3, 7.0)	8.80	4
B	(4.67, 4.0)	2.67	2
C	(1.75, 2.5)	7.75	3
All three	(2.91, 4.5)	15.32	2

SSE=sum squared error of all points from the centroid of either the cluster A, B, or C or the centroid of the three clusters for "all three." The degrees of freedom for each SSE is given by df, which is one less than the number of samples in each SSE calculation.

column 3, row 5. From Table 10.2, we use SSE/df to get mean-squared error (MSE) and use the formula $F\text{-Score}=(SSE_{between}/df_{between})/(SSE_{within}/df_{within})$. For Table 10.2, this value is $(15.32/2)/(19.22/9)=3.59$.

Next, we repeat this procedure for the situation where $k=4$, as shown in Fig. 10.3. Here, the arrows and ovals have the same meaning exactly as for Fig. 10.2, except that here, there are four arrows and four cluster ovals. The centroid, SSE, and df values for Fig. 10.3 are captured in Table 10.3. For these data, the $F\text{-Score}=(SSE_{between}/df_{between})/(SSE_{within}/df_{within})=(22.78/3)/(12.75/8)=4.76$. Comparing this value (4.76) to the value for $k=3$ (which was 3.59), we would recommend $k=4$ over $k=3$ without regularization. This illustrates the rise in fitness as more and more small clusters are "peeled" from the sample set and emphasizes the need for regularization.

Table 10.3 k-means clustering results for $k=4$, with clusters A, B, C, and D as shown in Fig. 10.3

Cluster	Centroid	SSE	df
A	(1.0, 6.5)	0.50	1
B	(3.17, 7.33)	1.83	2
C	(4.67, 4.0)	2.67	2
D	(1.75, 2.5)	7.75	3
All four	(2.65, 5.08)	22.78	3

SSE=sum squared error of all points from the centroid of either the cluster A, B, C, or D or the centroid of the four clusters for "all four." The degrees of freedom for each SSE is given by df, which is one less than the number of samples in each SSE calculation.

In this section, we propose five different types of regularization (penalties). These are representative, and not comprehensive. The goal is to provide five types of regularization penalties that cover a different interpretation of what it means to be (and not be) a cluster. Obviously, any unique weighted average of these five types also represents a different regularization penalty, but we'll address that later. For now, they will be simply introduced and their main feature(s) highlighted:

1. A coefficient, lambda (λ), times the norm (sum of squares) of the clusters—this can very simply just be the number of clusters, so that $\lambda(n_{clusters})^2$ is subtracted from the F-score: $F\text{-}score - \lambda_{1*}(n_{clusters})^2$.
2. Add a regularization term, lambda (λ), times the norm of the spread in the clusters. Suppose the spread is the variance (σ^2) around the centroids. Since ever-smaller clusters tend to have lower variance, we add this to penalize the smaller clusters: $F\text{-}score + \lambda_2{}^*\Sigma(\sigma_{cluster})^2$.
3. Subtract a regularization based on the cluster size. The coefficient, lambda (λ), is directly proportional to the number of clusters and is multiplied by the inverse of the size of the clusters: $F\text{-}score - \lambda_3{}^*(n_{clusters})^*\Sigma(1/size_{cluster})$.
4. Subtract a separate penalty for any noncluster clusters (cluster size$=1$ or cluster size $<10\%$ or 20% the mean size of the other clusters): $F\text{-}score - \lambda_4{}^*(n_{clusters\_of\_1})$
5. Divide the F-score directly by the number of clusters: $F\text{-}score + \lambda_5{}^*F\text{-}score/n_{clusters}$.

Combining these five into a single penalty equation, we arrive at Eq. (10.5):

$$F - score - \lambda_1 \cdot (n_{clusters})^2 + \lambda_2{}^*\Sigma(\sigma_{cluster})^2 - \lambda_3{}^*(n_{clusters})^*\Sigma(1/size_{cluster})$$
$$- \lambda_4{}^*(n_{clusters\_of\_1}) + \lambda_5{}^*F - score/n_{clusters} \qquad (10.5)$$

We next consider each of these regularization penalties in order.

10.3.1 Sum of squares regularization

The first one is straightforward. If the number of clusters is 3, we subtract $9\lambda_1$ from the F-score. If the number of clusters is 4, we subtract $16\lambda_1$ from the F-score. Typical values from my experience with medium to large size data sets are for λ_1 to be relatively small. Values for λ_1 are generally dependent on the size of the data sets. Since this is a (purposely very) small data set, we'll choose $\lambda_1 = 0.05$.

a. $F\text{-}score - \lambda_1 * (n_{clusters})^2 = 3.59 - 0.05(3)^2 = 3.14$
b. $F\text{-}score - \lambda_1 * (n_{clusters})^2 = 4.76 - 0.05(4)^2 = 3.96$

When does the regularized F-score of the two approaches become equal? This is an important value, which we will compute for every regularization approach. It is called the *equivalence point*. The equivalence point is by nature an isolated measurement, since if combined with other regularization techniques will not be able to drive which of the compared values for k has the highest value for fitness-penalty, or J. Nevertheless, it is important for us to get an understanding of a reasonable value for the lambda coefficient when two (or more) options for k seem reasonable. For the example at hand, the J score = fitness-penalty for $k = 3$ and $k = 4$ becomes equal when $4.76 - 16\lambda_1 = 3.59 - 9\lambda_1$ or $1.17 = 7\lambda_1$. Thus, the equivalence point is when $\lambda_1 = 0.17$. Our value of $\lambda_1 = 0.05$ seems reasonable, then. In general, we suggest the following guideline for selecting a good value for λ_1 where $J = F\text{-}score - \lambda_1 * (n_{clusters})^2$:

1. Determine how many regularization coefficients you're going to use $= n_{RC}$.
2. Determine the best two (or two of the best) clustering options—this can be done manually by looking for an F-score optimum region or "sweet spot" as k is varied from 2 to $\sqrt{n_{samples}}$.
3. Find the equivalence point and the corresponding value for λ_1 that we call $\lambda_1(equiv)$.
4. Select $\lambda_1(equiv)/n_{RC} < \lambda_1 < \lambda_1(equiv)$.
5. In our example $0.17/5 < \lambda_1 < 0.17$, or $0.034 < \lambda_1 < 0.17$.
6. Our value of 0.05 is conservative, that is, toward the lower end. Some will choose $\sqrt{(\lambda1(equiv)/n_{RC})(\lambda1(equiv))} = \lambda1(equiv)/\sqrt{n_{RC}} = 0.076$, the geometric mean of the range extremes: I like to err a little on the side of caution with regard to the regularization value, since I "trust" the F-scores in general and do not want the regularization to overly determine the final value of J.
7. The value of λ_1 can also be set automatically based on expert input, previous results, or training/validation.

10.3.2 Variance regularization

The second type of regularization is governed by $J = F\text{-}score + \lambda_2 * \Sigma(\sigma_{cluster})^2$, where we note that the variance $(\sigma^2) = SSE/df$. For our example data set, for the three clusters, we add $(6.12)\lambda_2$ to the F-score. For the four clusters, we add $(5.33)\lambda_2$ to the F-score. Typically, λ_2 is relatively small and unsurprisingly is dependent on the size of the data sets. Since this is a (again, purposely, very) small data set, we'll choose $\lambda_2 = 0.10$. This is larger than λ_1 since variance does not grow as the number of clusters increases, and so, the penalty will not grow with the scale of the sample set.

For $k=3$, $J=F\text{-}score+\lambda_2{}^*\Sigma(\sigma_{cluster})^2=3.59+\lambda_2{}^*(8.80/4+2.67/2+7.75/3)=3.59+\lambda_2{}^*$ $(6.12)=3.59+0.10{}^*(6.12)=4.20$. For $k=4$, $J=F\text{-}score+\lambda_2{}^*\Sigma(\sigma_{cluster})^2=4.76+\lambda_2{}^*$ $(0.50/1+1.83/2+2.67/2+7.75/3)=4.76+\lambda_2{}^*(5.33)=4.76+0.10{}^*(5.33)=5.29$. We are interested again in calculating the equivalence point, which is when 4.76 $+5.33\lambda_2=3.59+6.12\lambda_2$ or $1.17=0.79\lambda_2$. Therefore, the equivalence point for $\lambda_2=1.48$. Proceeding as above, our guideline for selecting λ_2 is as follows:

1. Determine how many regularization coefficients you're going to use $=n_{RC}$.
2. Determine the F-score sweet spot as k is varied from 2 to $\sqrt{n_{samples}}$.
3. Find the equivalence point and the corresponding value for λ_2 that we call $\lambda_2(equiv)$.
4. Select $\lambda_2(equiv)/n_{RC}<\lambda_2<\lambda_2(equiv)$.
5. In our example, $1.48/5<\lambda_2<1.48$ or $0.296<\lambda_2<1.48$.
6. Our value of 0.10 is conservative here and completely off the lower end. Some will choose $\sqrt{(\lambda2(equiv)/n_{RC})(\lambda2(equiv))}=\lambda2(equiv)/\sqrt{n_{RC}}=0.66$, the geometric mean of the range extremes. I like to err for this type of regularization quite a bit on the side of caution, since it is a regularization term, we add instead of subtracting, and we're really just trying to penalize very poorly clustered clusters.
7. The value of λ_2 can also be set automatically based on expert input, previous results, or training/validation.

10.3.3 Cluster size regularization

For this approach, $J=F\text{-}score-\lambda_3{}^*(n_{clusters}){}^*\Sigma(1/size_{cluster})$. Here, for the three clusters, we subtract $(2.35)\lambda_3$ from the F-score. For the four clusters, we subtract $(5.67)\lambda_3$ from the F-score. Typically, λ_3 is relatively small and of course is dependent on the size of the data sets. Since this is a very small data set, we'll choose $\lambda_3=0.20$. This is larger than λ_2 since the variances are larger than the inverse of cluster sizes. For $k=3$, $J=F\text{-}score-\lambda_3{}^*(n_{clusters}){}^*\Sigma(1/size_{cluster})=3.59-\lambda_3{}^*(3){}^*(1/5+1/3+$ $1/4)=3.59-2.35\lambda_2=3.59-2.35{}^*(0.20)=3.12$. For $k=4$, $F\text{-}score-\lambda_3{}^*(n_{clusters})$ ${}^*\Sigma(1/size_{cluster})=4.76-\lambda_3{}^*(4){}^*(1/2+1/3+1/3+1/4)=4.76-5.67\lambda_3=4.76-5.67{}^*$ $(0.20)=3.63$. The equivalence point is determined from when $4.76-$ $5.67\lambda_3=3.59-2.35\lambda_3$ or $1.17=3.32\lambda_3$. Thus, at the equivalence point, $\lambda_3=0.35$. This is a relatively small value, and our choice of lambda gets us over halfway to the equivalence point. Our now-familiar guidelines for selecting the lambda value follow:

1. Determine how many regularization coefficients you're going to use $=n_{RC}$.
2. Determine the best F-score sweet spot as k is varied from 2 to $\sqrt{n_{samples}}$.
3. Find the equivalence point and the corresponding value for λ_3 that we call $\lambda_3(equiv)$.
4. Select $\lambda_3(equiv)/n_{RC}<\lambda_3<\lambda_3(equiv)$.
5. In our example $0.35/5<\lambda_3<0.35$, or $0.07<\lambda_3<0.35$.

6. Our value of 0.20 is aggressive and toward the upper end of the recommended range. Some will choose $\sqrt{(\lambda 3(equiv)/n_{RC})(\lambda 3(equiv))} = \lambda 3(equiv)/\sqrt{n_{RC}} = 0.16$, the geometric mean of the range extremes. I like to err a little on the side of weighting this regularization factor higher, particularly when it is used as the only regularization factor, since greatly imbalanced cluster sizes are generally a worry for analytics (it may be the experimental design that is a problem, of course).

7. The value of λ_3 can also be set automatically based on expert input, previous results, or training/validation.

10.3.4 Small cluster regularization

Next, we consider the problem of small clusters or even unclustered samples. In our simple example, we have no clusters of one since there are no outliers—we would not have had any clusters less than 10% or 20% of the size of any of the other clusters, anyway, since the largest has just five samples. However, had we, we would have used $\lambda_4 = 0.15$. This is smaller than λ_3 because any cluster the size of 1 would have also had a substantial penalty in the λ_3 regularization. Needless to compute, for $k = 3$, $J = F\text{-}score - \lambda_4{}^*(n_{clusters\_of\_1}) = 3.59 - \lambda_4{}^*(0) = 3.59 - 0.15{}^*(0) = 3.59$ (unchanged).   For $k = 4$, $J = F\text{-}score - \lambda_4{}^*(n_{clusters\_of\_1}) = 4.76 - \lambda_4{}^*(0) = 4.76 - 0.15{}^*(0) = 4.76$ (also unchanged). There is no equivalence point here since the penalty $= 0$. Our guideline for selecting this value of lambda is included here for completeness:

1. Determine how many regularization coefficients you're going to use $= n_{RC}$.
2. Determine the best F-score sweet spot as k is varied from 2 to $\sqrt{n_{samples}}$.
3. Find the equivalence point and the corresponding value for λ_4 that we call $\lambda_4(equiv)$.
4. Select $\lambda_4(equiv)/n_{RC} < \lambda_4 < \lambda_4(equiv)$.
5. In our example, (3) and (4) don't work, since there are no clusters of size 1. So, instead, we noted that we would already penalize clusters of size 1 in the previous (λ_3) regularization, so that picking a value less than that value (75% as much here) is reasonable.
6. The value of λ_4, of course, can also be set automatically based on expert input, previous results, or training/validation.

10.3.5 Number of clusters regularization

Our last regularization example here is one that penalizes the number of clusters (assuming less is best, along the lines of Occam's razor, or at least his electric shaver). Here, we provide a penalty for having more clusters by adding less to the overall J score (our penalty is additive). For three clusters, we add $(\lambda_5/3)$ times the F-score, meaning we scale by $1+(\lambda_5/3)$. For four clusters, we add $(\lambda_5/4)$ times the F-score, meaning we scale by $1+(\lambda_5/4)$. For small numbers of clusters, the value for λ_5 can therefore be relatively large. We will use 0.25 here. For $k = 3$, $J = F\text{-}score +$

$\lambda_5 * F\text{-}score/n_{clusters} = 3.59 + \lambda_5 * (3.59/3) = 3.59 + 0.25 * (3.59/3) = 3.59 + 0.30 = 3.89$. For $k=4$, $J = F\text{-}score + \lambda_5 * F\text{-}score/n_{clusters} = 4.76 + \lambda_5 * (4.76/4) = 4.76 + 0.25 * (4.76/4) = 4.76 + 0.30 = 5.06$. These aren't moving much closer together, and indeed, the equivalence point, determined when $4.76 + 1.22\lambda_5 = 3.59 + 1.29\lambda_5$ or $1.17 = 0.07\lambda_5$, is given by $\lambda_5 = 16.71$. Clearly, this regularization approach isn't going to change much in this particular example. We nevertheless conclude with the recommended protocol to determine this lambda value:

1. Determine how many regularization coefficients you're going to use $= n_{RC}$.
2. Determine the F-score sweet spot as k is varied from 2 to $\sqrt{n_{samples}}$.
3. Find the equivalence point and the corresponding value for λ_5 that we call $\lambda_5(equiv)$.
4. Select $\lambda_5(equiv)/n_{RC} < \lambda_5 < \lambda_5(equiv)$.
5. In our example $16.71/5 < \lambda_5 < 16.71$ or $3.34 < \lambda_5 < 16.71$.
6. Our value of 0.25 seems conservative, but this is an accident of how closely matched the two clustering partitions are for this measure, and it is the largest coefficient we use in any of the five regularizations here—the hint is that the number of clusters regularization might not mean much for consecutive values of k.
7. The value of λ_5 can, of course, also be set automatically based on expert input, previous results, or training/validation.

10.3.6 Discussion of regularization methods

Between the five regularization approaches present, we account for the variability within the clusters (sum of squares and variance), the cluster size, the presence of small clusters or unclustered samples, and the overall number of clusters. These methods, combined, provide a robust set of checks and balances for ectopic optimization, accounting for within and between cluster variability, scale of the problem space, and unassigned samples.

Out of interest, what happens in this example if we apply all five regularizations simultaneously? The overall equation is given by Eq. (10.6):

$$J = F - score - \lambda_1 \cdot (n_{clusters})^2 + \lambda_2 * \Sigma(\sigma_{cluster})^2 - \lambda_3 * (n_{clusters}) * \Sigma(1/size_{cluster})$$
$$- \lambda_4 * (n_{clusters\_of\_1}) + \lambda_5 * F - score/n_{clusters} \qquad (10.6)$$

For $k=3$ clusters, $J = 3.59 - 0.05(9) + 0.10(6.12) - 0.20(2.35) - 0.15(0) + 0.25 * (1.20)$. Thus, $J = 3.59 - 0.45 + 0.61 - 0.47 - 0.00 + 0.30 = 3.58$. This really hasn't changed from its initial value of 3.59, but what of $k=4$ clusters? There, $J = 4.76 - 0.05(16) + 0.10(5.33) - 0.20(5.67) - 0.15(0) + 0.25 * (1.19)$. Thus, $J = 4.76 - 0.80 + 0.53 - 1.13 - 0.00 + 0.30 = 3.66$. All five regularizations combined have nearly moved the $k=4$ case to equality with the $k=3$ case, but not quite. In comparing, we see that the individual regularization terms never make up the difference of 1.17 between the two F-scores. But combined, they nearly do. We conclude that four clusters are only slightly better than three clusters in this problem, but would not be surprised if later data merged the upper clusters (A and B) in the four-cluster partitioning, resulting in the three-cluster partitioning. Regularization makes the confidence in $k=4$ a little less in comparison with $k=3$.

10.4 Analytic system optimization

We complete our consideration of system design optimization with a brief reconsideration of the variance and entropy measurements upon which so many of our analytics—and actions after performing the analytics—are based. In Table 10.4, two input spaces are compared for their suitability to being modeled by a first-, second-, and third-order regression equation. Firstly, the residual variance of the error drops significantly for both input spaces in going from first-, to second-, to third-order regression models. Even if we applied regularization, clearly the order three models are best. This is substantiated by the considerable increase in entropy of the residual error across the range $[\mu - \sigma, \mu + \sigma]$ of the error distribution. A large increase in entropy is observed for each increment in the order of the regression model. Greater entropy implies less "structure" to the residual entropy, meaning information gain has been achieved with the incremental model (e.g., third-order regression compared with second-order).

In Table 10.4, we can also see that the regression model is a better fit for input space A at third-order regression and probably at second-order regression when accounting for the entropy, than it is for input space B. First-order regression is a better model for input space B, however, than it is for input space A. Therefore, if we believe that the data should follow a first-order regression, we have a better fit for input space B. However, if we feel that more complicated regression models are acceptable (other factors that we do not yet know how to explain are in the data), we use the third-order (or higher) regression model and feel that input space A provides the better fit to the model.

Table 10.4 First-, second-, and third-order regression models for two sets of data and residual variability (variance of the error) and entropy (measured in evenly space bins across the range $[\mu - \sigma, \mu + \sigma]$ of the error distribution)

Order of regression	Input space A		Input space B	
	Residual variability	Residual entropy	Residual variability	Residual entropy
1	0.432	2.377	0.345	2.561
2	0.167	3.398	0.156	2.856
3	0.055	4.101	0.087	3.019

We can see that every order regression model is better for input space A than for input space B at order 3.

10.5 **Summary**

We reconsidered many of the system gains originally introduced in Chapter 3 herein with a broader perspective on system design empowered by meta-analytics as both hybrid analytics and as analytics about our analytics. We considered I/O gains and information gain, before turning to knowledge gain and efficiency seen in new light of increased value and in terms of conciseness of design choice, respectively. Robustness gain was introduced here and is defined in terms of the system's worst-case response to input.

Next, we revisited the key system design considerations—rank, accuracy, performance, cost, robustness, modularity, and scalability considering what we have covered over the past seven chapters. Rank and accuracy bias in a system were shown to be relatively assessed by the cost of their errors. The case for error gain over accuracy gain was further expostulated. Performance gain and later robustness gain were shown to be gains that benefit from k-fold training and validation in a way (I argue) accuracy- and rank-biased systems do not. A brief consideration of how errors in our model can greatly affect the overall lifetime cost of a system was shown through a simple example using freeware and pay-for software. In robustness gain, the use of 2-to-k enumerated training and validation design to provide a stronger estimate of robustness was described. Finally, additional considerations around modularity (popularity of adoption) and scalability (around popularity of a specific analytic) were overviewed.

Module optimization was specifically addressed using measurements of entropy, error variance, and sensitivity. These approaches are familiar from previous chapters; here, we show the process of using them along with analytics about the messaging, or communication, within and between modules.

Clustering, introduced in moderate depth in Chapter 1, was then augmented with regularization approaches. Regularization is a penalty subtracted from the fitness. The fitness is an F-score based on the relative variance within clusters compared with between clusters. Five regularization approaches are provided that, combined, account for the variability within the clusters (sum of squares and variance), the cluster size, the presence of small clusters or unclustered samples, and the overall number of clusters.

We conclude with a simple example of using variable complexity models along with measures of residual variance and entropy to determine which models are best and which data sets provide the best fit. Variance should decrease, and entropy should increase, as our model fitness improves.

References

[Sims13] Simske, S., 2013. Meta-Algorithmics: Patterns for Robust, Low-Cost, High-Quality Systems. IEEE Press and Wiley, Singapore.

[Wang09] Wang, F., Zhang, C., Li, T., 2009. Clustering with local and global regularization. IEEE Trans. Knowl. Data Eng. 21 (12), 1665–1678.

Aleatory and expert system techniques

11

An expert is a man who has made all the mistakes which can be made, in a narrow field
Niels Bohr

Psychohistory dealt not with man, but with man-masses. It was the science of mobs; mobs in their billions. It could forecast reactions to stimuli with something of the accuracy that a lesser science could bring to the forecast of a rebound of a billiard ball. The reaction of one man could be forecast by no known mathematics; the reaction of a billion is something else again
Isaac Asimov (1952)

11.1 Introduction

If you started reading this book with your only intention being to find out how to take a bag of data and convert it into labeled, indexed, clustered, or classified groups, you need read no further. You've got that. The clustering with regularization approach shown in Chapter 10 allows you to take unstructured data and turn them into clusters. The various analytic approaches of Chapter 1 allow you to mine these clusters and turn them into classes of structured, labeled information. That is a key to analytics, and in those key chapters, you learned how to build clusters, classifiers, and machine learning algorithms from the ground up. In between those chapters, you learned to better evaluate training data, to improve experimental design, to evaluate models for data, and to employ a wide range of hybrid analytic techniques—the core meta-analytic approaches from predictive selection to reinforce-void and a wide range between them. You've even learned how to analyze your analysis!

So what's left? It turns out rather a lot. In this chapter, aleatory techniques are elaborated. By aleatory, we mean depending on some source of randomness. Monte Carlo simulations use random sampling; random number generators can be used to provide full domain coverage of input, etc. But, in this chapter, randomness will be used in a variety of system-relevant applications. The mantra for aleatory approaches is that randomness results in coincidence with significance—or synchronicity if you prefer a Jungian view to a Jaccardian view. In order to find that coincidence with meaning, you usually have to actively search for it. Just as there is an obvious and important distinction between causality and correlation, there is also a very distinct difference between coincidence and luck. Luck just happens, and a part of the

Meta-Analytics. https://doi.org/10.1016/B978-0-12-814623-1.00011-3

reason it can have a negative connotation is there is often an unspoken impression that not enough attempts were made to receive the bounty of the "luck." Coincidence, however, often irks people the other way, with many a skeptic asserting that there is no such thing as coincidence; instead, we intentionally focus on the events that are the farthest from the norm and then look for connections between them to justify a (forced) claim of coincidence. In other words, if you seek luck, you can't find it, but if you seek coincidence, it is easy to find.

That might get too metaphysical for anyone but Sartre's or Camus's great-grandchildren, but I'll put a happy death to either of these interpretations. I prefer a much more mechanistic approach. Coincidence can indeed be forced, any time there are enough events to essentially guarantee a certain number will be X standard deviations away from the expected, where $X > 1.96$ or $X > 2.58$, for example. Those are special 95% and 99% values for two-tailed z-scores, and a Gaussian distribution should see such values either 5 or 1 time in 100. Coincidence? I think not. Now, we can mine these outliers for insight into the system. In this way, we use aleatory events to find out more about the behavior of the system in its extrema. As Niels Bohr noted, "an expert is a man who has made all the mistakes which can be made, in a narrow field." Viewing aleatory events as mistakes in central behavior, then, we learn from them.

As noted in Chapter 1, the concept of predictive analytics is the basis of the Foundation trilogy by Isaac Asimov, written a lifetime ago. In it, Asimov introduced the science of psychohistory, upon which I will overlay my own assumptions. Psychohistory used an extreme form of multivariate analysis both to predict specific events in the future and to eliminate from concern other events. Harry's science was meant to remove uncertainty as much as provide certainty for the future. But, his predictions broke down in the face of a personality stronger than that of Caesar, Christ, or Napoleon—named the "Mule," a genius of vision and manipulation. Or did it really matter? Were Hari Seldon's meta-analytic approaches sufficiently robust, scalable, modularizable, and accurate enough to estimate the future with sufficient probability? He did foresee the fall of the Galactic Empire and thus included a set of instructions for recovery from a millennium of anarchy that would follow. His systems were robust enough to overcome the "specific randomness" of the personality of the Mule. As mentioned in Chapter 1, this "preflight sensitivity analysis" of a predictive model is a suitable candidate for aleatory approaches. Kudos to Asimov for anticipating that hybrid systems—designed to follow the law of parsimony where possible and also modular and scalable enough to be able to handle much more complexity where appropriate—are more robust than simple or fully hybrid systems. These systems therefore remain relevant longer—maybe not for millennia as in Asimov's science fiction, but we are anyway more concerned with science facts. As Asimov envisioned psychohistory, he thought of it as a "science of mobs; mobs in their billions ... (which) could forecast reactions to stimuli with something of the accuracy that a lesser science could bring to the forecast of a rebound of a billiard ball." This sure sounds like a huge ensemble approach to me. And, the final tell is that Asimov recognized that the "reaction of one man could be forecast by no known mathematics; the reaction of a billion is something else again." In other words, Hari Seldon, via

Asimov, created a multibillion ensemble architecture that, as such systems do, percolated the correct rank of the future of history to the very top of the possibility stack. Hari Seldon fully understood the concept of a rank-biased system.

In this chapter, we will explore how aleatory techniques are able to "prestress test" a system to ensure that it will be robust to the unexpected. This is not a coincidence. It is a forced coincidence with meaning. Forget synchronicity, this is Seldonicity.

11.2 Revisiting two earlier aleatory patterns

Aleatory techniques were introduced in Chapter 4 in the context of entropy, or quantitative disorder, of a system. We will review the two approaches here and extend them based on the additional value multiple passes of adding randomness to a system can bring.

11.2.1 Sequential removal of features aleatory pattern

Insensitivity of a system is related to its robustness: the less sensitive a system is to added noise, the more robust it tends to be to new input. The difference between these two concepts is subtle but important to elaborate. Insensitivity to error describes how robust a system is to additive noise associated with existing input. Robustness describes how robust a system is to new input. Since the additive noise model is unlikely to match changes in input associated with new data (e.g., additive noise may be Gaussian, with a zero-mean difference from the current input, while new input is likely to see a drift in the mean value), these two measurements of system stability are almost always distinct. It is the former—intentional addition of randomness, following a particular model for the addition—that we are concerned with using aleatory approaches.

The first aleatory pattern described was used precisely to optimize a system's lack of sensitivity to random changes in specific portions of the input, termed the features. The process is termed, in a near-litotes fashion, *optimized insensitivity*. One way to approach this goal is to remove features that are more sensitive to the input, as in the *sequential removal of feature aleatory pattern*, which features these steps:

1. Identify the elements, usually different features being used together in an ensemble, which are candidates for removal (use feature ranking).
2. Construct the appropriate process for analysis (analytics, algorithm, system, etc.).
3. Complete the steps in the process.
4. Make the final recommendations, and deploy the recommended process for an analytic system.

The example used in Chapter 4 was a simple binary image classification, used for determining product authenticity and thus validating supply chain integrity. A set of a dozen image features—both color saturation (S) and intensity (I) measurements for the six colors red (R), green (G), blue (B), cyan (C), magenta (M), and yellow (Y)—were calculated. These are abbreviated RS, GS, BS, CS, YS, MS, RI, GI, BI, CI, YI, and MI as expected given the shorthand for each color and type of measurement in parentheses above.

Each of these features were used as a single classifier in an ensemble of binary classifiers for discriminating authentic from counterfeit products using images of specific regions of the labels. The individual classifiers in the ensemble ranged from near guesswork (0.55 accuracy for BS, or blue saturation, just above the "coin toss" value of 0.50) to near perfection (0.90 accuracy for GI, or green intensity, meaning 9 out of 10 samples were correctly classified). These values are recapitulated in Table 11.1. In our example, we are assuming higher error rates imply higher sensitivity to the input, but other measures of sensitivity (e.g., variance in error by class of input) could just as easily have been employed.

Based on the results of Table 11.1, there are four features (BS, CS, CI and BI, ranked 12, 11, 10, and 9, respectively) with values noticeably lower than the values of the other eight features (ranked 1–8) and are good candidates for removal. Among these, BS again stands out as being very far away indeed from the previous rank. The measurement of %Error Gain was introduced to show how much of the remaining error to be gained was gained by the increase in rank. The %Error Gain is given by equation 11.1. In order of rank 1–12, the %Error Gains are 0.20, 0.08, 0.11, 0.15, 0.04, 0.04, 0.08, 0.13, 0.19, 0.12, 0.20, and 0.58. The last 4–5 increases, particularly the last one (at 0.58), are anomalously high in comparison with the three (0.05, 0.04, and 0.08) right before it and indicate a fundamental change in the ability of the final four features to provide ensemble value:

$$\%ErrorGain[N] = \frac{(Error[Rank\,N] - Error[Rank\,N-1])}{(Max\,Error - Error[Rank\,N-1])} \quad (11.1)$$

In Eq. (11.1), Max Error is 0.50, which is pure guessing for a binary classifier. Also, when $N=1$, then Error[Rank $N-1$] = Error[Rank 0] is defined as 0.00 (perfection). As an example of applying Eq. (11.1), for rank 5 compared with rank 4, the %Error Gain = (0.23 − 0.22)/(0.50 − 0.22) = 0.04. Again, we see that BS (rank 12) makes 58% more of the "possible" error remaining compared with CS (rank 11).

Table 11.1 Twelve image features (R=red, G=green, B=blue, C=cyan, M=magenta, Y=yellow, S=saturation, and I=intensity) and the accuracy when each image feature is used as a binary classifier for distinguishing between images from authentic versus counterfeit labels

Image feature	RS	GS	BS	CS	MS	YS	RI	GI	BI	CI	MI	YI
Accuracy	0.71	0.77	0.55	0.62	0.76	0.87	0.83	0.90	0.67	0.65	0.74	0.78
Rank	8	5	12	11	6	2	3	1	9	10	7	4
%Error Gain	0.13	0.04	0.58	0.20	0.04	0.08	0.11	0.20	0.19	0.12	0.08	0.15

Some or all of the 12 features are then used together in an ensemble classifier, as described in the text. In addition to their ranks, the percent gain in error (which is 1.00 accuracy) for the given rank compared with the previous rank is given (please see text for details).

Table 11.2 Results when the least accurate features are removed in reverse-ranked order

Features removed	Overall accuracy (weighted voting)
None	0.948
BS	0.954
BS+CS	0.957
BS+CS+CI	0.962
BS+CS+CI+BI	0.963
BS+CS+CI+BI+RS	0.960
BS+CS+CI+BI+RS+MI	0.951
BS+CS+CI+BI+RS+MI+MS	0.941

The overall accuracy peaks using this approach when the four lowest accuracy features (BS+CS+CI+BI) are removed. After that, accuracy decreases when additional features are removed in this sequential approach.

Regardless, the features can now be individually ranked, and so, step 1 is complete. The appropriate instrument for analysis (step 2) is to then sequentially remove the features and observe the behavior (step 3). This is shown in Table 11.2.

In Table 11.2, a simple linear analytic instrument (sequential removal of the lowest ranked remaining feature) is used. Note that the error rate goes from $1.0 - 0.948 = 0.052$ to $1.0 - 0.955 = 0.045$ just by removing BS. Thus, BS is an easy first choice to remove. In this case, removing the four lowest accuracy features resulted in peak accuracy for the particular approach outlined in Table 11.2. For assessing accuracy, the features are combined using weighted voting, using the weighting of feature j proportional to the inverse of the error, that is $1.0 - a_j$ where a_j is the accuracy of feature j by itself, as already described in Eq. (4.15). The final recommendation (step 4) is to deploy the binary classification system with only eight of the twelve features, namely, RS, GS, YS, MS, RI, GI, YI, and MI. This example is incredibly simple and involves comparing only as many as 11 removal combinations, from {rank 12}, to (rank 12+rank 11}, ..., to {rank 12+rank 11+ ... +rank 2}. But, there are 12 features, and so $2^{12} - 12 = 4084$ different possibilities for removing 11 or less of the 12 features. While this set can be exhaustively searched for small data sets, when we move on to deep learning and potentially training and testing on millions of images, vides, etc., we might only really have time to test a few dozen or a few hundred combinations of features. When we start considering scores, hundreds or even thousands of features, of course, we do not have any such "exhaustive search" possibility, even with today's powerful processing and storage options.

Thus, we need a source of variation from the approach of Table 11.2. In Chapter 4, we noted that "multiple sequences for removal" are attempted, especially around the peak accuracy obtained from the method of Table 11.2. Four such candidates (with their accuracies in parentheses), each of which removes the two obvious outliers BS and CS, are given here:

1. {Rank 12+rank 11+rank 9} BS+CS+BI (0.963)
2. {Rank 12+rank 11+rank 9+rank 8} BS+CS+BI+RS (0.962)

3. {Rank 12+rank 11+rank 10+rank 8} BS+CS+CI+RS *(0.964)*
4. {Rank 12+rank 11+rank 10+rank 9+rank 7} BS+CS+CI+BI+MI (0.961)

Note that in this set of four, removing the combination "BS+CS+CI+RS," or {rank 12+rank 11+rank 9+rank 8}, gives the highest overall accuracy.

In reality, the training results are not very sensitive after removal of BS and CS to the next four lowest ranked features in accuracy. In order to test for what features to remove, we need to note discrepancies in selecting that features to remove, if any, when comparing individual to aggregate results. There are several methods to test for this systematically, rather than simply by trial and error and/or intuition, as in the four examples above. We will cover two of them here. The first is to look for flat regions in the %Error Gain metric and let each of these be the next jump from the current set. For the example that we are using, these are between ranks 5 and 8 (0.05, 0.04, 0.08, and 0.13) and again between ranks 9 and 11 (0.19, 0.12, 0.20). These two "runs" appear to be good candidates for "peerage" and thus parallel consideration for removal. The ranks 9–11 relatively similar %Error Gain zone implies we may wish to start with the following combinations:

1. {Rank 12+rank 11} BS+CS (0.957)
2. {Rank 12+rank 10} BS+CI *(0.965)*
3. {Rank 12+rank 9} BS+BI (0.962)

We see right away that we missed one of these in the above two approaches, and removing solely BS+CI results in the greatest improvement in error rate of any so far. Note that following up with removal of CS actually increases the error rate from 0.035 to 0.38 (see fourth row of Table 11.2). Thus, removing BS+CS+CI results in 0.962 accuracy. The other triad is BS+CI+BI, which results in 0.965 (no change from BS+CI).

The second method of testing systematically is to change the weightings based on the relative sensitivities of each of the features. We saw that removal of BS was ameliorating for the overall accuracy, reducing error from 0.052 to 0.045 when removed. But where do we reassign its weighting? One strategy is just to renormalize the weightings of the remaining features, acting as if the BS feature never existed. A second strategy is to enhance the weightings of those most poorly correlated with the feature removed, assuming they will lead to better overall behavior of the ensemble. A third approach is to enhance the weighting of features with similar sensitivities to that removed to ensure that any independence among the remaining features is not dampened. The choice of reweighting is a broad topic and relates to the discussion of bagging, boosting, and stacking in Section 1.7.8.

11.2.2 Sequential variation of feature output aleatory pattern

The second aleatory pattern described in Chapter 4 is also of interest here. This *sequential variation of feature output aleatory pattern* comprises varying the results of each of the features by a predetermined amount. This intentional randomness is another way to optimize a system's lack of sensitivity to random changes in specific portions of the input. This *optimized insensitivity* is performed using an intentional change in each feature (akin to "random" noise in one feature at a time) and then measuring the effect on overall accuracy (aggregated or broken out into a confusion matrix or other comprehensive analysis instrument). This is a form of sensitivity analysis in which the sensitivity to features is forced by intentionally adding errors to the (actual) measured values and will be referred to here as "forced aleatory sensitivity analysis." This differs from two other forms of sensitivity analysis worth mentioning here:

1. Sensitivity analysis in which two or more actual data with a given difference ("delta") between them is used to determine the relative sensitivity of an outcome to a given difference in input. This form of sensitivity analysis is often preferred to the aleatory one introduced above because it represents "real data" rather than altered data. However, it generally requires a large set of data to be able to ensure that deltas for multiple features can be found that are roughly equivalent in magnitude (or normalized magnitude). Regardless, this type of sensitivity analysis can be considered "natural sensitivity."

2. Sensitivity analysis in which the data are simulated. Simulated data are data that were created and not obtained by direct measurement. It is the other extreme from "natural sensitivity analysis" and often is used when anonymized (or "deidentified") data are needed (e.g., for privacy, security, or even unavailability of the needed data is an issue). Such "synthetic sensitivity analysis" is a form generally only used when there is a large set of data available, such that the simulated data can be carefully compared with the real data for important population behavior, such as mean, variance, shape of distribution, and correlation among the features.

We see from the discussion of natural and synthetic sensitivity analysis that our preferred approach, "forced aleatory sensitivity analysis," is somewhere between the two in terms of behavior. Like "natural sensitivity analysis," it is based on measured data (with error added). However, like "synthetic sensitivity analysis," our aleatory methods rely on synthesized differences being added to the measured data. It would be a little self-serving to say that aleatory sensitivity analysis is a hybrid of the other two common methods, but not to say that aleatory sensitivity analysis behavior should be between the other two behaviors.

So far, we have described aleatory methods at the focus level of a single feature. What happens when we account for all the features simultaneously? We know from using multiple feature categorization patterns that the features with a larger impact on the overall accuracy may be increased in relative rank, especially if the ranking is used subsequently on a pattern such as the *sequential removal of feature aleatory pattern* described in the previous section. But what about overall sensitivity of a feature? That is the output of the *sequential variation of feature output aleatory pattern*: a table of sensitivities. As we saw in the previous section, the features that are most sensitive to input variation are generally those that are less reliable as predictors for behavior of the deployed system. This means that, all other aspects of the analysis being equal, two features can be directly compared for their usefulness based on their sensitivities and their correlation with one another. If two features are very highly correlated, then, from a predictive standpoint, we should only need one of them to get the same predictive power. A good example of this is if two features are Fahrenheit temperature and Celsius temperature. While different in value (by the familiar $F = 32 + 1.8C$ equation), the two features are very highly correlated, differing presumably only by differences in measurement, calibration, and environment (humidity, amount of direct sunlight, etc.) procedures. But, if we were to use these two features as part of a categorization analytics, the two overall should have no better predictive power than either one by itself (assuming there is no systematic element to the differences between the two temperature measurements). Suppose, however, we find that the Celsius measurements are more sensitive to the variations in the input. This may be, for example, because they are recorded to the nearest degree Celsius, and so, they have an 80% larger expected value of error than do Fahrenheit recordings also made to the nearest degree. Whatever the case, the Fahrenheit values are better predictors of categorization of the weather, and so, they are chosen above the Celsius temperature to survive as a meaningful feature.

11.3 Adding random elements for testing

Systematically adding variability to the input data can be considered an aleatory technique, particularly if a specific noise model is assumed for the data and its distribution is applied to the deltas that are added to the actual (measured) data. This is analogous to some forms of Monte Carlo processes, of course. The use of this kind of aleatory technique can also be considered for the creation of synthetic data. Among the approaches that can be used to "randomly" vary data are the following:

1. For the first five in this list, we'll focus on numerical data. Dropping one or more significant figures in the data but allowing the mean of the data so altered to stay the same. This is effectively a data blurring operation, and it adds discretization error to the data. It is also a form of reliability testing.
2. Swapping two fields between two data elements. This is irrelevant when there is only one field in the data but makes a lot of sense when there are multiple fields (e.g., in image, this includes color channel intensity, saturation, and hue). Effecting enough of these swaps "uncorrelates" the fields stored in the data.
3. Using genetic programming inspired approaches to the data. Crossover, mutation, and inversion of digits in the data create a different type of error than those above. Crossover in terms of aleatory treatment of data can be used to exchange digits at limits of certainty (e.g., in the digits that are within 1–3 standard deviations from the mean). Crossover can be performed as a means of recrafting the distribution of the data to match the desired characteristics (e.g., fitting to a Gaussian), although in this case the crossovers will only be semirandom.

4. Mutation, similarly, can be viewed from a curve-fitting perspective. The strict aleatory approach performs random substitutions of digits, which will result in a distribution "uniform" across the digits affected. However, a uniform random distribution is not a necessary approach. Instead, the distributions of the random substitutions can be used to guide the distribution of the test data. If, for example, a Gaussian distribution is impacted by mutations and the mutations themselves are generated with equal probability across a given range, then the range of the data will be extended (since there is an equal probability of shifting away from the mean). The distribution will be changed entirely if the mutations are skewed or otherwise manipulated.

5. Inversions of digits are similar to the application of multiple mutations and so are of particular additional interest here. However, the fact that multiple digits are impacted simultaneously does mean this approach should converge to the desired distribution more quickly than the other two genetic-inspired approaches. The caveat is that inversions must affect at minimum two digits (or, i.e., at least two bits), and so, they may lead to an unacceptable level of data blurring.

6. Intentional introduction of errors. These approaches are particularly useful for text analytics. In that domain, the types of errors that can be introduced are rather extensive. At the mechanistic level, this includes substitution (replacing one letter or word with another), deletion (the loss of a letter or word), insertion (the addition of a letter or a word), and transposition (swapping two letters or words, usually next to each other). And, yes, transposition of two words in a document can make an enormous difference: consider New York City and New City York. One is a single compound noun designating the largest city in the United States, and the other is a new city named York.

7. In addition to these rudimentary operations (substitution, deletion, insertion, and transposition), more complex errors can be introduced for text and other "compound" data (which includes multiple-field data). In text analytics, this includes spelling (e.g., using "they're" in place of "their" or "there," which constitute several rudimentary operations concurrently), imputation, and normalization. Spelling is of particular interest, as some errors such as the parenthetically cited one (they're, their, and there) become rudimentary operations at another level of the data stack (these are word substitutions in addition to compound letter errors). Additionally, spelling errors include a wide range of spelling variants that are not tied to actual misspelling. Example includes pig Latin (or should I say "IgPay AtinLay?"), anagram ("I Sing And/Or Game" for "Imagine Dragons"), acronym ("MAKE MY DAY" for "Meta-Analytics Knowledge Educates Many Young Data Analysts Yearly"), slang/jargon (e.g., cockney rhyming slang such as "bubble and squeak" for "Greek" and texting slang such as "AAR8" for "at any rate"), pun ("data good thing to learn?"), and other context-dependent plays on words, engendered by people a lot more clever than whoever wrote these parenthetic examples. These types of "errors" are generally difficult to interject into documents, although there are increasingly available online and for pay lists of such specialized linguistics.

8. Imputation is a protocol for infilling missing data. Determining the correct values to substitute is an art as much as a science. For text analytics, many methods such as tf*idf and cosine models do not require imputation since they are based on the relative frequencies of terms. However, other natural language processing approaches, like part of speech tagging, suffer from missing words and/or letters. One method I've used with some success is to substitute words in order of their frequency into the corpus unless a certain level of confidence in the part of speech tagging is attained. Other methods for imputation are described in Section 5.3.

9. Normalization includes manipulating the statistical values of the data distributions, such as mean, median, mode, and variance. Section 3.3 covers many of the traditional normalization approaches. For introducing errors, normalization can involve equating one or more (dependent on the degrees of freedom in the data) of these values across multiple data groups.

11.4 Hyperspectral aleatory approaches

These are exciting times for imaging scientists, to be sure. Green fluorescent protein (GFP) made it possible to study aspects of the intracellular environment of living cells (such as analyte concentrations and pH). Lidar (radar + laser) and new imaging technologies based on CMOS and InGaAs have extended the gamut of imaging approaches available to scientists and engineers. In addition, hyperspectral (multi-spectral) and other hybrid imaging approaches, incorporating UV, IR, visible, and ultrasonic source signals, are now possible because of the explosion in sensing, processing, and storage over the past decade.

Taken together, hyperspectral approaches provide the means for interesting and in some cases novel ways to test systems for reliability, robustness, and sensitivity. These are described briefly here:

1. *Reliability* is the degree to which the result of a measurement, calculation, or specification can be depended on to be both accurate and precise—to not vary from one measurement of the same state to the next and to closely match the actual state. For hyperspectral approaches, this means that performing a measurement—for example, the height of a building or the width of a river—in two or more imaging modalities, results in an acceptably small difference from the measured value (and between the modalities). When the modalities are similar in etiology (say visible and IR light), this reliability is largely a *measurement* reliability—are the devices cocalibrated correctly, etc.? When the modalities are rather distinct in etiology (say ultrasound and lidar), this reliability is largely an *assumption* reliability—are the assumptions (about foreground vs background, about the boundaries, about the number of significant digits in the measurements, etc.) correct?

2. *Robustness* is tied to the variance in the system output for large changes in the system input. The formal definition is a system's ability to provide a similar

output with rigorous input testing. The output need not be a specific value, but can be consistent behavior. For example, the common-mode rejection ratio (CMRR) of a differential amplifier is the consistency of gain across a wide range of common-mode signals on the two inputs. Robustness can thus be thought of as the lack of unwanted (or at least unpredicted) gain from input to output.

3. *Sensitivity* is how much an output varies with a change in the input (first derivative). One pragmatic means of testing sensitivity is to determine ranges over which information from one data stream can be substituted for another. Full range substitutability implies that the measurements are redundant, so from a meta-analytics standpoint we may be "disappointed" to find no differences in sensitivity, as it may preclude an opportunity to gain system robustness, reliability, accuracy, precision, recall, etc., from two data streams being used together intelligently. From this perspective, sensitivity is an advantage to the meta-analytic system designer—the caveat being she must measure the sensitivity.

11.5 Other aleatory applications in machine and statistical learning

Maybe this section should have been entitled "random thoughts about randomness"? No, probably not. The key perspective for the meta-analyst about randomness is the flip side of the perspectives gained considering entropy. Randomness can be a source of system testing, as described for reliability, robustness, and sensitivity. The advantages of randomness, of course, extend to the unknown. Without providing sources of randomness, unexpected system flaws cannot be identified before deployment (think of the Tacoma Narrows Bridge disaster and aeroelastic instability, which was difficult to diagnose even after the famous 1940 collapse), and so, a system architect is less likely to be able to predict failure modes.

As discussed in previous chapters in this book, along with many others [Hast09] [Mars09], one of the most important considerations for any machine learning design is how the available training data are used. In this chapter, we have talked about means to modify, synthesize, and normalize additional training data, but another important aspect of training data is to recognize the "global" constraints placed on its generation, measurement, and history. If all the ground truth data are obtained in one small time window, for example, then later knowledge about how the input should be varied cannot be fed back to the generation. If the measurements are taken with nonrepresentative settings (filtering, precision, gain, etc.), the appropriate additional bits required by the system cannot be added with confidence later. Finally, the history of the data is important. This means when, how (settings), with what equipment, with what operator, etc. data were collected. This emphasizes the importance of tagging and metadata. All of these conditions can be treated as variables that can be treated with any of the aleatory techniques described earlier in this chapter.

11.6 Expert system techniques

Turning now to expert system techniques, our concern is on validating the domain expertise by calculating the effect of applying it on overall system measurements such as entropy, accuracy, robustness, cost, performance, and other system optimizations of interest. As mentioned above with regard to entropy, aleatory approaches are—or at least can be—the flip side of traditional expert system techniques. Random changes in the expert system rules can be added to determine their effects on the overall system measurements at any point in a system design. The sensitivity of the overall system to random changes in the rules may help provide a more robust, cost-sensitive, or otherwise optimized system than would be the case without testing the impact of random changes. Suppose, for example, that we have two system models that provide the same basic performance on a data set. We can then add aleatory changes to the system in, at minimum, the following ways:

1. Change the coefficients of each model by the same percentage.
2. Change the training data along the lines of Section 11.3.
3. Randomly delete percentages of the training data.
4. Apply the inverse of the expert system rules to the inverse of the data with the same sets of aleatory approaches as in 1, 2, and 3.

The most robust system will show the smallest mean change to these aleatory approaches. The most cost-sensitive system will show the overall lowest cost. The most accurate system will show the overall lowest mean error.

11.7 Summary

In this chapter, we revisited in-depth two aleatory patterns originally presented in Chapter 4. For the *sequential removal of feature aleatory pattern*, we extended the rudimentary approach of removing features sequentially based on their rank for a figure of merit such as accuracy. We performed this by looking for inflection points in the %Error Gain metric. At the inflection points, a simple analytic approach designated sequential removal of the lowest ranked remaining feature is used to provide a sensitivity analysis for the sequential removal of features (until an optimum set is determined).

The *sequential variation of feature output aleatory pattern* is a form of sensitivity analysis in which the sensitivity to features is forced by intentionally adding errors to the measured values. This is termed forced aleatory sensitivity analysis and is a reasonable middle ground between sensitivity analysis performed using actual data with a given difference ("delta") between them (designated natural sensitivity) and sensitivity analysis performed on simulated data (designated synthetic sensitivity analysis).

In Section 11.3, a variety of ways to add randomness to existing (measured) data were presented: dropping significant figures; swapping two fields between two data elements; using genetic approaches such as crossover, mutation, and inversion; rudimentary introduced errors (substitution, deletion, insertion, and transposition);

compound introduced errors (spelling, anagram, acronym, slang, jargon, pun, and other context-dependent plays on words); imputation; and normalization.

Hyperspectral aleatory approaches were considered with respect to the important system measurements of reliability, robustness, and sensitivity. The distinction between measurement and assumption reliability was described, and sensitivity was considered in terms of substitutability. We concluded with a brief mention of aleatory techniques applied to expert system rules.

References

[Hast09] Hastie, T., Tibshirani, R., Friedman, J., 2009. The Elements of Statistical Learning, second ed. Springer.

[Mars09] Marsland, S., 2009. Machine Learning. Chapman & Hall/CRC, Boca Raton FL.

Further reading

Simske, S., 2013. Meta-Algorithmics: Patterns for Robust, Low-Cost, High-Quality Systems. IEEE Press and Wiley, Singapore.

Application I: Topics and challenges in machine translation, robotics, and biological sciences

12

Everything that can be invented has already been invented
Charles Duell (1899)
I visualize a time when we will be to robots what dogs are to humans, and I'm rooting for the machines
Claude Shannon (1987)

12.1 Introduction

If Charles Duell had been correct in 1899, then this chapter would not be needed. But then, neither would the past 11 chapters nor this book at all, because there were no computerized analytics even though "everything that can be invented" existed. This was from a man who at the time was the director of the US Patent Office. Was he a steampunk ahead of his time, thinking that the steam-run world of 1899 would extend far into the future? Well, 10 million patents later, we're still going strong on invention, and steam is still used—but is possibly more often punked these days. This chapter is meant to stimulate further invention using analytics as a driving factor to improve many (or any!) other fields of science, technology, engineering, art, and mathematics (together known today as STEAM). One can support this form of STEAM without being a steampunk.

On the other side of the spectrum is the mechanophilia of Claude Shannon, who I was more than happy to attribute a quote to, since he is so important to the history of entropy calculations in analytics. But I have to wonder if the quote really makes sense in composite, since coevolution has guided the relationship between people and puppies, and you really can't root for one without simultaneously rooting for the other. So, unlike Claude, I wish to root for the combination of robots and us and hope that we continue to coevolve and provide for a better world. One thing is certain—robots and their central nervous systems, from Arduino (C/C++) to Python to LISP—will continue to evolve. In this chapter, we hope to provide the punctuated equilibrium to effect evolutionary changes in machine translation, robotics, and biological sciences. We will do this by applying the meta-analytic techniques learned in the previous chapters together with the approaches native to translation, robotics, and biology. We begin with machine translation.

Meta-Analytics. https://doi.org/10.1016/B978-0-12-814623-1.00012-5

12.2 **Machine translation**

Machine translation offers an innately meta-analytic experience, since the number of stages in machine translation can be so extensive. Keeping it to 10 steps in this section, I will highlight the touch points for analytics in each of them:

1. The first step is image/speech to text and language translation. Here, the original sentences are created from whatever the input media is. This could be speech, in which case an automatic speech recognition engine (voice to text, or ASR) is used. It could be words in an image, in which case character extraction and recognition are needed. Regardless, the common ground ends up being the native language of the person using the system. This is a perfect step in which to engage the ground truthing approaches described in Chapter 2. Specifically, prevalidation (Section 2.2) approaches can be used to determine which input is of insufficient quality to remain part of the training set. This prevalidation should result in better, more robust behavior since the system will not be partially "randomized" by low-quality input. Applying pruning of training data approaches (Section 3.3) can help in the prevalidation approach by singling out time windows for the data to be tested using the prevalidation methods. Regardless, during the input phase is the best time to eliminate obviously anomalous data. The language translation step is largely independent of the quality of the input and so can be viewed as a second substep. As briefly discussed in Section 9.2.2, translation quality can be determined by using the same translation approach on a separate, usually smaller set of text, and then automating the quality of the output obtained, that is, by determining the quality based on how closely the language translating engine matches the search responses before and after translation.

2. The second step in machine translation is in grading of the sentences by difficulty. This is an excellent candidate for a meta-analytic-as-hybrid approach. Analytics for grading sentences can be based on content, sequence, or proximity. The content basis rates sentences based on the rareness of the terms (a variant of the *TF*IDF* methods described in Section 2.2), the complexity of the part of speech (e.g., compound nouns and verbs score higher than simple nouns and verbs and gerunds rank higher than progressive tenses), or the mean length of the terms in syllables, for three examples. The sequence basis can also use rareness of the sequence, rareness of the consecutive parts of speech in the sequence, or the length of the sequence—for example, phrase—in syllables, as three examples. Finally, proximity or other co-occurrence approaches can be used to rate sentence complexity based on the cumulative complexity of the terms in them.

3. The third step in machine translation is editing. Editing consists of correcting spelling errors and punctuation errors and then preparing the corrected text for more effective downstream processing by algorithm. This preparation can include removing stop words (such as very common words that do not affect the meaning, "the," "or," "and," "how," etc. being good examples) and

performing stemming and/or lemmatization to ensure that terms with the same semantic meaning aggregate and so are properly weighted for occurrence frequency. The spelling errors can be guided by a ground truth data set so that "intended misspellings" such as those concerning slang, shorthand, and texting are not corrected and thus lose their contextual meanings.

4. Morphological analysis is the fourth step in our somewhat simplified set of machine translation processes. This step may be performed in advance of Step 2 to enable some of the meta-analytic approaches outlined there. Inflection, number, part of speech, and tense are the primary morphological outputs. Meta-analytic approaches such as weighted voting are helpful for the improved accuracy of this step.

5. Determining the inflection of the words is broken out as a separate step here because of its amenability to meta-analytic approaches. Inflection metadata include the aspect, case, comparative, gender, mood, number, person, tense, and voice of the word and provide an interesting opportunity for consensus approaches. Within a specific partition of text, the different components of inflection can be individually analyzed word after word and then the sequential tallies analyzed to determine if there is consistency and also for categorizing the type of text. The former—consistency—can be used to determine the inflection-related tagging to perform when several options are available.

6. Syntactic analysis comprises part of speech (POS) tagging, grouping of words into phrases (or clauses), and the relationships between words, particularly when a pronoun refers to a known noun ("he" for "Eisenhower," "it" for "world peace," etc.). Often, the POS tagging can be performed twice—once in Step 2 above to help determine the complexity of the sentences, clauses, and phrases and a second time in this step where it can take advantage of the inflection metadata assigned to better decide on borderline POS tags. Grouping words into phrases can benefit from the POS tagging, since often phrases begin and end with specific speech parts; for example, conjunctive adverbs such as "for example" divide sentences into two clauses. Pronoun referents can be resolved using weighted voting of algorithms such as closest noun, inflection-matching noun, and closest proper noun.

7. Grammar determination can be considered in some ways as the inverse of Steps 4, 5, and 6, since grammar checks that the morphology, inflection, and syntax are correct. Interestingly, the information obtained during this phase can be fed back to Steps 4, 5, and 6, which may improve their accuracies.

8. After grammar and syntactic analysis are performed, the words are tagged. Tagging is used to identify the linguistic properties of the individual words (POS tagging) and to identify the clauses, phrases, and their categories (e.g., a Reed-Kellogg system diagram) [Aart06]. Parsing here can be considered an "aggregate" analytics that incorporates output from the previous steps (morphology, syntax, POS tagging, grammar, etc.) and determines the overall parsing of the sentences. Like grammar, its results can be fed back to the earlier steps for validation and consensus.

9.   Semantic analysis generates the meaning representations, which can be considered metadata that allow the definition of important linguistic relationships such as synonym and antonym; metaphor and simile; litotes and synecdoche; kenning and metonymy; chiasmus and antithesis; and irony, sarcasm, and satire, among other "higher level" linguistic output. Semantic analysis is readily supported by meta-algorithmic approaches such as expert feedback (e.g., using slang, sarcasm, and irony dictionaries) and extended predicted selection (e.g., analyzing word content and then deciding which type of figure of speech to search for), patterns originally introduced in [Sims13]. Semantic analysis is therefore a very broad area of analytics, determining the meaning of words, the meanings associated with grammatical structures, and commonsense knowledge and/or dictionaries of semantic associations of idiomatic expressions.

10.   In the final step, the analysis is mapped to the language into which it is translated, if necessary. Not surprisingly, since all of the variability added up in the previous nine steps can potentially affect this step, it is particularly prone to noise and error. There are a number of reasons for this, including the fact that idiomatic expressions, which are consistently prone to syntactic and semantic error, need to be translated *idiomatically*, that is, not in direct word-for-word translation. Different translation engines can be automatically rated for quality, fortunately, in several ways. The first, covered in Section 9.2.2, ranks the translation engines after using them to translate both the document corpus and the corpus' search terms. The corpus/search query set that provides the search behavior most closely matching that of the original (untranslated) document set is deemed the best translator [Sims14]. The second involves a "round-trip" from one language (original) to another (desired language of translation) and back to the original. Then, the word error rate (and other linguistic error rates, including morphology, grammar, and syntax) can be computed, and the translator with the lowest round-trip error rate is selected as the best. An example of this approach is given in Table 12.1.

Clearly, in the relatively complicated process of machine translation, we find that different analytic approaches are valuable at each stage of the translation. We also see that errors can be cumulative, and in order to reduce the overall errors, we may wish to feed back information from later steps back to earlier steps.

Table 12.1 Round-trip of a single sentence with several idiomatic expressions using a web-based translator.

Sentence type	Sentence text
Original	Bob gave me the lowdown on what's shaking
Translated	Bob me dio lo mejor de lo que está temblando
Back to original	Bob gave me the best of what is shaking

Note that there are several errors after the "there and back again" translations. In particular, the idiomatic expression "lowdown" has been changed in meaning from "true facts or most salient details" to "the best."

12.3 Robotics

Robotics is a huge field and includes a wide range of subfields, including industrial robotics, service robotics, software-based robotics (artificial intelligence, bots, etc.), autonomous robotics, bionics, and warfare robotics. The definition of what constitutes a robot varies between individuals, but it is clear that they are becoming more pervasive and will continue to become more pervasive for the foreseeable future. Meta-analytics are particularly applicable to the intelligence associated with robotics and in particular when one considers five of the arguably most important aspects of employing robotics in society: human-robot interface, manipulation, mobility, programming, and sensors. We herein consider these five aspects of robotics in light of meta-analytic approaches that we have introduced previously and then elaborate upon the same:

1. Human-robot interface (HRI) is a particularly important consideration, since the rate and depth of adoption of a robot depends on how comfortable a human is with using it. With a software bot, the human-computer interface (HCI) is already a very highly developed field, and this includes the user interface together with the means in which a user continues inputting to the bot. With the advent of ambient computing, input has become more "natural" (e.g., voice-based) and ubiquitous for many HCI touch points. However, not every user considers personalization of HCI to be natural, and so, an opportunity for the meta-analytic designer is to customize the HCI to the specific preferences of the user. A useful approach for HCI is to employ a form of the predictive selection meta-analytic wherein the predictive portion assesses the context of the HCI and the selection portion modifies the types of HCI allowed for the given context. Suppose an ambient computing bot assesses whether the person is having a conversation in the room or with a remote person (e.g., on the phone or via a communication app). Then, it may decide to remain mildly interactive (in the room condition) or go into nonrecording mode (remote conversation condition) based on the user's historical preferences. For a physical robot or "physibot" to engage a neologism, the HRI is even more important a consideration, since the physibot may have the potential to do bodily injury to the user, may frighten the user by its actions, or may impact a user financially (e.g., by depleting a consumable such as fuel, medicine, and bandwidth). In the case of a physibot, the predictive selection algorithm may be an oversimplification, because the predictive phase of the algorithm has its categories defined *a priori*, while we may be concerned with nascent context that requires a more "averaged" or smooth response. Thus, contextual mixing algorithms such as weighted voting or the variety of confusion matrix [Sims13] approaches, with intermediate categories being defined *a posteriori*, may be more appropriate to the task.

2. For manipulation, an articulated robotic limb is controlled at one or more joints, with each joint carefully controlling the location $\{x,y,z\}$ and the direction $\{\Theta_1,\Theta_2,\Theta_3\}$ that the attached robotic link points. If the joints and link are rigid, three of these values will determine the other three but in the presence of a load on

the effector end (or abutting anywhere else). When a load (e.g., sensor and object to be moved) is firmly grasped by the effector end, the robot can control the position and velocity of the part with only periodic sensing and position correction/recalibration. The position error is due to a number of factors, including part state, part geometry, part mass, friction in the environment, coefficient(s) of restitution as applicable, and the robot's own control errors. The part state can change with time; for example, the part can be damaged and repaired, changing its mass and/or moments of inertia. Internal wear can also change the robot's velocity, resistance to movement, etc. Part geometry can change permanently (e.g., due to damage), temporarily (e.g., due to humidity, temperature, or pressure change), or actively (e.g., due to load-induced bending). Part mass automatically changes when a load is grasped by the effector end of the link. Friction in the environment can include having to overcome resistance in wires and pneumatics, which are part of the overall system configuration. For the coefficient of restitution, which is the ratio of the relative speed after to the relative speed before a collision, a full kinetic model of the collision would be required. In reality, a quick postcollision calibration verification is the minimum required. Finally, the robot's own control errors are often difficult to calibrate: they may vary, often appreciably, based on the septet of task values $\{x,y,z,\Theta_1,\Theta_2,\Theta_3,L\}$, where $L=$mass of the load. A seven-space calibration for even coarse resolution—for example, 100 values in x, y, and z, by 1.0 degree increment in Θ_1, Θ_2, and Θ_3, and from 0.1 to 10.0 kg in 100 g increments—requires 4.666×10^{15} calibration measurements. Obviously, a large amount of interpolation and often extrapolation is needed for a full-range calibration to be applied. Because each of these manipulation concerns has some degree of independence from the others, a hybrid intelligence engine that simultaneously accounts for models of each is generally preferred to a single model that maps the behavior of the robot under different measured conditions to its salient outputs $\{x,y,z,\Theta_1,\Theta_2,\Theta_3\}$. This is perhaps intuitive based on the coarse resolution of any calibration of the robot as described above. Further, having a model for each of these main manipulation factors—part state, part geometry, part mass, friction in the environment, coefficient(s) of restitution, and control errors—is more robust to changes in the inputs over time and of course can more readily internalize enhanced data sets (adaptability).

3. Robot mobility is a hallmark of service robots, since industrial robots are usually locked in place, in a track, or within a confined range of motion for safety, calibration, repair, and other cost-optimization concerns. Service robots include wheeled, tracked, multilegged, aerial, and underwater autonomous vehicles/devices. Adding motion to a sensor-laden device (why would one have a robot with no sensors on it?) requires the use of odometry (visual, inertial, etc.) so that the data collected by the other sensors on the mobile unit are calibrated for their new locations. The analytics involved are combining the movement of the robot with the movement of the sensors (e.g., imaging device) on the robot. Unless these motions are correlated (and there is no reason that they have to be), the two forms of movement have independent variability, and thus, the overall variance is

roughly the sum of the two separate variances. One way to reduce the amount of variability of these added motions is to use a hybrid system for measuring odometry (e.g., adding an ultrasound motion sensor to the visual imaging sensor). A second, independent means of calibrating the two motions is to perform object or feature map identification and then measure changes in angle and position based on the relative location of the objects. This can be based on RANSAC along the lines of previous work [Garc08] [Golb12] [Kitt10].

4. Robot programming, among the five broad aspects of robotics addressed, is ostensibly the one that will benefit most from hybrid, ensemble, combinatorial, or other meta-analytic approaches. In addition, these approaches will benefit the users of the robotics, since they will lead to less "fringe" behavior and thus a safer, more "smooth" behavior. Among the main system-level, or functional, concerns of any well-engineered analytics, algorithm, process, or system are the familiar septet of cost, accuracy, rank bias, robustness, adaptability, modularity, and scalability. Cost can readily be addressed by producing multiple robotic control software projects and using an approach such as constrained substitution [Sims13] to replace a more expensive (e.g., pay-for-use) process with a less expensive (e.g., open source and in-house developed) process when the contextual analytics indicate this is allowable. Accuracy of the robot includes accuracy of motion, mentioned above, which usually benefits from the existence of several trajectory algorithms (for motion and measurement) to better estimate the location of robotic elements. This is extremely important for safety concerns, such as ensuring that a robot effector will not move beyond taped-off safety-labeled boundaries. Accuracy of purely software concerns is perhaps as important for safety, as the robotic "brain" must understand the simple safety rules that govern how much force is needed to trigger automatic retraction or even shutdown. Additionally, this artificial brain must understand more complex rules such as when to recognize that a human user/interactor requires emergency attention and when the robot needs unscheduled service. In each of these cases, being able to hybridize domain expertise-driven rules with machine intelligence algorithms is particularly beneficial. Rank bias is a particularly salient concern for robotic control systems, since well-designed robotic programming involves constant feedback of the robot's impact on its environment and immediate correction when indicated. Invoking multiple analytics to determine the reasonable next state under contextual feedback benefits from the central limit theorem and usually ensures that the correct response to a changing environment is higher on the list, making safe and appropriate response faster and more accurate than when using only a single analytics. Having multiple analytics contribute to the robot's next state often increases the adaptability of the robot, as well. This is because the combination of analytics will generally be more sensitive to changes in the input than a single analytics. One simple example of this is when each analytics has only two output states. When there is one analytics, there are only two possible outputs, but when there are N analytics, there are 2^N maximum output states for even these simple binary decision

analytics. Modularity is usually directly correlated with cost, since modular approaches can be reused with little or no development costs. However, modularity includes more than simple reusability. Repurposability, where the modules are defined at a sufficiently atomic level such that they can be recombined for purposes for which they were not intentionally designed, is a huge advantage of creating multiple analytics for the same combination of {input, output} specifications. This is effectively analytic polymorphism, or being able to use analytics with different internal details for the same transformation between one node (input) and another (output) depending on contextual variables, preferences, regulations, and other factors. The last consideration in this short section is scalability, which is how well the robotic analytic approach handles scale in one or more aspects, including size of data set to analyze, range of input types, and task list. Often, an increase in scale or scope requires the use of two or more analytics in place of one, in which case a smooth transition between the two (e.g., a sliding pair of coefficients over the transition range) can be effective. If needed, a more adaptable scaling approach, for example, using a predictive selection approach whereby a different configuration of analytics is used for each subrange of input, can be selected. The scope of the robot's tasks requires a lot more attention than this short section provides, since there is currently a transformation of an appreciable part of the manufacturing sector from mass production to a hybrid of mass production and mass customization. This means a significant fraction of industrial robots must now be concerned with actual accuracy of motion, rather than simple repeatability. The $\{x,y,z,\Theta_1,\Theta_2,\Theta_3\}$ values can vary by as much as two orders of magnitude for movement to an arbitrary position in comparison with moving to the same position multiple times [Kats17]. Thus, the "accuracy" values currently reported for articulated robotic arms are in reality "repeatability" values, and new analytics are required to provide the required precision of motion as the number of locations to support moves from one to many. We see here in particular how assigning analytics at the same level of modularity as the subsystems of the robotics leads to improved efficiency, robustness, and adaptability.

5. Our final aspect of robotics considered here is the sensors and the sensing performed. Arguably, a machine without sensors cannot be a robot, since sensors are generally required to perform complex series of actions automatically—the hallmark of robots. Sensing is of course a primary analytics in any system: it is the input. Among the hybrid analytic opportunities for sensing are employing two or more sensors with partially overlapping sensitivities to magnitude, frequency, frequency ranges (filtering), spatial resolution, width of field, and directionality (sensitivity to direction). The overlap between multiple sensors is important, as it can be used to determine when one or more sensors is out of calibration or damaged. Additionally, sensors of different modalities (e.g., a thermal sensor and an infrared light imager) can be used to analyze distinct aspects of the same physical continuum (in this case, radiated energy). Another example is the interplay between ultrasound, inertial accelerometer, and seismometer sensors.

The importance of robotics would be difficult to overstate in today's monitoring, manufacturing, mobility, and marketing environments. One thing that can be said with certainty is that robotics will continue to increase in importance in the near future. This means that hybrid systems that provide redundant safety to the programs and the physical aspects of the robots are of paramount importance, because as robots become more pervasive, they will also be treated with less novelty. Safety will at some point change from a concern to an assumption on behalf of the users of the technology, as is human nature. It is therefore so important to build systems from the beginning—that is, from the ground up—that provide robustness, adaptability, rank bias, modularity, and scalability. Building systems for these user and human characteristics, as I hope I have shown throughout this book, will naturally lead to systems with the robotics provider's goals of both competitive cost and accuracy.

12.4 **Biological sciences**

For the biological sciences, a useful starting point for any in-depth meta-analytic approach is to model the analytics on the biological processes unto which they are being applied. Biological sciences are particularly interesting due to the richness of biological diversity and adaptability. Most physiological systems include a high degree of redundancy to failure, fail-safe mechanisms, and robustness to changing environments. In Sections 1.8.3 and 7.4, brief overviews of immunologic and biological analogues for analytics were reviewed. These complemented the other great biologically inspired analytics, artificial neural networks and genetic programming. These concepts will not be repeated here, wherein we extend them to the larger fields of biology, including enzymes, ecology, and evolution.

Enzymes are biologically manufactured polymers, all of which are proteins except for ribozymes, which are composed of ribosomal RNA (thus nucleotide polymers instead of amino acid polymers). Enzymes catalyze specific—usually quite specific—biological reactions such as those involved in metabolism, growth, and cell differentiation. Thus, enzymes are used to accelerate the completion of targeted biochemical reactions. Enzymes act upon target molecules that are designated substrates, and the enzyme converts the substrates into one or more different molecules known as the product(s). The simplest enzymatic effect may be creating a conformational change in the molecule, but often, the enzyme changes the molecular formula of the substrate, for example, by adding or removing phosphate groups, by oxidation and reduction, by splitting lipids into fatty acids, by splitting complex carbohydrates into simpler sugars, by splitting proteins into peptides, and by splitting nucleic acids into their nucleotide bases. You get the idea—enzymes rapidly upgrade the amount of information in an environment by combining, separating, mixing, or transforming the "information" in the substrates. The primary products of enzymes can be second messengers, which themselves go on to perform more information identification and generation than perhaps the enzymes themselves did. This is a key analogue for sequential analytic systems, in which the unlocking of one or more findings triggers a more in-depth search downstream. Examples of such "sequential reactions" include finding keywords for a partition (cluster, class, or category) and then performing a more thorough search to see if a document belongs to the partition. By having the right keyword, the upfront search is swift and reliable; by allowing the scaling, the partition assignment is as accurate as possible. This can be viewed as a form of sequential refinement, but the refinement need not follow the same algorithmic path as the initial knowledge discovery.

The field of evolution, of course, has not gone unnoticed in the field of analytics. Genetic algorithms (Section 1.8.1) are the grandparents of many of today's evolutionary approaches [Bäck93][Banz98]. In this section, we consider evolutionary approaches at the more macroscopic level. Three topics will be covered here: reproductive isolation, punctuated equilibrium, and CRISPR-Cas9.

Reproductive isolation is a means of forming new species. In nature, isolating a subset of an existing species, such as in a proverbial tidal pool, eventually is accompanied with enough genetic changes (mutations, the loss of allele, etc.) that speciation occurs, and even if the isolated population was brought in contact with the original "stock" species, interbreeding would be unsuccessful. Genetic isolation can occur due to behavioral (e.g., nocturnal vs. diurnal), gametic (incompatibility of germ cells), habitat (geographic isolation), or mechanical incompatibility (e.g., chihuahua and mastiff). Regardless, reproductive isolation allows two groups (categories, clusters, or classes) to grow in isolation to each other. Using this principle for meta-analytics is relatively straightforward. Partitions of the data (whether clusters, categories, or classes) can be left in isolation after they are formed on the original training data. Then, new samples can be assigned to one or more partitions based on the statistical characteristics of the partitions alone, each partition gaining new samples without consideration or knowledge of whether the new samples are multiply assigned. After this has run for a relevant number of samples, the partitions can then be recalculated (using, e.g., expectation-optimization). The potential multiple assignment steps provide a different type of optimization that only allows single assignments, as in traditional expectation-maximization approaches. This method can be used to perform a multiple expectation-optimization approach followed by voting for final partition assignment and in this way shares some behavior with bagging.

The second evolutionary approach considered in this section is punctuated equilibrium, a widely accepted theory for how evolution works in response to environmental changes, originally outlined by Eldredge and Gould in the 1970s [Goul77]. Punctuated equilibrium proposes that the rate of evolution is decidedly nonconstant; in particular, the rate is usually relatively low except at times of great environmental stress. During stressful times, the evolutionary rate is greatly accelerated. We can readily apply punctuated equilibrium to the genetic algorithms overviewed in Section 1.8.1, by changing the mutation, crossover, and/or inversion rates based on how far the population of chromosomes is from the optimum. However, to do this, we must have some idea of what the optimum would be, and that may not be the case for many genetic programming situations. However, the concept of punctuated equilibrium is extensible to other types of analytics. For example, we can punctuate the feedback in a neural network to use a higher weight for the feedback in an artificial neural network (see, e.g., the discussion on the value of eta, η, in Section 1.8.2) during early learning to prevent early "locking" on a local optimum and then reduce the value of η over time (e.g., from 0.3, to 0.2, to 0.1 over the three-thirds of the expected number of iterations). Punctuated equilibrium can also be applied to simple meta-algorithmic patterns, such as weighted voting. Here, the weights used can favor the features that performed best on the training data when the system is deployed but then be relaxed somewhat over time, assuming that the samples will drift a bit from the training data over time. Suppose we have four features being used and their relative weights after training and validation are {0.4, 0.3, 0.2, 0.1}. Then, by exchanging the training and validation sets, we find them to be {0.38, 0.33, 0.19, 0.10}. We see the largest change is 0.03, and so, we assume that after deployment, we will "collapse" by 0.03 in weighting. So, we deploy the system with {0.4, 0.3, 0.2, 0.1} and allow these weights to change to {0.37, 0.285, 0.215, 0.13} over time.

As our last example, we note that clustered regularly interspaced short palindromic repeats (CRISPR) and CRISPR-associated (Cas) genes [Ran13] were discovered in the adaptive immunity processes of certain species of archaea and bacteria (e.g., *Escherichia coli* and *Streptococcus thermophilus*), where the CRISPR-Cas9 system is used to eliminate invading genetic material. CRISPR-Cas9 is part of the explanation for why bacteria can acquire resistance so quickly against a bacteriophage—it is used to integrate a genome fragment of the infecting virus into its CRISPR locus. An analytic analogue for the CRISPR system is to use an information injection process whereby data elements are substituted or inserted into an existing data set, and the altered data structure is then reassessed for categorization, clustering, classification, etc. The fact that information of varying length can be inserted (or substituted) into the data set supports a variable evolution rate. Where does the slice and splice approach of CRISPR work best? Noisy input data come to mind. In this case, CRISPR-inspired substitution can be used to inject a hypothetical outcome into the data, such as filling in details in a noisy area for a biometric evaluation (this is the only area in which I have applied this particular approach to date, by the way); a spectra for an analyte; and other signal, image, video, or 3-D image analysis tasks.

12.5 **Summary**

In this chapter, we addressed meta-analytics and machine translation, robotics, and the biological sciences. In the machine translation section, we divided this complicated system into 10 sequential processes, pointing out the variety of analytic approaches that can be applied at each step. Also of note are the points in the 10-step sequence where information calculated can be fed back to "earlier" stages to improve the overall behavior of the system. We concluded with a new example of functional reliability assessing, the "translation round-trip" approach.

Next, the field of robotics was shown to potentially benefit highly from meta-analytic approaches. Our argument is to apply analytics at the same level of modularity as the subsystems of the robotics and targeted for particular aspects of the robotics (human-robot interface, manipulation, mobility, programming, and sensors). The application of predictive selection and weighted voting patterns to physical robot ("physibot") motion and manipulation is perhaps obvious: being able to simultaneously address cost, accuracy, rank bias, robustness, adaptability, modularity, and scalability in robot programming may be less intuitive. Using multiple sensors for richer analytics is also an important meta-analytic consideration.

For the biological sciences, we see that using analytics modeled after the biological processes that they are being applied to is a logical approach. Rather than rehash biological approaches inspired by neural networks, genetics, or the immune system, in this chapter, we discussed using enzymes and previously undiscussed (in this text) the evolutionary concepts of reproductive isolation, punctuated equilibrium, and CRISPR-Cas9. These biological systems are used to provide insight into the robust design of certain types of intelligent analytic systems. Punctuated equilibrium is especially repurposable to other analytics, including ANNs and meta-algorithmics.

References

[Aart06] Aarts, B., McMahon, A. (Eds.), 2006. The Handbook of English Linguistics. Wiley-Blackwell.

[Bäck93] Bäck, T., Schwefel, H.P., 1993. An overview of evolutionary algorithms for parameter optimization. Evol. Comput. 1 (1), 1–23.

[Banz98] Banzhaf, W., Nordin, P., Keller, R.E., Francone, F.D., 1998. Genetic Programming—An Introduction. Morgan Kaufmann.

[Garc08] García-García, R., Sotelo, M.A., Parra, I., Fernández, D., Eugenio Naranjo, J., Gavilán, M., 2008. 3D visual odometry for road vehicles. J. Intell. Robot. Syst. 51 (1), 113–134.

[Golb12] Golban, C., Istvan, S., Nedevschi, S., 2012. Stereo based visual odometry in difficult traffic scenes. In: IEEE Intelligent Vehicles Symposium (IV), pp. 736–741.

[Goul77] Gould, S.J., Eldredge, N., 1977. Punctuated equilibria: the tempo and mode of evolution reconsidered. Paleobiology 3 (2), 115–151.

[Kats17] Katsiaris, P.T., Adams, G.B., Pollard, S., Simske, S.J., 2017. A kinematic calibration technique for robotic manipulators with multiple degrees of freedom. In: Advanced Intelligent Mechatronics 2017 (AIM 2017), pp. 358–363.

[Kitt10] Kitt, B., Geiger, A., Lategahn, H., 2010. Visual odometry based on stereo image sequences with ransac-based outlier rejection scheme. In: IEEE Intelligent Vehicles Symposium (IV), pp. 486–492.

[Ran13] Ran, F.A., Hsu, P.D., Wright, J., Agarwala, V., Scott, D.A., Zheng, F., 2013. Genome engineering using the CRISPR-Cas9 system. Nat. Protoc. 8, 2281–2308.

[Sims13] Simske, S.J., 2013. Meta-Algorithmics: Patterns for Robust, Low-Cost, High-Quality Systems. IEEE Press and Wiley, Singapore.

[Sims14] Simske, S.J., Boyko, I.M., Koutrika, G., 2014. Multi-engine search and language translation. In: EDBT/ICDT Workshops, pp. 188–190.

Application II: Medical and health-care informatics, economics, business, and finance

13

Diseased nature oftentimes breaks forth in strange eruptions
William Shakespeare (1597)
In the business world, the rearview mirror is always clearer than the windshield
Warren Buffett
We want the world and we want it now
Jim Morrison (1967)
I think if you look back through time, the history of income, wealth and taxation is full of surprise. So I am not terribly impressed by those who know in advance what will or will not happen
Thomas Piketty

13.1 Introduction

Hotspur (young Henry IV) notes in the eponymous Henry IV, Part 1, that "diseased nature oftentimes breaks forth in strange eruptions." While this can be read as the disease being correlated with eruptions, from a predictive analytic standpoint, we are more interested in how the eruption can be anticipated by the symptoms (features) of the disease. Disease progression currently justifies a tremendous amount of expense, but much of this expense is arguably misplaced, because we are incapable of simultaneously treating and not treating the same patient to assess the actual benefit of treatment. While control groups are increasingly effective in health-care studies, the impossibility of simultaneously treating and not treating an individual means that we will always need case studies and explicitly planned experiments for our analytic approaches.

Famous Nebraskan Warren Buffett notes that the rearview mirror is always clearer, implying that we have 20/20 hindsight but may be a bit myopic looking ahead. However, I would note that the windshield is much larger than the rearview mirror, and so, the future is brighter than the past. This also means that the future is filled with more bugs, especially if your windshield is traveling at 75 miles/hour on Interstate 80 in Nebraska. Overall, then, it is a good time to be a meta-analytics professional. We are creating so much data at such a high speed, all the while accepting the fact that there are bugs with the data collected that we must correct real time.

Meta-Analytics. https://doi.org/10.1016/B978-0-12-814623-1.00013-7

This is because the rate of data collection continues to increase, with no end in sight. This "data revolution" has changed business faster than many businesses can visualize, and so, we have increasingly the data "haves" and the data "have nots." Those who can collect, store, interpret, and act upon the real-time data are rewarded handsomely, at least in market capitalization and/or venture capital investment if not directly in revenue or margin. We thus surmise that Mr. Buffett's quote is more relevant to business before the data revolution. We are now in the "reign of error" stage of the data revolution, but that also means that business as usual will never regress to a prerevolutionary model. Consumers expect their information immediately; in effect, they want the world, and they want it now. Given the way prediction and estimation work, this means that consumers want the world and they want it yesterday, since our algorithms must anticipate the now. Business today is more than real-time data processing: it is the processing of today's data in anticipation of tomorrow's requests.

French economist Thomas Piketty notes that "if you look back through time, the history of income, wealth and taxation is full of surprise. So I am not terribly impressed by those who know in advance what will or will not happen." Does this mean that finance and economics do not benefit from predictive analytics? Absolutely not. Instead, it means that these fields are precisely those in which a new perspective on how to reliably predict and how to effectively estimate is needed. Piketty is expressing his dissatisfaction with the current state of economic and financial predictive analytics. In this chapter, we reach out from the current means of performing analytics in these broad fields to a new set of approaches based on meta-analytics. To use business terminology, we hope that you profit from it.

13.2 Healthcare

In health care, we are particularly interested in the anonymization (or deidentification) of data, ostensibly for patient privacy concerns but, in reality, more for legal/auditing concerns. Privacy is often opposed to other desired attributes of health-care data, such as instant feedback on exercise goals and ease of access to the data for legitimate consumers of the data (health-care professionals, patients, etc.). The Internet, particularly the social Internet, often sacrifices privacy at the expense of narcissism (being able to share all your latest news but allowing strangers to monitor you) and convenience (being able to locate nearby resources but allowing the app provider, the mobile device manufacturer, and/or the cloud service provider to log your position, preferences, and purchasing). One life insurance company has pushed the limits even further, allowing its policyholders to "score premium discounts for hitting exercise targets tracked on wearable devices such as a Fitbit or Apple Watch." Presumably, then, when you miss your exercise targets, you suffer a double hit to your self-esteem of knowing that your insurance company might decide to change the cost of your premium. The insurance company aims to incent its customers with gift cards and discounts [Barl18], so there is a "carrot" and the "stick" here; however, one has to wonder if the overall strategy isn't a bit analogous to letting the fox guard the henhouse.

On a different thread and as noted in the introduction to this chapter, monitoring a person's disease state and disease progression—irrespective of the amount of privacy sacrificed—is generally viewed as a justifiable expense, since an accurate understanding of a patient's health state is aligned, at least in theory, with an optimal preventative or therapeutic treatment regimen. Much of the overall health-care expense, however, may be speculative since we are incapable of simultaneously treating and *not* treating the same patient in order to assess the actual benefit of treatment. Or are we? What if, instead of designing treatment regimens to be relatively static (even if customized to the patient), we designed them to be dynamic? Let's describe this for two situations: a pharmacological regimen used to treat a particular endocrine disease and a thermal regimen used to treat a joint sprain.

For the pharmacological regimen, the generic dose is a standard amount such as "take two tablets each morning." The specific, or customized, dose may well be the two tablets normalized to body mass, with two tablets being employed prescribed for 120–180 pounds and the overall number of tablets being defined as the integer nearest the person's mass divided by 75; that is, if the person weighs 200 pounds, then $200/75 = 2.67$, and so, the person is instructed to ingest three tablets. A person who weighs 100 pounds is instructed to ingest $100/75 = 1.33$ or 1 tablet. Both of these regimens are static, however. The patient either takes three tablets or takes one tablet, but that amount doesn't change (unless their weight does). A dynamic regimen, on the other hand, adjusts based on some sensing/measurement and feedback from the patient, for example, the serum level of the previous dose. If the serum level is above some upper threshold, then the patient adds two pills to their next dose. If the serum level is above some lower threshold but below the upper threshold, then they add one pill to their next dose. Finally, below the lower threshold, the patient takes the standard dose. Note that this is easily extensible to ranges below thresholds, too. Thus, for a pharmaceutical regimen, any of the four strategies {generic, static}; {generic, dynamic}; {specific, static); and {specific, dynamic} is possible for the given situation.

For the thermal regimen, there is a similar breadth of strategy. A generic approach might use ice on days 1, 2, and 3 after injury, while a specific regimen might assess the recovery rate of the individual and switch from ice to heat at day 2 or day 4, instead of the switch at day 3. A static approach would switch from the use of anti-inflammatories to the use of cytokines when the sensing of the amount of extracellular histamine present in the wound indicates a late stage in inflammation, while a dynamic approach might include the sensing of the amount of extracellular histamine present in the wound region but adjust the mixture of anti-inflammatories and cytokines according to the stage.

What is almost certain to happen in health care is that regimens will become, as a percentage of all treatments, more customized, more dynamic, more personalized, and more data-driven as time progresses forward. In other words, more types of data and more types of analytics—that is, meta-analytics—will be used to drive treatment success. The future of medicine is in the hands of the data collected. The human body is a highly complex system involving many feedback systems; the analytics used to fine-tune this system should take advantage of the same adaptive, closed loop designs.

13.3 Economics

Economics represent an application space in which the input sets are decidedly broad and diverse. Economies are simultaneously fragile and robust, and this contradiction is perhaps tautologically innate to economies: The fragility is a consequence of the ability of virtually any negative event in the perception of a relevant set of citizens in the economic zone to pejoratively impact sales, pricing, and/or confidence; the robustness is a consequence of the ability of virtually any well-received event to positively impact the same. This means, from a system standpoint, that economies have an effective limitless number of inputs, a tremendous breadth of outputs, and multiple feedback mechanisms whereby the output can be measured, compared with a particular value, and fed back to the input to adjust its value. Because the inputs are measured and the outputs created in parallel, economics is seemingly designed with meta-analytic approaches in mind. We'll start this off with a brief example, that is, the use of Piketty's model to predict the percentage of people living under the poverty line (in terms of income).

As an example of applying meta-analytics to economics, I here consider Piketty's excellent book on Capital in the 21st Century [Pike13]. I do this for several reasons: (1) Piketty assimilates a massive amount of data into his formulations, so his book's scope is already one of big data; (2) Piketty's analyses are generally compelling and accurate; (3) Piketty's analysis can be readily expanded into meta-analytic approaches; and (4) the starting point that Piketty provides for meta-analytic elaboration should be interesting to a broad audience.

Piketty [Pike13] uses as the principal formula for much of his economic theories on capital and income a simple one that relates the rate of return on capital (designated r) to economic growth (designated g), where r includes profits, dividends, interest, rents, and other income from capital and where g is the amount of income. Piketty notes in his statistical models that when the rate of growth is low, wealth tends to accrue more quickly from r than from labor and additionally tends to accrue more among the top 1 and 10 percentiles in terms of capital ownership, increasing inequality in capital across the range of wage earners. Piketty's premise is that the primary force for separation and greater wealth inequality is the degree to which $r > g$. There is no doubt truth to what Piketty claims; however, from the standpoint of meta-analytics, it is unsatisfactorily simple to focus on only these two factors. While Piketty further elaborates on the inheritance of capital using the same approach [Pike13]—and this surely counts as meta-analytics—he may have been served well to include other factors in his analysis as an additional and likely more powerful, meta-analytic approach. Among the critiques of his work is included the fact that other economists can also explain the growing disparity in wealth of the wealthiest 1% of population in comparison with the lower 20, 50, or even 80% of population with the circumstances of globalization and technological change. These, in turn, are relatively broad factors that can be readily broken up into component, or subfactors. For globalization, the subfactors can be the percentages of gross domestic product (GDP) that imports and, separately, exports comprise. These factors can be further subfactored by market segment—for example, agriculture, food, transportation, housing, electronics, and health care—and this can continue for several further levels, perhaps ending at the level of an individual imported or exported item (say, a particular brand and type of cheese). The entire hierarchy of the factor can be indicated as easily as, for example, Import.Food.Dairy.Cheese.FamilyFarmsInc.Brie, which provides the factor Import, subfactor Food, and further sub-subfactors Dairy, Cheese, FamilyFarmsInc (brand), and Brie (type of cheese). Another subfactor of globalization may be the amount (absolute amount and percentage amount) of taxes, tariffs, and other transfer pricings associated with any/all levels of the hierarchy of factors and subfactors.

Similarly, we can assign subfactors to "technological change" including communication technologies, artificial intelligence (AI) technologies, and data access technologies. Sub-subfactors of these include different types of communications, including road, train, and air (in addition to the Internet), and for AI access to different types of advanced computing (supercomputers, desktop computers, mobile computing, etc.). These factors are captured in Table 13.1.

Determining the optimal level of subfactoring to consider in the final economic model is a meta-analytic approach. We illustrate the means to assess this in Table 13.2, which replaces the labels assigned to the factors, subfactors, and sub-subfactors of Table 13.1 with their distinctly measured predictive accuracies.

In Table 13.2, we make the decision on the predictive powers based on the reported accuracies. We see that for the column in Table 13.1 labeled "return on capital (r) versus growth (g)," which is columns 2 and 3 (second and third from the left) in Table 13.2, the sample subfactors provide better accuracy (0.678 and 0.813) than the factor itself (0.663). The sub-subfactors of columns 2 and 3—that is, {0.645,

Table 13.1 Example of factorization and subfactorization of economy-relevant factors, illustrating the ability to effectively scale up the number of factors considered for the economic model in a hierarchical or recursive manner.

Factor	Return on capital (r) versus growth (g)		Globalization		Technological change	
Sample subfactors	$r > g$?	Ratio r/g	%GDP imports	%GDP exports	Communication technologies	AI
Sample sub-subfactor 1	For individuals	Ratio < 1	Agriculture	Food	Roadway coverage	Access to supercomputing
Sample sub-subfactor 2	For new corporations	$1 \leq \text{Ratio} < 2$	Transportation	Housing	Railway coverage	Access to desktop computing
Sample sub-subfactor 3	For existing corporations	Ratio ≥ 2	Electronics	Health care	Air travel coverage	Access to mobile phones

Table 13.2 Example of Table 13.1 with the predictive accuracies of each step indicated.

Factor	0.663		0.734		0.567	
Sample subfactors	**0.678**	**0.813**	0.745	**0.794**	**0.613**	0.622
Sample sub-subfactor 1	0.645	0.778	**0.834**	0.767	0.555	**0.561**
Sample sub-subfactor 2	0.693	0.756	**0.876**	0.645	0.435	**0.654**
Sample sub-subfactor 3	0.655	0.873	**0.819**	0.808	0.632	**0.836**

Boldface accuracies indicate those chosen for the final analysis. Please see text for details.

0.693, 0.655} and {0.778, 0.756, and 0.873}—do not provide better mean accuracy than the subfactors to which they belong, and so, factoring into these three subfactors for predictive behavior is not apparently a refinement of the model. However, in the columns fourth and seventh from the left, we see that modeling based on the sub-subfactors does improve the overall accuracy of the model.

Obviously, Table 13.2 is a simplification of the actual process of building a model matched to the problem. Much further analysis of factors and various levels of subfactor are possible. For example, we may have a related subfactor (or sub-subfactor, etc., collectively "child" factors) in two different columns, since, for example, both agriculture and food imports/exports may both have a wide variety of food types as overlapped categories. This is considered the search for a confounding factor—a subfactor affecting multiple parent factors. Also, as we know from the more general field of classification, our optimal set of factors may be weighted combinations of parent and child factors at several levels. Regardless, this example illustrates the use of a meta-analytic approach to build an economic model.

Importantly, this model is not the same as principal component analysis approaches. We are not looking for an orthogonal set of basis functions; instead, we are looking for a model that can be described in terms of the actual factors themselves. This means that the models are directly based on the measured factors and their combinations. In the example of Tables 13.1 and 13.2, then, we may build our model as a very simple linear combination of the factors and subfactors that are most promising; for example, the output $= c_1*(r-g) + c_2*(r/g) + c_3*$(agricultural imports) $+$ c_4*(transportation imports) $+ c_5*$(electronics imports) $+ c_6*$(%GDP exports) $+ c_7*$ (communication technologies) $+ c_8*$(access to supercomputing) $+ c_9*$(access to desktop computing) $+ c_{10}*$(access to mobile phones). Because the ranges of the 10 subfactors will differ largely—for example, r/g may only be in a range of 0.1–10, while "agricultural imports" will range from $0 to perhaps many hundreds of billions of dollars—we will expect to see widely varying values for the individual coefficients c_1–c_{10}. The products of the coefficients and the subfactors will, however, be more similar in magnitude (e.g., the range of accuracies in Table 13.2 for the boldface terms that comprise the selected subfactors is only from 0.561 to 0.876).

In building economic models, we can simultaneously consider the production, distribution, and consumption of goods and services using two or more analytic approaches, one of which may be the factor/subfactor approach shown in Tables 13.1 and 13.2. For example, in addition to a "constructive" model based on the relative accuracies of the factors/subfactors, we may wish to incorporate the use of a "sensitivity"-based model in which the relative changes in the economic output based on changes in factors across their respective ranges are considered. This is highly relevant for deploying a system that will be valuable for predictive assessment of the behavior and interplay of different economic variables. Using the example of Piketty's model, we may decide to include all of the various factors and subfactors at once and remove them based on the insensitivity of the overall economic model to changes across the entire range for each variable. In other words, samples are pruned by larger sensitivities rather than greater accuracies.

13.4 Business and finance

In business and finance, analytics are already *de rigueur* for any successful organization. Profitability in many ventures is dependent on an estimate not only of the mean but also of the variability of a particular asset, commodity, stock, etc. This is the basis of the "buy low, sell high" adage in stocks, which is irritating to hear about after the fact but wonderful to have seen coming. Whether or not predictive analytics constitutes insider trading in the future is a question worth asking at this point, as surely there will be a time—if indeed that time has not already occurred—when predictive analytics will surpass the abilities of even financial department employees at predicting the market capitalization of a corporation. The use of analytics to predict future outcomes and gain deeper insights into current behavioral patterns and how they will help shape the future is an important part of any organization's strategy in this age of analytics, and this helps explain the enthusiasm around such technologies as blockchain [Nara16], which might otherwise be no more than a quotidian, incremental incarnation of a distributed ledger. Blockchain's volatility (and, admittedly, its usefulness in allowing transaction parties to hide behind anonymity) is a large part of its charm. Financial institutions perform better when there is volatility in the market, and blockchain in its first decade has been all about volatility. An important predictive analytic for any financial institution is the volatility of the markets in which they can choose to participate. The most profitable markets are the ones with the highest volatility. The mean doesn't mean as much as the variance.

For businesses, determining the level of volatility is essential for such prosaic reasons as ordering, inventory, shipping, and marketing. Unpredictability in sales leads to inefficiencies in myriad aspects of planning a business. Staff can be unoccupied, draining revenue, or staff can be overworked, draining their spirit. Inventory can sit unpurchased, increasing the footprint of stock and increasing the urgency of scaling up marketing efforts. In other words, volatility in the market leads to a larger footprint for the entire supply chain—volatility in the market corresponds to variance in resources and a concomitant expended range of contingencies to anticipate downstream.

For business and finance applications, we are most interested in reducing the volatility around the mean predicted behavior. This differs from the benefits of most hybrid, ensemble, combinatorial, and meta-algorithmic approaches, which tend to elevate the rank of the correct output irrespective of an improvement in the overall accuracy, precision, recall, or other concerns. In business and finance, the top concern for the intelligent system designer is usually the amount of risk incurred in the near term. Multiple approaches to risk management are relevant, including the following four that will be touched upon in this section:

1. Historical simulation
2. Extreme value theory
3. Worst-performing algorithm
4. Consensus hybrid model

The first two of these are existing approaches, well known and well adapted in the financial community. For (1), predicting the value at risk is accomplished through the simulation of a cumulative distribution function (CDF) of asset returns over time, a process named *historical simulation*. The CDF can be sampled from in a time series, along the lines of a Monte Carlo simulation, and from it, a population of returns over time is estimated. From this plurality of simulations, a consensus expected return and variance (risk) can be computed. In its basic form, historical simulation equally weights all asset returns of the whole period and does not allow data further in the past to be less heavily weighted. This is inconsistent with our recommendations for the pruning of aging data as described in Section 3.3. More appropriately, *weighted historical simulation* ages older data to overcome the inconsistencies of basic historical simulation. Another modification of historical simulation, *filtered historical simulation*, is concerned with the volatility in the history of asset returns and uses a model-based treatment of volatility with a nonparametric specification of the CDF to provide a broader estimate of the range of risks than basic historical simulation. From a meta-analytic standpoint, of course, some linear combination of weighted and filtered historical simulation is almost certain to provide a more robust estimate of risk. Whether a robust estimate of risk is the preferred assessment of risk, of course, is open to debate. The extremes of risk may be most important.

If so, then (2) above—that is, *extreme value theory*—may be the approach best for the financial segment. Extreme value theory incorporates the probability of events that are more extreme than any previously observed in the historical return on assets into its calculations. Extreme value analysis (EVA) is not just used in business and financial models; in addition, it is employed in structural engineering, earth sciences, traffic prediction, and geologic engineering. In meteorology and hydrology, EVA is employed to estimate the probability of the so-called "100 year" and "1000 year" floods, the "50 year" waves, and the "100 year" coastal swellings. EVA relies on straightforward but powerful approaches, such as daily/weekly/monthly/annual maxima series. There is some art involved in the calculation of these series—that is, the maxima and minima can be represented based on day, week, month, or other partitioning—but in the end, a high and low end of overall risk can be estimated. Generally, when absolute maximum risk is important to estimate, the time window for the series approaches an infinitesimal slice of time, akin to the computing of compound interest.

For (3), the *worst-performing algorithm* approach, we employ multiple models, which might include the variants of historical simulations and extreme value approaches, along with Bayesian networks, neural networks, evolutionary algorithms, and others. In terms of reliability, we are concerned with the differences between models and not just on the different data sets. Therefore, the "worst-performing algorithm" is the one that provides the highest negative risk. This is a relatively simplistic model and is only used if the user is extremely risk-averse (e.g., someone planning a military action). For less conservative hybrid approaches, we will use the fourth approach.

For the fourth approach, namely, the *consensus hybrid model*, we focus on the use of clustering and classification algorithms in multiple combinations in order to generate the most robust financial models. Here, a wide variety of the meta-algorithmic approaches described in the previous 12 chapters can be brought to bear on the multiple models described in the previous paragraph regarding the *worst-performing algorithm* approach. The consensus hybrid model is a traditional meta-algorithmic [Sims13] approach to risk analysis and thus performs a process such as weighted voting, predictive selection, or weighted confusion matrix to provide the highest accuracy + robustness estimate of risk. This approach tends to centralize the estimate and so by definition blurs the outliers and underestimates the extreme risks.

All told, it is clear that the business and financial sectors are especially predisposed to meta-analytic approaches. There is a rather inelegant reason for this: business and finance analytics have so many potential influencing factors that estimations related to returns on assets almost certainly do not optimally balance the influences of these factors—if in fact they consider all of the relevant factors. More concerningly, financial models are incapable of pinpointing "random" events such as earthquakes, tsunamis, major sporting winners, election results, and a wide variety of other outcomes, which can, upon occurring, cause larger effects on finances than all the other factors combined. One might note that financial prediction is more akin to trench warfare than to a siege—long periods of boredom punctuated by moments of sheer terror. Even the most extreme of extreme value analyses are unlikely to effectively anticipate these events. Thus, we are ultimately left with an unsatisfying amount of control over business and financial analytics. The best that we can do is optimize the cost models for the predictable and accept that the unpredicted can and will occur. Using historical data, we can at least estimate the cost of the unpredictable, add that to the range of our predictions, and so define the worst-case risk.

13.5 Summary

In this chapter, several novel (to this book) application domains for meta-analytics were considered. For health care, we considered the means by which to deidentify potential privacy-compromising information (this is applying analytics to the on-ramp of health-care analytics). We also considered the trade-offs in generic versus personalized health care (applying health care to the off-ramp of health-care analytics). For economics, we started with the relatively simple economic model of Piketty and extended it through the incorporation of new factors and subfactors. The advantages of such an approach include its inclusiveness (new factors easily incorporated) and its ease of retraining. Since health-care regimens are almost certain to continue to become progressively more customized, dynamic, and personalized, we can certainly anticipate them to become progressively more data-driven for the foreseeable future.

In economics, we begin with a consideration of Piketty's straightforward but effective model for capital and income by incorporating factors and various levels of subfactors in the areas of globalization and technological change. We show how a table of accuracies for the factors can be used to select a model that can be described in terms of the actual factors themselves. This means that the models are directly based on the measured factors and their combinations and thus can be conveyed to a nonmathematically inclined audience in the terms of their trade.

In business and finance, the difference between an estimate of the mean and the variance of the risk was described. Four different means of analytics or meta-analytics for assessing risk on asset returns were described, including historical simulation and its variants (weighted and filtered historical simulation), extreme value theory, the worst-performing algorithm (or "greatest risk"), and the consensus hybrid model. Each of these approaches has different value depending on the nature of the risk, the size of the financial investment, and the willingness of the asset investor to take on risk.

13.6 Postscript: Psychology

Psychology is a field that has gone largely undiscussed in these 13 chapters. It is, however, one of the fields in which analytics have been historically of paramount importance. This includes the tried and true approaches of collecting surveys (in which case percentages are the customary analytics), performing longitudinal and cross-sectional analyses, and performing archival analyses. Tying behavior, mental state, and personality together has helped drive a lot of the advanced regression techniques now so common to the field of analytics. More recently, the field of behavioral analytics has extended analytics to the (very!) personal level of suggesting entire streams of information for an individual to consume. Are these streams always relevant? No, but the large data collectors—think of the companies above $500 billion in market capitalization—are very good at insinuating more information out of their users. So, the analytics continue to get better—meaning more personalized, more accurate, and not incidentally more creepy.

Other elements of psychological research are generalizable to the overall field of meta-analytics. One of the most important is the concept of confounding factors, in which two correlated measurements are actually unrelated. For example, we might see that square feet in a person's house is highly correlated ($r > 0.95$) with the number of trips to Europe taken by the household. It is clear in this example that the size of the house is not causing the family to go to Europe, nor is going to Europe making the family purchase a larger house. Instead, there is a rather obvious confounding factor—the net income of the family—that is very highly ($r > 0.99$) correlated with both square feet of house and trips to Europe. A simple rule of correlation is as follows: there is almost always a confounding or at least partially confounding factor. Setting up a table of correlation coefficients is, therefore, essential to better understanding the relationships between your features.

Another concern to any earnest psychological researcher is the fact that in many cases, a quasi-experimental approach, rather than a proper experimental approach, must be employed. A quasi-experiment is empirical—that is, control and experimental group assignment is *a posteriori*, so that it is used to estimate the causal impact of an experimental factor but without random assignment. This means such an experiment is almost certain to be impacted by one or more confounding factors. However, there are usually ethical and/or structural exigencies that prevent a proper experimental design in many psychology-related research areas. One example is to test the impact of smoking on the development of another disorder such as lung cancer. It would be unethical to randomly assign participants in the experiment to either the control or one of the experimental (e.g., 0.5, 1, or 2 packs per day) groups, since assignment to an experimental group would have considerable health risks (not to mention it may be difficult to enforce). Thus, for this experiment, the assignments are after the fact, and the experiment designer does not have the ability or choice to change the independent variable. Thus, if only such a study were available, a cigarette manufacturer might argue that there may be a predisposition of people to smoke who already have a higher than average genetic risk of lung cancer. Some might argue that this is statistical apologetics, giving the cigarette manufacturers a loophole. It's not—I'll close that loophole shortly. However, from the standpoint of a quasi-experiment, it can reasonably be argued that a physiological lung defect such as weakened alveolar linings and dilated bronchi may make a person more likely to smoke: the smoking might constrict the bronchi to normal levels and so alleviate discomfort. The onus should then be on the cigarette manufacturers to establish that constricted bronchi lead to a higher lung cancer rate but that only delays the creation of another confounding factor to keep the argument going. Fortunately, there are means of establishing a proper experiment *a posteriori*. Perhaps a biological anomaly, identical twins are an absolute boon to psychological research. Because they are born with equivalent genetic information (epigenetics dissuades us from ever truly arrogating the term "identical" here, but the expression is more mellifluous than monozygotic, isn't it?), if we find identical twins with different smoking behavior, we can act as if they were assigned to these different groups *a priori* (since from the genetic standpoint, their assignment is random). This elevates the quasi-experiment to an experiment.

From the perspective of meta-analytics, this discussion of quasi-experiment versus proper experiment is illuminating, not to mention interesting. We can use a meta-analytic (i.e., hybrid) approach to establish that the quasi-experimental data (experimental output of the *a posteriori* quasi-experiment) match that of the identical twin experiments. In so doing, we can justifiably augment the size of each of our experimental groups with the non-identical-twin individuals. That is, if the two groups are not statistically significantly different, we can combine them, and in so doing, the quasi-experiment becomes a reasonable proxy for the true experiment.

Finally, with meta-analytic approaches such as the cumulative gain, or lift, curves (Chapter 4); sensitivity analysis (Chapter 5); predictive selection (Chapter 6); model fitting (Chapter 7); design patterns (Chapter 8); analytics about analytics (Chapter 9); analytic system design (Chapter 10); and aleatory techniques (Chapter 11) at hand, we can craft the meta-analytics equivalent of "identical twin" research. Combinatorial approaches drive meta-analytics, and for psychological and other complex behavioral research, creating multiple hypotheses and finding intelligent means of creating consensus among these hypotheses are a good approach if one aims to create a robust overall knowledge base.

References

[Barl18] Barlyn S, 2018. Strap on the Fitbit: John Hancock to Sell Only Interactive Life Insurance. Reuters.com, 19 September 2018, 4:11 PM, at https://www.reuters.com/article/us-manulife-financi-john-hancock-lifeins/strap-on-the-fitbit-john-hancock-to-sell-only-interactive-life-insurance-idUSKCN1LZ1WL (Accessed 24 September 2018).

[Nara16] Narayanan, A., Bonneau, J., Felten, E., Andrew, M., Goldfeder, S., 2016]. Bitcoin and Cryptocurrency Technologies: A Comprehensive Introduction. Princeton University Press, Princeton. ISBN 978-0-691-17169-2. 336 p.

[Pike13] Piketty, T., 2013]. Capital in the Twenty-First Century. Harvard University Press. 696 p.

[Sims13] Simske, S., 2013]. Meta-Algorithmics: Patterns for Robust, Low-Cost, High-Quality Systems. IEEE Press and Wiley, Singapore.

Discussion, conclusions, and the future of data

14

14.1 Chapter 1

The first chapter provided a sweeping consideration of the field of analytics, which is essential to an understanding of meta-analytics. Statistical estimation compares uncertainty in the independent and dependent variables, which is directly related to sensitivity analysis. The calculation of residual entropy is used to determine model definition sensitivity. Clustering k-means and k-nearest neighbor clustering are introduced to illustrate the conversion of unstructured data into structured data. The addition of regularization approaches to clustering to "optimize" the clustering is considered in Chapter 10. The process of unclustering was also introduced as a form of "tessellation and recombination" (a meta-algorithmic pattern) for clusters.

Additional topics in Chapter 1 introduced the reader to a set of analytic tools. A four-state Markov model was used to illustrate how system optimization can be garnered from the behavior of individual states and their transitions. This model can also be applied to time series data. Next, "nonbiological" machine learning approaches were overviewed. Entropy as a means of assessing how close to optimization a system is was discussed. Support vector machines (SVMs) and Bayesian approaches were reviewed. Dimensionality reduction for assessing the complexity of a system was covered, along with its link to information gain. Optimization, search, data mining, and knowledge discovery approaches were introduced. Recognition was covered along with processes of binarization, segmentation, key-point detection, classification, and the consideration of training data. These were applied to 1D and 3D recognition in addition to the 2D image recognition. The main forms of ensemble learning (bagging, boosting, and stacking) were introduced along with a novel ensemble method, the spatial-continuity hybrid.

Next, artificial intelligence (AI) approaches were introduced: genetic algorithms (GAs), artificial neural networks (ANNs), and immunologic approaches. Only the most rudimentary of evolutionary approaches were covered, but the basics of populations, mutations, crossovers, and inversions were described. For ANNs, multilayer

Meta-Analytics. https://doi.org/10.1016/B978-0-12-814623-1.00014-9

perceptrons were used to illustrate the concepts of nodes, gains, back-propagation, and thresholding at each consecutive layer.

The chapter concluded with the introduction of a simple but very adaptable classifier approach. The degenerate binary case was covered first. Then, the general case was described, in which training and testing, weighting samples based on distances from all class populations, and the derivation of features from measured features are considered. Taken as a unit, this chapter introduces analytic approaches not often seen in traditional analytic books, including the following:

(1) Design patterns and approaches for combining a multiplicity of analytic approaches.
(2) Application to a wide range of fields.
(3) Pragmatically, statistics-, and heuristic-driven evaluation approaches (such as for the ground-up classifier in Section 1.10).

This chapter intends to provide the means for all practitioners of data analytics to build better systems. The aim is to allow someone with a moderate understanding of statistics, calculus, logic, linear systems, and design patterns to be able to architect and deploy more intelligent systems than even the best individual intelligent algorithm designer can achieve—by using such a superior algorithm as the starting point. This meta-architect understands the relative advantages and disadvantages and both the flexibility and the limitations, of each of the component systems, and thus how to make them more valuable within a larger system involving two or more intelligent components.

14.2 Chapter 2

Ground truth is, in fact, only part of the truth. While we cannot prejudicially eliminate ground truth data, we can employ an approach analogous to boosting (one of the original meta-analytics), wherein different weighting of the ground truth is used to better train and validate an intelligent system. Traditional training approaches are problematic: Many use *k-fold* cross validation, wherein $\frac{(k-1)100\%}{k}$ of the ground truth is used for training and the k subsets of the training data are used for testing; these k tests are averaged to report the (overtrained) test accuracy. This is really a teleological measurement, showing the maximum possible performance of the algorithm. As such, it should be complemented with more thorough training+validation+testing approaches, which are more robust.

Training data can be used for many purposes; for example, the first round of training can be used for the optimization of accuracy, while the second round (or "validation") of training can be used for robustness. We introduced the use of prevalidation wherein a subset of ground truth data define a set of weak classifiers (improved robustness), and when all the training data are used, we tune the accuracy of the entire data set. Sequential consideration of meta-analytic patterns was shown to be a form of validation: training sets are herein used to select the appropriate *pattern* for the analytics. The validation set evaluates paired meta-algorithmic behavior.

Iterative training on multiple meta-algorithmic patterns can be followed by using the validation set for robustness rather than accuracy: validation explores which meta-analytic approach provides the best system output, whether it is accuracy, robustness, or some other measurement or combination of measurements.

14.3 Chapter 3

Experimental design of analytic systems may, by necessity, occur after the data are collected. Data normalization is used to even the playing field so that, before weighted, distinct features or dimensions will contribute to an analytic task equally. An advanced form of normalization—bias normalization—and its design considerations are means of preventing asymmetrical data collection from distorting the conclusions. Systems should be designed cognizant that cost, time, availability, and even ethics may preclude the desired rigor in an analysis (see also the discussion around quasi-experiments in Chapter 13). Ground truthing, or training set normalization, is employed to prevent one or a few ill-behaved data sets from steering the architect into a poor design choice. Gracefully aging data involve a backward-in-time (BIT) or a combined forward-in-time/backward-in-time (FIT-BIT) approach and is based on the data analogue of a moving average filter.

There is also an "engineering practice" that is defined around meta-analytics. Componentization, modularity, and the amenability to series and parallel construction provide many potential system designs, as in other fields (and software in general). The application of linear system theory, particularly sensitivity analysis, allows us to compare and contrast different models to fit the data: the one least sensitive to instantaneous changes in the input (domain) data is likely to be more useful in deployment phase.

14.4 Chapter 4

Data analytics is, in some sense, the act of removing the "personality" from data—be it raw data or cumulative data such as represented by a confusion matrix. One means of extracting this structure is to generate a cumulative response curve (CRC). In aligning two or more CRCs, we identify zones of interest for *sequence-dependent predictive selection* (a meta-analytic pattern based on the meta-algorithmic patterns on predictive selection), which is based on sorted differential-conditional CRCs, or SD-CCRCs. The start and end zones of the SD-CCRC are especially useful to mine for predictors. The simple (and traditional) cumulative gain curve (CGC), or lift curve, complements the powerful analytic tool, the confusion matrix, in illustrating classification error, precision, recall, and accuracy with any percentage of the samples assigned to a particular class.

Maximum information gain was applied to the optimization of a "decision tree" for biometrics: while the number of possible biometrics is relatively small, the number of meta-analytic approaches that can use these biometrics is shown to be very large. *Sequencing, weighted linear combinations*, and *predictive selection preclustering* patterns provide the possibility for billions of customized analytics, even with only 10 measured biometrics. Here, information gain is the differential ability of a custom pattern to identify an individual from a large population. The custom biometric approach and settings are the individual's "public key" and their biometric response to a form of private key.

Model agreement patterns were discussed: Residual entropy removes the personality from a data set, while the regression-based approach to temporal, scaling, distribution, and reliability parameters adds robustness. System design theory-based—particularly co-occurrence and similarity-based ensemble—approaches are shown to provide excellent *rank-biased systems*, moving the correct answer closer to the top of the stack. These are not always *accuracy-biased systems* and in fact at times can decrease accuracy while reducing the mean guesswork to find the correct response.

Two sensitivity analysis meta-analytic design patterns were introduced: (1) the *sensitivity-driven ensemble selection pattern* uses the partial derivative and a confidence weighting for each factor to create a weighted significance coefficient for each factor, enabling more productive boosting, bagging, or even weighted voting. (2) The *sensitivity-driven dimensionality reduction pattern* is a feature selection, not a feature extraction, form of dimensionality reduction (through feature pruning). This type of dimensionality reduction is compared with that driven by confusion matrices. The latter employs "within pair" and "outside pair" confusion matrix-based techniques to target dimensionality reduction from D-dimensions through the replacement of two classes with a binary classifier that follows a D-1 dimension-reduced classification.

Aleatory approaches—insensitive as possible to errors in individual parts of the analysis—provide us with a so-called optimized insensitivity, providing sequential removal of features by two different means. This enables dimensionality reduction even while identifying likely correlations. A second aleatory approach, the *sequential variation of feature output aleatory pattern*, is a form of sensitivity analysis that intentionally introduces error to see what the system insensitivity to errors of each feature is. Finally, a "veil of ignorance" approach to expert system-inspired weighting of features and rules together is provided.

The value of confusion matrices is further enhanced when they are shown to apply to the determination of independence in probability theory. Here, confusion matrices are employed to minimize the difference between the off-diagonal elements from their independence-optimal values (i.e., those values predicted by independence).

14.5 Chapter 5

Sensitivity analysis approaches are used to assign individual models to portions of the domain, creating hybrid models or metamodels. Relatedly, destabilization of data groups was discussed for four situations: (a) when one set of ground truth has largely different entropy than the other sets, (b) when one set of ground truth is more or less discretized than the other sets, (c) when one set of ground truth is created by different means than the other sets, and (d) when the grouped behavior of the data is too similar by analytic evaluation. Sensitivity analysis was also applied to the system model and to individual algorithms in an ensemble, combinatorial, or other hybrid system. By varying the weights in a weighted voting system, we could compute absolute, relative, and directional effects. A matrix approach to sensitivity analysis was used to determine when adding another algorithm or meta-algorithm is warranted in a hybrid design. Three types of sensitivity were evaluated for this purpose. Sensitivity analysis of path was shown to be particularly applicable to Markov models and Bayesian networks. Clearly, sensitivity-based approaches are one of the most important families of meta-analytics, providing not only better analysis but also better system testing and configuration.

14.6 Chapter 6

Predictive selection is often used to improve system decision-making accuracy, although the approach of intelligent partitioning followed by the differential deployment of selection tasks based on maximizing precision is broadly useful in optimizing any system objective function. Six major approaches to partitioning were described: (1) yes/no or pass/fail; (2) threshold-based partitioning; (3) subrange-based partitioning; (4) conditional/Boolean partitioning; (5) sequential partitioning, which may result in changing subrange definitions; and (6) consensus partitioning, a conditional partitioning based on both the data and the metadata. Predictive selection applies to ensembles of classifiers (or any other analytics), so long as the configuration providing the highest precision can be assessed. The trade-off for predictive selection is adding more rules to improve precision versus running the risk of over-training the system. Partitioning of the input can use a "separation of task" approach, wherein an auxiliary data feature is used to assign the sample to one of a plurality of partitions. The overall improvement in system behavior depends on how the features interact together, although this is not directly addressed by predictive selection. For predictive selection, there is one focus: maximizing precision for every decision.

We concluded with multipath predictive selection, wherein a number of possible decisions are made and a goodness of fit score computed for each path that is robust to the utility of the output. Again, some form of analytic regularization is needed so that this algorithm does not devolve into creating as many partitions as possible. A functional measurement such as the range of precisions for the entire ensemble of algorithms, analytics, or systems in each partition was shown to work well in this role of regularization. This emphasizes the need for regularization as a "check and balance" for a wide number of meta-analytic processes.

14.7 Chapter 7

Most advanced fields of science, engineering, and technology can be employed for defining data system models of utility in dynamic, scalable, modular, and robust systems. In this short chapter, we focused on chemistry, organic chemistry, and immunology approaches and showed how anonymization can be employed as a means of testing the optimization of a model. Chemistry analogues used for analytics include the five simplest chemical reactions: composition, decomposition, combustion, single substitution, and double substitution. One strategy is to apply all five equations to data sets and evaluate the percent of the theoretical improvement in the analytic output that is gained. The concept of limiting reagents, which provide a sort of sensitivity analysis for the overall analytic model, was introduced. The analogy between a sequence of reversible/bidirectional organic chemistry reactions (oxidation-reduction) and the need for robust analytics was made: One direction is the addition of new tagging information, and the other is the removal of ectopic tagging information. Immune cell differentiation is shown analogous to the continual refinement of analytics. The stage of maturation corresponds to an increasing precision of classification or indexing. We also described the ability of data categorization to "rewind" a level (or more) and be recommitted to an alternate path.

Anonymization of data was shown to be consistent with the measurements of system error entropy, least squared error (LSE), and variance. Anonymization's utility in providing both secure and reliable voice biometry was briefly discussed. The model error metrics of LSE, variance, and entropy were defined, and their employment for determining model goodness of fit is provided.

14.8 Chapter 8

Two different, though related, approaches to categorization analytics were introduced. The first, *synonym-antonym*, focuses on the weighting of synonyms and antonyms based on their similarity or dissimilarity to categorization terms, multiplied by the relative rareness of the terms. The overall summed weights of synonymic and antonymic behavior can be used for assignment purposes. Secondly, the *reinforce-void* pattern family is discussed. Residual entropy, expectation-maximization (EM), and varying the coefficients for the ratio of occurrences to nonoccurrences can be used to generate effective features for this pattern. The analogy to the Hegelian dialectic is highlighted. The behavior of reinforcement/void ratios compared with their expected values can be used as a criterion for feature selection and for multicategory discrimination. Finally, an extension of the familiar expectation-maximization (E-M) algorithm; "define, assign, and refine"; or expectation-maximization-elimination (E-M-E) was introduced.

14.9 Chapter 9

Meta-analytics is more than just coordinating two or more analytics to improve the overall analytic behavior (cost, accuracy, robustness, etc.). They are also analytics around analytics, including the application of methods based on entropy to difference sets; the application of entropy to descriptive distributions such as histograms; and the use of occurrence vectors, which merge the best of Jaccard and correlative approaches. Functional metrics in which one or more measurable processes give us insight into other analytics we wish to evaluate were considered. The recommendation is to use primary functional metrics where possible: one such functional metric design pattern designated the "inverse predictive selection," which is used in numerous applications to provide better forward estimation as part of optimizing the analytics. We reinforced the value of connecting analytics around important system design concerns of (a) performance; (b) robustness; (c) accuracy; (d) cost; (e) modularity and repurposability; (f) testing, measurement, and validation; (g) scalability; and (h) reliability.

We should ensure that the data set used for training or testing is both as broad and as uniformly deep as needed to ensure optimal system robustness. Training data are also useful for defining representative samples and for defining new categories from outlier data. Finally, training and testing can be regularized for swifter and more robust optimization. Expectation-optimization approaches are augmented with regularization to create an expectation-optimization-regularization, or E-O-R ("Eeyore") algorithm. This enables a two-factor optimization based on iterative assignment to representative sample (E-O) and the optimization of the number of clusters with an F-score calculation.

14.10 Chapter 10

A broader perspective on system design is empowered by meta-analytics as both hybrid analytics and as analytics about our analytics. I/O gains, information gain, knowledge gain, and efficiency can be measured in new light of increased system value and in terms of conciseness of design choice. Robustness gain was introduced here, defined as the system's worst-case response to input. In revisiting key system design considerations—rank, accuracy, performance, cost, robustness, modularity, and scalability—we showed that rank and accuracy bias in a system are relatively comparable by the cost of their errors. The case for error gain over accuracy gain as a means of weighting was further expostulated. Performance gain and later robustness gain are gains that benefit from k-fold training and validation in a way that accuracy and rank-biased systems do not. In robustness gain, the use of 2-to-k enumerated training and validation design provided a stronger estimate of robustness.

Module optimization uses measurements of entropy, error variance, and sensitivity. Using them along with analytics about the messaging, or communication, within and between modules adds more insight into system functionality. We further elaborated on the benefits of regularization applied to clustering. Regularization is defined as a penalty subtracted from the fitness. The fitness is an F-score based on the relative variance within clusters compared with between clusters. Five regularization approaches account for the variability within the clusters (sum of squares and variance), the cluster size, the presence of small clusters or unclustered samples, and the overall number of clusters. In clustering and other partitioning processes, variance should decrease, and entropy should increase, as our model fitness improves.

14.11 **Chapter 11**

For the *sequential removal of feature aleatory pattern* introduced in Chapter 4, we introduced a figure of merit (such as accuracy) approach to dimensionality reduction, looking for inflection points in the %Error Gain metric. At these points, sequential removal of the lowest-ranked remaining feature is used to provide a sensitivity analysis for the reduced dimensionality. For the *sequential variation of feature output aleatory pattern*, the sensitivity to features is determined by intentionally adding errors to the measured values. This "forced aleatory sensitivity analysis" is a reasonable middle ground between sensitivity analysis performed using actual data with a given difference ("delta") between them (designated natural sensitivity) and sensitivity analysis performed on simulated data (designated synthetic sensitivity analysis).

A variety of ways to add randomness to existing (measured) data were overviewed: dropping significant figures; swapping two fields between two data elements; using genetic approaches such as crossover, mutation, and inversion; rudimentary introduced errors (substitution, deletion, insertion, and transposition); compound introduced errors (spelling, anagram, acronym, slang, jargon, pun, and other context-dependent plays on words); imputation; and normalization. Combined, these tests are recommended means of assessing the robustness of a system. Lastly, hyperspectral aleatory approaches were considered with respect to measurements of reliability, robustness, and sensitivity. The distinction between measurement and assumption reliability was described, and sensitivity was considered in terms of *substitutability*.

14.12 **Chapter 12**

For machine translation, we pointed out the variety of analytic approaches that can be applied at each of 10 identified major steps. There are multiple nodes in the sequence where information calculated can be fed back to "earlier" stages to improve the overall behavior of the system, an approach termed "translation round-trip."

Robotics was shown to benefit from meta-analytic approaches. Applying analytics at the same level of modularity as the subsystems of the robotics, we can use the predictive selection and weighted voting patterns for physical robot ("physibot") motion and manipulation. Using multiple sensors for richer analytics is also an important meta-analytic consideration and argues for robotics being "meta-analytic" by nature.

Using analytics modeled after the biological processes that they are being applied to is a logical approach, analogous to the chemistry analogues in Chapter 7. Using enzymes and evolution as two systems for design insight, we showed how reproductive isolation, punctuated equilibrium, and CRISPR-Cas9 processes provide insight into the robust design of certain types of intelligent analytic systems. Punctuated equilibrium is especially repurposable to other analytics, including ANNs and meta-algorithmics, where it can be used to break recalcitrant nonglobal "optimization."

14.13 **Chapter 13**

In Chapter 13, we considered applying meta-analytics to health care, economics, business, and finance. We specifically focused on how hybrid approaches enable simultaneously generic and personalized health care. Meta-analytics were then shown to have the potential to greatly extend existing economic models, such as Piketty's, through the incorporation of new factors and subfactors in a recursive hierarchy. This meta-analytic system is inclusive to new factors and is easy to retrain. In our specific example, we showed how factors in globalization and technological change could be used to augment Piketty's model based on capital and income. Our model extensions are based on directly measured factors and their combinations, which means their structure can be explained to an audience in the terms of their trade. In business and finance, four different meta-analytics for assessing risk on asset returns were described, including the historical simulation and its variants (weighted and filtered historical simulation), the extreme value theory, the worst-performing algorithm (or "greatest risk"), and the consensus hybrid model. We completed the new content of the book with a discussion of quasi-experimental approaches in psychological and other research. Most importantly, we considered the approaches allowing us to combine the two data sets through establishing statistical equivalence (or, rather, showing the lack of statistical differences) between these two populations. This approach is closely related to the approaches for pruning low-quality training data (Section 2.2) and aging training data (Section 3.3).

14.14 **The future of meta-analytics**

Despite living in the age of big data, our future is perhaps more uncertain than it has been in a long time. Is this a mirage only seeming more uncertain because we now understand better the power of predictive analytics? That may well be the case. Regardless of the certainty of what is to come, I can predict with high accuracy that the end is very near, just as it was, regrettably, for Jim Morrison when he penned those lyrics in 1970. The end of this book, that is, which is in just a few short sentences. If this book accomplishes nothing else, it should show the reader that there is a lot of room for creativity, for argument, and for discussion in the future of data analytics, that is, in meta-analytics. As Joseph Joubert noted, the aim of this creative argumentation and discussion is not for one analytic to "claim victory" in a particular area of application. Instead, meta-analytics is all about progress. *Understanding on the shoulders of the giants* of analytic experts who have come before you. Using their findings, their insights, and their wisdom as the launchpad in a career guided by dataphilia. The love of data. If you are not already smitten, find Cupid's dart—or should I say data?—and feel its barb. Because data are here to stay. I hope that this book helps launch your dataphilia in creative ways.

Index

Note: Page numbers followed by *f* indicate figures and *t* indicate tables.

Printed in the United States
By Bookmasters